D1383427

TRADE PROTECTION IN THE UNITED STATES

THE LOCKE INSTITUTE

General Director
Charles K. Rowley, PhD

Editorial Director
Arthur Seldon, BSc, CBE

Director of Legal Studies
Amanda J. Owens

Financial Director
Robert S. Elgin, MA

Program Director
Marjorie I. Rowley

Founded in 1989, The Locke Institute is an independent, non-partisan, educational and research organization. The Institute is named for John Locke (1632–1704), philosopher and political theorist, who based his theory of society on natural law which required that the ultimate source of political sovereignty was with the individual. Individuals are possessed of inalienable rights variously defined by Locke as 'life, health, liberty and possession,' or, more directly, 'life, liberty and property.' It is the function of the state to uphold these rights since individuals would not enter into a political society unless they believed that it would protect their lives, liberties and properties.

The Locke Institute seeks to engender a greater understanding of the concept of natural rights, its implications for constitutional democracy and for economic organization in modern society. The Institute encourages high-quality research utilizing in particular modern theories of property rights, public choice, law and economics, and the new institutional economics as a basis for a more profound understanding of important and controversial issues in political economy. To this end, it commissions books, monographs, and shorter studies involving substantive scholarship written for a wider audience, organizes major conferences on fundamental topics in political economy, and supports independent research. The Institute maintains a publishing relationship with Edward Elgar, the international publisher in the social sciences.

In order to maintain independence, the Locke Institute accepts no government funding. Funding for the Institute is solicited from private foundations, corporations, and individuals. In addition, the Institute raises funds from the sale of publications and from conference fees. The Institute is incorporated in the State of Virginia, USA, and has applied for non-profit, tax-exempt educational status under Section 501(c)3 of the United States Internal Revenue Code.

Officers of the Institute are listed above. Please direct all enquiries to the address given below.

4084 University Drive, Suite 103 • Fairfax, Virginia 22030, USA

Trade Protection in the United States

Charles K. Rowley, Willem Thorbecke and
Richard E. Wagner

The Locke Institute and George Mason University, US

THE LOCKE INSTITUTE

Edward Elgar
Aldershot, UK • Brookfield, US

© Charles K. Rowley, Willem Thorbecke and Richard E. Wagner 1995

All rights reserved. No part of this publication may be reproduced, stored in a retrieval system, or transmitted in any form or by any means, electronic, mechanical, photocopying, recording, or otherwise without the prior permission of the publisher.

Published by
Edward Elgar Publishing Limited
Gower House
Croft Road
Aldershot
Hants GU11 3HR
UK

Edward Elgar Publishing Company
Old Post Road
Brookfield
Vermont 05036
US

British Library Cataloguing in Publication Data
Rowley, Charles K.
    Trade Protection in the United States. –
    (John Locke Series)
    I. Title II. Series
    382.730973

Library of Congress Cataloguing in Publication Data
Rowley, Charles Kershaw.
    Trade protection in the United States / Charles K. Rowley with
Willem Thorbecke and Richard E. Wagner.
        p.   cm. — (The John Locke series)
    Includes bibliographical references and index.
    1. Protectionism—United States.   2. Free trade—United States.
I. Thorbecke, Willem, 1958–   .   II. Wagner, Richard E.   III. Title.
IV. Series: John Locke series in classical liberal political economy.
HF1716.R68 1995
382'.73'0973—dc20   95–7196
                                                                                                CIP

ISBN 1 85898 198 0

Printed and bound in Great Britain by
Hartnolls Limited, Bodmin, Cornwall

For Gordon Tullock

Contents

Figures and tables

Preface

This is a book about the political organization of free individuals. More specifically, it is concerned with an apparent paradox: why would free individuals choose a political organization that deprives each of them of the opportunity to trade with other individuals on terms freely negotiated between themselves? In attempting to resolve this paradox the authors must probe deeply into the organic, nation-state predilections of the very large majority of writings on trade protection. They must analyse in some detail the institution that facilitates redistributionist rather than wealth-enhancing exchanges in the political markets of the United States. They must ask probing questions as to why the United States has failed to deliver on the promises of the Founding Fathers.

The analytical approach of the book can be described by the term 'methodological individualism'. Human beings are conceived as the only decision-makers in determining group as well as private action. All issues of political organization are reduced to the individual's confrontation with alternatives and his choice among alternatives. The individual's logic of choice constitutes the central part of the analysis, and no external position is taken concerning the ultimate goals or criteria that should direct that choice. Indeed, all attempts to socially engineer policy outcomes are anathema to this methodology, reflecting the fatal conceit of elite decision-makers. In this sense, the book falls squarely within the tradition of Virginia political economy, deploying the building blocks provided by James M. Buchanan and Gordon Tullock to a centrally important policy issue confronting Americans at the present time.

This book began as a small eight chapter primer designed to place a public choice gloss on trade policy. Intensive preliminary discussions between the three authors resulted in the unique combination of public choice and constitutional political economy that permeates the final product. As work on the book advanced, it became apparent to the authors that a more substantial involvement with trade theory and policy would be desirable and that this in turn would create a lengthier book. Dr Wagner, who had drafted three of the initial chapters, declined to participate in this larger enterprise because of other commitments. His initial contributions have been distributed throughout Chapters 1–3 and 13 of this book. Charles Rowley bore full responsibility for the final draft of the book, contributed to Chapters 2, 3 and 13, was fully responsible for Chapters 4–7 and worked equally with Willem Thorbecke in preparing Chapters 8–12.

At the outset of this project, none of us was expert in international economics, although we have worked hard to master the intricacies of the discipline. Certainly, we have been more than usually dependent on the acknowledged giants in the field, Robert Baldwin, Jagdish Bhagwati and John Jackson, each of whom has carried the flag of free trade in a hostile environment. Although our policy recommendations are more unequivocally free trade than theirs, our arguments would be less convincing without their contributions. We are proud to stand on their shoulders in the battle against mercantilism.

Initial drafts of the various chapters were presented at meetings of the Southern Economic Association in New Orleans (1993) and Orlando (1994), at a meeting of the Public Choice Society in New Orleans (1992), at a meeting of the European Public Choice Society in Valencia (1994), at meetings of the Henry Simons Society in New Orleans (1993) and Vancouver (1994), at a meeting of the Western Economic Association in Vancouver (1994), at Colloquies of the Locke Institute in Fairfax (1993 and 1994), and at meetings of the Center for Study of Public Choice in Fairfax (1993 and 1994). We are grateful for constructive criticisms offered on these occasions.

We are grateful to Susan Bloom, James M. Buchanan, Nisan Ceran, Alejandro Chafuen, Mark Crain, Kent Grote, Carl Helstrom, Harpreet Kaur, Leonard Liggio, William C. Mitchell, Anthony Santelli, Robert D. Tollison, Gordon Tullock and Michael Walker for helpful suggestions. We are grateful to Marjorie I. Rowley, administrative assistant of the Locke Institute, for typing the book and organizing the project with unfailing enthusiasm.

The project would not have been completed without financial support from the Lynde and Harry Bradley Foundation and the Sunmark Foundation. Atlas Economic Research Foundation provides congenial, scholarly facilities which are greatly appreciated.

Prologue

What is prudence in the conduct of every private family, can scarce be folly in that of a great kingdom. If a foreign country can supply us with a commodity cheaper than we ourselves can make it, better buy it of them with some part of the produce of our own industry, employed in a way in which we have some advantage. The general industry of the country, being always in proportion to the capital which employs it, will not thereby be diminished, no more than that of the above-mentioned artificers; but only left to find out the way in which it can be employed with the greatest advantage. It is certainly not employed to the greatest advantage, when it is thus directed towards an object which it can buy cheaper than it can make. The value of its annual produce is certainly more or less diminished, when it is thus turned away from producing commodities evidently of more value than the commodity which it is directed to produce. According to the supposition, that commodity could be purchased from foreign countries cheaper than it can be made at home. It could, therefore, have been purchased with a part only of the commodities, or, what is the same thing, with a part only of the price of the commodities, which the industry employed by an equal capital would have produced at home, had it been left to follow its natural course. The industry of the country, therefore, is thus turned away from a more, to a less advantageous employment, and the exchangeable value of its annual produce, instead of being increased according to the intention of the lawgiver, must necessarily be diminished by every such regulation.

(Adam Smith, *The Wealth of Nations* (1776), vol. I, ed. Edwin Cannan (London: University Paperbacks, 1961), Book IV, Ch. ii, pp. 478–9.)

PART I

BASIC PRINCIPLES

1 Trade, national borders and individual welfare

1 Introduction

Many people have enjoyed reading *Robinson Crusoe* since its publication in 1719. Daniel Defoe's story of Crusoe's shipwreck, survival and subsequent meeting with Friday is truly an absorbing tale. One must be careful, however, not to form an exaggerated impression of an individual's economic capacity from reading the story. Crusoe got along pretty well on his island, at least as judged by 1719 standards of living. Even though he lived alone until he met Friday, he was none the less able to secure the cooperation of countless other people. Much of that cooperation Crusoe carried with him on his ship.

No individual truly left to his own devices could make a rifle, bullets and gunpowder, or a saw, hammer and nails. Crusoe also carried much social cooperation in his head, for no truly solitary individual could ever have developed the knowledge Crusoe possessed about how to use such implements. Even while he was alone, Crusoe derived large gains from trade and social cooperation that multiplied many times over his standard of living from what it could have been had he been truly left exclusively to his own wits and devices. Crusoe's standard of living was testimony to gains from trade, much more so than it was testimony to his individual economic prowess.

In his noted essay *I, Pencil*, Leonard Read describes how it would be impossible for a single individual to produce even such a simple item as a lead pencil. Lead must be mined, combined with graphite which must also be mined, and fashioned into a form suitable for writing. Trees must be felled, shaped into pencil lengths for which cores to hold the lead must be bored. All these activities require the creation of many tools. Any effort even to describe fully how a pencil is made would show quickly that no solitary individual could make one. To make a pencil requires a cooperative effort among millions of people scattered throughout the world and brought together through a complex network of trades and contractual relationships.

Economics is the study of how such social cooperation is achieved through a process that, in a somewhat paradoxical use of language, is usually described as competitive. Individuals, in seeking to promote their particular economic interests, typically promote and advance the well-being of others in the process. A market economy entails the use of a process of free and open competition as a means of organizing social cooperation. Specialization through a division of labor increases everyone's productive capacities from what they would otherwise be. This proposition about the gains from specialization holds as strongly for trade across national borders as it does within a particular nation. In this chapter we shall review some of the central ideas of the gains from specialization and trade, both within a nation and among nations, after which we shall explore the appropriate place of government and public policy in securing those gains.

2   Specialization, trade and economic welfare

That people gain from uncoerced trade is practically a self-evident proposition. This potential for gain exists even if, as between two people, one is more productive than the other across all activities. Friday, for instance, might be more productive than Crusoe in all the activities that take place on their island. To illustrate, suppose Crusoe and Friday engage in two economic activities: catching fish and gathering coconuts. Further, suppose that on an hourly basis Crusoe can catch one fish or gather three coconuts, while Friday can catch three fish or gather four coconuts. Friday is more productive than Crusoe in both economic activities, as Table 1.1 outlines.

[The example is drawn from Daniel Defoe, Robinson Crusoe, 1719]

Table 1.1   Harvest per hour

	Fish	Coconuts
Crusoe	1	3
Friday	3	4

Friday's greater productivity means that in an autarkic situation without trade, he would enjoy a better standard of living than Crusoe. Suppose in their primitive state of society that Crusoe and Friday each works ten hours per day, and that each seeks to obtain an equal number of fish and coconuts. To do this would require Crusoe to spend three-quarters of his day fishing and Friday to devote four-sevenths of his day to fishing. For their efforts, Crusoe's daily harvest would be 7.5 fish and 7.5 coconuts. Friday's daily harvest would be more than double that of Crusoe, for he would obtain 17.1 fish and 17.1 coconuts per day. Friday's higher standard of living reflects his greater absolute productivity in both activities.

Despite Friday's greater absolute productivity, Crusoe and Friday can still both improve their standards of living through specialization and trade. The key to understanding this is to recognize that while Friday has an *absolute advantage* in both activities, Crusoe has a relative or *comparative advantage* in gathering coconuts. While Friday is more productive in absolute terms in each activity than is Crusoe, Friday is relatively more productive in catching fish. Crusoe thus has a comparative advantage in gathering coconuts. We can see this by comparing the cost of fish and coconuts produced by each person. Each fish Crusoe produces requires him to sacrifice three coconuts that he could otherwise have produced. In contrast, each fish Friday produces requires him to sacrifice only 1.33 coconuts. Friday produces fish at a lower cost in terms of sacrificed coconuts than Crusoe. For each coconut he produces, Crusoe must sacrifice one-third of a fish. However, Friday must sacrifice three-quarters of a fish to produce a coconut. Crusoe is the lower-cost producer of coconuts, even though Friday can gather more coconuts per hour than Crusoe.

Consider again the situation under autarky where each apportions his time so as to harvest equal numbers of fish and coconuts. Aggregate output per day is 24.6 units each of fish and coconuts. Should Crusoe specialize wholly in gathering coconuts and Friday in catching fish, aggregate daily output would be 30 units each of fish and coconuts. To be sure, Crusoe and Friday might not wish to consume more coconuts and fish. Some of that potential increase in output might be converted to leisure. Alternatively, instead of taking more leisure, one or other of them might invest some of that time in making a boat. Regardless of the particular use they might make of the added productive capacity that specialization and trade brings, the central point is that there will be mutual gains from social cooperation through trade, even if one participant has an absolute advantage across all activities.[1] What holds for the two-person society constituted by Crusoe and Friday holds for larger societies as well: specialization in production combined with trade leads to vastly multiplied standards of living over what would result in the absence of specialization and trade. Restrictions on trade constrict the gains from specialization and nudge a society in the direction of autarky.

The modern study of economics is customarily dated from the publication in 1776 of Adam Smith's *An Inquiry into the Nature and Causes of the Wealth of Nations.*[2] Smith sought to explain how it was that economic progress and human welfare were best promoted within a social environment of open competition and free trade, because such an environment would support more fully than any other the mutual gains from specialization and trade. Smith brought his arguments to bear against the mercantilistic restrictions on trade that were prevalent at his time. Open competition would harness people's natural partiality toward their own ends to the service of the ends of others. Within a market economy, any person's economic well-being varies directly with the value of the services that that person supplies to others. People do well for themselves by doing good for others, as revealed by the willingness of those other people to pay for the services rendered. The specialization of economic activities in a market economy also means that knowledge is highly fragmented and divided. Specialization allows people to be experts in limited areas and amateurs elsewhere. Someone can know a lot about mining diamonds without knowing anything about how to cut them or market them. Similarly, someone may know a lot about cutting them, while knowing little about how they are mined or distributed. An expert in marketing diamonds might be an amateur when it comes to rubies. The ability of a market economy to use knowledge that is widely dispersed throughout the economy and is available in no central location was used a century and a half after Smith by Ludwig von Mises to explain why a centrally planned economy would be impossible.[3]

The fundamental paradox that economics seeks to explain is how it is that competition, within a framework of private property and freedom of contract and association, is the most effective process ever discovered for organizing social cooperation on a large scale. If each of us was to make up a wish list of what we would like to have, the aggregation of those lists would exceed many times our capacity to produce. Some wants will be fulfilled, others will not. Competition among us is inescapable; however, competition within a legal framework characterized by private property and freedom of contract will allow people generally to fulfil those wants more fully than any other form of social organization, because it will harness individual interest to the service of social cooperation. A market economy is a competitive process for organizing social cooperation.

3   The state and the legal framework for market exchange

What is true for economic relationships between Crusoe and Friday holds for economic relationships generally: specialization and trade promote general economic well-being, while impediments to specialization and trade retard it. While our central interest in this book is with the subset of trading relationships that cross national boundaries, it will prove helpful to consider briefly the place of the state in market exchange generally. There is little if any economic distinction between domestic and international trade, so a brief consideration of market exchange generally may prove helpful in subsequent discussion.

What is the place of the state, and of state policy regarding trade, in a society where economic activities are organized predominantly through market exchange? It is generally acknowledged that the state has a strong role in supporting and maintaining the framework of legal institutions within which trade takes place. For trade to take place, rights of property must be clear and contracts must be enforced. The state maintains these legal institutions, without which the scope for market exchange would be considerably narrower than it actually is. This view of the state is sometimes referred to as the *nightwatchman state* or the *protective state* (Buchanan 1975). The principal economic function of government in a classical liberal order is to preserve and protect individual rights against infringement from one another and from outsiders.[4] Protection against one another requires police and courts; protection from outsiders requires a military force. Such a nightwatchman state is fully consistent with the classical liberal order embodied in the American Declaration of Independence, in which it is affirmed that government is not a source of rights for people but rather is an instrument that people can use to protect and preserve their rights. Those rights themselves, however, belong initially to people as free individuals and not to the state or its officers. Such a state provides and maintains a protective framework within which trade can take place.

While there is a generally strong presumption that trade enhances economic welfare, neoclassical economists subject this presumption to exceptions. For the most part, these alleged exceptions cover cases where the parties to a trade impose costs on others who are not parties to that trade. In such cases as these, the claim that trade enhances welfare is subject to challenge, and state policy that restricts trade is seen to be capable of enhancing the general welfare. For instance, a paper mill might deposit wastes into a river, and in turn impose costs on downstream users of the river. Under certain circumstances, it is possible to claim that this will result in too much output from the paper mill, along with an underutilization of the river for alternative purposes.

To be sure, and following Coase (1960), if the paper mill had to buy permission from downstream users, the mill would use the river less fully as a receptacle for its wastes, provided those other uses were more valuable than use of the river as such a receptacle. It might do this in any of several ways: it might produce less paper; it might develop a network of holding tanks and treatment facilities for cleaning its wastes before returning them to the river; or it might locate elsewhere. In any case, it is claimed that better economic decisions will result when people must take such costs into account when they make their economic choices.

Arguments based on economic policy grounded in claims of external cost are not the only weapons deployed by economists anxious to justify roles for government that exceed those generally consistent with a nightwatchman or protective state. Many economists also argue that a more positive and expansive role for the state is also justified. Market arrangements fare well, they acknowledge, in accommodating exchanges where it is easy to charge people for their usage and to prevent their usage if they do not pay. But there are cases where it is difficult if not impossible to charge people, and where people can consume services even if they do not pay from them. In some instances, the consumption of such services by one individual imposes no costs upon others. Such services are often called *public goods* and the justifications for state activity that such services invoke can be summarized by the notion of a *productive state*.

The provision of protection against flooding is not the same kind of business as the provision of protection against roaches and similar pests. The protection given by an exterminator is restricted to that house, and people who will not pay for such services will not receive protection. Such selectivity is impossible with flood protection. A project to control flooding in some low-lying, flood-prone area, if implemented effectively, will protect everyone who lives in the protected area. If a levy or a spillway is built, everyone who lives in the affected area receives protection. In such a setting, ordinary market transactions, it is alleged, typically will not operate very effectively to organize the provision of flood protection and similar services.[5]

Such public-goods notions are often used to justify state provision of services. Even here, however, it is important to note that the common justification for such provision has the state somehow acting in conformity with classical liberal values, and most certainly not acting contrary to those values. The very reason for public provision is that there are market trades that people would like to make if only they could, but which they cannot make because of technological circumstances. State provision of public goods is justified as a means of bringing about those transactions that would have been made had technology been somehow different, and doing so at non-prohibitive transaction costs.[6]

4   Knowledge, incentive and state policy

A system of economic organization based on private property requires some measure of government activity, notably to protect individuals' rights of person and property. Even though there may be general agreement about the proper principles of such governmental activity, that agreement often dissolves in the specifics of particular implementation. It would doubtless be agreed that someone who pipes exhaust gases from his car into his neighbor's house violates his neighbor's rights of property. Government action to prevent this violation would be consistent with the principles of the protective state. But what about the effect of millions of drivers doing the same thing to each other, just as surely even if not so directly and dramatically? In the absence of clearly defined and enforceable property rights in air, government efforts to counter air pollution may seem to many economists to be clearly consistent with the principles of private property and the protection of individual rights.

Yet government action often follows perverse patterns in practice. For instance, the Environmental Protection Agency (EPA) requires all coal-fired power plants to install gas scrubbers to remove sulfur dioxide. While eastern coal is high in sulfur, western coal has low sulfur content; sulfur dioxide comes predominantly from eastern and not western coal. A policy of reducing sulfur emissions would thus shift demand from eastern to western coal. However, the EPA offset this shift in demand by requiring the installation of scrubbers in plants that use western coal as well. The EPA did this even though the sulfur emissions from those that use western coal would have been lower without scrubbers than emissions from plants using eastern coal with scrubbers. At the time of this regulation, the chairmen of the EPA authorizing committees in Congress were both from West Virginia. Moreover, eastern, but not western, coal workers belonged to the United Mine Workers. A principled case conceivably can be made for environmental regulation; but the actual course of regulation typically has little or nothing to do with those principles.[7]

To advance normative arguments based on public goods or externalities is not to say that state policies that restrict trade will automatically or necessarily operate as conventional models of public goods and of external cost would prescribe. Actual state policies will differ from those envisioned by the normative arguments either because state officials lack the knowledge required to do so or because they do not truly want to pursue such policies in the first place. These problems of knowledge and incentive, which we shall pursue throughout this book, can be illustrated briefly here with reference to the paper-mill and flood-control illustrations noted above.

There is a substantial economic literature on the properties of different techniques for controlling external costs. Much of this literature concerns the comparative properties of taxing and regulating, and the particular methods that might be used in each case. Hence, the paper mill could be taxed in any of several ways: on the amount of its production of paper, or on the volume of effluent it discharges. Similarly, regulation could limit the amount of effluent discharge, it could require the mill to invest in facilities for treating the effluent, or it could rely upon zoning to restrict the location of paper mills.

Even if it is assumed that policy measures are adopted in a spirit of benevolence, which means that policy measures would seek to replicate the market transactions that would have taken place had transaction costs been absent, the knowledge necessary to implement such measures will not exist. For if such knowledge were to exist, markets would have been unnecessary for the organization of economic activity and collectivist planning would have been possible.[8] Whether the mill should reduce its discharge of effluents, and if so, to what extent, depends on the cost to the mill of such reductions relative to the value that users of the river would place upon having a cleaner river. If transaction costs are low, the economically more valuable use of the river will result regardless of the initial pattern of ownership rights, for reasons that Coase (1960) makes clear.

Suppose a single mill discharges effluent into the river, with there being only a few people affected downstream by the discharge. It should not be too difficult for those people to organize some process of bidding and negotiation with the mill over its discharge. The downstream users might be able to bid enough to get the mill to institute some more costly method of effluent treatment than open discharge. If so, it can be reasonably inferred that the cost imposed on the downstream users by the discharge exceeded the cost to the mill of reducing its discharge of pollutants into the river. Similarly, should those downstream users be unable to reach an agreement with the mill, it can be inferred equally reasonably that the cost imposed on the downstream users was less than the cost that the mill would have to bear in reducing its discharges. In any case, the positive Coase Theorem explains how market transactions will tend to replace less-valuable with more-valuable uses of resources in situations where conflicts arise among resource owners, provided that rights of ownership are clear and that transaction costs are low.

However, if transaction costs are high and efficient trades do not take place, a conundrum arises. Transaction costs may be high because there are a number of mills or other activities that discharge effluents into the river. Alternatively, costs may be high because there are a large number of downstream users of the river affected by the upstream discharges.[9] In either case, the cost of any effort to organize negotiation and bidding among large numbers of people may well exceed the potential gains from such an effort. There is simply no way to determine what the outcome would have been in this case had transaction costs been low.

A disinterested, benevolent politician cannot replace the market as a process for generating the knowledge on which choices regarding the possible uses of the river are based. Even Solomon recognized this lack of knowledge when faced with the contending claims of two women to a single child. He assigned each woman a right to half the child and let the women negotiate a solution between themselves. In the absence of some market process for the generation of knowledge, policy choices will be open to two types of error even in the presence of Solomonic benevolence. One error will be to allow the paper mill to continue to discharge effluents, even though a cleaner river is more valuable to downstream users than would be the cost to the mills of reducing their discharges. The other error will force the mills to reduce their discharges, even though the cost of doing so will exceed the values that the downstream users would place on the cleaner river.

The situation becomes significantly more difficult once it is recognized that Solomonic disinterestedness is rare. For instance, a politician whose support is drawn primarily from among downstream users is almost surely going to read the same 'evidence' differently from a politician whose support comes primarily from the upstream mills. In such cases politicians will have a powerful incentive to see a situation in the same way as their strongest supporters. With knowledge always being incomplete, almost any position becomes defensible on some claim of advancing the common interest in situations that deal with external costs.

It is the same with situations pertaining to public goods, and for essentially the same reasons. Is a proposed flood-control project worthwhile? If the value that the affected parties would place on the added protection exceeds the cost they would have to pay, the proposed project would be worthwhile. If flood protection is not sold through ordinary market processes, there is no way to tell what kind of flood-control projects should be generated.

In this situation, or in any situation where a public good is alleged to exist, there are two types of error. One involves the creation of a flood-control project when the value that people place on the reduction in flooding is less than the cost they would have to bear. The other error occurs when a flood-control project is not created, even though the value that individuals place on a reduction in flooding exceeds the cost they must bear to achieve it.

5   National borders and international trade

With respect to the economic gains from specialization and trade, national borders are generally pretty much economically irrelevant. The same principles that explain the economic advantages from specialization and trade within a particular society or nation explain the similar gains across them. The law of comparative advantage was first articulated by David Ricardo in his 1817 book *Principles of Political Economy and Taxation*. Even a nation that is an inferior producer of all products can participate in international trade and can gain thereby. Free trade among nations promotes general economic prosperity through increasing international specialization and the division of labor.

Ricardo (1817) illustrated the law of comparative advantage for England and Portugal with respect to cloth and wine. Portugal was assumed to be the more efficient producer of both products, but to be relatively more efficient in producing wine than cloth. Ricardo gave the particular illustration shown in Table 1.2, whereby a particular quantity of cloth could be produced in

Table 1.2   Man-years required for given output

	Cloth	Wine
Portugal	90	80
England	100	120

Portugal with 90 man-years of labor, which required 100 man-years in England. A particular quantity of wine requiring 80 man-years in Portugal would require 120 man-years in England.

In this illustration, Portugal has an absolute cost advantage in producing both products, but it has a relative cost advantage in producing wine. A unit of cloth produced in Portugal requires the sacrifice of nine-eighths units of wine. England can produce a unit of cloth at a sacrifice of only five-sixths of a unit of wine. England is the relatively cheaper producer of cloth. Ricardo showed how England and Portugal could both become better off if Portugal specialized in producing wine and England cloth, and with England buying wine from Portugal in exchange for cloth.

In terms of basic economic principle, national boundaries are irrelevant. Whether the specific illustration is Crusoe and Friday trading between fish and coconuts, or England and Portugal trading between wine and cloth, the economic principles are identical. England and Portugal could have been portrayed as trading between coconuts and fish, and Crusoe and Friday trading between wine and cloth, and nothing would have been changed. In either case, specialization and trade provide economic gains; restrictions on trade impede specialization and generate economic losses, as compared with what would have resulted under open trade. A physician who is also a superior weaver might none the less buy sweaters from a less-gifted weaver, because the value of the sweater would be much less than the value of the medical services that he could have rendered in the time it would take him to make the sweater. Whether that sweater is bought from a weaver who resides within the same nation as the physician or from a foreign weaver is irrelevant from the standpoint of the principles of specialization and gains from trade.

6   Nations do not trade, people do

Issues of international trade are commonly framed in terms of nations trading. This, for instance, was the framework that David Ricardo used in formulating and presenting the law of comparative advantage. And it is the way that the theory of international trade is typically presented today. Despite the widespread use of a language that speaks of nations trading, this usage has some problematic features.

To be sure, we recognize that a model of trade between nations can, like any analytical model, serve simply as a means of simplifying arguments. Some Americans might buy beer produced in Germany, while some Germans buy software programs made in America. Not all Americans by any means would buy German beer, and some Germans would even buy American beer. Similarly, not all Germans would buy software made in America, and some Americans would buy software made in Germany. A simple characterization of the United States' (*sic*) export of software to Germany in exchange for beer would make for a simple model that was true to two primary facts: Americans spend more on German beer than Germans spend on American beer, and Germans spend more on American software than Americans spend on German software.

As with any model, its value depends on how carefully it is used. A model that speaks of nations trading is simpler and more economical to describe than one that presents all such trades as being among individuals who happen to live in different nations. The use of a model of nations, and not people, trading would probably do little, if any, harm if it were regarded simply as a statistical statement, similar to the one that notes that the average family has 1.8 children. In the case of children, there is no danger that anyone would claim that this statement of an average family provides any basis for normative analysis.

The same cannot be said, however, for models of international trade, so long as those models are kept at the aggregative level of nations trading. There is an extensive literature on trade and commercial policy that is written from the perspective that nations trade. If America is viewed as trading software to Germany in exchange for beer, various lines of questioning arise concerning such things as whether an American tariff on German beer might improve the terms of trade for America; and if it might, whether that improvement would be more valuable than the reduced volume of trade that results from the tariff. This is a problematical line of questioning, unless it is assumed that all Americans, and all Germans, are identical – an assumption that, in turn, is equivalent to assuming that America and Germany are one-person nations.

Models that construe trades as between nations and not as between persons can easily lead to a form of economic nationalism that in turn can easily degenerate into a justification for neomercantilism. Mercantilism was an economic doctrine that arose in a period of large empires headed by kings, as illustrated primarily by England, France, Spain and Holland. Economic policy was construed principally as a means of promoting the king's interests in such things as personal and court consumption and foreign conquests. The well-being of individual citizens was incidental and mattered only to the extent that such well-being supported the king's interests.

Suetonius noted in his biographical essays on *The Twelve Caesars* that the Roman Emperor Tiberius once remarked, in response to a proposed tax increase: 'A good shepherd shears his flock; he does not flay them' (1957: 131). The king was the shepherd, lord or owner, the people were his subjects, and he should shear but not skin them, because if they were skinned they would not be as productive for the king, and they might even be enlisted in some rebellious or seditious cause. What may be wise counsel for a mercantilist king is not sensible for a liberal democracy, where government is viewed not as a source of rights but as a protector.

It is very easy to use economically nationalistic arguments to support neomercantalist practices, once the fiction that nations trade is invoked. If America is construed as trading software for German beer, rather than as some Americans buying beer from Germans and some Americans selling software to Germans, it seems almost natural to construe American commercial policy in terms of how it promotes some fictionalized aggregate or average American interest. The debate over terms of trade is thus regarded in principle as being determinative, with the only question being whether the improvement in the terms of trade is worth the restriction in trade. Such a focus on nations trading obscures all of the variations among individuals that are a central feature of the division of labor and knowledge in a complex society.

Suppose an American tariff on German beer were found to improve the terms of trade, which means that the amount of beer imported per unit of software exported increases. In what sense is this a desirable objective of trade policy? Americans who drink German beer are harmed because the tariff raises the price, thereby leading those Americans to drink less German beer and to drink more American beer which they find less desirable. Domestic producers of substitute beer will gain from an increased market for their product. The tariff thus worsens the position of beer-drinkers relative to beer-producers. It also worsens the position of American software exporters, because the reduced volume of German beer exports to America will in turn reduce the German demand for American software. In this case, this will result primarily because the decreased American demand for Deutschmarks that results from the tariff will lead to an appreciation in the value of the dollar, which will make American software more expensive in Germany.

In short, once it is recognized that it is people that trade and not nations, the conventional analysis of trade policy that operates in terms of national aggregates becomes questionable and problematical. Statements about national aggregates will generally bury vast differences among individuals in how they are affected by different trade policies. The economic nationalism that aggregate statements about trade policy seem almost naturally to promote fails to consider some important issues concerning the relation between individual citizens and the state in a liberal polity.

7   Trade policy and human welfare in a liberal polity

The problem of economic policy is starkly different for a mercantilist than for a classical liberal polity. The mercantilist polity has *subjects*, who in turn are simply objects or inputs into the king's own production function. Some kings may turn out to be ordinarily despotic, while others prove to be enlightenedly so. Regardless of the substance of the king's rule, however, individuals will be subjects and not citizens, and the problem of state policy will be something for the king to resolve however he sees fit. This is not to say that the king's choice of policy will be a simple matter. It could be quite difficult, reflecting some deep and difficult questions of knowledge. For instance, the king might be an enlightened despot who wants only to promote the well-being of his subjects, but faces much uncertainty in seeking to do so. For one thing, the impact of a tariff on the well-being of the king's subjects will depend on whether other nations take retaliatory action. Even if the king feels confident about what foreigners will do in response to a tariff, the king could be unsure about the relative extent of the harm to those of his subjects who consume the taxed product and the benefit to those who produce substitutes for the taxed product. He could also be uncertain about his own evaluation or assessment of those benefits and harms, not least because he is uncertain about whether the benefits to some will generate more support for his rule than the harms to others will generate by way of opposition.

Regardless of the difficulties the king may face, they are *his* difficulties. He faces an administrative decision about how to use his resources so as best to promote his ends. The setting is complex, in that he has no simple recipe to follow, so the consequences of his choices cannot be known in advance. Uncertainty is unavoidable. Therefore, he may choose trade policies in the belief that they will secure more support than they will cost, only to find himself exiled or beheaded three years later through what becomes recognized as a miscalculation.

A classical liberal polity, however, has *citizens* and not subjects, and the problem of policy is not a matter of administrative choices, regardless of how deeply veiled in uncertainty those choices might be. Such a classical liberal polity as the United States once was is one that is founded upon the logically prior rights of its citizens. As such, government is not a source of rights, but rather is a reflection of people's use of their rights. There is no doubt that international issues are important elements in a classical liberal polity. Many of these are pursued through treaties and conventions. The extent of territorial limits, the ownership of Antarctica, and mining in the ocean are examples. Yet the presence of trade across national boundaries does not provide great areas of concern or interest that differ significantly from purely domestic trade.

8   The division of knowledge in commerce and politics

While it is common in textbook presentations of economics to portray a competitive market as one where participants have full knowledge of relevant market opportunities, a growing literature on the economics of information and knowledge has developed over the past two decades.[10] For the most part, this literature takes the presumption of full information as a point of departure or orientation, and examines the operation of market processes as departures are made from full information.

Obscured by this approach is the recognition, articulated by Hayek (1945), that there is no such thing as full knowledge. Economic processes are far too complex for anyone ever to have anything even remotely approaching full knowledge. If such a fullness of knowledge were possible, markets would be unnecessary. Hayek's central insight offers an alternative point of analytical departure to starting with some presumption of full knowledge and then reducing the amount of knowledge that people are presumed to possess. This alternative perspective starts with a case where individual participants know a great deal about their narrow areas of greatest concern, and know quite little about almost everything else.[11]

A commercial society is characterized by a division of knowledge at least as much as it is characterized by a division of labor. People specialize in what they know as much as they specialize in what they do. Markets do not require full knowledge for their operation, nor do they generate anything approaching full knowledge as a result of their operation. Rather, they generate a sufficient distribution and specialization of knowledge that enables people to fare well despite their general ignorance, because experts are harnessed to the service of the amateurs through the operation of market institutions.

This point about the division and specialization of knowledge is the normal situation in all human affairs, in the usual commercial market places as well as in the political market place. In both the commercial and political market places, the distribution of information is strongly asymmetric. In all such settings, most people know little about most of the choices they make while knowing quite a lot about a few. The consequences of this specialization and division of knowledge, however, may differ significantly as between commercial and political market places, due to the different institutional settings within which those market places operate.

In the commercial market place for word-processing software, for instance, buyers typically will know little about how such software works; but through such avenues as reading magazines and talking with friends and colleagues, buyers will recognize that some software seems easier to use or has more interesting capabilities than other software. By contrast, producers of software programs will know a lot about the operation of their programs. Yet, to prosper in the commercial market place, they will have to serve the particular preferences of their customers.

Although customers typically know little about how software programs work, they are able to judge how satisfied they are with particular programs. Producers must be alert continually to the prospect of losing customers to other producers, as well as seeking to locate new customers. As a result of the operations of a market for software, consumers are able bring together a volume of expertise that is in no one's capacity to acquire. In the commercial market place, the ignorance of consumers threatens only limited harm; for the institutions of property and contract law operate to prevent producers from taking advantage of their superior knowledge.

The political market place differs in important respects. To illustrate, suppose that a familiar component of the commercial market place such as the consumer purchase of groceries were transferred to the political market place. The supply of groceries would now be directed through legislative processes. In a two-party system of government, candidates would compete during the election period for the right to operate retail stores during the subsequent period. The competing candidates would offer competing bundles of grocery items as their platforms, and voters would choose between the candidates on the basis of their evaluation of the promises and platforms offered by the candidates, possibly with those evaluations tempered by some assessment of the reliability of the candidates' platforms. In any case, the political market place, at the stage of voter choice, involves a form of full-line forcing, in contrast to the commercial market place where voters can pick and choose among the various items offered by competing suppliers.[12]

In the commercial market place, unfulfilled promises will lead to a loss of business as customers go elsewhere. In some cases they may lead to law suits, if the unfulfilment is in breach of contract. In the political market place, however, unfulfilled promises are immune from legal challenge, and they will result in a loss of business only to the extent that they lead voters to change the way they vote in the next election.

In the commercial market place, claims made by sellers must survive in a competitive process in which buyers are usually able to experiment with alternative options if they choose to do so. A particular seller who advertises a better software program that integrates all existing database and spreadsheet programs, and which can be learned by anyone in 60 minutes, may sell some copies on the basis of such a claim. However, the simultaneous existence of other software producers provides a setting in which any particular producer's claims will be tested. The contrary experiences of customers who have had better success with the products of other sellers will redound to the detriment of the claimant.

It would be different, though, if software were instead provided through the political market place. In the general-fund analogue to this setting, software would be financed through taxation and distributed to users free of charge or at a charge that was subsidized by taxes. In any case, there would no longer exist competing alternatives to raise questions about whether or not the government's software is really the best that people can expect. Information about price would no longer exist. All that existed would be claims about quality. Yet, information about quality is more difficult to acquire and to assess than is information about price, particularly when competing alternatives are absent, which reduces the force of competition in the political market place.

Furthermore, political market places encourage a greater variance in the acquisition of knowledge than would occur in a commercial market place. The reason for this is that, for the most part, individuals cannot trade on the knowledge they acquire in the political market place. In the commercial market place, a potential consumer can trade upon the knowledge he acquires about software programs. More-careful shopping translates directly into lower prices or more-suitable products. Whatever choices people make about how much information to acquire, it is they who bear the consequences of their choices. Moreover, they do so in an environment where producers have strong incentives to advance contending claims relative to other producers. Competition among suppliers generates a supply of information, and the situation whereby consumers bear the consequences of their choices generates a demand for information.

A consumer faced with full-line forcing in the commercial market place still bears the value consequences of his choice. He can either accept the entire package the producer offers, or he can pursue other options, but in either case he is free to act directly upon whatever knowledge he acquires. If, through the acquisition of more knowledge, the consumer should come to regret a prior choice, this is unfortunate from that consumer's perspective; but, still, it is his choice. A consumer in the commercial market place will stop well short of becoming fully informed as a rational response to positive information costs.

It is different in the political market place, particularly in the presence of full-line forcing, where bundles of commodities or programs and not individual commodities or programs are offered for choice. In two-party systems, two competing candidates offer different platforms containing different bundles of programs. In a political market place, however, the voter is not able to act upon whatever information he acquires. For his choice is rarely, if ever, decisive in choosing which candidate gets elected. In elections, there is practically no connection between the individual's acquisition of knowledge and the political choices that result.

This situation weakens the position of consumers and strengthens the position of producers. In all market places, commercial and political, producers are better informed about their offerings than are consumers. This is simply one aspect of the division and specialization of knowledge. In political markets, this asymmetry is vastly increased. The incentives of producers in the political market place are changed accordingly. With consumers less interested and less diligent, producers respond by selling more image than substance.

9   Interest groups, rent-seeking and the political market place

There is one significant exception to the general principle that consumers will be less informed about producer offerings in the political market place than in the commercial market place. This concerns cases where the consumers of political offerings take the form of concentrated interest groups. For instance, a quota limiting the amount of sugar that can be imported into the United States keeps the domestic price of sugar above its world market price. As a result, the typical American consumer pays a few dollars more each year, while the 10,000 or so sugar farmers in the United States on average gain more than $100,000 per year from the quota program.

In this case, as with many programs that restrict international trade, small harms are placed on many people while large benefits are conferred on a few. The sugar program illustrates this situation well; but numerous other programs have this same central character. Even if sugar farmers have large families, and even if distant relatives are taken into account, the beneficiaries from the program would constitute far fewer than 1 per cent of the population. For more than 99 per cent of the population, the sugar program would be a source of harm, though a small harm, for each individual consumer. When those harms are aggregated across consumers, however, they become substantial, and generally are much greater in magnitude than the gains to the sugar farmers.

Sugar quota programs, along with numerous similar programs that have the same impact, are part of a bundle of programs that voters may appear to select in the political market place. Yet hardly anyone even knows that such programs exist. Those who do know are those who gain much from them.[13] A few participants in the political market place with specialized interests know what the program accomplishes, while the remaining participants know next to nothing about it.

Economists use the term *rent* differently from everyone else; they use it to describe a situation where some productive input, a person, a piece of equipment or a parcel of land, is receiving a price beyond what would be required to induce the owner of that input to allow its services to be supplied. Rents, as used by economists, could be taken away without affecting the supply choices that owners of those inputs would make. Gordon Tullock (1967) developed the economic theory of rent-seeking, although the concept he developed was not actually called rent-seeking until a publication by Krueger in 1974. Suppose a legislature has the ability to restrict market competition by imposing quotas. One way of analysing such a program is to say that it enriches producers at the expense of consumers, which is to say that it redistributes wealth. Regulatory redistributions of this kind tend to be extremely inefficient and, as such, are unexplainable conundrums for economists who are not acquainted with public choice and who fail to apply rent-seeking analysis.

In reality, the political market place acts systematically and not randomly. As potential recipients of rents, people will seek to secure a competitive advantage by undertaking expenditures that will enhance their prospects. It is even easy to construct cases where politically established rents benefit no one. A substantial literature has now developed on rent-seeking. It suffices here to note that the ability of a legislature to change the locus of property rights will change the structure of economic activity. Inputs will shift into the creation of political relationships.

Washington DC leads the nation in the location of national trade associations. The preponderant majority of chief executive officers of large corporations pass through Washington DC on business on at least a monthly basis. Little direct production takes place in Washington. Yet governmental authority is a necessary input in almost all productive activities: producers use government to secure privileged market restrictions, to prevent such privileges from being removed, and to prevent competitors from securing similar privileges.

It is commonly alleged that a democratic polity is the natural political complement of a market economy. Freedom of trade in the economic sphere may readily seem to be complementary to freedom of participation in the political sphere. However, there is good reason to think that the relation between classical liberalism and democracy is a difficult one to maintain. From a number of directions, the contemporary literature on public choice articulates how a mercantilist economic regime is a 'natural' outcome of democratic political processes.

Democratic political institutions do not lead necessarily to the creation and maintenance of internal free trade; they do so only to the extent that the existing constitutional rules of the game block the natural mercantilist tendencies of democratic institutions. To illustrate, suppose an economy is divided into 100 interest groups of equal size. The internal structure of the economy of this isolated state is such that there are 100 industries of equal size. Suppose further that the economy is organized competitively. The interest-group model of government, along with the theory of rent-seeking, views competing interests as endeavoring to carve out islands of protection in this competitive sea. One simple way of doing so is to cartelize an industry.

The members of each industry are in a position to capture a share of the monopoly rents that would be created by successful cartelization. A successful effort to do so on the part of a single industry would bring about the best of all possible worlds for its members: the ability to sell at a monopoly price while being able to buy at competitive prices. However, what holds for one industry holds for all. The members of each industry are in the same position of being better off as a monopolist in an otherwise competitive economy. In such circumstances, a prisoners' dilemma situation clearly exists. All members of the society are better off living under a competitive institutional order than they are living under an inclusive mercantilist order.

10 Principle, expediency and trade policy

For the most part, government in a classical liberal order is primarily engaged in protecting rights and preserving order. This leads unequivocally to the support of trade, both domestically and internationally. Are there cases where restrictions on trade are consistent with a market-oriented but not a classical liberal polity? In the case of domestic trade, it is usually claimed that external costs may provide instances where a restriction on trade is consistent with market principles.

Clearly, there are possible cases of external cost on an international level. Claims and allegations about ozone holes, chloroflurocarbons and the like are some examples. For the most part these situations lead to discussions of treaties. They are not readily amenable to restrictions on trade. A few cases, hypothetical or not, can always be given. But many, if not most or all, such cases face a problem of demonstrating their applicability. It is far easier to articulate cases of external cost as support for protection than it is to demonstrate their applicability. What often happens is that interest groups secure protection for their benefit at public expense, mainly because they have cogent-sounding arguments on their side in a setting where there are no strongly organized interests in opposition.

Nice thoughts and high principle do motivate people, often quite strongly. But it is unwise to rely to any extent upon such sentiments. The strong forces of self-interest will never be denied their presence. The constitutional trick is to arrange the organs and bodies of governance in such a way that self-interest tends to conform to the pursuit of high ideals. This works out pretty well in a market economy. A person interested in increasing his net worth is able to do so only by providing services of value to other people, and with those other people paying for those services from their own property.

Government, however, operates under different incentives. Such political programs as trade restrictions are almost always secured by a favoured few to the detriment of the politically unorganized majority. The extent to which democratic political processes support individual rights depends importantly on how political institutions operate to generate knowledge and channel incentive.

As Vincent Ostrom (1987) explains, government represents a Faustian bargain. It represents the use of an instrument of evil – force over people – for the good that such evil might accomplish: peace and prosperity. While an instrument of evil can be used to accomplish good, it can also accomplish much evil. The mixture of good and evil that is likely to be accomplished depends significantly on the manner in which government authority is constituted. This the American Founding Fathers recognized clearly, as the essays in *The Federalist* show. This book seeks to demonstrate the wisdom of the Founding Fathers with regard to trade and its protection, and to confound the forces of protectionism that have seized control of the United States political process.

Notes

1   The only exception to this statement arises if one person's absolute advantage is of the same relative strength across all activities. In terms of the illustration developed in the text, no trade would arise if Friday could gather nine coconuts per hour. In this case, he would be three times as productive as Crusoe in both activities, and there would be no potential gains from specialization between them.

2   There was a voluminous amount of economic writing before Smith, as a perusal of any text on the history of economic thought will show. Yet *The Wealth of Nations* is widely regarded as the first major treatise setting forth the idea of a largely self-regulating economic order.

3   A good collection of essays on this theme is Hayek (1945). While Marxist ideology projected the image of a centrally planned economy as a replacement for a market economy, it was never a planned economy because such an economy would have been impossible. Rather, it was a corrupt and inefficient form of market economy, which generated much lower standards of living and greater terror than would have resulted in a true market economy. See, for instance, Roberts (1971). These themes are treated from the perspective of general economic theory in Sowell (1980).

4   This is not to deny that contracts can be enforced without state authority. There is substantial evidence to the contrary, much of which is surveyed in Benson (1990). Rather, this liberal claim is only to note that the state has come to play a large, though not exclusive, rule in such enforcement.

5   Market provision in such cases is not impossible, however, as Coase (1974) shows for the case of lighthouses in seventeenth-century England. Even in this case, though, it is notable that the state collected tolls from ships as they came into harbor, and passed along the revenues to the lighthouse owners. This was market provision, but still with a discernible presence of the state.

6   Epstein (1985) uses the construct of 'forced exchanges' to convey this idea.

7   This case is discussed in Stroup and Baden (1983).

8   This theme is developed clearly in Cordato (1992). For a collection of essays from essentially the same perspective, see Wagner (1991).

9   Such illustrations as this one should not be taken to imply the absence of property rights in water. For an interesting analysis of common law processes for the control of water pollution, and how the development of those processes were stunted by the Clean Water Act of 1972, see Meiners and Yandle (1992).

10 This literature is surveyed clearly and crisply in Phlips (1988).

11 For an effort to examine some of the consequences for economic analysis of adopting this kind of Hayekian perspective, see O'Driscoll and Rizzo (1985).

12 Full-line forcing is explored in Burstein (1960). The importance of full-line forcing for politics is examined in Breton (1974), and Wagner and Weber (1975).

13 Or who would lose much if the program were repealed. It is possible for someone to lose if a program is repealed without gaining from the program. The value of the program is capitalized into the value of sugar farms. Someone who bought a farm after the quota program was enacted would not gain anything from it, but would lose should the program be repealed.

References

Benson, Bruce (1990) *The Enterprise of Law* (San Francisco: Pacific Research Institute).

Breton, Albert (1974) *The Economic Theory of Representative Government* (Chicago: Aldine).

Buchanan, James M. (1975) *The Limits of Liberty* (Chicago: University of Chicago Press).

Burstein, M.L. (1960) 'A theory of full-line forcing', *Northwestern University Law Review*, 55: 62–95.

Coase, Ronald H. (1960) 'The problem of social cost', *Journal of Law and Economics*, 3 (October): 1–44.

Coase, Ronald H. (1974) 'The lighthouse in economics', *Journal of Law and Economics* 17 (October): 357–76.

Cordato, Roy E. (1992) *Welfare Economics and Externalities in an Open Ended Universe* (Boston: Kluwer).

Darby, Michael R. and Karni, Edi (1973) 'Free competition and the optimal amount of fraud', *Journal of Law and Economics*, 16 (April): 67–88.

De Jasay, Anthony (1985) *The State* (Oxford: Basil Blackwell).

De Jouvenal, Bertrand (1961) 'The chairman's problem', *American Political Science Review*, 55 (June): 368–72.

Epstein, Richard A. (1985) *Takings: Private Property and the Power of Eminent Domain* (Cambridge, Mass.: Harvard University Press).

Hayek, Friedrich (ed.) (1945) *Collectivist Economic Planning* (London: George Routledge).

Krueger, Anne O. (1974) 'The political economy of the rent-seeking society', *American Economic Review*, 64 (June): 291–303.

McKean, Roland N. (1973) 'Government and the consumer', *Southern Economic Journal*, 39 (April).

Meiners, Roger E. and Yandle, Bruce (1992) 'Constitutional choice for the control of water pollution', *Constitutional Political Economy*, 3 (Fall): 359–80.

Nelson, Philip (1971) 'Information and consumer behavior', *Journal of Political Economy*, 78 (April): 311–29.

O'Driscoll, G.P. and Rizzo, M. (1985) *The Economics of Time and Ignorance* (Oxford: Basil Blackwell).

Ostrom, Vincent (1987) *The Political Theory of a Compound Republic,* 2nd edn. (Lincoln: University of Nebraska Press).

Phlips, Louis (1988) *The Economics of Imperfect Information* (Cambridge: Cambridge University Press).

Ricardo, David (1817) *Principles of Political Economy and Taxation* (London: J.M. Dent, 1911).

Roberts, Paul Craig (1971) *Alienation and the Soviet Economy* (Albuquerque: University of New Mexico Press).

Smith, Adam (1776) *An Inquiry into the Nature and Causes of the Wealth of Nations* (New York: Modern Library, 1937).

Sowell, Thomas (1980) *Knowledge and Decisions* (New York: Basic Books).

Stigler, George J. (1975) *The Citizen and the State* (Chicago: University of Chicago Press).

Stroup, Richard L. and Baden, John A. (1983) *Natural Resources: Bureaucratic Myths and Environmental Management* (San Francisco: Pacific Research Institute).

Suetonius (1957) *The Twelve Caesars*, trans. Robert Graves (Harmondsworth, Middx: Penguin Books).

Tullock, Gordon (1967) 'The welfare costs of tariffs, monopolies and theft', *Western Economic Journal* 5: 224–32.

Wagner, Richard E. (1977) 'Advertising and the state', in David G. Tuerck (ed.), *The Political Economy of Advertising* (Washington, DC: American Enterprise Institute).

Wagner, Richard E. (ed.) (1991) *Charging for Government: User Charges and Earmarked Taxes in Principle and Practice* (London: Routledge).

Wagner Richard E. and Weber, Warren E. (1975) 'Competition, monopoly and the organization of government in metropolitan areas', *Journal of Law and Economics* 18: 661–84

2 The case for free trade

1 Introduction

Few countries have anything approaching completely free trade. The city-state of Hong Kong may be the only modern nation with absolutely no tariffs, import quotas or other non-tariff barriers to trade. Spectacular as the economic success of that country has been, no other late twentieth-century government has dared to embrace free trade, however powerful the arguments that can be marshalled in its support.

Yet the importance of trade as a means of enabling individuals to specialize in producing what they are good at has a long pedigree stretching all the way back to the Ancient Greeks. Plato (1974), for example, advocated this principle when arguing in *The Republic* that the quantity and quality of the goods available to society would increase substantially if farmers specialized in growing food, builders in constructing houses and weavers in producing clothes.

If the increased output from specialization was to benefit society at large, it must be accompanied by trade. Trade would enable each of Plato's workers to diversify their consumption into food, accommodation, and clothing. Presumably such uncoerced exchanges would make each participant better off, since otherwise they would not occur. This would be true whether exchange took the primitive form of barter or the more sophisticated form available within a money-based economy.

Writing in 1776, in *The Wealth of Nations*, the book that first formalized economics as a discipline worthy of specialized study, Adam Smith refocused attention on Plato's important insight. His famous pin factory example demonstrated the empirical fact that ten workers, each specializing in different tasks, collectively could produce thousands of times more pins than was possible by each worker producing pins in a non-specialized manner. Smith, of course, was the ultimate advocate of free trade. As Bagehot (1880) was to state, Smith's name can no more be dissociated from free trade than Homer's from the siege of Troy:

> So long as the doctrines of protection exist – and they seem likely to do so, as human interests are what they are, and human nature is what it is – Adam Smith will always be quoted as the great authority on Anti-Protectionism, as the man who first told the world the truth, so that the world could learn and believe it. (Bagehot 1880)

The notion that unilateral free trade is a desirable objective of policy irrespective of the behavior of other national governments, advanced by Smith in 1776, was formalized by David Ricardo into the doctrine of comparative advantage, as outlined in Chapter 1 of this book. Since Ricardo's case is critically dependent on the assumption that market prices reflect social costs, it is not at all surprising that the various challenges to the doctrine of free trade have come over the last two centuries from theorists who have focused on one or another market failure (Bhagwati 1994: 232).

In Sections 2 and 3 of this chapter we set out some fundamental principles of economic and political philosophy that guide our thinking on the issue of free trade and that, at least in part, set us apart from the mainstream thinking of neoclassical economics. In section 4, we identify the predictable economic gains from free trade, including benefits typically ignored in standard treatments. In section 5, we distinguish between nationalist and cosmopolitan formulations of the free-trade argument. In sections 6 and 7 we distinguish between the various instruments of trade protection and outline the differing impacts of these instruments on market and political process. Section 8 concludes the chapter with a plea that economic liberty should be accorded the high moral ground in the debate over free trade versus protection.

2   Methodological individualism

Individualism is a social theory or ideology which assigns a higher moral value to the individual than to the community or to society and which consequently advocates leaving individuals free to act as they think most conducive to their self-interest (MacPherson 1987: 790). The term was also used descriptively during the nineteenth century to denote the competitive market system which allows the direction of the economy to be the unintended outcome of the decisions made by myriad individuals about the uses to which they will put their own labor and resources.

The individualism that informs analysis in this book takes its modern form in the writings of Friedrich von Hayek (1945) and James M Buchanan (1966). The intellectual tradition to which it belongs begins with the scholarship of John Locke, Bernard Mandeville and David Hume. It achieves its full stature in the works of Josiah Tucker, Adam Ferguson and Adam Smith and in that of their great contemporary, Edmund Burke. It is carried forward into the nineteenth century in the writings of two of that century's greatest historians and political philosophers: Alexis de Tocqueville and Lord Acton. It was all but destroyed during the twentieth century by philosophical radicals who followed Benthamite utilitarian principles that trapped them under the influence of another kind of individualism of a quite different origin (Hayek 1945: 4).

This alternative influence, ultimately so dangerous for true individualism, found its strongest early representation in the works of French and other continental writers – the Encyclopedists, Rousseau and the Physiocrats – with Cartesian rationalism playing a dominant role in its composition. It is a major source of modern socialism, and has been castigated by Hayek as constructivist rationalism, a doctrine of fatal conceit, based on the synoptic delusion of its would-be social engineering disciples (Hayek 1988).

True individualism is primarily a theory of society, an attempt to understand the forces which determine the social life of man. Only secondarily is it a set of political maxims derived from this view of society. Its basic contention is that there is no other way to understand social phenomena but through an understanding of individual actions directed toward other people and guided by their expected behavior (Hayek 1945: 6). By tracing the combined effects of individual actions, we discover that many of the institutions on which human achievements rest have arisen and are functioning without a designing and directing mind; that the spontaneous collaboration of free men often creates things which are greater than their individual minds can ever fully comprehend.

True individualism contends that man has achieved what he has in spite of the fact that he is only partly guided by reason and that his individual reason is bounded and imperfect. This somewhat antirationalist approach, which regards man as a very fallible being whose errors are corrected only in the course of a spontaneous social process, and which aims at making the best of very imperfect material, is probably the most characteristic feature of English individualism (Hayek 1945: 9).

Indeed, this viewpoint strongly influenced Adam Smith, whose chief concern was not so much with what man occasionally might achieve when he was at his best, but that he should have as little opportunity as possible to do harm when he was at his worst. Indeed it is scarcely too much to claim that the main merit of the individualism which Smith and his contemporaries advocated is that it is a system under which bad men do least harm (Hayek 1945: 9).

The chief concern of the great individualist writers, indeed, was to find a set of institutions by which man could be induced, by his own choice and from motives which determined his ordinary conduct, to contribute as much as possible to the wealth of a nation. In such an endeavor, these scholars were well aware of the conflicts as well as the harmony of individual interests and stressed the importance of facilitating institutions where rules and principles would reconcile conflicting interests without giving any one group power to make their views and interests always prevail over those of others.

From such concerns, the main practical conclusion of true individualism is a demand for strict limitation of all coercive or exclusive power. This conclusion is not to be read as an endorsement of anarchism, which itself is a product of the fatal conceit to which individualism is irrevocably opposed. It does not deny the necessity of coercive power, certainly does not reject the minimal state; rather, it seeks to limit coercion to these areas where it is indispensable. It seeks to enable us to distinguish between the acceptable agenda and the non-agenda of government.

Specifically, individualism emphasizes the acceptance of formal principles or rules which enable man to distinguish between mine and thine and from which he and his fellows can ascertain what is his and what is somebody else's sphere of responsibility. An individualist system thus is based on universal acceptance of general principles as the means of creating order in social affairs; and not on the enforcement of specific orders.

Individualism affirms that all government should be democratic. It does not share in any belief in the omnicompetence of majority decisions. It argues that, under democracy, the sphere of enforced command ought to be restricted within fixed limits. In the individualistic approach, the political structure is conceived as something that emerges from the choice processes of individual participants (Buchanan 1966). The state is viewed as if it ultimately derives from individual consent. There exists no social welfare function, no public interest as such in a society of freely choosing individuals; and there seems to be no reason to invent such a conception for analytical convenience.

This rejection of any organic notion of the state does not imply necessarily that the political process reduces to a simple struggle for power among individuals and groups or that it must culminate in the tyranny of the majority as feared by Tocqueville, although it may do either or both. It is necessary to distinguish sharply between day-to-day political decision-making, where the struggle often does reduce to that among conflicting individuals or group interests, and constitutional decision-making where individuals choose the set of rules under which subsequent day-to-day decisions are to be made.

In making choices at the constitutional level, the individual does not know, nor can he easily predict, what particular issues will be presented subsequent to the adoption of a rule. Even if he can predict with some accuracy the sort of issues that may arise, he will be less able to predict his own position *vis-à-vis* the other members of society. Faced with such uncertainty, an individual will try to select a rule that will work reasonably well for an unpredictable series of events. In such circumstances, self-interest imposes on the individual an attitude and a behavior pattern that is not identical with that dictated by the same self-interest when an individual makes choices on specific political issues (Buchanan and Tullock 1962).

We shall return to this constitutional perspective in the final chapter of this book following a detailed public-choice analysis of trade politics in the United States. In that chapter, we shall confront the individual American with a constitutional choice over trade policy rules, having fully informed him of the historical path of US trade policy in the absence of binding constitutional constraints. If the reader will then engage in this conceptual constitutional experiment, we do not doubt that enlightened self-interest will lead him to make the free trade choice.

3   The right to life, liberty and property

In 1703, John Locke wrote a letter to a relative, anticipating a judgement of posterity with the commendation: 'Property I have nowhere found more clearly explained than in a book entitled, *Two Treatises of Government.*' It is to this text that we now turn to review the relationship between property rights and civil government from the perspective of social contract theory. For this perceived relationship also plays a major role in our approach to the issue of free trade.

The Lockeian allegory starts unequivocally prior to the establishment of civil society, with man still in the state of nature:

> To understand Political Power right, and derive it from its Original, we must consider what State all Men are naturally in, and that is a *state of perfect Freedom* to order their Actions, and dispose of their Possessions and Persons, as they think fit, within the bounds of the Law of Nature, without asking leave, or depending upon the Will of any other Man. (Locke 1690: 269)

The state of nature is a state of liberty in the negative sense of that term, implying the absence of coercion of one individual by another. It is not a state of license. Rather, it is subject to natural law which requires that no one ought to harm another in his *life, liberty and property*. In the state of nature, where there is no government, each individual has executive authority to enforce this law:

> And that all Men may be restrained from invading others Rights and from doing hurt to one another, and the Law of Nature be observed, which willeth the Peace and *Preservation of Mankind*, the *Execution* of the Law of Nature is in that State, put into every Man's hands, whereby every one has a right to punish the transgressors of that Law to such a degree, as may hinder its Violation. (Locke 1690: 271)

The existence of natural law would not eliminate all inconveniences from the state of nature. Indeed, such inconveniences must certainly be great since men may be judges in their own case. Yet, this is a much better situation than that in which men are bound to submit to the unjust will of another. At least in the state of nature, if an individual judges wrongly in his own case he is answerable to the rest of mankind. For the most part, Locke had a favorable impression of man and judged the state of nature to be 'a state of peace, goodwill, mutual assistance and preservation'.

Mankind is always vulnerable in the state of nature to the state of war which is 'a state of enmity, malice, violence and mutual destruction'. The state of war is characterized by the use of force, or a declared design of force, upon the peace of another, where there is no common superior, on earth, to appeal to for relief. To avoid this depicted state of war is a major reason individuals quit the state of nature and put themselves into society. For the state of war fundamentally threaten's each individual's natural right to life, liberty and property.

In Locke's view, each individual has a right to the property in his own person and a right to the product of his own labor. In addition, individuals create property rights for themselves out of the common pool of available resources by mixing their labor with such resources and, in this way, annexing them:

> Whatsoever then he moves out of the State that Nature hath provided, and left it in, he hath mixed his *labour* with, and joyned to it something that is his own, and thereby makes it his *Property*. It being by him removed from the common state Nature placed it in, it hath by this *labour* something annexed to it, that excludes the common right of other Men. For this *labour* being the unquestionable Property of the Labourer, no Man but he can have a right to what that is once joyned to, at least where there is enough and as good left in common for others. (Locke: 1690, 288)

Locke offered a religious justification for his theory of natural rights based on a careful interpretation of the Old Testament, emphasizing that although God gave the world to men in common he also gave it to the use of the industrious and rational. Only a system of private property rights could ensure the latter outcome. Of course, many people in a more secular age would not accept Locke's religious justification of natural rights. There is an alternative justification, based on the classical liberal objective of human flourishing, that has been advanced by Rasmussen and Den Uyl (1991).

Rasmussen and Den Uyl draw upon Aristotelian ethics to develop an account of human well-being that emphasizes the importance of self-directedness. Living rationally is described as *eudaimonia*, a state of well-being achieved by self-actualization and characterized by the satisfaction of those desires and wants which lead to successful human living, or human flourishing.

Living rationally or intelligently is the over-arching end which integrates and unifies all the other ends of human flourishing. The individual needs to act from his own knowledge and understanding and, thereby, to exercise control and direction over his actions. Thus 'autonomy or self-directedness is an inherent feature of any activity constitutive of human well-being' (Rasmussen and Den Uyl 1991: 71).

From this perspective, it is possible to defend the moral claim that individuals have natural rights that precede any political constitution and that cannot be alienated by any social contract. These natural rights reflect the principle that individuals may not be used for attaining ends not of their own choosing. The rights relevant to human flourishing are negative rights, placing duties upon others designed to protect an individual's autonomy. The natural right to private property arguably is the most important of all such natural rights when viewed from this perspective of human flourishing (Rowley 1993: 72).

The natural right to property is simply another name for the freedom to act according to one's choices, defining allowable acts of transformation of the material world. In this perspective, even the Lockeian proviso is moot. For there can never be 'enough and as good' left for others if every action results in a unique transformation. No one has a right to the acts of transformation of others, since there can be no pre-existing claim to that which does not yet exist.

If individuals are endowed with natural rights in the state of nature, it is no small matter to leave that state and to enter into civil society. By agreeing to leave the state of nature, the individual sacrifices his right to judge and to punish the breaches of natural law by others. This is no mean sacrifice. It will not be countenanced by those with property unless political society assumes full responsibility for protecting property rights and for punishing those who transgress upon these rights:

> For the preservation of Property being the end of Government, and that for which Men enter into Society, it necessarily supposes and requires, that the people should *have property*, without which they must be suppos'd to lose that by entering into Society, which was the end for which they entered into it, too gross an absurdity for any Man to own. (Locke 1690: 360)

If the right to life, liberty and property is acknowledged as fundamental to a constitutional republic such as the United States, significant implications follow for the debate over free trade versus protectionism. Specifically, even if an economic case for protection can be mounted, which we seriously doubt, that case must then somehow overwhelm human flourishing arguments that defend private property from the corrosive tendencies of political society.

4   The economic gains from free trade

Probably the most important insight in all of international economics is the idea that there are *gains from trade* – that is, that when individuals in different countries sell goods and services to one another, this is almost always to their mutual benefit. As Chapter 1 demonstrates, the range of circumstances under which international trade is beneficial is much wider than most people appreciate.

For example, many US businessmen fear that if Japanese productivity overtakes that of the United States, trade with Japan will damage the US economy, because none of the US industries will be able to compete. Similarly, US labor leaders argue that United States workers are hurt by trade with less-advanced countries whose industries are less efficient than those in the US, but whose wages are so much lower that they can undersell US producers.

The theory of comparative advantage conclusively demonstrates, however, that trade between two countries can be mutually beneficial even when one country is more efficient than the other at producing everything and when producers in the less-efficient economy can compete only by paying lower wages. Trade provides benefits by stimulating exports whose production makes relatively heavy use of resources that are locally abundant and by stimulating imports whose production makes heavy use of resources that are locally scarce. Adam Smith recognized this truth, without formalizing it into a general theory, as early as 1776:

> If a foreign country can supply us with a commodity cheaper than we ourselves can make it, better buy it off them with some part of the produce of our own industry, employed in a way in which we have some advantage ... In every country, it always is and must be in the interest of the great body of the people to buy whatever they must of those who sell it the cheapest. (Smith 1776: 422)

In thus arguing for specialization and free trade, Smith was reacting against the mercantilist system then in place in eighteenth-century Britain. Mercantilists viewed international trade as a means of constructing unilateral gains for one country at the expense of others. They argued that a government should use protection to ensure that the country exported more by value than it imported, thus allowing it to accumulate gold. The increased holding of gold was thought to make the nation-state richer and more powerful.

Smith, Ricardo and many other classical economists demonstrated that trade, by enabling countries (or rather their citizens) to exploit differences in the productivity of labor, land and capital, in climate and in mineral resources, would be beneficial overall. For this reason, at least until the last quarter century, non-Marxist economists generally viewed interference with international trade as being against the public interest. Significantly, they tended to hold to this position irrespective of political ideology and irrespective of their willingness or not to recommend activist government intervention with respect to the domestic economy.

Let us illustrate the economic costs and benefits of free trade using as measuring rods two concepts common to neoclassical microeconomics, namely

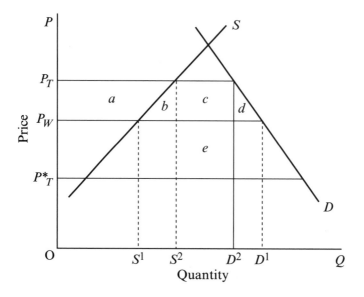

Figure 2.1   The costs and benefits of a tariff

consumer and producer surplus. Figure 2.1 illustrates the costs and benefits of a tariff for the importing country. We interpret these costs and benefits separately for the large country that may be able to shift its terms of trade by tariff impositions and for the small country that cannot do so (Krugman and Obstfeld 1987: 183).

In Figure 2.1, the world price for the commodity under consideration is P_W. A tariff raises the domestic price from P_W to P_T. In the large-country case, it lowers the foreign export price from P_W to P_T^*. In the small-country case, the foreign export price remains at P_W. As a consequence of the tariff imposition, domestic production rises from S^1 to S^2, while domestic consumption falls from D^1 to D^2. The costs and benefits to different groups can be expressed as sums of the areas of five regions, labelled *a,b,c,d,e*.

Consider first the gain to domestic producers. They receive a higher price and a higher producer surplus measured by region *a*. Domestic consumers face a higher price and a loss of consumer surplus equal to the combined regions *a + b + c + d*. The government gains by collecting tariff revenue equal to the combined regions *c + e*.

Evidently, these gains and losses accrue to different individuals. Problems of making interpersonal comparisons of utility make it difficult to reach an overall balance of gain or loss from the tariff. Despite these problems, it is common for analysts of trade policy to attempt to compute the net effect of a tariff on national welfare by assuming that at the margin a dollar's worth of gain or loss is of the same social worth.

On this basis, the net cost of a tariff on welfare is equal to the loss of consumer surplus ($a + b + c + d$) less the increase in producer surplus (a) less the increase in government revenue ($c + e$). In the large-country case, there are two triangles of welfare loss ($b + d$) offset by a rectangle of offsetting gain (e). The triangles represent the efficiency loss that arises because a tariff distorts incentives. The rectangle represents the terms of trade gain that arises because a tariff lowers foreign export prices.

The offsetting gain depends on the ability of the tariff-imposing country to drive down foreign export prices. If the country cannot affect world prices (the typical case), region e disappears, and it is clear that the tariff reduces welfare. It distorts the incentives of both producers and consumers by inducing them to act as if imports are more expensive than they actually are. The perfect-competition, constant-returns-to-scale assumptions implicit in the classical model deny relevance to the terms-of-trade effect and confirm the comparative-advantage result.

At first sight, it may seem that the gains from free trade are surprisingly small, perhaps too small to justify the fuss that economists make about free trade. After all, the triangles $b + d$ do not appear to be large relative to the total consumer and producer surplus under consideration in Figure 2.1. Product by product that may be so, but overall the triangles mount up. One estimate of the overall gain from tariff reductions negotiated in the Uruguay Round, for example, puts the annual gain at $200 billion, or roughly 1 percent of world product (*The Economist* 18 December 1993). Clearly this is not peanuts.

In reality, this measure of welfare loss is much too low, for two reasons. First, as Paul Romer (1994) recently has shown, the conventional analysis implicitly assumes that the set of goods is both fixed and complete. Prices in an economy may be changed by government intervention, and quantities will change as a result – but the list of goods that are traded at some price, in some quantity, will not change. On this assumption, changes at the margin are what matter and the triangles capture all the losses from import barriers.

However, suppose that introducing a new good to a market entails a fixed cost. Then some substantial amount of revenue will be required for the good to be sold at all. By reducing the quantity demanded a little, a tariff may cause the good never to appear. In such circumstances, Romer (1994) argues, the loss is not merely the efficiency triangles, but the entire social surplus.

To illustrate his point, Romer sets out a model of an economy which uses labor and many different kinds of imported capital to produce goods. With fixed costs of the kind just described, tariffs reduce the variety of capital available to domestic producers. On the basis of plausible guesses for the parameters of his model (the elasticity of demand for capital, etc.), Romer compares the cost of protection in a world with a fixed list of capital imputs and in a world with a changeable list. In the first, conventional, case, a tariff of 10 percent reduces national income by 1 percent. But, in the second case, the same tariff reduces national income by 20 percent.

For the advanced nations, the implicit assumption of the conventional model of a fixed list of goods, including capital goods may not be implausible. For the underdeveloped nations, it is plainly wrong. Developing countries do not use smaller amounts of the full range of goods available in the rich countries. They use smaller amounts of a much smaller range. According to Romer (1994): 'a rough guide to the welfare losses in any country will ... be the difference between the range of productive inputs that are available there and the range of productive inputs that could be put to use there'. Seen this way, the cost of bad government in the third world looks vast. And economists have been right, even without fully knowing why, to care so passionately about trade (*The Economist* 16 July 1994: 65).

A second reason conventional measures of the welfare loss associated with protection are too low is their failure to account for rent-seeking costs (Tullock 1967). Rents are here defined as returns in excess of opportunity cost made available to some individuals as a consequence of government intervention. For our purposes, rents may be viewed as the rectangles a, c and e in Figure 2.1 made available to producers and to the potential suppliants for government revenues as a consequence of a tariff imposition. The conventional analysis treats these regions simply as transfers from consumers.

As Tullock (1967) noted, however, the opportunity to obtain rents will induce rational individuals to outlay real resources in search of such rents (rent-seeking). Under certain conditions (Tullock 1980) competitive rent-seeking will dissipate resources equal to the present value of the rents under consideration (rectangles $a + c + e$ in our timeless example). In such circumstances, the welfare cost of tariffs is far higher than conventional analysis suggests (regions $a + b + c + d + e$ in the extreme case). Such costs of rent-seeking predictably occur in advanced as well as in underdeveloped countries and constitute a major argument in the economic case for free trade (Rowley and Tollison 1986).

5   Free trade: national versus cosmopolitan formulations

The economic theory of free trade, outlined in section 4 above, focuses attention on free trade for one country rather than on free trade for all. It makes a strong case for unilateral free trade policy on the part of any single nation state. As such, it offers no direct guidance for the design of an international trading system in circumstances where many or all of the nations under consideration fail to reflect the logic of comparative advantage in their individual trade laws. Are there any indications in this body of economic thought as to what rules might be sought for the governing of trade among nations? To approach this question, Bhagwati (1988, 1993, 1994) cleverly has distinguished between the *national* and the *cosmopolitan* version of the theory of free trade.

The national formulation of the case for free trade is the one that predominantly shapes the policy debate. 'It posits national welfare as the objective of policy and proceeds to demonstrate that free trade will maximize national welfare' (Bhagwati 1993: 18), at least where market prices reflect social costs. 'Premised again on the assumption that prices reflect social costs, the cosmopolitan argument simply elevates to the world level what the national argument did at the level of the nation state' (Bhagwati 1993: 19). If one applies the logic of efficiency to the allocation of activity among all trading nations, and not merely within one's own nation state, it is easy to see that it yields the prescription of free trade everywhere. If any nation uses tariffs or subsidies to drive a wedge between market prices and social costs, then surely this is not consonant with an efficient world allocation of activity.

The two arguments thus share common foundations. Yet they have different implications for matters that have proved to be contentious in the continuing debate over trade policy. If the case for national free trade holds as stated, then it really is irrelevant whether other nations follow free trade or not. *Fair trade* and *reciprocity*, defined as the requirement that others follow free trade if one's own free trade is to make economic sense, are incompatible with the national argument. The prescription that emerges then is for *unilateral* free trade. Not so, however, under the cosmopolitan argument. 'World efficiency requires that *everyone* follow free trade. It is simply not enough that one or more do so The prescription now is *universal* free trade' (Bhagwati 1993: 20).

It is intuitively obvious that if the trade barriers imposed by other nations can be regarded as changeable by the closure of one's own markets, then a nationalist case can be made for departing from unilateral free trade in pursuit of national advantage. Adam Smith acknowledged this possibility in 1776:

> The case in which it may sometimes be a matter of deliberation how far it is proper to continue the free importation of certain foreign goods, is, when some foreign nation restrains by high duties or prohibitions the importation of some of our manufacturers into their country. Revenge in this case naturally dictates retaliation and that we should impose the like duties and prohibitions upon the importation of some or all of their manufactures into ours. Nations accordingly seldom fail to retaliate in the manner. (Smith 1776: 434)

Smith was not fully convinced, however, that such a policy would not fall foul of the exigencies of short-term political pressures:

There may be good policy in retaliations of this kind, when there is a probability that they will procure the repeal of the high duties or prohibitions complained of. The recovery of a great foreign market will generally more than compensate the transitory inconveniency of paying dearer during a short time of some sorts of goods. To judge whether such retaliations are likely to produce such an effect, does not, perhaps belong so much to the science of a legislator, whose deliberations ought to be governed by general principles which are always the same, as to the skill of that insidious and crafty animal, vulgarly called a statesman or politician, whose councils are directed by the momentary fluctuations of affairs. When there is no probability that any such repeal can be procured, it seems a bad method of compensating the injury done to certain classes of our people, to do another injury ourselves, not only to those classes, but to almost all the other classes of them. (Smith 1776: 435)

As Bhagwati (1993) has noted, this argument for the use of one's own trade barriers to remove those of others raises important questions of political economy that tend to be ignored or down-played by economists who engage in the welfare economics of strategic trade policy. Specifically, one question that should be answered is whether the one nation really has the power to pry open others' markets; or whether this power is exaggerated by the self-interest-induced optimism of the lobbies that energize such aggressive policies. Another relevant question is whether such a trade policy will be captured by domestic protectionists, saddling the nation in question with tariffs. A third question that should inform the debate is whether the power of example, rather than sanction, might not induce others to follow free trade, making unilateral free trade a more efficacious and less dangerous path to reciprocity.

How these questions are answered politically will have major implications for trade policy at the national level. In late nineteenth-century, Britain, for example, despite considerable discord and debate, unilateralism survived as the basic tenet of trade policy. In late twentieth-century United States, in contrast, with far less discord and debate, reciprocity dominates trade policy, and the use of muscle via threats to close markets in the absence of concessions on unilateral demands has become the basic tenet of US trade policy.

The key questions outlined above in connection with the nationalist arena of trade policy debate are also relevant within the cosmopolitan arena. Specifically, it should be asked whether the use of power to extract unilateral concessions threatens the rule of law under which a trading regime should function; whether it must lead to concessions granted to the powerful by the less powerful, replacing economic competitiveness by political clout as the guiding force behind international trade; whether such use of power will deteriorate into a unilateral self-serving determination of the closedness or openness of other nations' borders; and whether impartial observers should regret the impact on world efficiency if the strong nations fully indulge their own interests by browbeating the weak into removing protection and/or cutting export subsidies (Bhagwati 1993: 22).

The cosmopolitan argument more forcibly than its nationalist counterpart, because it focuses more directly on issues of reciprocity, raises an emotional issue of fairness that tends to be glossed over in the nationalist argument. Adam Smith (1776) talked about revenge as motivating the demand for reciprocity and restricting a nation's ability to pursue a policy of unilateral free trade. This sense that reciprocity is required by *fairness* is much more pronounced today.

As a result, it can be argued that there now exists a prudential argument for seeking reciprocity in free trade (Bhagwati 1988: 1993). This argument cannot be resolved until the public choice issues in US trade policy have been thoroughly reviewed.

6   The instruments of trade protection

The three main instruments of trade protection are tariffs, quotas and voluntary export restraints (VERs). The tariff is doubtless the instrument that most people have in mind when they think of trade protection. The postwar period has seen considerable tariff reductions, from an average level of around 40 percent to one of about 4 percent, largely under the sponsorship of several rounds of negotiations under the General Agreement on Tariffs and Trade (GATT). Other forms of trade protection, however, have been growing in the postwar period. These instruments of protection differ in several important respects that will be relevant to some of our subsequent analysis.

Tariffs

A tariff is a form of excise tax and, like any excise tax, may be expressed as either a flat amount per unit of a product or a percentage of the value of a product. For instance, a tariff on automobiles might be set at 10 percent of the wholesale value of the product or it might be set at $1,000 per vehicle. Until the mid-nineteenth century, tariff revenues were almost the sole source of tax revenue for the US federal government. Even in the last two decades of the nineteenth century and the first decade of the twentieth, tariff revenues continued to generate around half of all federal tax revenues. It was only after the introduction of the federal income tax in 1913 that tariff revenues began to dwindle in relative significance. Tariffs now generate only some $16 billion annually, which is less than 1 percent of total federal revenues. Tariffs could be abolished entirely, and the lost revenues would be made up through the normal growth in federal revenues in the following tax year.

The protective impact of a tariff varies directly with its rate. The higher the rate of tariff, the higher will be the domestic selling price of the imported product and, hence, the greater will be the protection offered to domestic

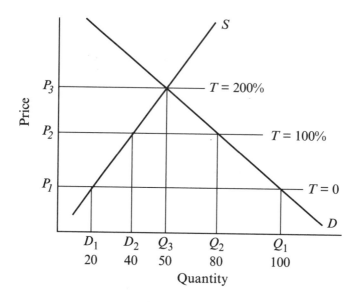

Figure 2.2   The protective impact of a tariff

producers of competing products. This point can be illustrated by Figure 2.2, which illustrates a situation where, in the absence of a tariff, the price of automobiles would be P_1, and the quantity of automobiles sold would be Q_1. The domestic supply of automobiles is illustrated by S so that at a price of P_1, D_1 would be the domestic production of automobiles. The number of auto-mobiles imported would be $Q_1 - D_1$. If a tariff of 100 percent is imposed on automobiles, the price would double to P_2. At this higher price, Americans would buy fewer automobiles, as illustrated by Q_2, and domestic producers would expand their production to D_2. The number of automobiles imported would shrink to $Q_2 - D_2$.

The tariff accomplishes a number of things. It raises revenue for the government, illustrated by $(P_2 - P_1)(Q_2 - D_2)$ It harms consumers, who must pay higher prices for automobiles and who thus buy fewer of them. It in-creases the earnings of those producers who receive the higher prices the tariff brings about, including owners of inputs specialized in the production of automobiles. Figure 2.2 shows that if the tariff is raised to 200 percent, which would yield a price of P_3, the tariff would eliminate imports entirely. The domestic market for automobiles would shrink to Q_3, and all of it would be supplied by domestic producers.

It is helpful to refer to the output consequences of a tariff in index fashion. Accordingly, in the absence of a tariff, the size of a market is indexed at 100.

The domestic share of this market is 20, which implies that imports account for 80 percent of the market. The 100 percent tariff reduces the total size of the market to 80 percent of its original size, while increasing domestic production to 40 percent of the original market size. Imports thus shrink from 80 percent of the original market to 40 percent. The 100 percent tariff thus cuts imports in half and allows domestic production to double. The tariff of 200 percent reduces the total size of the market to 50 percent of its original size, all of it occupied by domestic producers.

Quotas

Whatever can be accomplished by a tariff can be accomplished alternatively by a quota, at least as a blackboard exercise. This is illustrated by Figure 2.2. Rather than imposing a 100 percent tariff on automobiles, a quota that re-duces imports by 50 percent has the same effect. By reducing imports from 80 percent of the initial automobile market to 40 percent, the quota allows domestic production to double and price to rise to P_2.

To be sure, there are various circumstances concerning market conditions under which this first-order equivalence between a tariff and a quota van-ishes. For instance, whether markets are modeled as being competitive or monopolistic matters, as Figure 2.3 shows.

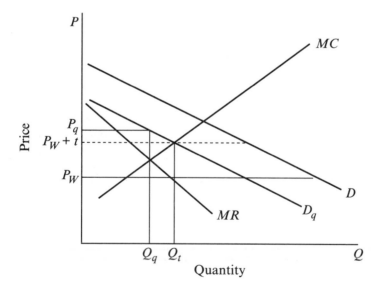

Figure 2.3 Comparing a tariff and a quota

In Figure 2.3, D is the demand for a product by domestic residents; P_W is the world price of the product. Imports, under free trade, are available in unlimited quantities at that price. The domestic industry consists of a single firm, whose marginal cost is given by MC. Under free trade, monopoly behavior is not possible. The domestic firm supplies quantity Q_f at price P_W. Imports are $D_f - Q_f$. The outcome is identical with that of perfect competition.

If a specific tariff is charged on imports, the domestic firm can charge $P_W + t$. The profit-maximizing monopolist will set price equal to marginal cost, supplying quantity Q_t. Domestic demand falls to D_t. The domestic firm still produces the same quantity as would a perfectly competitive industry: imports decline to $D_t - Q_t$.

Suppose instead that the government imposes a limit on imports, restricting their quantity to a fixed level equal to $D_t - Q_t$ (the same as that induced by the tariff t in the previous example). The post-quota demand curve now confronting the monopolist is D_q, shifted $D_t - Q_t$ to the left of Q. Corresponding to D_q is a marginal revenue curve MR_q. The domestic firm supplies quantity Q_q at price P_q, thus equating marginal revenue with marginal cost.

Figure 2.3 clearly shows that a tariff and a quota designed to generate the same level of imports are not identical in other respects. Specifically, the quota leads to a lower level of domestic production (Q_q rather than Q_t) and to a higher price (P_q rather than $P_W + t$). The reason for this difference is that an import quota creates more monopoly power than a tariff, by offering absolute protection to the domestic firm no matter how high the domestic price. Given this result, it is an interesting commentary on the inefficiency of political markets that protection has shifted systematically during the postwar period from tariffs to quantitative restrictions.

Further, any equivalence that may exist between a tariff and a quota can be undone as circumstances change through time, even if competitive assumptions are maintained. An increase in demand, for instance, will leave price unchanged with a tariff and will be accommodated through an expansion in imports. Domestic production will occupy a decreasing share of the market as demand increases under a tariff. With a quota, however imports will be unchanged and price will rise. Domestic production will occupy an increasing share of the market as demand increases under a quota.

Voluntary export restraints (VERs)
A VER is a quota imposed and enforced by the exporting government. Under a regular quota, imports are allowed only to the extent that those who wish to receive the imports can obtain licenses from the government. Under a VER, a license to export is required from the foreign government. Since a VER is simply a quota that is administered by the nation of export and not the nation of import, there will be a first-order equivalence between quotas and VERs.

Just as there is a quota equivalent to a 100 percent tariff, there is VER equivalent to that quota. In this case, the exporting government would limit exports to 50 percent of what they would otherwise have been.

To speak of a first-order equivalence is not to speak of an actual equivalence. It is only to say that there are circumstances under which an equivalence will hold. If those circumstances do not hold, the equivalence may not exist. This is certainly the case with tariffs, quotas and VERs. Conditions of equivalence among the three can be constructed. However, these instruments also differ in important respects, both economically and politically.

7   Trade protection and market processes

A market economy is one where such outcomes as the types of products produced, their amounts, and their prices are not imposed by any central authority, but rather emerge through the activities of market participants who relate to one another within an institutional framework grounded on the legal principles of property and contract. A fundamental economic difference between tariffs and quotas, whether imposed on imports or on exports, is that tariffs are consistent with the operation of market processes while quotas are not. A tariff changes market outcomes, but it does not violate the operating principles of market processes. The imposition of a 100 percent tariff on automobiles leaves the basic operation of market processes unchanged, and simply represents a new piece of datum to which market participants respond in their own ways as they see best. Such a tariff operates in the same way as some exogenous deterioration in the ability of people in foreign lands to produce automobiles.

Which particular types of automobiles are impacted, and to what extent, as well as the impact on prices, are not direct objects of choice for anyone, but rather represent an unintended end-product of the actions and choices of market participants. With the 100 percent tariff, the 50 percent reduction in imports is accomplished in decentralized fashion. How that 50 percent reduction ends up being distributed among producers and types of vehicles is determined by the market participants. Some producers may stop exporting automobiles to the United States entirely, because the demand for these vehicles vanishes or because the producer decides to sell in other markets. Other producers may undergo little reduction in their American sales, possibly because buyers are strongly attracted to those vehicles and are willing to pay the higher prices, or possibly because the producer absorbs a good deal of the price increase that the tariff would otherwise have dictated.

It is a wholly different situation with a quota, because quotas replace market processes with those of a command economy. This replacement is not readily apparent from the virtual reality that such a blackboard exercise as Figure 2.2 mimics, but it becomes quickly apparent from an examination of actual reality. Quotas replace property and contract as central organizing institutions with governmental dictation.

The scholars of economic policy associated with the approach of ORDO-liberalism (Eucken 1952), sought to distinguish between economic policies that were compatible with the principles of a market economy and policies that conflicted with those principles. The ORDO-liberals did not reject the crafting of economic policies by governments, but sought to articulate principles governing those policies that would ensure that they did not violate and undercut the principles of a market economy. The distinction between a tariff and a quota illustrates this ORDO-liberal distinction between market-congruent and market-incongruent policy measures.

To be sure, it is always possible to set up initial conditions where a tariff and a quota appear to be identical. To illustrate, consider a simple two-economy framework where shoes are exported from China to the United States. Suppose in the absence of any trade restrictions that the average price of a pair of shoes imported from China is $30, with 10 million pairs imported annually. Now suppose this free-market setting is altered by the imposition of a tariff of 100 percent on the value of shoes. With shoes imported from China now selling for $60 per pair, Americans would buy fewer shoes, say only 3 million pairs. A quota limit of 3 million set on the importation of shoes from China would achieve the same outcome.

In the example just given, a tariff of 100 percent and a quota set at 3 million pairs gives the same outcome: only 3 million shoes are imported from China and they sell for $60 per pair. This identity between a tariff and a quota is true by construction, as a blackboard exercise. It is easy to conclude from the mechanics of this construction that tariffs and quotas are essentially identical, with any differences between them being but secondary differences concerning the details of their respective operations. But in these differences of detail reside significant differences for the character of the economic order of a society.

In a market economy, economic activities are self-organized by the participants who themselves operate according to the principles of property, contract, and liability. The tariff on imported shoes is a tax that leads people to substitute non-taxed transactions for the purchase of imported shoes. The injection of state authority in the case of a tariff, significant though it is, is limited to the stipulation of a tax rate and the collection of revenues.

It is much different for a quota. While a tariff relies upon the self-organizing processes of a market economy, a quota imposes political direction in place of self-organization. When a tariff of 100 percent is imposed and Chinese shoes become more expensive, some people will continue to buy Chinese shoes while others switch to American-made shoes, and yet others will make their existing shoes last longer through visits to the repair shops.

The reduction in American purchases of Chinese-made shoes from 10 million to 3 million pairs is a by-product of the choices of individual American consumers who react to the tariff-induced rise in price. There is no way before-the-fact to know exactly what the aggregate response to the 100 percent tariff would be. It may be that 4 million pairs would be bought, or 2.5 million pairs for that matter. What makes it possible to say that a quota of 3 million pairs is equivalent to a tariff of 100 percent is the fact that *the tariff, and not the quota, is the instrument of protection.*

Furthermore, shoes are not identical with one another, even though economists might often leave this impression in their discourse. There are thousands of varieties of shoes produced by hundreds of manufacturers. A tariff of 100 percent may reduce imports from 10 million to 3 million pairs. The odds that this 70 percent reduction in the aggregate volume of imports will be accompanied by 70 percent reductions in each variety of shoe and from each manufacturer are probably equivalent to the odds that random strikes of a piano keyboard for three minutes will produce a hit tune.

For a quota truly to be identical with a tariff, it is necessary that it produce the same results in detail, and not just at some aggregate level of shoes, independently of styles, sizes and the like. Such an identity is, however, impossible to achieve, as all the failures of all the communist economies have demonstrated. What the implications of a 100 percent tariff will be in terms of reduced purchases of particular styles and sizes, and from which particular manufacturers, can only be gauged by observing the choices that people actually make in response to a tariff.

It is possible to observe and record market reactions to a tariff on shoes in terms of the amounts that people buy of different styles and sizes from different producers. From this information, it might be possible, under limited conditions, to construct a blackboard exercise where a quota system duplicates the outcome of the tariff. But the information necessary to impose the equivalent quota can be pieced together only by observing the market reactions to the tariff. If a quota is imposed directly, there is no informational basis for replicating the market outcome. This is just one illustration of the well-known theme that true central planning is impossible, so long as planning is assessed in terms of its ability to replicate what people would have achieved through markets.

8   Trade protection and political processes

There are some significant political differences between tariffs and quotas, with quotas generally being more valuable to holders of political offices than tariffs. This proposition about relative value is a corollary of quotas being a component of a command economy. The state obviously plays a greater role in a command economy than in a market economy. Along many margins of choice, quotas can generate more 'business' for the holders of state offices than can tariffs.

Tariff revenues add to the general fund, while quotas do not. On this score alone, tariffs would muster stronger political support than quotas. Indeed, quotas would muster no support because they generate no revenue. Obviously, there is much more to the determination of political support than revenues generated for the Treasury. Revenues that accrue to the general fund, as tariff revenues do, generally elicit weaker political support than revenues that are earmarked for particular purposes. The reason for this is that revenues that accrue to the general fund create a form of common property, the distribution of which depends on the outcome of appropriations processes and politics. Earmarked revenues, by contrast, become the property of those interest groups that support the programs financed by those revenues. Interest groups will generate more pressure in support of tax increases when those revenues are earmarked for programs they favor than they would of those revenues accrued to the general fund (Hettich and Winer 1988; Hunter and Nelson 1989; Seiglie 1990; Athanassakos 1990).

This is not to deny the obvious fact that political pressure can be generated to support revenues that accrue to the general fund. However, such pressures are generally more intense when particular interests are involved. In the case of a tariff, stronger political pressure will be exerted when the proposed object of taxation is produced domestically than when it is not. If there is no domestic production, proposed tariff revenues accrue to the general fund. Who would lobby for such a tax? The revenues involved in any tariff are small, and interest groups seeking large appropriations are better advised to put their resources into lobbying for larger appropriations from the general fund than in seeking to expand that general fund. For to expand the general fund makes more revenue available for all interest groups who seek to exploit the budgetary commons.

There may also be little opposition to such a tariff. Consumers of the imported product are harmed by the tariff, but typically they exert little political pressure. Generally, consumers generate political pressure only where large producers with similar interests act on their behalf. For instance, suppose there is no domestic production of sugar and no import quota. A proposed tariff on sugar would harm consumers, but would also thereby harm producers who use sugar as an input in their production. Major soft-drink manufacturers may then provide some opposition to a tariff increase.

It is customary to distinguish between a revenue tariff and a protective tariff, where the intent of a revenue tariff is simply to gather revenue while the intent of a protective tariff is to protect domestic manufacturers from foreign competition. In this respect, a thoroughly protective tariff collects no revenue because it is set so high as to eliminate all imports. The conventional distinction between a revenue tariff and a protective tariff is also grounded on a distinction between whether or not the product subject to the tariff is produced domestically.

Sugar is produced both in the United States and in other nations. Hence, a tariff on sugar is classified as a protective tariff. If sugar were not produced in the United States, a tariff would be classified as a revenue tariff. However, even if there were no American production of sugar, a tariff on imported sugar would almost certainly give a protective advantage to some American producers relative to others. For instance, such a tariff makes beverages that use sugar more expensive, which in turn increases the demand for beverages that do not use sugar. Once the ubiquity of substitution in production and in consumption is recognized, the distinction between a revenue and a protective tariff loses any categorical significance.

We do not deny that tariffs generate political business; for if they failed to do so there would be no tariffs. Rather, we assert that quotas generate even more valuable business, not least because they open up various opportunities for the cultivation of special interests, the award of special favors, and the use of administrative discretion.

Consider once again Figure 2.2, with a quota equivalent to the 100 percent tariff, which restricts imports to half of what they would otherwise be. If one million automobiles would formerly have been imported, now only 500,000 will be allowed into the country. Various foreign producers are willing to supply one million automobiles to the domestic market, but only 500,000 will be allowed in. Which 500,000 will be allowed in? Which will be excluded? In this situation, political power and favoritism will operate on both sides of the market. Foreign producers will compete among themselves to secure better positions under the quota system. They might do this through any number of ways, most of which go under the generic heading of lobbying and public relations, and in any event are designed to secure a larger share of the quota. Politicians and officials in the position to award quotas are on the other side of this market, and will likewise be guided to some extent by the abilities of different foreign aspirants to appeal to their interests.

It is easy to envision a situation where the aspirants spend as much in trying to seek a favorable quota as they would have paid in tax under a 100 percent tariff. However, these expenditures do not accrue as revenues to the general fund, but take the form of income to the purveyors of those activities financed to improve prospects under the quota. Public relations firms may be hired to direct advertising campaigns. Conferences may be sponsored. Contributions may be made to Political Action Committees (PACs). A quota changes the particular forms that competition takes, but it generally does not eliminate that competition which is inherent in scarcity. The revenues that accrue to the Treasury's general fund under a tariff accrue instead as personal incomes to those who participate in the market for legislation under the quota.

With a quota, market forces are prevented from operating, and political favoritism and discrimination take precedence. The quota starts by imposing an aggregate limit on the volume of imports. But that aggregate limit will not be sufficient to operate the quota. Each producer of imported automobiles must be given a quota. An opportunity thus exists for some producers to be given more lenient treatment than other producers. Some producers will be given a quota that is 80 percent of what they were formerly exporting, while others will be given a quota of only 20 percent. And some producers will be denied any opportunity to export to America. How these quotas will be distributed will depend on the outcome of political processes through which quota negotiations operate and outcomes established (Tollison 1988; Babcock *et al.* 1990; Lenway *et al.* 1990; McChesney 1991).

In many ways, the opportunity for discrimination enhances the power of the state relative to what would exist under a non-discriminatory regime. When discrimination is possible, democratic processes become a form of auction through which legislative outcomes are those that favor highest bidders. A tariff leaves to impersonal market processes the determination of how the reduction in imports will come about. A quota gives that power of determination to some political figure or agency. In consequence, producers will seek to demonstrate that they deserve especially good treatment by appealing to the politicians who will make the quota determinations, and the politicians will likewise render their verdicts. If those politicians are strongly pecuniary in their motivation, something close to outright bribery may result. If they are more circumspect, contributions to PACs, campaign contributions, participation in campaigns, and networking activities may increase. A market can have many currencies when property rights are indefinite. But a market for legislation there will be.

9   Conclusions

Few would now dispute that events since 1989 have demonstrated the practical desirability of markets over socialism. Yet there is good reason to doubt that capitalism has achieved a total victory (Sirico 1994). Despite the efforts of many great economists, political philosophers and historians, economic liberty had failed to capture the moral high ground in public debate. In consequence, its security as a system of economic organization is not guaranteed anywhere in the world. Although economists typically are more sympathetic to free trade than to any other aspect of market process, their sympathies rest much more on the narrow calculus of economic gain and loss than on any respect for life, liberty and property.

As long as economic liberty, together with its requisite institutions of private property, free exchange, and contract enforcement is not supported by a generally held set of norms by which it can be defended, it cannot be sustained long-term. Into the moral vacuum left by its advocates rush notions hostile to economic liberty, notions drawn largely from the values and vocabularies of intervention and socialism (Sirico 1994). Such hostile notions not infrequently are rationalized in the language of economics.

The moral defense of liberty must make a series of distinctions: between rights and privileges, between society and government, between community and the collective. Rights, society and community are all part of the natural order of liberty. Privileges, government and the collective rest on pre-emptive coercion. Rightly understood, capitalism is the name for the economic component of the natural order of liberty, the economic application of the principle that every human person has dignity and should have that dignity respected.

Free trade is an indispensable component of capitalism rightly understood. As such, free trade is to be defended morally on grounds of liberty as much, if not more, than it is to be defended morally on grounds of economic efficiency. Indeed, it is to be defended on grounds of liberty even in those rare instances where the economic calculus of gains and losses may suggest a case for protection.

References

Athanassokos, A. (1990) 'General fund financing versus earmarked taxes: an alternative model of budgetary choice in a democracy', *Public Choice*, 278.

Babcock, B.A., Carter, C.A. and Schmitz, A. (1990) 'The political economy of US wheat legislation', *Economic Inquiry*, 28: 335–53.

Bagehot, W. (1880) *Economic Studies* (London).

Bhagwati, J.N. (1988) *Protectionism* (Cambridge, Mass.: MIT Press).

Bhagwati, J. (1994) 'Free trade: old and new challenges', *Economic Journal*: 231–46.

Bhagwati, J.N. (1993) 'Fair trade, reciprocity and harmonization: the novel challenge to the theory and policy of free trade', in D. Salvatore (ed.), *Protectionism and World Welfare* (Cambridge: Cambridge University Press), pp. 17–54.

Buchanan, J.M. (1966) 'An individualistic theory of political process', in D. Easton (ed.), *Varieties of Political Theory* (Englewood Cliffs, N.J.: Prentice-Hall).

Buchanan, J.M. and Tullock, G. (1962) *The Calculus of Consent* (Ann Arbor: University of Michigan Press).

Eucken, W. (1952) *Grundsatze der Wirtschaftspolitik* (Tübingen: J.C.B. Mohr).

Hayek, F.A. (1945) 'Individualism: true or false', in F.A. Hayek (ed.), *Individualism and Economic Order* (Chicago: University of Chicago Press), pp. 1–32.

Hayek, F.A. (1988) *The Fatal Conceit* (Chicago: University of Chicago Press).

Hettich, W. and Winer, S. (1988) 'Economic and political foundations of tax structure', *American Economic Review*, 78: 701–12.

Hunter, W.J. and Nelson, M.A. (1989) 'Interest group demand for taxation. *Public Choice*, 62: 41–61.

Krugman, P.R. and Obstfeld, M. (1987) *International Economics* (Boston: Scott Foresman and Co.).

Lenway, S., Rehbein, K. and Starks, L. (1990) 'The impact of protection on firm wealth: the experience of the steel industry', *Southern Economic Journal*, 56: 1079–93.

Locke, J. (1690) *Two Treatises of Government* (New York: Cambridge University Press, 1991).

Macpherson, C.B. (1987) 'Individualism', in J. Eatwell, M. Milgate and P. Newman (eds), *The New Palgrave* (London: Macmillan), vol. 2, pp. 790–3.

McChesney, F.S. (1991) 'Rent extraction and interest-group organization in a Coasian model of regulation', *Journal of Legal Studies*, 20: 73–90.

Plato (1974) *The Republic* (Harmondsworth, Middx: Penguin).

Rasmussen, D.B. and Den Uyl, D.J. (1991) *Liberty and Nature: An Aristotelian Defense of Liberal Order* (La Salle: Open Court).

Romer, P. (1994) 'New goods, old theory and welfare costs of trade restrictions', *Journal of Development Economics.*

Rowley, C.K. (1993) *Liberty and the State*, Shaftesbury Paper no. 4 (Aldershot, Hants: Edward Elgar).

Rowley, C.K. and Tollison, R.D. (1986) 'Rent-seeking and Trade Protection', Swiss Journal of International Relations 41, Fall: 141–66.

Seiglie, C. (1990) 'A theory of the politically optimal commodity tax', *Economic Inquiry*, 28: 586–603.

Sirico, R.A. (1994) 'Capitalism must seize the high ground', *The Financial Times*, 9 August.

Smith, A. (1776) *The Wealth of Nations*, Cannan Edition, (New York: Modern Library, 1937).

Tollison, R.D. (1988) 'Public choice and legislation', *Virginia Law Review*, 74: 339–71.

Tullock, G. (1967) 'The welfare cost of tariffs, monopolies and theft', *Western Economic Journal*, 5: 224–32.

Tullock, G. (1980) 'Efficient rent-seeking' in J. Buchanan, R.D. Tollison and G. Tullock (eds), *Toward a Theory of the Rent-seeking Society* (College Station: Texas A & M University Press).

Wagner, R.E. (1991) *Charging for Government: User Charges and Earmarked Taxes in Principle and Practice* (London: Routledge).

3 The rhetoric of trade protection

1 Introduction

Chapter 2 argued the case for free trade, centering attention on Adam Smith's discussion of the division of labor and on David Ricardo's and James Mill's formulation of the doctrine of comparative advantage. Taken together, the contributions of these scholars still provide the essential theoretical case for free trade.

As we noted in Chapter 2, this case is dependent, at least in part, on the assumption that market prices reflect social costs. It is not at all surprising, therefore, that the challenges to the free trade doctrine over the past two centuries have come from economists who have focused on one or the another form of market imperfection (Bhagwati 1994: 232). If Pareto-relevant externalities can be identified, economists who are uneasy with the free trade doctrine, and who believe in the existence of impartial, omniscient and benevolent government, can mount a market-failure argument that comparative advantage impulses must be assisted by government intervention and that various forms of trade protection can be justified as welfare improving.

Such economists have proven to be devilishly clever in exploiting this lacuna in the free trade doctrine to mount a dazzling, if ultimately unconvincing, rhetoric of trade protection. It is our intention in this chapter to set out the key contributions to the protectionist literature, to give them a fair trial, and yet to demolish them. In so doing, our primary concern is with economic arguments, although we shall also confront and confound a number of non-economic arguments.

We start our discussion with the earliest theoretical arguments, deployed in the first half of the nineteenth century, and prominent in the writings of John Stuart Mill and Robert Torrens, that looked to protection to support infant industries and national defense or to exploit monopoly power in trade. We then review the theoretical arguments advanced by the new welfare economists in the mid-twentieth century on the basis of perceived factor-market and product-market imperfections. We then turn to the theoretical developments of the 1980s that recouched conventional protectionist arguments in terms of small group models of strategic interaction. We bring our review of economic arguments to a close by discussing the new challenges to free trade mounted in the 1990s that come from altogether different directions and that bear little relation to conventional market-failure arguments.

2   The infant-industry argument

The infant-industry argument for trade protection holds that temporary protection may be necessary to allow an industry to reach maturity, to reap the full benefits of learning by doing, and thus to achieve its comparative advantage. In the absence of temporary protection, it is argued, the industry will not be competitive with foreign producers. As a conceptual possibility such a situation cannot be rejected out of hand. There is a large economics literature on learning by doing that suggests that the sheer volume of output as distinguished from the scale of activity, in some circumstances, affects production costs. There is yet another large literature that suggests that the promotion of a brand image and the cultivation of the market for the output of a newly established firm may be time-related. It does not follow necessarily, however, that such circumstances justify trade protection.

Let us illustrate the weakness of such infant-industry arguments by reference to the problems associated with establishing and promoting a domestic wine industry. Suppose that potential winegrowers determine that some location is blessed with climate and soil conditions suited to growing grapes and making wine. Evidently, a decision recorded now to plant vineyards will not lead to saleable output for several years. Doubtless, a further period of experimentation will be required before the wines produced meet their full potential, and a yet further lapse of time will be necessary before a reliable brand image is established.

The situation is not one that calls for protective tariffs against foreign imports. Rather, it represents a common problem of capital investment that is confronted by myriad industries every day. The problem of any capital investment is that monies must be set aside now for revenues that will accrue in the future. Private entrepreneurs resolve the problem by undertaking present-value estimates to determine profitability and by raising venture capital to finance the profitable opportunities. Current losses are borne in the short term in the expectation that they will be overwhelmed by time-discounted future surpluses. Capital markets emerge to take care of such time-related problems. In the absence of some Pareto-relevant externality, there is no justification even in principle for protecting entrepreneurs from competition by some form of government instrument.

There can be no doubt that a government offering tariff protection against foreign competition will induce more investment, at least in the short run, in that particular area than would a government that allowed market forces free rein. But this does not imply that such investment is economically advantageous. With a sufficiently high rate of protection, entrepreneurs might even be induced to grow bananas in Minnesota hot houses or to nurture orange groves in Alaska. Never should any such misadventure be labelled as an infant industry on its way to maturity.

Only in circumstances where the development of an infant industry promises to confer external benefits on other industries is there a valid conceptual argument for protection. Even here, the case is far from watertight. Suppose, for example, that the expansion a protected industry does promise to lower costs or to provide other benefits for existing industries. Why would such externalities not be internalized by ordinary market processes? Is there some capital market impediment to the integration of the new activity into the existing industries through the purchase of equity? If so, why not remove that impediment? If the existing industries do not choose to merge with the new venture, what is to stop them from subsidizing it, substituting their own resources for those of the taxpayer in the pursuit of external benefits that they will eventually reap?

The argument for infant-industry protection should always face a high burden of proof. It is easy for politicians and bureaucrats to perceive infancy problems that do not exist, when pressured by special interests to spend taxpayers money. It is difficult, if not impossible, for them to make highly complex investment judgements successfully when, for the most part, they have escaped into public service because they have no comparative advantage in the private sector.

3   The national defense argument

If the infant-industry argument holds that temporary protection may be justified to allow an industry to reach maturity and to achieve its comparative advantage, the national defense argument maintains that it may be prudent to retain some domestic productive capacity even though comparative advantage calls for the product's importation. For example, if steel is thought to be essential to national defense, and yet a country has no comparative advantage in steel production, the national defense argument would justify tariff protection against steel imports arguably for an indefinite time-span.

This is a conceptual line of argument that depends on a number of empirical assumptions. First, there is the question as to what is essential to national defense. Suppose that it can be justly determined that a particular product, let us say oil, is essential to national defense. The question remains as to how much domestic production is truly necessary. If the product is one that can be stored at low cost in terms of storage and spoilage, a policy of stockpiling may be much more economical than one of tariff protection A program of purchasing the commodity cheaply on world markets during times of peace for deployment during periods of war may be much more cost-effective than maintaining an inefficient industry indefinitely by artificial means.

The very essence of the national defense argument rests on the notion of organic state welfare economics condemned in earlier chapters of this book. A nation is no more than an aggregate of the individuals who comprise it. If individual citizens do not sense the urgency of paying higher prices so that a domestic industry can be sustained against the contingency of war, a very high burden of proof should rest on those who would deploy the political process to counteract their lack of such concern.

Of course, a domestic industry can organize itself as a special interest and muster electoral support for its essential status whereas stockpiles involve visible costs to taxpayers and do not readily accommodate significant interest groups in their expansion. Political market pressures generally operate against principled economic arguments, therefore tilting policy towards excessive protectionism. Knowledge of such a bias, however, underlines rather than mutes the urgency of our principled economic case against the national defense argument.

4   The terms of trade argument

As Chapter 2 demonstrates, almost all tariffs impose deadweight losses or excess burdens upon individuals in excess of the amount of revenue generated by the tariff. The excess burden arises because the tariff causes individuals to shift consumption away from more highly valued toward less highly valued products, with some consequential loss of consumers' surplus. Only where demand is completely inelastic will the substitution effect and the implicit excess burden fail to materialize.

The degree of the excess burden varies directly with the absolute value of the elasticity of demand for the product. The more elastic the demand, the greater the shift in quantity demanded that the tariff induces and the larger the excess burden of the tariff. The idea of an optimal tariff relates to this excess burden insight, recognizing in the case of a large country that can exert a monopsony influence over its imports that a tariff has two effects: it reduces the volume of trade on the one hand; and it may improve the terms of trade on the other.

An improvement in the terms of trade is defined as an increase in export price relative to import price, which implies that the country in question (or rather its citizens) generates more imports per unit of exports. The theory of the optimal tariff holds that there may be a range over which an increase in a tariff generates greater benefits through improvements in the terms of trade than losses through excess burden. Figure 3.1 illustrates the nature of this trade-off.

Consider a two-good economy in which (in the aggregate) there is a monopsony buyer in the world market for that country's importable good. In Figure 3.1, *DD* is the country's aggregated demand curve for imports and *SS* is the foreign supply curve of that product Although *SS* represents the marginal cost curve for foreign exporters, it represents the average cost curve for the importing country. The marginal cost of imports is represented by MC_M.

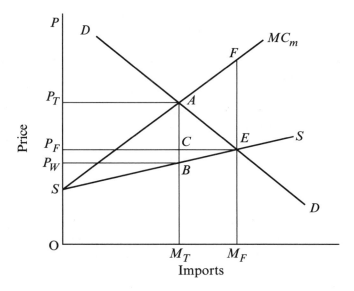

Figure 3.1   Tariffs and the terms of trade

In a free trade situation, trade equilibrium is at point *E*, given by the intersection of *DD* and *SS* at price P_F and quantity imported M_F. However, at this equilibrium, the value to the importing country of an extra unit of imports is less than the marginal cost of that unit by an amount *EF*. The importing country evidently can increase the welfare of its citizens by reducing imports to M_T, determined by the point of intersection *A* of *DD* and MC_M.

The potential gain is equal to the area *FAE*, and arises as a consequence of improvements in the terms of trade, from P_F to P_W. In order to shift the equilibrium from *E* to *A*, the importing country may decide to impose a tariff of *AB* per unit. Equilibrium is then realized at *B* with a world price P_W and domestic price P_T. The tariff wedge, of $P_W P_T$ per unit, is referred to as the optimal tariff, producing a terms of trade gain of *FAE* and an excess burden loss of *ABE* in Figure 3.1. The optimum tariff maximizes the differences between *FAE* and *ABE*.

There are a number of weaknesses in the terms of trade argument which, taken together, render it a dangerous route for any nation state to follow. First is the question whether any country, even one as economically large as the United States, can significantly influence more than a relatively few product prices on world markets. Most products are purchased by consumers in many countries and a reduction in consumption by one country will not much influence the equilibrium price unless really high tariffs (and excess burdens) are imposed.

Moreover, if one large country does enjoy a modest degree of monopoly power, other nations also are likely to enjoy similar pockets of monopoly power. In such circumstances, a tariff hike by one country will provoke retaliation, removing initial terms of trade gains in a wealth-destructive trade war. Such was the experience of the United States during the early 1930s following the imposition of the infamous Smoot–Hawley tariff increase in the 1930 Trade Act. Although Harry Johnson (1953) was able to identify circumstances in which the initiating country would not lose out entirely from a tariff war, the probability of such a loss is too high in practice to be lightly ignored.

Organic state welfare economics once again rears its ugly head in the terms of trade argument. Once it is recognized that a nation is composed of heterogeneous individuals and that property rights in free trade are violated by tariff interventions, optimal tariff theory becomes extremely problematic. Suppose that a US tariff on German beer imports benefits 'Americans' by improving the terms of trade sufficiently to compensate for the reduction in trade between the two countries. Specifically, the US exploits its monopoly in computer software products, using the tariff to extract a monopoly rent from German citizens.

Where is the compelling force in such an argument? Individual Americans who enjoy German beer are harmed by the tariff. Individual Americans who supply computer software products gain. Third parties who access the tax revenues generated by the tariff also gain. Compensation is never paid. In the absence of such compensation there is no way to tell whether those who gain actually could over-compensate the losers. In short, the entire gains from trade argument is a sham, serving as a rationalization for using government as an instrument to infringe some individuals' rights for the benefit of others.

Suppose, nevertheless, that potential compensation is rationalized by some social welfare function, and the terms of trade argument thus resuscitated. The question once again arises how some political organization, composed of individuals who have escaped into public service to avoid the discipline of private markets, could possibly make the complex market evaluations necessary to elicit whether terms of trade advantages actually exist and to calculate the optimal tariffs that would effectively exploit foreign markets. To the extent that such terms of trade validations emanate from special interests, the entire exercise will be self-serving, although no less politically effective for all that, at least in the current US political environment.

5   The employment protection argument

The employment protection argument against free trade first seriously was mounted at the onset of the Great Depression. Maynard Keynes, in particular, abandoned his early belief in free trade in February 1930, in evidence before the Macmillan Committee, offering the view that tariffs, while unwise as long-term policy, could immediately alleviate a slump (Bhagwati 1994: 233). Keynes' protectionist predilections intensified throughout 1931, leading to a celebrated controversy with Lionel Robbins and John Hicks in 1932 (Beveridge 1932). The naive notion that tariffs would effectively export the consequences of business cycles (real or monetary) to other countries was cruelly falsified by the experience of the 1930s following the Smoot–Hawley tariff of 1930. Even at that time, Keynes dimly recognized that beggar-thy-neighbor politics might be technically inferior to policies of domestic reflation (Bhagwati 1994: 233).

Subsequent theoretical analysis established that, under fixed exchange rates, reflation policies alone would create external imbalance and that two policies, reflation and devaluation, generally would be necessary to achieve the two targets of internal and external balance. Tariffs then became widely recognized as inferior to an optimal combination of devaluation and reflation as the policy solution to unemployment (Bhagwati 1994: 234).

Prior to the adoption of flexible exchange rates in 1973, the foremost proponents of floating rates predicted that their adoption would result in a diminution of pressures for tariff protection. More recently, economists have attributed rising protectionist pressures to the very system that was supposed to see to their abatement (Aschheim *et al.* 1993) What has happened to the system of floating exchange rates that was supposed to provide stable exchange rates and to facilitate external adjustment?

Since 1973, world financial markets have been characterized by large movements in nominal exchange rates. These movements have been considerably larger than the early advocates of floating had anticipated. They have been accompanied by large swings in real exchange rates since nominal exchange rate variations have not followed very closely changes in relative prices of traded goods. In consequence, purchasing power parity has not systematically been maintained.

Three different schools of thought have emerged concerning this unforeseen development and its implications for trade development. The first school argues that movements in real exchange rates produce adverse real effects on the economy. The so-called *misalignments* lead to a boom in the traded-goods sectors of countries whose currencies have become undervalued. Correspondingly, in the countries whose currencies have become overvalued, the traded-goods sector is squeezed, leading to losses of output and employment that are not easily absorbed in the short run by other sectors of the economy (De Grauwe 1989: 228). According to this school, individuals adversely affected by these developments organize to generate trade protection. Unless governments respond by managing exchange rates, international trade will be negatively affected.

The second school of thought, expressed by proponents of floating rates, takes a more benign view of exchange rate history. The fact that exchange rate movements have been large and unpredictable does not necessarily imply that they have been harmful (Frenkel 1983: 8). The central insight of this school is the notion that the exchange rate is best analysed within an asset price framework. Since exchange rates are financial-asset prices, they are flexible and forward-looking. Volatility is to be expected in such an auction market because of the continual arrival of new information. The ability of flexible exchange rates to absorb shocks has eased quantity and price adjustments in goods and labor markets, actually lowering protectionist pressures by comparison with what would have occurred in a fixed exchange rate system exposed to equivalent outside shocks. In this view, any unemployment argument for trade protection is decisively lowered by a floating exchange rate system.

The third school focuses attention on the large trade deficits that have become a fixture of the US economy since 1981, and which themselves have become a focal point for the trade protection movement. This school views trade deficits as a direct counterpart of continuing federal budget deficits rather than as the product of exchange rate imbalance and unfair trade practices by foreign competitors. Few economists believe in a simple one-to-one linkage between the budget and trade deficits. Yet a revised version of the twin deficit story may well be the best explanation for the post-1981 US experience (Krugman 1992: 43).

The basic story runs as follows. Beginning in 1981, US national saving began to fall sharply, falling well short of US investment demand. In the absence of international borrowing, this saving shortfall would have driven interest rates sharply upwards. Instead, much of US investment was financed through the sale of assets to foreigners. If a country sells foreigners more assets than it buys, it must correspondingly buy more goods than it sells. The ultimate cause of the trade deficit, therefore, lies in the decline in US saving, partly, although not entirely, due to the budget deficit.

This school of thought rejects trade protection as a solution to the trade deficit problem and focuses instead on the prospects for federal budget reforms. Its proponents emphasize that the trade deficit problem is not an unemployment problem, since unemployment in the United States, for most of the period 1981 to 1994, has been at or below its natural level. Nevertheless, they recognize that special interest groups will exploit trade deficits for self-serving protectionist purposes and that they will find a ready brokering response in Congress unless the savings rate issue is clearly explained to the voting public.

6 The imperfect competition argument

The 1930s witnessed the emergence of yet another threat to free trade, this time from a theoretical source (Bhagwati 1994: 234). Edward Chamberlin (1929) and Joan Robinson (1931) independently developed a theory of imperfect competition that opened up a systematic exploration of the middle ground between perfect competition and monopoly. The result was the undermining of the notion that market prices reflected social costs and the calling into question of the virtues of the *laissez-faire* invisible hand in general and, with it, the merit of free trade (Bhagwati 1994: 234).

The skepticism about prices not reflecting social costs due to imperfect competition never made much of an inroad into the thinking of the general public: the insight was too complex for that to happen. It was to remain a powerful source of erosion in the belief that free trade was desirable among professional economists and economics students, especially among those predisposed in favor of government intervention (Hicks 1959: 46). In its initial form, the imperfect competition argument made little practical impact. It was vastly overshadowed by the circumstance of high unemployment and by Keynes' much-vaunted desertion of the comparative-advantage justification of free trade (Bhagwati 1994: 235).

In 1949, the Chicago School opened up a devastating critique of imperfect competition theory that has never been satisfactorily answered. Stigler did not deny the logic of Chamberlin's analysis for the many-firm industry. However, he contended that the implications of this model differed only trivially from those of perfect competition theory, because the model was only tractable where the demand elasticities for the products of individual firms were extremely high. This line of criticism was taken further by Archibald (1961), who demonstrated that Chamberlin's model yielded no qualitative comparative static predictions, and therefore was unscientific. The analytical weakness of the model was its failure to specify completely the demand relationships within each group.

The Chicago Group proceeded further to counter the threat from imperfect competition theory by demonstrating empirically that although markets seemed to be imperfect at some superficial level, in reality competition satisfied an *as if* criterion, in that imperfections were simply not of sufficient consequence to require policy intervention (Friedman 1963). By the early 1960s, the original imperfect competition theory, rightly or wrongly, had been relegated to the role of a *curiosum* in the trade protection rhetoric.

7 The argument from factor market imperfections

The 1950s to 1970s were decades of increasingly freer trade in the developed countries, characterized by successive rounds of GATT negotiations that resulted in dramatic reductions in tariffs. From the particular perspective of the United States, this was a heyday of freer trade. Yet the increasing trade liberalization of the developed countries contrasted sharply with policies of import substitution and protectionism that enveloped much of the underdeveloped world.

For the most part, politicians in the underdeveloped countries resorted to the infant-industry argument in defense of their trade protection policies. Alternatively, they argued that the protected industries were necessary features of any modern economy, implying a non-economic preference for their support and development. Leading international economists, dissatisfied with such pragmatic justifications, inferred on behalf of underdeveloped countries a range of factor market imperfections that justified trade protection policies (Corden 1957; Johnson 1965; Bhagwati and Srinivasan 1969).

Foremost among such justifications were the perceived presence of disturbing intersectoral wage differentials, sticky wages such that the market wage exceeded the shadow wage, sector-specific minimum wages and monopsony (Bhagwati 1994: 235). In the spirit of the times, few economists suggested the removal of the root causes of market failure. Instead, they pursued a second-best logic of piling regulation on regulation in a manner guaranteed to stifle all entrepreneurship in already largely lifeless economies. There was an explosion of theoretical developments concerning optimal and second-best policies to remedy the distorting effects of a wide range of self-imposed factor market imperfections in the third world economies.

For the most part, the factor market imperfections argument was not directed to the advanced economies, although it might well have been, given the thicket of factor market interventions that strangled economic growth in many such economies throughout the 1960s and 1970s. In the international community, however, this argument served as a shield to protect socialist dictators and left-leaning democracies in the third world as they scuttled their economies in pursuit of self-serving, rent-seeking objectives. In particular, the major aid-granting international agencies became major conduits for such thinking, deploying international aid to prop up governments that supplied trade protection in response to rent-seeking special interests, destroying private property rights that should have served as the engine of economic development.

8   The argument for strategic trade policy

The 1980s shared with the 1950s to 1970s the distinction of having the theory of trade protection extended in the realm of imperfect competition. In this later period, however, the development was concerned with product market imperfections and was directed at the trade policies of the advanced nations, most notably the United States (Bhagwati 1994: 237).

Three reasons can be identified for the economic analysis of US trade policy shifting so sharply during the 1980s (Krugman 1988: 5). First, the role of trade in the US economy and the role of the United States in the world economy changed significantly. In a simple quantitative measure of this change, the shares of imports and exports in US manufacturing value-added both more than doubled between 1960 and 1980. Qualitatively, international considerations became much more important, with most US firms much more reliant on export sales or facing keen foreign competition in their US markets. Inevitably, a range of industrial policy debates that had been viewed as domestic in nature were transformed into debates that contained a vital trade policy component.

Second was the perception among an influential body of economists that a change had occurred in the character of trade, which no longer resembled the kind of exchange envisaged in classical theory. Specifically, a large and growing part of world trade was viewed as consisting of exchanges that could not be attributed easily to underlying comparative advantage. Instead, trade seemed to reflect arbitrary or temporary advantages resulting from economies of scale and scope or shifting leads in close technological races (Krugman 1988: 7). Since technological innovation is an activity that may generate external benefits to the rest of the economy, its growing importance in international trade, it is argued, reinforces the need to rethink the analytical basis for trade policy.

Third was the application to international trade theory of major innovations in the field of industrial organization designed to analyze industries in which only a small number of firms are competing – oligopolies, in the jargon of economics. In such industries, firms do not act like atomistic competitors. Instead, they face a few identifiable rivals, they have some direct ability to affect prices, and they make strategic moves designed to affect their rivals' actions. Imperfect competition is the term coined to denote such interactive competition. Major US exporters such as Boeing and Caterpillar find themselves in this kind of imperfect competition in world as well as in US markets.

Taken together, these three factors were harnessed during the 1980s into a powerful attack on the comparative advantage justification for unilateral free trade. On the one side, it was argued, much of trade appears to require an explanation in terms of economies of scale, learning curves and the dynamics of innovation, phenomena that are incompatible with the kind of idealization under which free trade is always the best policy. On the other side, the increased sophistication of the analytical tool-box suggests two ways in which an activist trade policy can benefit a country relative to free trade, perhaps at the expense of its competitors.

The first such way is through the ability of government policies to secure for a nation a larger share of available rent, where rent is defined as payment to any factor input higher than what that factor could earn in an alternative activity. Rent may mean a higher rate of profit in an industry than is available elsewhere in industries of equivalent riskiness; or it may mean higher wages in an industry than equally skilled workers earn elsewhere. If certain industries earn significant rents, it is argued that trade policy can increase national income by securing for a country a larger share of rent-yielding industries.

The classical political economy view is that such rents are unimportant in a competitive market. If profits or wages temporarily are unusually high in an industry, capital or labor will quickly enter and compete them back to normal levels. Imperfect competition theory is less sanguine on this issue. If there are important advantages to large-scale production, or a steep learning curve, for example, new entry into an industry may be unprofitable even if incumbent firms are making high profits or paying high wages, or both. In such circumstances, subsidies or protection may be viewed as desirable policy instruments to provide *first-mover advantages* to domestic firms.

The second justification for activist trade policy is through the ability of government to secure for a nation external economies that would be sacrificed by free trade. External economies are defined as benefits from some activity that accrue to individuals or firms other than those engaging in that activity. An often-quoted example is the diffusion of knowledge generated in one activity to other firms and other sections within an economy. If such external economies exist, capital or labor in the sector itself may not earn exceptional returns; rather, that sector will yield high returns elsewhere within the economy by providing specific benefits to capital and labor deployed on other industries:

> Suppose, for example, that we conclude that certain high-technology sectors generate large technology spillovers to the rest of the economy. We could then conclude that promoting these sectors through protection, export subsidies and so on, might raise national income. Conversely, foreign promotion of these sectors might be depriving us of valuable spillovers and should be countered, contrary to the conventional argument that free trade is appropriate to whatever other countries do. (Krugman 1988: 14)

Neither the rent nor the external-effects argument is unambiguously favorable to strategic trade policy, even at the level of pure theory. Let us dissect each in turn. Let us accept that certain activities may manifest natural monopoly characteristics evidenced by strict sub-additivity of costs (Baumol *et al.* 1982). Let us suppose, however, that such industries are contestable, in the sense that they are characterized by zero or near-zero costs of entry and exit. In such circumstances, a necessary condition for sustainability of the natural monopoly is that the firm in question should post Ramsey prices designed to achieve break-even across its product line. There is no possibility of earning rents under such circumstances.

Let us relax the contestability assumption and acknowledge that a natural monopolist may earn rents in equilibrium equal to its sunk costs of entry. Let us assert, however, that the condition of non-contestability depends on some form of government protection. In such circumstances, the equilibrium rents may be illusory, dissipated by rent-seeking outlays necessary to secure government protection (see Chapter 4). The strategic rent-seeking justification for trade protection then vanishes.

Let us now accept the argument that a certain category of activities provides external benefits to the economy as a whole. By no means is this a sufficient argument for trade protection or export subsidies even at the level of pure theory. First, there is the question whether the externalities are Pareto-relevant. The world is full of externalities that are not and that present no threat to efficiency in the *laissez-faire* economy (Buchanan and Stubblebine 1962). Second, there is the question whether transaction costs are too high for individuals to internalize the externality through private negotiations. Third, there is the question whether high transaction costs that block a private resolution can be lowered sufficiently by government to justify a regulatory response. If any of these questions is not answered positively, the conventional case for intervention simply disintegrates.

Let us now play devil's advocate by conceding that certain activities may satisfy the necessary conditions at the level of pure theory to justify some form of strategic trade protection. How might this be translated into political action and with what likelihood of economic success? The first question that must be raised is whether even an efficiency-driven government is equipped to identify strategic sectors and to pick winners for the nation. The answer is that government is highly unlikely to measure up well to such a responsibility.

Suppose that a government determines to seek out strategic sectors where there is substantial rent, that is, where the return to labor or to capital is exceptionally high. Several factors tend to confuse such an investigation (Krugman 1988: 16). First, there is the problem of separating rent from quality differences in markets where labor is of diverse quality. If one industry pays higher wages than another, does that represent rent or does it merely reflect the fact that the high-wage industry employs higher-skilled and better-qualified workers? A national policy of targeting sectors that yield high value-added per worker (one that is frequently advocated) is entirely inappropriate if that policy fails to identify whether high value-added simply reflects high input.

Second, there is the problem of evaluating high rates of return as indicators of wealth. If certain industries appear to earn high rates of return, they may do so because only the successful firms remain while the failures have simply vanished. To evaluate *ex ante* risk may require an in-depth investigation that would be time-consuming and costly. To ignore it would be to run the risk of targeting for strategic trade protection industries that are bereft of rent in the meaningful *ex ante* sense of that term.

Third, there is the danger that observed rents may be a transitory phenomenon, the consequence of good luck that may not repeat itself. If favorable technological developments or shifts in demand benefit an industry, firms and workers already in that industry typically will receive windfall gains. Such gains may well not accrue to new entrants. Thus, a policy of promoting such an industry may fail to move resources to sectors where they can earn high returns. Evidently, the task of identifying strategic rent sectors is not a simple matter of looking at profit rates and wage rates over the past five years (Krugman 1988: 17). It is probably beyond the technical competence of any government.

Similar measurement problems exist with respect to external economies. By definition, a spillover does not command a market price and therefore is not directly traceable. Almost all attempts to measure external economies have been based on historical studies of past relationships. Always, such studies are shot through with the subjective prejudices of investigators. For trade policy, what is necessary is a forward-looking assessment which requires highly detailed knowledge of often rapidly changing market conditions. It does not take Friedrich Hayek (1945) to remind us that planning systems simply cannot apprise themselves effectively of the relevant information which is available, if at all, only in a diffused decentralized form. We doubt if one government economist in a hundred could even supply a passably accurate definition of the positive Coase theorem. We would lay bets that not a single member of Congress could do so.

Suppose, however, that by some form of divine intervention a set of industries somehow were to be successfully identified as candidates for strategic trade protection or export subsidies. Problems would still remain as to how an impartial but not omniscient government would devise policies effectively to promote such sectors.

The first potential problem arises where the sectors that government wishes to support compete with each other for such scarce resources as technically trained manpower. This is particularly likely in the case of external economy sectors involving research and development expertise. In such circumstances, evident government prejudices for supporting firms with formal research departments over entrepreneurs with genuine insights may have disastrous long-term consequences for economic performance.

The second potential problem arises, when devising policies to assist high-value industries, of predicting the effects of such intervention in a complex strategic environment. Will an export subsidy raise the factor returns to the subsidized firms or will it provoke retaliation and increased competition?

Will a tariff protect the rents of a threatened domestic industry, or will it induce sloth and be wasted in technical inefficiency? Will it provoke a tariff war of a prisoners' dilemma nature?

Bureaucrats with no comparative advantage in entrepreneurship are ill-suited to making such decisions. That they must do so with other people's wealth predictably makes them careless as well as incompetent in such decision-making. There are likely to be serious agency problems when people use other people's money to make investments, to award subsidies and the like.

The third problem that arises when governments decide to pick winners is that the rule of law (Hayek 1960) typically is violated. Known individuals and known sectors are selected for specific privileges and, by inference, known individuals and known sectors suffer adverse discrimination. This provides bureaucrats with discretionary power that *must* be exercised to violate a fundamental precept of liberty. If that discretionary power is significant the road to serfdom (Hayek 1944) evidently is wide open and will be ridden hard by those government officials who have no innate respect for negative freedom.

Finally, we should recognize that strategic trade policy is never implemented by impartial, efficiency-motivated government. It is exploited by special interests that take advantage of the logic of collective action (Olson 1965) and rational voter ignorance (Downs 1957) to distort the political process by rent-seeking outlays. Once it becomes recognized by industries that government may be prepared to supply trade protection and export subsidies, the demand for such policies will manifest itself with entrepreneurial and managerial talent diverting itself from productive endeavors into non-productive lobbying of the political process.

9 The fair trade argument

Comparative advantage theory suggests that diversity among trading nations is good rather than bad for mutually gainful trade; indeed, that international trade exists in significant part because of differences in tastes and endowments between countries. Yet new challenges to the free trade idea target such diversity, demanding fair trade and harmonization of domestic policies and institutions (if not the homogenization of all individuals) as preconditions for free trade.

The argument for a level playing field involves a claim that trade should take place only among people who somehow are equally situated. Much of this claim to trade restriction involves charges that lower labor costs give an advantage to foreign over United States producers, that free trade under such circumstances must pit American against foreign workers 'in a race to the bottom' (Bhagwati, 1994: 238). Lost amid this claim is any recognition that gains from trade are grounded in differentiation and specialization. Where labor is cheap – *for whatever reason* – there is a comparative advantage in the production of commodities that make relatively intensive use of labor. Where labor is expensive and capital plentiful, there is a comparative advantage in the production of commodities that make relatively intensive use of capital. The logic of this argument is surely not so difficult to understand.

Claims about securing a level playing field have much the same flavor as claims to promote equality of opportunity through tax and transfer programs of the welfare state. Superficially, both claims seem reasonable if not unexceptional. But this apparent reasonableness is because both claims are devoid of content. Once an effort is made to provide content to the claims, it becomes quickly apparent that the claims are extremely unreasonable.

With respect to equality of opportunity, for example, it is often argued that all individuals should start at the same point in the race to accumulate wealth. What does this really mean? Evidently, some individuals inherit a superior gene pool to others, by being born relatively intelligent or physically well-endowed. Should these people be handicapped to start behind the intellectually slow, the halt and the lame? What would be the implications for the wealth of any nation whose government invested in such an experiment?

Suppose even that genetic and environmental advantages were neutralized. What happens when those who are harder-working or who sacrifice hedonism for long-term advantage begin to surge ahead of those who fail to do so? Are the shackles once again to be imposed? If so, what are the implications for the human capital stock as outward and inward migration respond to the signals that have been imposed? Surely *that* is a clear-cut race to the bottom.

It is much the same with arguments in favor of a level playing field. With respect to an athletic field, it is easy to determine whether or not it is level. Anyone can buy a carpenter's level at a hardware store and make such a determination. But what would such a requirement mean with respect to international trade? In a word, nothing. Producers situated in different locations throughout the world differ among themselves in all kinds of ways. Some are located where labor costs are lower than those faced by other producers. Some are located in places where individuals have a strong work ethic, whereas others are in areas where individuals indulge themselves in idleness, quitting work early and slipping away for extended weekend rest-periods.

Producers in some areas (notably the Pacific Rim) enjoy political systems where people value commerce highly and thus tightly restrict the scope of government action. By contrast, producers in other areas (for example, the United States) suffer under political systems that do not value commerce highly, that evidence a strong preference for affirmative action and welfare policies over wealth creation and that impose highly intrusive, meddlesome and taxing governments designed to quell the entrepreneurial instincts of their most highly endowed members.

In such circumstances, discourse about a level playing field is meaningless. In practice, what such discourse seems to imply, once the rhetoric is set aside, is that producers in areas where government is less taxing and less meddlesome with respect to commerce seem to have an advantage over American producers. That such is the case is hardly surprising. If Singapore sets a top marginal income tax at 15 percent and the United States sets a top marginal income tax at over 50 percent, a child in diapers could explain the significance for productive effort.

The claim for a level playing field thus is an effort to reduce the advantages that producers have because they enjoy good government. Such a policy, if implemented, would work its wealth-reducing mission, not by increasing the commercial orientation of United States citizens, but by suppressing that commercial orientation elsewhere. Surely *that* is a clear-cut *race to the bottom*.

10 The argument against dumping and foreign export subsidies

A popular variant on the level playing field argument is the case for protection based on claims that foreign producers are selling their products at prices that are too low. Evidently, this is not an argument that emanates from domestic consumers. Such 'unfair' competition may arise, it is argued, because foreign exporters dump their products onto the domestic market at prices that are below those charged in their own markets or because foreign governments subsidize the production of goods targeted significantly for export markets.

Such activities, it is argued, must be countered by countervailing tariffs or by other trade-impeding penalties. The fact that such interventions violate the principles of an extended market order and impose the principles of a command economy either is not recognized or is a matter of unimportance to those who advocate recourse to fair trade laws.

Dumping is usually defined for policy purposes as selling below cost. This sounds straightforward, but is not. As a long-run proposition, a firm cannot stay in business if it does not cover its costs. Any firm that persists in truly selling below cost is a firm whose owners are transferring wealth to their customers. They are practicing charity and not business. Certainly, charity is not objectionable; and it is a permissible activity within the context of a market economy. It is surely a rare occurrence, however, for firms to engage in charity to the point of endangering their own existence.

Cost is a concept that is applicable to long-term planning but that has no applicability to production that has already taken place. The cost of any item which has already been produced is zero, since those costs have already been borne. That is one reason domestic producers engage in activities identical to dumping that go under the name of 'sales'.

Immediately after Christmas, for example, retailers typically 'dump' a variety of Christmas decorations onto the market. For some consumers, the opportunity to buy Christmas decorations a year in advance, at perhaps a discount of 50 percent, proves to be a good investment. The retailers who offer these sales presumably find such disposal to be more profitable than packing and storing the goods until the following year. In a great many cases, sales of such items at deep discounts, at prices that are less than some irrelevant accounting measure of cost, is a rational business strategy, beneficial both for sellers and for buyers. This is also the case with much of what is labelled foreign dumping.

It is sometimes claimed that dumping is a component of predatory pricing, whereby low prices today that drive competitors out of business will lead to high, monopolistic prices tomorrow. Once again, the argument is suspect, as Chapter 10 explains in some detail, not least because the predator must suffer greater losses than his victims, if he is to act as residual supplier to the market throughout the period of predation.

While claims of predatory pricing are often advanced, no such episodes have actually been recorded. The claim that was most vociferously advanced, concerning the behavior of Standard Oil in the early twentieth century turns out to have been entirely bogus. Standard Oil did not run competitors out of business by charging below-cost prices. Instead, it bought out its competitors. The general point this makes is that predatory pricing is far more costly than a simple purchase of assets. Rational producers thus will follow the latter route. Whether government officials are prepared to recognize this logic is more a matter of public-choice pressures than of clear economic analysis.

11   The argument for securing wages and working conditions

Another recent, highly potent challenge to free trade focuses on the income distribution effects of trade with underdeveloped countries. Ironically, economists who press this argument typically agitate for egalitarian policies domestically. Presumably, for them all charity stops at the borders. Starting with the late 1980s, such economists have raised fearful voices in the North, dreading trade with the poor South as a recipe for descent into the wages and working conditions of these impoverished nations (Bhagwati 1994: 241)

The major theoretical constructs providing intellectual support for such fears in the North are the Factor Price Equalization (FPE) theorem and the Stolper–Samuelson (SS) theorem which show an adverse impact of free trade on the factor of production that is scarce in the domestic country relative to elsewhere among a country's trading partners. Presumably, for the Cassandras of the North, this is identified as unskilled labor in the North *vis-à-vis* unskilled labor in the South, relative to other factors of production such as capital (Bhagwati 1994: 241).

Although FPE was considered to be implausible, if not wrong, when first presented by Samuelson in 1948, the current tendency is to regard it as an inescapable destiny, implying for the unskilled an inevitable immiseration of their real wages under conditions of free trade. As Bhagwati (1994: 242) rightly reminds us, however, the original view of the FPE theorem was correct. Its assumptions are extraordinarily demanding; and it is not a compelling, or even adequate, guide to real-world phenomena.

Bhagwati (1994: 242) sets out three reasons why the presumption that real wages in the North and South will converge under conditions of free trade can be considered to be unrealistic. His arguments relate to the Stolper–Samuelson theorem, assuming that the rich country imports unskilled labor-intensive goods and exports human and physical capital-intensive goods. He further assumes that the terms of trade improve when trade is freed. In the (2 × 2) version of the theorem, which is consistent with the FPE theorem, the real wage of labor falls in the rich country.

First, scale economies can invalidate this outcome, causing both factors' real wages to rise. They do so by raising the marginal products, and hence the real wages, of both factors, effectively countering the redistributive effect which militates against the real wage of unskilled labor. This effect will occur both when the economies are external to the firm but internal to the industry (Panagariya 1981) and when the economies are internal to the firm but due to added variety rather than to reduced cost (Helpman and Krugman 1985).

Second, specialization in production can also invalidate the real wage effect of the Stolper–Samuelson theorem, by breaking down the unique relationship between goods and factor prices. While factor prices are unique at complete specialization on a good, goods prices are not, since raising prices for the good will be compatible with continued specialization. Furthermore, while the redistributive effect operates as long as trade shifts production toward a good, once complete specialization is achieved, any further rise in that good's relative price means that both factors gain.

The lifting-all-boats effect from this improvement in the terms of trade will then ensue, helping each factor proportionally to how much it consumes of the cheaper imported goods. In this respect, evidence suggests that groups at the bottom of the income distribution fare particularly well from free trade (Cline 1990). Since protection in the United States typically is provided for industries that are not intensive in the incidence of poverty among their workforce, this argument suggests that it works specifically to the disadvantage of the poor.

Third, the lifting-all-boats effect can also occur if free trade brings with it more competition causing *x*-efficiency effects which take the form of Hicks-neutral technical change. If this effect operates throughout the economy, it will serve to raise real wages in both sectors, potentially reversing any fall in the real wage due to the Stolper–Samuelson effect. Even if the effect occurs differentially in the import-competing sectors, as we may predict, work on the general equilibrium income-elasticities of supply under technical change (Findley and Grubert 1959) indicates that the effect will raise the real wage of the factor intensively used in these sectors, i.e. of unskilled labor.

Undoubtedly, the real wages of unskilled labor in the United States have been subjected to downward pressure since the early 1980s. The culprit, however, is not trade but rather technology and technical change (Bhagwati and Dehejia 1993). The new information technology is strongly reinforcing Griliches' (1969) insight that skilled labor is relatively more complementary to capital. A computer may displace several unskilled workers while creating a job for one skilled operator. In such circumstances, the impact both of capital accumulation and of technical change serves to reduce rather than to increase the real wages of the unskilled. As with free trade, so with the new information technology, any Luddite attempt to reverse this trend most certainly would be a *race to the bottom*.

12   The new protectionism and the welfare state

Since the early 1970s there has been a notable change in the frame of reference within which trade protection is advanced in the United States. As Melvin Krauss (1978) and Jan Tumlir (1979) both observe, the old protectionism largely has given way to the new.

The old protectionism operated within a vision of an international system consisting of free enterprise market economies, based on the price system, linked to one another by unrestricted international economic exchange. Governments seldom intervened in the private economy except when protectionist pressures became politically irresistible. When they were forced to do so, protection was rendered by an instrument least harmful to the workings of the market economy – namely the non-discriminatory tariff.

The new protectionism, in contrast, emerges out of the logic of the welfare state; indeed, it represents elements of the welfare state applied to international trade. It reflects the almost complete demise within the United States of rugged individualism, of the frontier spirit with which individual Americans prided themselves when dealing with economic change and unexpected adversity. It reflects the replacing of those admirable characteristics with growing dependence upon government to ameliorate or to stave off the adverse consequences of change even at some considerable cost to the wealth of the nation.

While too many economists are fascinated with theoretical proofs of the existence, uniqueness and stability of equilibrium conditions in economic models, one of the most notable features of real economic life is the presence of continual change. This latter characteristic is what George Shackle (1972) meant when he referred to an economy as being *kaleidic*. Much of this continual change comes about as producers seek to develop new products and to expand their markets. Many of these initiatives involve the creation of new knowledge and the development of new technologies.

Among the consequences of such change are the shrinkage and death of some business enterprises and the birth and expansion of others. It is increasingly rare in such circumstances for individuals to enter a particular career in the possession of a particular set of skills with any expectation that they will be able to employ these skills until retirement. Knowledge changes too rapidly and individuals confront the prospect of retooling perhaps several times during their productive lifetimes. Wiseman (1953) has argued that much of the demand for market closure stems from resistance to such change and represents the use of protection as a form of insurance.

One consequence of this welfare-state approach to protectionism is that the non-discriminatory tariff becomes less important than discriminatory tariffs, quotas and voluntary export restraints as instruments of protection. In this way, the new protectionism constitutes a clear and present danger to the market economy, representing the replacement of non-discrimination with a process of political discrimination in which those individuals who are politically influential secure advantages at the expense of those who are not. The outcome of the new protectionism, as subsequent chapters of this book demonstrate, is a set of discriminating trade provisions in direct conflict with the rule of law, which requires that rules and practices should apply equally to all individuals, including those who design and enforce those rules.

13   The new protectionism and the extended order

The term *extended order* is the concept Hayek (1988) eventually came to prefer over terms such as the *open society* which he used in the same sense. It is used in contradistinction to the *restricted order* of the small horde or tribe (Curzon-Price 1994). The extended order is one in which millions of individuals interact. It is an order because within it individuals can form correct expectations, or at least expectations which have a good chance of proving correct. It is spontaneous because it is the product of the action of many individuals but not the result of human design.

Hayek's key insight is that it is knowledge that is the central issue in organizing peaceful and prosperous human societies. The extended order coordinates and puts to good use knowledge that is scattered among millions of individuals. It does so through the mechanism of the market. The restricted order, in contrast, can only solve simple, local problems on the basis of very limited information. That is why societies that attempt to replace the market order by central commands fail so miserably. It also explains why societies that place serious obstacles in the path of the market order deprive themselves of its information processing capacity and thus impoverish themselves.

The extended order accomplishes the dual feat of coordinating dispersed knowledge and generating new knowledge through an interlocking system of rules and institutions. Within this set of institutions is one of overriding importance: that of private property. Without private property there can be no concept of honesty, of exchange or of privacy. More important, without private property there can be no liberty, defined by Hayek as independence of the arbitrary will of another.

The new protectionism is a clear infringement of the extended order, attempting to regulate in a highly discriminatory fashion free exchange among individuals, using border controls as social engineering instruments in pursuit of arbitrary objectives. Even if the new protectionism were not invaded by the pressures of public choice it must be extremely harmful to liberty, extremely invasive of private property, and extremely damaging to the coordination and generation of knowledge. If it is distorted by public choice pressures it must constitute the kind of ultimate threat to the extended order that Hayek so skillfully outlined in *The Road to Serfdom* (1944).

References

Archibald, G.C. (1961) 'Chamberlin versus Chicago', *Review of Economic Studies*, xxix (October): 2–28.

Archibald, G.C. (1963) 'Reply to Chicago', *Review of Economic Studies*, xxx (February): 68–71.

Aschheim, J., Tavlas, G.S and Ulan, M. (1993) 'The relationship between exchange-rate variability and protection', in D. Salvatore (ed.), *Protectionism and World Welfare* (Cambridge: Cambridge University Press), pp. 290–308.

Baumol, W.J., Panzar, J.C. and Willig, R.D. (1982) *Contestable Markets and the Theory of Industry Structure* (New York: Harcourt Brace Jovanovich).

Beveridge, W. (ed.) (1932) *Tariffs: The Case Examined* (New York: Longmans, Green).

Bhagwati, J. (1994) 'Free trade: old and new challenges', *Economic Journal*, 104(3): 231–46.

Bhagwati, J. and Dehejia, V. (1993) *Freer Trade and Wages of the Unskilled: Is Marx Striking Again?* (Washington, D.C.: American Enterprise Institute).

Bhagwati, J. and Srinivasan, T.N. (1969) 'Optimal intervention to achieve non-economic objectives', *Review of Economic Studies*, 36: 27–38.

Buchanan, J.M. and Stubblebine, W.C. (1962) 'Externality'. *Economica*, xxix (November), 29: 371–84.

Chamberlin, E. (1929) *The Theory of Monopolistic Competition* (Cambridge, Mass.: Harvard University Press).

Cline, W.R. (1990) *The Future of World Trade in Textiles and Apparel* (Washington, D.C.: Institute for International Economics).

Corden, W.M. (1957) 'Tariffs, subsidies and the terms of trade', *Economica*, 24.

Curzon-Price, V. (1994) *Hayek's Extended Order*, University of Geneva Working Paper.

De Grauwe, P. (1989) *International Money: Postwar Trends and Theories* (Oxford: Clarendon Press).

Downs, A. (1957) *An Economic Theory of Democracy* (New York: Harper & Row).

Findley, R. and Grubert, H. (1959) 'Factor intensities, technological progress and the terms of trade', *Oxford Economic Papers*, II: 111–21.

Frenkel, J. (1983) 'Turbulence in foreign exchange markets and macro-economic policies', in

D. Bigman and T. Taya (eds), *Exchange Rate and Trade Instability: Cases, Consequences and Remedies* (Cambridge: Ballinger).

Friedman, M. (1963) 'More on Archibald versus Chicago', *Review of Economic Studies*, xxx (February): 65–7.

Griliches, Z. (1969) 'Capital–skill complimentarity', *Review of Economics and Statistics*, 51: 465–8.

Hayek, F.A. (1944) *The Road to Serfdom* (London: Routledge).

Hayek, F.A. (1945) 'The use of knowledge in society', *American Economic Review*, xxxv (4): 519–30.

Hayek, F.A. (1960) *The Constitution of Liberty* (London: Routledge & Kegan Paul).

Hayek, F.A. (1988) *The Fatal Conceit: The Errors of Socialism* (Chicago: University of Chicago Press).

Helpman, E. and Krugman, P.R. (1985) *Market Structure and Foreign Trade* (Cambridge, Mass.: MIT Press).

Hicks, J.R. (1959) *Essays in World Economics* (Oxford: Clarendon Press).

Johnson, H.G. (1953) 'Optimal tariffs and retaliation', *Review of Economic Studies*, 21: 142–53.

Johnson, H.G. (1965) 'Optimal trade intervention in the presence of domestic distortions', in R.E. Caves, H.G. Johnson and P.B. Kenen (eds), *Trade, Growth and the Balance of Payments* (Amsterdam: North-Holland).

Krauss, M.B. (1978) *The New Protectionism* (New York: New York University Press).

Krugman, P.R. (1987) 'Is free trade passé?', *Journal of Economic Perspectives*, i (Fall): 131–44.

Krugman, P.R. (1988) 'New thinking about trade policy', in P.R. Krugman (ed.), *Strategic Trade Policy and the New International Economics* (Cambridge, Mass.: MIT Press), 1-22.

Krugman, P.R. (1992) *The Age of Diminished Expectations* (Cambridge, Mass.: MIT Press).

Mill, J.S. (1848) *Principles of Political Economy* (London: Longman, Green).

Olson, M. (1965) *The Logic of Collective Action* (Cambridge, Mass.: Harvard University Press).

Panagariya, A. (1981) 'Variable returns to scale in general equilibrium theory once again', *Journal of International Economics*, 10: 499–526.

Robinson, J. (1931) *The Economics of Imperfect Competition* (London: Macmillan).

Samuelson, P.A. (1948) 'International trade and the equalisation of factor prices', *Economic Journal*, 58: 163–84.

Samuelson, P.A. (1949) 'International factor-price equalisation once again', *Economic Journal*, 59: 181–97.

Shackle, G.L.S. (1972) *Epistemics and Economics* (Cambridge: Cambridge University Press).

Stigler, G.T. (1963) 'Archibald versus Chicago', *Review of Economic Studies*, xxx (February): 64–6.

Stolper, W. and Samuelson, P.A. (1941) 'Protection and real wages', *Review of Economic Studies*, 9: 58–73.

Torrens, R. (1844) *The Budget: On Commercial and Colonial Policy* (London: Smith, Elder).

Tumlir, J. (1979) 'The new protectionism, cartels and the international order', in R.C. Amacher, G. Haberler and T.D. Willett (eds), *Challenges to a Liberal Economic Order* (Washington, D.C.: American Enterprise Institute).

Wiseman, J. (1953) 'Uncertainty, costs and collectivist economic planning', *Economica*, 20 (May), 118–28.

4 The political economy of trade protection

1 Introduction

The welfare economics of the theory of international trade implies, with only trivial and inconsequential qualifications, that unilateral free trade policies serve to maximize the overall wealth of a nation and to provide individuals with maximum possible consumption opportunities. With rare exceptions, the world's leading economists, despite differences in political preferences, unite in the fair-trade corner and mount a powerful case against trade protection on the basis of widely endorsed efficiency theorems derived from neoclassical economics. The trade-protection corner, for the most part, is populated by a motley crew of economic journalists, interventionist-minded lawyers, political scientists and economic scribblers from the Kennedy School of Government with minds unexposed to, or insufficiently nimble to comprehend, the comparative advantage theorem.

Yet the world that these leading economists inhabit is largely and extensively a world of trade protection, a world in which wealth is diminished and consumption opportunities curtailed not by the exigencies of fate but by the misguided hand of man. Why is it, we may well ask, that the big economic guns, like the massive well-fortified guns that comprised the ill-fated Maginot Line, appear to be pointing futilely in the wrong direction? Why is it, when economists for once find themselves overwhelmingly united and supported by a clear and apparently compelling logic, that their arguments seemingly carry so little weight in the market place of politics?

Our search for answers to these questions starts out with an acknowledgement that the welfare economics theorems which underpin the case for free trade are efficiency-orientated, that they depend upon the existence both of an efficient market in information and of an effective network of compensating lump-sum transfers. If the information market fails, voters will not necessarily be cognizant with the theory of comparative advantage when they pull the levers in their voting booths. If lump-sum transfers are not available, those who perceive personal losses from any movement to free trade will not necessarily anticipate receiving compensation from those who feasibly might remedy their suffering while themselves retaining net benefits from the policy adjustment.

In political markets characterized by incomplete information and by incomplete compensation mechanisms, the opportunities for gains-from-trade that motivate the efficiency calculus will be challenged and frequently will be overwhelmed by distributional conflicts. The extent to which the one or the other motivation dominates depends not only on the extent of the failure of the information and compensation mechanisms, but also on the organization of legislatures, including the composition of legislative committees and the procedures under which legislation is considered. The decisive factor rarely will be the particular motivation of the actors that comprise the political market place. In our analysis, *Homo economicus* thrives in this environment and self-seeking man is the universal specter.

2   Identifying the gainers and losers from trade protection

The traditional theory of international trade derives its conclusions from one of three alternative models (Magee *et al.* 1989). The first model, known as the *Ricardian* or *classical model*, postulates an economy characterized by a single homogeneous and intersectorally mobile factor of production – labor. In such an economy, the only source of income derives from labor services and there is no conflict concerning trade policy. Each individual gains from free trade and loses from protection. The second model, known as the *Heckscher–Ohlin model*, postulates an economy characterized by at least two intersectorally mobile factors of production – labor and capital. Since the source of income in this case derives from more than one factor, there may be gainers as well as losers from trade protection. The third model allows for the presence of industry-specific as well as intersectorally mobile factors of production and once again provides for gainers as well as losers from trade protection. In the cases of models two and three, differences between those who gain and those who lose may result in coalitions that have conflicting interests regarding trade policy.

In the Heckscher–Ohlin model, the potential conflict between labor and capital arises through the link between relative output, prices and real factor returns. In a competitive economy, with two goods and two intersectorally mobile factors, trade protection will increase the real income of the owners of the economy's relatively scarce factor at the expense of owners of the relatively abundant factor whose real incomes will fall. This result, known as the *Stolper–Samuelson theorem*, is intensified by the fact that the deadweight costs of protection are also borne by owners of the economy's relatively abundant factor. In this manner, the real incomes of owners of the economy's relatively scarce factor increase even as aggregate real income declines as a consequence of trade protection. Extension of this model to encompass many goods produced by two factors does not affect the basic Stolper–Samuelson result. Stolper–Samuelson thus suggests that lobbying for and against trade protection will occur along factor lines – capital versus labor.

However, industry-specific interests and not factor-based coalitions in general are observed to be active in seeking trade protection. Industry-specific interests are associated with industry-specific factors, and these are associated, not with Stolper–Samuelson, but with the theory of non-competing groups first advanced by Cairnes (1884) and now referred to as the *Ricardo–Viner model*. Returns to industry-specific factors consist of the rents remaining after the mobile factors have been paid their competitively determined returns. Industry-specific factors thus have a particular interest in seeking to influence trade policy, in order to protect or to increase their rents, whereas a mobile factor owner's *consumption preferences* establish the factor's position on trade policy. In the absence of information on consumption preferences, the policy stance of a mobile factor is uncertain – the so-called 'neoclassical ambiguity'.

There is no ambiguity in the case of industry-specific factors: individuals with claims on factors specific to the import-competing sector gain; individuals with claims on factors specific to the export sector lose. Protection increases the real return to the factor specific to the import-competing sector in terms of the protected good whose relative price has increased and also in terms of the export good whose relative price has fallen. In the export sector, the return to the specific factor declines in terms of either good. This identification of gainers and losers from protection extends to any number of goods. Factors specific to any import-competing industry have an interest in seeking protection for their industry and save where logrolling opportunities emerge, only for their industry, while opposing protection for any other industry.

Given that intersectoral factor immobility typically is a short-run characteristic, the Heckscher–Ohlin and the Ricardo–Viner models respectively identify such factor owners' long- and short-run interests in the conduct of a country's international trade policy. Long- and short-run interests so defined may evidently be in conflict. Only by a careful testing of the two rival models is it possible to determine the balance between these potentially conflicting interests in any specific country. Stolper–Samuelson suggests that lobbying for and against trade protection will occur along factor lines – capital versus labor. Ricardo–Viner suggests that it will occur along industry lines – import-competing versus export.

The evidence, at least with respect to the US, strongly favors Ricardo–Viner. As Magee *et al.* (1989) note, the US labor movement has always been active in lobbying on trade policy, and has been markedly so since the early 1970s. Although most of the headlines place labor on the side of greater protection, as we shall see, this is not always true. Management in many US industries also lobbies actively, presumably on behalf of their stockholders. By observing the nature of such lobbying, it is possible to determine whether Heckscher–Ohlin or Ricardo–Viner is more reflective of the experience.

Following Magee *et al.* (1989), the alternative implications of the two models for US lobbying are set out in Figure 4.1. In terms of Stolper–Samuelson, since the United States is capital-abundant and labor-scarce, capital should favor free trade or even export expansion, and labor should favor protection. Thus, Stolper–Samuelson asserts that the lower left quadrant

Position of industry's labor

1.Protectionist   2. Free trade

	1.Protectionist	2. Free trade
1.Protectionist	11 Ricardo–Viner Import-competing industries	12
2. Free trade	21 Stolper–Samuelson All industries	22 Ricardo–Viner Export industries

Position of industry's capital

Figure 4.1   Implications of traditional international economic theories for US lobbying

Position of industry's labor

1.Protectionist   2. Free trade

	1.Protectionist	2. Free trade
1.Protectionist	11 Distilling Textiles Apparel Chemicals Plastics Rubber shoes Leather Shoes Stone products Iron and steel Cutlery Hardware Bearings Watches	12 Tobacco
2. Free trade	21 Petroleum	22 Paper Machinery Tractors Trucks Aviation

Position of industry's capital

Source: Magee, S.P., Brock, W.A. and Young, L. (1989), *Black Hole Tariffs and Endogenous Policy Theory*, New York: Cambridge University Press, p. 108.

Figure 4.2   Empirical results for lobbying on the Trade Reform Act of 1974

in Figure 4.1 will contain all US industries, while the other quadrants are empty. In terms of Ricardo–Viner, however, with immobility of both factors, capital and labor in an industry will work together on trade policy. This implies that import-competing industries will be in quadrant 11 and export industries in quadrant 12, with the two diagonal quadrants empty.

Magee *et al.* (1989) tested these alternative hypotheses against evidence drawn from the testimony of 29 trade associations (representing management) and 23 unions (representing labor) for either trade or greater protection before Congress on the Trade Reform Act of 1974. The results of this test for 21 US industries are outlined in Figure 4.2. It is crystal clear that the data are dominant diagonal and strongly supportive of the Ricardo–Viner model. In only two industries were labor and management opposed to each other. Management was in favor of free trade in petroleum and protectionist in tobacco, with labor in each case the reverse. The petroleum industry was complicated by a split between the major oil companies which favored free trade and the independents which did not. Given the overwhelming weight of the evidence in favor of Ricardo–Viner, the authors declined to perform a test of statistical significance, tartly noting that to do so would simply belabor the obvious. Capital and labor in a given industry typically do not oppose each other on the issue of protection or free trade for that industry.

A second implication of Stolper–Samuelson, but not of Ricardo–Viner, is that, for the country as a whole, each factor will favor either free trade or protection, but not both. Magee *et al.* (1989) tested this hypothesis against US evidence and found it wanting. In only 63 percent of the industries under review was it the case that capital supported its supposedly preferred alternative (protectionism) whereas Stolper–Samuelson predicts 100 percent support. The results reject the factor mobility hypothesis implicit in Stolper–Samuelson, but cannot reject the factor specific hypothesis implicit in Ricardo–Viner. The sample proportion of labor favoring protection was 0.76. Both Stolper–Samuelson and Ricardo–Viner are rejected by this evidence, with the latter rejected more decisively. The results for labor, therefore, are inconclusive with respect to the choice between the two models, in terms of this implication.

A third implication of Stolper–Samuelson, but not of Ricardo–Viner, is that the position taken by capital or labor in an industry on the issue of protection will be independent of whether the industry is export or import competing. Magee *et al.* (1989) tested this implication against US evidence and found that both capital and labor responses differed significantly from the Stolper–Samuelson prediction.

Furthermore, they determined that the average trade balance in industries in which capital supported free trade was $689 million whereas the average trade balance was –$245 million in industries where capital was protectionist. This difference was highly significant statistically. The average trade balance in industries in which labor supported free trade was $1,985 million, whereas it was –$321 million in labor-protectionist industries. These differences were significant statistically. Overall, Magee *et al.* (1989) concluded that both capital and labor lobbied for protection in ways more consistent with the Ricardo–Viner model.

Finally, as Hillman (1989) observes, a categorization of the various gainers and losers from protection is incomplete without a consideration of foreign interests. Protectionist policies restrict the access of foreign industries to domestic markets and affect the profits of foreign corporations. For this reason, foreign corporations have a direct interest and foreign nationals an indirect interest in the conduct of a country's international trade policy. The foreign interest is not necessarily exclusively in favor of free trade policies, since an appropriately orchestrated contraction of trade, through voluntary export restraints (VER) or other 'orderly marketing arrangements', may increase the profits of foreign exporters, while simultaneously benefiting domestic import-competing interests.

3 Efficient choices among the alternative instruments of trade protection

Although much of the literature on trade protection focuses on the tariff, protection can take many forms. Imports may be restricted by specific or *ad valorem* tariffs, import quotas, quota-tariff combinations, variable import levies, voluntary export restraints (VERs), domestic-content requirement schemes, government purchasing restrictions, and by a variety of more or less subtle ways that increase the cost of imports relative to domestically produced substitutes.

In this section, the nature of the problems that might confront a benevolent, but not omniscient, efficiency-oriented government in its choice among alternative trade protection instruments is outlined. To motivate the analysis, we shall assume that the United States is a sufficiently large trading nation as to be able to influence its terms of trade by its own actions. Specifically, we shall assume that, although all individual producers and consumers are atomistic price-takers, the US government can act with monopsony power on its trade protection initiatives (Vousden 1990).

Consider a two-good economy which (in the aggregate) is a large buyer in the world market for its importable good. In Figure 4.3, DD is the country's aggregated demand curve for imports, and the foreign supply curve is SS, upward-sloping because foreign producers export more only at a higher price. Although SS represents the marginal cost curve for foreign exporters, for the US it represents the average cost of imports, with the marginal cost of imports, MC_M, also upward-sloping and above SS.

In a free-trade situation, world equilibrium is at point E, given by the intersection of DD and SS, at price P_F and quantity imported M_F. However, at

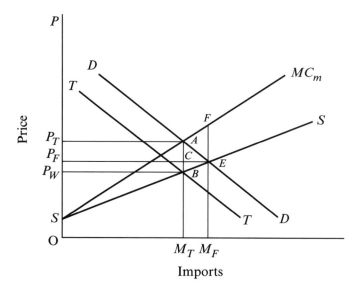

Figure 4.3   The optimal tariff

this point, the value to the US of an extra unit of imports is less than the marginal cost of that unit by an amount *EF*. The US apparently can increase its welfare by reducing imports to M_T, determined by the point of intersection *A* of *DD* and MC_M.

The resulting US gain is equal to the area *FAE*, and arises as a consequence of improvements in the terms of trade, from P_F to P_W. In order to shift the equilibrium from *E* to *A*, the US government may decide to impose a trade-restricting tariff of *AB* per unit. Equilibrium in the world market is then realized at *B* with world price P_W and domestic price P_T. The tariff wedge, of $P_W P_T$ per unit is referred to as the *optimal tariff*. This tariff reduces welfare by an amount equal to the area *ABE*.

It is worthy of note that the optimal tariff is not identical with the tariff which yields the government the highest possible revenue, the so-called *maximum revenue tariff*. The difference is illustrated in Figure 4.4. The government, as collector of the tariff revenue, is equivalent to a monopolistic firm which buys imports from abroad at an average cost given by the curve *SS* and which sells them at a price given by the curve *DD*. The profit is the tariff revenue. In Figure 4.4, the maximum revenue is attained at point *R* where the marginal revenue curve *MR* intersects MC_M. This outcome in-volves a lower level of imports than under the optimal tariff (M_R as opposed to M_T) and a higher tariff per unit (*MN* as opposed to *AB*). A government

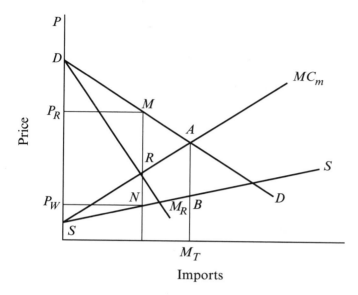

Figure 4.4   The maximum revenue tariff

which uses tariffs primarily as a revenue–raising device, as was the US situation in the nineteenth century, will restrict trade more than is optimal from the efficiency perspective.

Figures 4.3 and 4.4 indicate the difficulty that confronts an efficiency-orientated government in selecting the optimal tariff under conditions of uncertainty. Neither the demand nor the supply curve for imports can be precisely known, even at one point in time, and both are likely to shift over time in response to changes in consumer preferences and in supply techno-logies, as well as in response to changes in exchange rates. All these meas-urement problems are likely to intensify as the number of products under consideration increases and as the number of foreign countries involved rises. Even the most careful of calculations must be rendered hypothetical because of actuarially non-calculable prospects of retaliation on the part of foreign governments. Even if *Nash equilibria* exist under conditions of tariff wars they may not be unique. Unstable tariff cycles may well be the norm.

It has been demonstrated, at least with respect to tariff wars, that interna-tional trade is not likely to be eliminated completely. It is by no means evident, however, that the US would benefit from optimal tariff impositions, even where terms of trade factors are favorable, in the event of foreign retaliation. The rest of the world, in any event, would experience welfare and wealth losses as a consequence of US trade protection.

It was customary in analytical discussion, until Bhagwati (1965), to argue that tariffs and quotas were equivalent – that if a tariff were to be replaced by a quota equal to the import level associated with the tariff, the quota would lead to a domestic price that would exceed the landed, CIF price of the imported good by an implicit tariff that would equal the explicit tariff that the quota replaced; and the real outcome would be identical (Bhagwati and Srinivasan 1984: 119). The only partial equilibrium difference, it was argued, would be that in the case of the tariff the revenue would accrue to the government, whereas in the case of an equivalent quota an equal amount of *rent* would accrue to those receiving the import quotas, at least if the quotas are not auctioned. For general equilibrium equivalence, it would be necessary for the government to dispose of the tariff revenue in the same way as the recipients of the rent on import licenses – and that is highly implausible.

Bhagwati (1965, 1969) first raised the question of the breakdown of the equivalence proposition, noting that it was valid in the context of a model that assumes competitive foreign supply, perfect competition in domestic production and a quota allocated to ensure perfect competition among quota holders in the disposal of the quotas. If any of these conditions did not hold, the equivalence could break down.

Suppose, for example, that the domestic producer is a monopolist. The replacement of a tariff by a quota designed to achieve the tariff-associated level of imports will result in an implicit tariff that exceeds the explicit tariff. For marginal revenue at any given output is higher with the tariff than with the quota. This occurs because the tariff leads to an increase in domestic output which lowers the domestic price and thus reduces the quantity of imports supplied; whereas with a quota imports are fixed and the entire increase in domestic sales comes from the increase in quantity demanded. Therefore, output is higher and domestic price is lower under a tariff than under a quota that provides the same level of imports.

Suppose, alternatively, that the Cournot–type tariff retaliation process outlined above is compared with a similar retaliation process in which the protagonists employ optimal quotas rather than optimal tariffs each time. Rodriguez (1974) has demonstrated that such a process leads to a radically different equilibrium outcome in which trade is asymptotically reduced to zero and in which neither country can gain relative to free trade by initiating quota warfare. Although trade is never actually eliminated, under quotas there exists no *Nash equilibrium* associated with a non-zero level of trade, contrary to the case with tariffs.

Thus in contrast to the case in which tariffs are the sole retaliatory device, use of quotas in a trade war will induce a severe contraction in the volume of international trade and will be very harmful to all participants. Yet, despite this clear disadvantage, quantitative restrictions of various kinds have been in favor over the past twenty years, both by individual governments and in bilateral trade negotiations. A pervasive form of such quantitative restrictions of trade is the so-called voluntary export restraint (VER).

A VER is a quota imposed by an exporting country on its exports to another country in response to pressure by the importing country. Because VERs are the outcome of negotiations between two countries, they may reflect some constrained preferences of the government of the exporting country. Because they remove any threat of retaliation, they are often viewed as a cooperative alternative to the elimination of trade which may occur when non-cooperative quota wars are initiated.

A VER differs from other forms of trade restriction in several respects (Vousden 1990: 96). First, it is a policy, designed to protect producers in the importing country, which is administered by the government of the exporting country. Second, it is a source specific restriction in the sense that it applies to a small number of specified exporters, possibly even opening up exploitable export opportunities for foreign producers that are not covered by a particular VER. Third, VERs are usually implemented for a specified period of time, in contrast to other types of trade restrictions which are imposed for indefinite periods.

Figure 4.5 illustrates the effects of a VER for a large country, H, such as the United States, which imports a product from one other country, A. DD

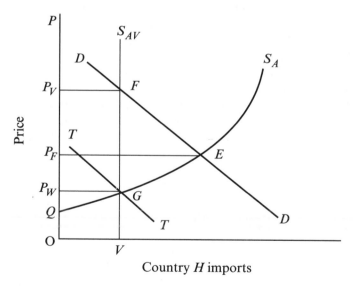

Country H imports

Figure 4.5   The voluntary export restraint

represents country H's demand curve for imports and S_A is country A's supply curve of exports in free trade. All markets are assumed to be competitive. Under free trade, equilibrium is at E, and the price in both countries is P_F. A VER restricting exports to OV units restricts A's supply curve to QGS_{AV}. Equilibrium moves from E to F with the world price of the commodity rising to P_V. This is also the domestic price in country H.

Let us compare this outcome with a tariff (or its import quota equivalent) which yields the same level of imports (OV) for country H. This is achieved by a tariff which shifts country H's demand curve for imports from DD to TT, intersecting S_A at G. In this outcome, the world price is P_W, whereas the domestic price in country H is P_V, the same as under the VER. Relative to a tariff or a quota, the VER implies worsened terms of trade for the importing country. Under the tariff, country H captures the tariff-revenue rectangle $P_V F G P_W$ as indeed would be the case under the quota. However, under the VER, the rectangle goes to the exporting country. Indeed, this is one reason why an exporting country's government may accede to a VER. The government of a major importing country like the United States may accept this rent-loss as a tolerable price to pay to avoid GATT regulations and to avert the prospect of a retaliatory trade war, even given the sacrifice of terms of trade advantage that the VER also implies.

4   The rent-seeking insight

Although neoclassical economic theory suggests that a policy of free trade usually maximizes aggregate welfare even in the case of a major trading nation, the welfare losses incurred as a consequence of trade protection, at first sight, do not appear to be large. Figure 4.6 illustrates the relatively insignificant magnitude of the loss of Marshallian surplus associated with the imposition of a protective tariff, under conditions of increasing cost production.

In Figure 4.6, under conditions of free trade, the world price of the commodity in question is P_W, domestic production is Q_D, domestic consumption is C_D and the level of imports is $C_D - Q_D$. By imposing a tariff of magnitude $P_W T$, the government increases domestic production from Q_D to Q_{DT} and reduces domestic consumption from C_D to C_{DT}. The level of imports falls to $C_{DT} - Q_{DT}$. The tariff reduces consumers' surplus from DPF to DTE.

In the conventional view, however, not all of this represents social waste. Consumers' surplus in the amount $TP_W AC$ is transferred to domestic producers whose producers' surplus rises from $SP_W A$ to STC. Consumers' surplus in the amount $BCEG$ is transferred to the government as tariff revenue. Only the shaded triangles, ABC and EFG constitute welfare loss due to an inefficient allocation of resources and a distorted pattern of consumption. Evidently, these triangles jointly represent only a small proportion of the total consumers' surplus displaced by the protective tariff.

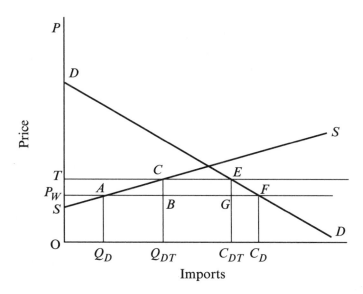

Figure 4.6   The conventional measure of welfare loss

Let us suppose, however, in the initial free-trade perspective, that rational wealth-seeking domestic producers as well as rational government-revenue-seeking interests, identify the rents that become available as transfers from domestic consumers if the government can be persuaded to impose a protective tariff. Might it not then be the case that such interests would outlay resources up to the full present value of the areas $TP_WAC + BCEG$ in lobbying and other forms of pressure designed to persuade government that the protective tariff is an appropriate form of intervention? Might it not further be the case that such outlays waste otherwise productive resources and dissipate the wealth of the nation to the full present value of the transfers that appear to be contestable?

This was the original rent-seeking insight provided by Gordon Tullock in two seminal articles published in 1967a and 1971, although the term *rent-seeking* itself was coined later, in 1974, by Ann Krueger in an article that failed to cite Tullock's earlier contributions. As we shall demonstrate in sections 5 and 6, the rent-seeking insight opens up trade protection policy to public-choice analysis. For the moment, however, let us explore its implications for the efficiency of the various instruments of trade protection, assuming, however unrealistically, that the choice among such instruments is exogenously determined. This is the approach of Jagdish Bhagwati and T.N. Srinivasan (1984) in their adaptation of Tullock's rent-seeking insight into a reformulation of the welfare economics of trade protection designated as DUP (or directly unproductive profit-seeking) activities.

Central to the DUP approach is the paradox that DUP activities may sometimes be indirectly productive or welfare improving while they are always directly unproductive. Four critical classes of DUP activities are distinguished (Bhagwati and Srinivasan 1984: 326):

Category I: The initial and final situations are both distorted.
Category II: The initial situation is distorted but the final situation (thanks to the DUP) is distortion free.
Category III: The initial situation is distortion-free, but the final situation is distorted.
Category IV: The initial situation is distortion free, and so is the final situation (despite the DUP activity).

Bhagwati and Srinivasan made a fundamental distinction between categories I and II, where DUP activities can be welfare-enhancing and categories III and IV where they must be welfare-immiserating. Crucial to this distinction is the nature of the initial situation, specifically whether it is distorted or distortion-free, prior to the trade protection intervention. Let us briefly review each of the four categories in turn.

In category I, DUP activities are analysed within the context of an economy that is initially distorted by the presence either of an import quota or of a protective tariff. In the import quota case, Krueger (1974) noted that the premium-fetching licenses generate resource-using competition among potential beneficiaries of the license allocation. In the protective tariff case, Bhagwati and Srinivasan (1984) noted that the tariff revenues would generate resource-using competition among potential beneficiaries of the revenue disbursements. In both cases, the lobbying activity despite being wasteful of scarce resources, paradoxically may be beneficial if it leads to second-best welfare improvements.

In category II, DUP activities are analyzed within the same context of an initially distorted economy but are viewed as eliminating the initial distortion. A good example of such activity is smuggling, which effectively destroys the protectionist impact of the quota or tariff under consideration. The overall welfare impact of such a DUP activity is the sum of two effects: the welfare effect of a withdrawal of resources into the directly unproductive activity, with the distortion held unchanged (category I type analysis), and the welfare impact of the elimination of the distortion in the final situation. The former is either positive or negative; the latter is necessarily positive. The net outcome may be either positive or negative.

The paradox of beneficial DUP activities disappears when the initial situation is free of distortion. Category III identifies the circumstance where DUP activities create a distorted outcome. Two classic examples (Tullock 1967b) of such legal DUP activities are successful lobbying for the creation of a government-sanctioned monopoly, and lobbying to secure tariff protection. In each case, the total social loss imposed by the DUP activity under consideration can be decomposed into the sum of two effects: the negative welfare effect of the withdrawal of resources into the directly unproductive activity, if no distortion results, and the negative welfare effect of the imposition of the distortion itself. Evidently, there is no potential source of gain in this situation.

The final category of DUP activities, category IV, relates to those which start and end with a distortion-free situation. A classic example, suggested by Tullock (1967b), is the situation where tariff-seeking by one lobby is offset by anti-tariff lobbying by another group. The diversion of resources from productive use when the first-best policy of free trade is in place throughout must be welfare immiserating.

Bhagwati and Srinivasan (1984) concluded that the welfare-improving paradox will never arise if a pure quantity distortion (such as that posited by Krueger 1974) is the only distortion in place. Hence, the scope of the paradox is reduced, is then narrowed to the case of the tariff, although it is not eliminated. If the quantity constraint is impure, however, for example if the quota is fixed in terms of domestic values, then the paradox may arise even with respect to premium-seeking activities. The DUP insight, therefore, does not affect decisively the debate outlined in section 3 concerning the choice that might be made by a welfare-maximizing government among the alternative instruments of trade protection in the terms of trade special case. It strongly suggests, however, that a welfare-maximizing government, aware of rent-seeking implications of any trade protection instrument, typically will choose the free trade option.

The fact that governments typically do not choose this option is hardly because they sense the existence of a DUP paradox. Governments that broker trade protection typically do so because they are in the grip of political market forces that demonstrate minimal regard for economic efficiency but that are fuelled instead by wealth redistribution goals.

5 Public choice I: The relevance of the vote motive
The public-interest theory of government, which dominated political economy throughout the middle years of the twentieth century, is jettisoned henceforth in this chapter. Indeed, it is the systemic target of the Virginia political economy program (Rowley 1993). Instead, all individuals are analysed as interacting in political markets as rational utility maximizers just as they are

in private markets. The commodity under consideration is trade policy, defined as protectionism versus free trade. The market brokers are politicians, whether in the legislative or in the executive branch. The suppliers and demanders of trade protection are individual voters, groups of individuals organized as special interests, and groups of bureaucrats with interests vested on one side or the other of the market (Rowley and Thorbecke 1993).

Such individuals and groups may be motivated by ideology as well as by wealth while engaging in the market for trade protection. Politically efficient markets would register the appropriate balance between such preferences as manifested by those who engage in such trades. Politically efficient markets are unlikely to be economically efficient for reasons that will be explained. The United States political market is not necessarily even politically efficient for reasons that also will be explained (Rowley and Vachris 1992).

It is important to note that the terms 'supply' and 'demand' consist of the willingness to pay, in the currency of votes or of money transfers, by individuals and groups, in return for wealth or ideology transfers that carry a positive net expected present value to those concerned. 'Supply' consists of the inability or unwillingness of those from whom wealth or ideology transfers are sought, at the relevant margin of policy, to protect themselves by generating sufficient offers to the brokers. As such, the concept entails connotations of coercion that are absent in the conventional market definition.

Early analysts of public choice believed that the vote motive rigorously controlled political markets in systems of representative government. Downs (1957) suggested that political parties were vote-seekers, formulating policies to win elections, rather than seeking political victory in order to implement preferred policies. Under assumptions specified in his model, Downs deduced the *median voter theorem*, which indicated that competing parties would be driven by vote considerations to converge in policy space to a unique and stable political equilibrium which reflected the policy preferences of the median voter. This equilibrium would offer no discretion to political parties unless they were to lose their will to govern.

The median voter theorem was attractive to those who endorsed majoritarian outcomes, although not necessarily to those who feared, with Tocqueville and Madison, that such outcomes might constitute a tyranny over the minority. Oddly enough, it was anathema to most conventional political scientists, who typically were great advocates of majoritarian democracy, because it introduced rational-choice notions into the analysis of political behavior. In any event, it has turned out to be less robust than many early public-choice scholars had anticipated, highly dependent on a stringent set of assumptions that rarely coincide in real political markets (Rowley 1984):

1.   the election must be contested only by two political parties;

2. the policies at issue must collapse into one dimension of left–right political space;
3. voters must be well-informed regarding the policy positions of political parties;
4. voter preferences must be single-peaked over the relevant policy space;
5. voters must not abstain in significant numbers through alienation from voting in elections;
6. political parties must be well-informed regarding voters' policy positions;
7. political parties must be able and willing to move across policy space;
8. voters must punish governments that deviate from successful electoral manifestos.

Although the United States political system superficially is a two-party system, the situation is complicated by the fact that the Southern Democrats often behave like a separate third party. Moreover, party allegiance is much weaker in the US Congress than in most European parliamentary systems, with few penalties applied to those who deviate from the pre-announced party position. Tullock (1967a) has established that multi-party competition will not necessarily converge on the median, and, indeed, that an equilibrium may not exist under such conditions. Furthermore, the United States is a constitutional republic, not a majoritarian democracy. As we shall demonstrate in section 7, this has significant implications for interest group politics.

If the policies at issue fail to collapse into a single dimension of left–right political space, political cycles may exist in multi-dimensional space, even if single-peaked preferences hold in each dimension on its own (Riker and Ordeshook 1973). In such circumstances, the median is not the unique equilibrium, nor is it stable. If voter preferences are not single-peaked in single issue space, as may well be the case with redistributionist policies, political cycles will dominate and the median voter theorem will not prevail (Black 1948; Arrow 1950) .

If voters are not well-informed regarding the policy positions of the political parties, the median outcome may not hold since the parties may deviate from that position without penalty. The *rational ignorance hypothesis* reflects the fact that the probability that an individual vote will prove to be decisive in a major election is minute – less than one in a million in US presidential elections. This implies that the differential expected benefit to any voter from voting in an election is trivial, typically much less than 1 cent. Only some notion of civil duty, or some gross miscalculation of probabilities, will drive the rational voter to the polls. Only an active consumption interest will motivate the rational individual to become informed about politics. Otherwise, he will remain rationally ignorant, whether or not he casts his electoral vote, relying upon opaque ideology indicators or candidate valences to determine his electoral position. This paradox, more than any other, opens up opportunities for interest groups to seize control of the political process.

Elections are discrete events in a continuous political process. The vote motive, even at its most potent, is only as influential as elections are in controlling the behavior of political parties between elections. There are good reasons to doubt the effectiveness of such controls. One potential weakness lies in the ability of political parties to full-line force a bundle of policy proposals onto voters, protecting relatively unpopular policies by wrapping them together with attractive proposals. A second potential weakness is the irrelevance to political parties of long-term voter preferences that extend across several elections, and a consequential tendency towards myopia in political decision-making (Lee 1987).

A third potential weakness is the high rate of voter memory decay which protects incumbents from the full electoral consequences of deviating, while in office, from political pledges. A fourth potential weakness is the difficulty that incumbents experience in achieving voter credibility if they move significantly in electoral space from policy positions that they have become identified with while in office. Severally and jointly, these potential weaknesses loosen the voters' grip over political markets and open up opportunities for interest groups to influence the political process. The rational ignorance of voters makes advertising, funded by campaign contributions, a particularly potent instrument of competition in political markets.

Let us now analyze the behavior of a political market in trade protection in terms of the voting models outlined in this section, emphasizing the median voter model posited in its most robust form. Although this model is clearly unrealistic, it does offer an insight into the forces which are at work when voting is not totally dominated by the lobbying of interest groups, and when rational voter ignorance does not obstruct the centripedal tendencies of a competitive political system.

Suppose that individuals have diverse claims to an economy's factor endowments and that they have no means of diversifying their factor-ownership portfolios (Hillman 1989: 37). Each factor owner then has an optimal trade policy that is individually welfare-maximizing. Only those individuals who hold claims over factors in proportions duplicating the relative factor endowment of the economy necessarily have an interest in supporting a policy of free trade. With majority voting and no voting costs, a country's trade policy is determined by the welfare-maximizing policy of the median voter, and hence by the relation between the median voter's claims over factors and the aggregate endowment. Since the median voter generally will not have claims to factor ownership in the same proportion to the country's relative factor endowments, there is no necessary reason to expect a direct free-trade outcome.

Let us review the proposals for tariff protection under conditions of majority voting, first under conditions of the Heckscher–Ohlin model, and second, under conditions of the multi-sector specific-factors model of international trade. In the Heckscher–Ohlin case, the economy is endowed with given quantities of intersectorally mobile labor and capital. Suppose that each individual owns one unit of labor and a non-negative amount of capital. His capital–labor ratio then equals his stock of capital; and his total income consists of income derived from factor ownership plus his share of any tariff revenues. Suppose that tariff revenues are distributed neutrally, *pro rata* with individual factor incomes (Mayer 1984).

Suppose that the importable good is capital-intensive. If a tariff is imposed, the real wage falls and the real return to capital rises. Individuals with a higher ratio of capital to labor are more likely to gain. Specifically, individuals gain from a tariff if their capital–labor ratio exceeds the economy's capital–labor ratio, and individuals where the reverse situation holds benefit from an import subsidy. The higher an individual's capital–labor ratio, the higher the tariff level that maximizes his utility. Under a non-distorted voting system, the tariff level adopted will be that which maximizes the utility of the median voter. A positive tariff will prevail if the median voter has a higher capital–labor ratio than the economy as a whole.

As we have noted earlier, even though the Stolper–Samuelson approach may be useful for evaluating long-term equilibrium, it is inappropriate when analyzing the attitudes of factor owners to protection in real-world economies where protection support tends to be industry- rather than factor-based. Moreover, it fails to explain how an industry whose factor owners constitute a small number of voters can successfully secure tariff protection. To resolve both these problems, we must turn to a multi-sector version of the specific factors model (Vousden 1990: 179).

Suppose that each potential voter owns one unit of labor (the mobile factor) and some of at most one industry-specific factor. Starting from a free trade situation, it is proposed that a tariff be introduced for one sector. Assuming that the cost of voting is uniform across individuals, under what circumstances will a majority vote confirm the tariff proposal? The answer depends on (a) the magnitude of the stakes for the various voters relative to voting costs; (b) the way in which the tariff changes the wage rate relative to average factor returns; and (c) the magnitude of the deadweight loss of the tariff.

Suppose that the deadweight loss effect is small and that the tariff increases the wage relative to the weighted average of all factor prices. Then it is likely that a large number of voters who do not own the sector's specific factor will gain from the tariff and, if voting costs are not too high, will support it at the ballot box. Suppose, alternatively, that the tariff changes the wage in the same proportion as the weighted average of all factor prices. Then owners of specific factors in all other sectors lose, the owners of the sector's specific factor gain and owners of labor are unaffected. In such circumstances, a majority will vote against the tariff as long as voting costs are not too high.

However, if the deadweight loss of the tariff is low, the gains to the protected specific factor are approximately equal to the total losses of the unprotected specific factors (redistribution). If there is more than one unprotected sector, the loss imposed on any one of them by a small tariff is less than the gain to the specific factor in the protected sector. It follows that the gains to an owner of a given share of the protected sector's specific factor are larger than the losses to an owner of the same share of a specific factor outside the protected sector when the number of sectors exceeds two. If individuals face the same positive cost of voting, those for whom the stakes are smaller may abstain from voting, making it more likely that a majority of those who vote will approve the tariff.

This ingenious voting model explanation of how a small minority of the population could succeed in gaining acceptance of a policy which favors them at the expense of the rest of the community rests on a set of somewhat unrealistic assumptions. It relies upon the existence of very low deadweight losses distributed uniformly across society, whereas in reality adverse tariff effects tend to be asymmetrically distributed. It assumes that tariff protection is voted on either in a single-issue election or as the dominant issue in a multi-issue election, which is more or less absurd. It completely ignores the ability of those who gain significantly from protection to influence election outcomes by expenditures designed to influence the vote behavior of rationally ignorant voters or to forestall political parties from locating the median voter. In order to remedy these weaknesses, we now must turn to other public-choice theories of tariff determination in which the principal actors are political parties and pressure groups, and in which voters play only a secondary role.

6   Public choice II: The relevance of interest groups

The analysis presented in section 5 suggests that, under conditions of representative democracy, the links between the policy preferences of an individual voter, the exercise of the right to vote and policy outcomes concerning trade protection are tenuous (Hillman 1989). In such circumstances, coalitions of individuals seeking a common objective may be much more effective. Such coalitions may offer blocks of organized votes or sizeable campaign contributions as a means of asserting pressure on the policy brokers and of providing a degree of political effectiveness that individuals by themselves simply cannot achieve. The relevant coalitions, composed of those who lose and those who gain from particular measures of trade protection, are referred to henceforth in this section as interest groups. Those who gain from such measures are also referred to as special interests.

A special interest issue is one that generates substantial benefits for a relatively small number of constituents while imposing a small individual cost on a relatively large number of other constituents (Gwartney and Wagner 1988). As James Madison recognized, in *The Federalist, No.* 51 (1787), a majoritarian system of representative government is biased toward the adoption of special interest policies even when such policies are unambiguously harmful to the citizens at large. The separation of powers and the bicameral legislature were written into the United States Constitution in no small part to curtail this bias. The Ninth and Tenth Amendments were designed to protect individuals from the excesses of the federal and state governments. Arguably, these constitutional constraints have failed to hold firm against the battering that they have received from the special interests in the two centuries that have passed since the Philadelphia resolutions. Parchment has ceded victory to guns within the governance structure created by the Founding Fathers (Wagner 1987).

Special interests emerge to take advantage of rational ignorance within the electorate and the limited information available to the legislature to obtain political advantages for members more than commensurate with their relative combined voting strength. Their success depends on their ability to offer rewards (votes or wealth transfers) to politicians and to engage in persuasive advertising among potential voters to engage their active support through the ballot box. As we shall show in section 7, legislatures effectively infiltrated by special interests typically manifest weak party allegiances and evidence relatively high incumbent success ratios in the election process.

Special interests may be viewed as rent-seekers or as rent-protectors, whose principal objective is that of creating or of maintaining rents through the political process and of securing such rents in the form of transfers from the general interest to their own constituencies. Such rents, by definition, are returns in excess of opportunity cost, and special interest groups do not engage primarily in productive activity. Indeed, rent-seeking by special interests typically occurs in institutional settings where the pursuit of private gain generates social waste rather than social surplus (Buchanan 1980) and in which the competition between scarce resources focuses on the redistribution rather than the enhancement of a nation's wealth.

It might be thought, and it has been argued (Becker 1983), that competition between interest groups eliminates inefficient forms of lobbying and secures policies that minimize deadweight social costs. Such thoughts are misplaced and are based on erroneous beliefs as to the symmetric access to political markets available to different kinds of interest groups.

The logic of collective action (Olson 1965) indicates to the contrary that competition between interest groups introduces significant bias into political markets. Such bias is a direct consequence of the differential impact of the free-rider problem on various kinds of interest groups which in turn results in asymmetric access to political markets. The free-rider problem threatens interest group lobbying because the policy benefits coveted by interest groups are endowed with publicness characteristics in that individuals cannot be denied access to the benefits if they fail to make an appropriate contribution to the lobbying effort. A number of hypotheses can be derived from this important insight.

First, it is predictable that existing interest groups generally will have significant incumbency advantages over potential competitors because of the sunk costs associated with pressure group formation. Second, it is predictable that well-established interest groups generally will have significant membership size advantages over newly established rivals since there is a region of increasing returns to pressure group activity. Small groups of non-wealthy and non-vocal members are unlikely to exert effective political pressure. Third, it is predictable that membership size advantages will be seriously eroded by the free-rider problem once interest groups grow beyond the point where individuals are motivated to supply an optimal amount of effort. Fourth it is predictable, for organization cost reasons, that geographically concentrated interest groups will outperform geographically dispersed groups when other lobbying conditions are comparable. Fifth, it is predictable that interest groups that provide high per capita benefits to members will outperform interest groups that provide low per capita returns, when other lobbying returns are comparable.

Although the publicness characteristics of lobbying returns always pose a conflict between collective and individual rational behavior, indicative of a prisoners' dilemma, not all interest groups are equally affected. In some cases, interest groups may be able to avoid free-riding by coercing members to supply pressure. Coercive potential of this kind is most notably available to trade unions and professional associations, either in the form of legal sanctions or of illegal violence against those who attempt to free-ride. In other cases, interest groups may be able to byproduct the provision of pressure by providing selective benefits to members, although there must be limits to the ability to cross-subsidize in this way under competitive conditions (Stigler 1974). In yet other cases, the benefits may be sufficiently high on a per capita basis to enable astute political entrepreneurs to overcome the free-riding incentive without recourse either to coercion or to selective benefits. Corporations seeking trade protection benefits for specific factors of production evidently fall into this category.

These observations help explain why consumer interests, for example, are notoriously unsuccessful in forming coalitions to oppose tariffs and other instruments of trade protection and why special interests successfully lobby for such outcomes against the large majority of individuals who stand to lose from the abandonment of free trade. Those groups that are best able to mobilize their members predictably will deflect legislative action away from the preferred position of the median voter by an astute use of campaign contributions designed to compensate key politicians for any direct loss of votes and to manipulate rationally ignorant voters to embrace their special interest objectives. They will also systematically target for retribution those key politicians who have displayed past independence and who have attempted to pursue public rather than special interest policy objectives.

7 Public choice III: The relevance of the Congress

The individuals who broker the legislative market in protectionist policies are politicians, members either of the United States Senate or the House of Representatives. They pair demanders and suppliers of protectionist legislation, those who want a law or a regulation the most with those who object the least. Typically, they concentrate on legal arrangements that benefit well-organized and geographically concentrated interests for whom *pro rata* benefits are high at the expense of poorly organized, geographically diffuse interests each of whom is taxed a little to finance the wealth-reducing law or regulation.

The political brokers are at the heart of the legislative process, seeking out equilibria, with varying degrees of error, reflecting the preferences of the principal actors, conditioned by the constitutional rules and international laws that define the market place in trade protection. Competition among the brokers and the contestability of brokerage positions constrain the ability of individual politicians to make manifest their own ideologies, to purvey rather than simply to broker policies. Nevertheless, ideology plays a role, as does error, in the political market place (Rowley 1993; Rowley and Thorbecke 1993). Fundamentally, political markets in trade protection broker wealth transfers. If wealth is ever created, as for example by a tariff reduction law, it is usually an unintended consequence of transfer activities (Stigler 1988; Tollison 1988).

The United States political system is not a majoritarian democracy in the sense of Downs (1957) but a constitutional republic in the sense of Buchanan and Tullock (1962). In order to pass a trade protection bill, the minimum winning coalition is either a majority of both houses of Congress plus approval by the president, or a two-thirds override by both houses of Congress when the president disapproves. Thus when the president approves a measure, the minimal winning coalition comprises 218 representatives, 51 senators and the president. When the president opposes, however, the minimum winning coalition comprises 290 representatives and 67 senators. The president, therefore, is as powerful as a combination of 72 representatives and 16 senators (Magee *et al.* 1989).

Although there are more representatives than senators, since there are 33 senators excluded from the winning coalition who would compete to vote for most proposals at a low price, it has been argued (Young 1978) that it should require no more money to purchase the vote of a senator than that of a representative. If representatives and senators are equally influential, then the president's influence is 88 times as great as that of an individual representative or senator. The rational lobby therefore is indifferent between paying $88 million to the president in return for a vote versus paying $1 million to each of 88 representatives and senators to vote for the override of a veto (Young 1978).

Politicians expend real resources in specific wealth transfer markets in return for brokerage fees which typically take the form of some mixture of campaign contributions, post-political career remuneration and promised votes. The size and continuity of such brokerage fees depend significantly upon the perceived durability of legislation, which itself depends on constitutional interpretations and the specific rules and institutions of the legislature. Durability of legislation is a prized attribute for most politicians since interest groups rationally will not bid much for any statute that is expected to be repealed in some forthcoming legislative session. Interest groups and politicians thus have a common interest in promoting institutional arrangements that enhance the durability of laws.

One institution which serves this common interest is the separation of powers. The role of the presidential veto in lowering the probabilities that statutes will be repealed has already been alluded to. Crain and Tollison (1979) use this insight to explain why presidential vetoes appear to vary positively with respect to the size of majorities in the US House and Senate, whether or not the president is a member of the majority party. From the perspective of maintaining the durability of laws, it is argued that presidents have as much to fear from large majorities of their own party as from the opposition party. In such a setting, the relative value of the presidential veto in prohibiting the overturn of existing legislative contracts with special interests is high, since the veto can be applied immediately on the threat of repeal of a legislative contract and not only after protracted legal proceedings. Cross-sectional evidence concerning gubernatorial vetoes at the state level does not refute this hypothesis (Crain and Tollison 1979).

The fact that vetoes are sometimes overridden provides a rationale for the role of the independent judiciary as an additional facet of the separation of powers also serving as a longer-term guarantor of legislative bargains. Landes and Posner (1975) have argued that the institutional circumstances surrounding federal judgeships – notably life tenure and security from nominal income reductions – encourage judges to resolve disputes in terms of the intentions of the original legislature. Anderson *et al.* (1988) have strengthened this insight, deploying the modern public-choice approach. The judicial branch receives its budget from the legislative branch. If judges act so as to sustain or to increase the durability of legislation, their budgets and judicial salaries increase. If they act to lower durability, they pay the appropriate penalty. Cross-section regressions analysis at state level does not refute the implications of this theory (ibid.).

The broader implications of the works cited above are important and disturbing (although they are not shared by all scholars of public choice; see Rowley 1992). They suggest that the United States system of government is better characterized as a collusion of, rather than a separation of, powers; that the federal government has obtained, by constitutional malpractice, powers which the Founding Fathers had meant to deny it. If so, then this first attempt to secure individual liberty by constitutional means has lamentably failed.

The pure majority rule (PMR) theory of public choice focuses on the extreme and special nature of the conditions necessary for the existence of equilibrium. It demonstrates that generally no such equilibrium exists (Plott 1973). The absence of equilibrium implies that majority rule cycles exist, cycles which can be shown to extend over the entire policy space (McKelvey 1979). No form of legislative exchange can obviate these results as long as the pure majority rule structure is maintained. In particular, no form of logrolling, whether implicit or explicit, coalition formation, or individual bargaining can eliminate the inherent instability that follows from the non-existence of a majority rule equilibrium (MRE). As long as losers are not denied access to the agenda, there is no natural stopping point in the voting cycle. Coalitions and agreements simply unravel as quickly as they are established.

Yet the United States legislature is characterized by a quite remarkable degree of stability, by a marked absence of the cycling implied by the pure majority rule theory (Tullock 1981). Evidently, the rules and procedures that have evolved in the United States Congress over its two hundred years of existence induce a degree of legislative stability that defies the logic of cycling theory. It is our contention, following Shepsle and Weingast (1987), that stability is induced by institutional restrictions on the domain of legislative exchange and not by legislative exchange *per se*.

In this perspective, the instability of majority rule is seen to hinge on the unrestricted richness of coalition and logrolling possibilities under PMR and the non-enforceability of contracts designed to foreclose on the cycling process. Institutions that differ from PMR may exhibit stability because they restrict logrolling behavior and, therefore, the potential for some subsequent legislative exchange to upset an equilibrium. A number of rules employed in the United States Congress exert such an influence. It is unlikely that all such restrictions are accidental, the unintended consequences of blind evolution.

One such rule is the requirement that in pairwise voting over policy alternatives the status quo is voted on last. This implies that, no matter where votes on alternatives prior to the final vote move through policy space – and according to McKelvey this process can lead anywhere – the last vote is against the prevailing social state. PMR as amended by this rule is a restricted and well-behaved decision process.

Another such rule is that providing committee proposal powers. In the House of Representatives, committees (with minor exceptions) initiate the proposal process within their respective areas of policy jurisdiction. The rules of the House require that, in addition to voting the status quo last, a committee proposal is voted on second to last. This implies that any successful amendment to a committee's proposal must defeat that proposal in the penultimate vote and then proceed to defeat the status quo. This clearly constrains the PMR process yet further.

Yet another rule relates to the Rules Committee itself in the House of Representatives. Each bill must go to the Rules Committee after being passed by its committee and before it reaches the House Floor. The purpose is to grant the bill a *rule* governing debate and the amendment process. If a rule is not granted, the bill is effectively killed since it may not be forwarded to the full House for a vote. This rule requirement further restricts the range of outcomes of an institutional majority vote system since a committee bill must lie within the preferred set of a majority of members of the Rules Committee if it is to evade a Rules Committee veto.

Shepsle and Weingast (1987) identify several other features of the US legislative process that significantly restrict potential outcomes and secure stability in circumstances where majority rule cycles might otherwise prevail. In particular, conference committee agreements, germaneness rules, and rules of recognition serve to prevent elements of the majority rule win-sets from ever arising for comparison, thus leaving other elements invulnerable.

If the structure-induced equilibrium outlined above is to be sustainable in the longer term, the choice processes that gave rise to the existing structure of the US Congress must not be vulnerable to the same instabilities found in PMR. This potential vulnerability is referred to as the *Riker Objection* (Riker 1980). In practice, however, an endless cycling at the level of institutional choice is unlikely for a number of reasons.

First, the choice of new rules typically is not made through the PMR process. Second, any attempt to change the status quo in a manner contrary to the interests of those currently in control is high risk since failure may lead to the imposition of sanctions. Third, there often exists a well-defined status quo alternative that *de facto* narrows the choice set and, therefore, the prospect of a cycle. Even at the constitutional level, restrictions on the ability of individuals to make proposals may help to induce equilibrium and avoid chaos.

The precise manner in which the legislature brokers trade protection policy depends on the relative importance of political parties *vis-à vis* the oversight committees in channelling interest group pressures. Since 1930, Congress has manifested a slow but systematic shift away from political party importance towards committee control.

Let us suppose, following Brock and Magee (1978), that two political parties select tariff *quotations* designed to maximize their respective election probabilities, each taking the other party's tariff quote as given. The outcome is a Nash equilibrium in tariff quotes and election probabilities for each party, from which an equilibrium expected tariff emerges. Let us suppose that the parties are competing in an environment characterized by two opposing pressure groups, one pro-tariff and the other anti-tariff. It does not matter for analytical purposes whether the division of interest is Stolper–Samuelson (labor versus capital) or Ricardo–Viner (industry-specific).

Each party associates itself with one of the two interests (not the same) but finds its policy position constrained by general voter dissatisfaction with the dispensing of political favors (Hillman 1989). Each lobby supports its position by contributing campaign funds to the party whose tariff position is more favorable to its members. Let us suppose that it does not pay either lobby to contribute to more than one party. A party can increase its probability of winning by (a) attracting more campaign funds from the lobby which supports it (to buy votes); (b) reducing the funds going to the other party; and (c) winning more votes directly by preferring a low tariff quote (the general voter effect).

In this model, (a) tends to drive the tariff quotes of the two parties further apart; (b) tends to drive the two parties' tariff quotes closer together; and (c) works to reduce the tariff quotes of both parties. In the absence of a very powerful general voter effect, it is unlikely that the two parties will converge in policy issue space or that lobbying competition will result in trade protection policies tailored to the preferences of the median voter. If the lobbies are evenly matched and expend large resources in rent-seeking competition, both lobbies may end up worse off than under free trade, unable to cooperate in order to release themselves from the resulting prisoners' dilemma.

The US Congress is now characterized, however, by much weaker political parties than is typical of parliamentary models such as that of the United Kingdom. In their place has developed a complex committee and subcommittee structure that has not been replicated elsewhere among the Western democracies. In these circumstances, it is relevant to ask why such committees exist and what roles they play that straightforward political party competition cannot provide. The public choice response is that they represent an efficient division of legislative labor (Tollison 1988).

Committees enable the legislature to specialize, given time and resource constraints, in searching for efficient pairings of demanders and suppliers of legislation. By holding hearings to determine what legislation to initiate, and by holding trial votes to test the political climate, committees facilitate the creation of a successful menu of legislation carefully molded to reflect the preferences of relevant constituents. In this role, committees may be viewed as 'engines for finding out what laws people want and who will pay for them, conducting preliminary votes, screening and controlling bureaucratic appointments, and so on' (Tollison 1988: 358).

If the committees perform these functions well, they facilitate *political efficiency*, matching the policies brokered with the preferences of those individuals who control the most powerful lobbies. By screening effectively, they minimize the number of bills that fail to make their way through the full chamber of the legislature, and maximize the rate at which the bills released to the House or the Senate make their way to the president for his acceptance or veto. In a political system that does not manifest tight party control over elected representatives, committees may offer significant advantages in terms of political efficiency and of structure-induced equilibrium over the individualistic logrolling alternative that might emerge in its absence.

In the absence of congressional committees, it can be argued that classical contracting will fail to provide an efficient political nexus between special interest groups and individual members of Congress given the weakness of the political parties and the strong spatial characteristics of the Senate and, even more especially, of the House membership. Contracting is further hindered by the presence in political markets of bounded rationality and opportunism on the part of all parties and of extreme specificity of the assets under negotiation, conditions that in combination pose serious problems for classical contracting (Williamson 1985). The problem is especially relevant for logrolling contracts.

Suppose that two tradeable bills arise simultaneously in the Congress, but offer a non-contemporaneous flow of benefits – one a pork-barrel automobile tariff to protect Detroit and the other a fair-trade bill designed to enhance the protectionist behavior of the International Trade Commission (ITC). Interest groups seek to logroll in order to move these bills onto the statute books in the absence of separate majority support. Evidently, the fair-trade benefits depend on the future behavior of the ITC, which will reflect future congressional monitoring, whereas the tariff benefits are instantaneous. The Detroit auto interests, if they are opportunistic, have an opportunity to renege on the deal once the tariff bill has been enacted. In the absence of an efficient governance mechanism, trades across such margins might not take place.

Suppose, alternatively, that two potentially tradeable bills – both pork-barrel tariff bills – do not proceed to a vote simultaneously and that there is no prospect of packaging the legislation subsequently into an omnibus bill. In the absence of an enforceable market in IOUs sufficiently explicit as to encompass all contingencies, *ex post* opportunism on the part of the special interest that first moves its bill through Congress poses a serious threat to efficient *ex ante* trades, especially in the absence of repeat trading prospects.

The committee system of the US Congress has been rationalized as a governance response to such potential problems of contract failure (Weingast and Marshall 1988). It is argued that the committee system establishes enforceable property rights over legislation, thus ameliorating the problems for classical contracting that we have outlined above. Each committee is assigned a specific area of policy jurisdiction within the House or the Senate. It is allocated a near-monopoly right (but see Rowley and Vachris 1992 for doubts on this assertion) to move legislation within its jurisdiction to the floor of the chamber.

Committees are made up of a specified number of seats, each held by a specified member of the chamber who typically has a pronounced constituency interest in the affairs of that committee and who has successfully accessed the committee through the bidding system maintained by the two parties. Committee members usually retain their seats as long as they choose, subject to continued electoral success. Seniority privileges are an increasing function of the length of committee service. Leadership positions within a committee – and the agenda power thus accorded – come with seniority buttressed by willingness to redeem the campaign debts of significant chamber members.

The committee system exerts important effects on coalition formation, narrowing the set of feasible policy initiatives and extending the durability of those that are enacted. Agenda power ensures that effective coalitions must include a majority of members of the relevant committee. Trades among committee members, in these circumstances, are more important than trades across committees, because committee members have high, specialized stakes in their own jurisdictions. The committee system thus shields the special interests from the full adverse impact even of major political party electoral reversals, thus elevating the brokerage fees that can be extracted in return for moving special interest laws onto the statute books.

Although the congressional committee system provides the most effective governance system available in political markets – as the comparative stability of US legislation *vis-à-vis* parliamentary alternatives clearly attests – this does not imply that it is comparable in any way to the capital market governance arrangements that have evolved as conduits of private market efficiency in capitalist economies. Property rights are never as clearly vested nor as easily transferred in politics as in private markets, nor are they as divisible.

Members of Congress cannot auction committee seats, nor can they diversify their portfolios. They must instead specialize in their holdings, which are not easily alienable. Their rights are not exclusive, both because of the bicameral legislature and separation of powers and because committee jurisdictions not infrequently overlap. The efficient capital market has no political market counterpart.

8   The choice of protective instrument

The pure theory of international trade strongly suggests that a unilateral shift from protection to free trade will increase overall real income in a country unless it induces a significant, counterbalancing deterioration in that country's terms of trade (Johnson 1965). The theory infers that once governments become informed of the clear net benefits of unilateral trade liberalization, they will always do away with trade protection, compensating losers if necessary by non-distortionary lump-sum, tax-subsidy interventions.

There is compelling evidence to support the pure theory, namely the dazzling success of the British economy following its embrace of free trade in 1846 symbolized by the repeal of the protectionist Corn Laws. Even in this evidence, however, there lurks the embryo of a public-choice problem. In the end, the repeal of the Corn Laws turned on Prime Minister Robert Peel's intellectual conversion to the idea of free trade, which led him to abandon the sectional protectionist interests of the Conservative Party. Despite his great service to the nation, Peel was charged by his rival Disraeli with having betrayed his party for the principles of political economy. Peel's political career was irreparably destroyed (Bhagwati 1988).

For the most part, governments patently do not respond as the pure theory suggests they should. The earlier public-choice analysis of this chapter explains theoretically why governments choose to accept generalized wealth destruction by maintaining and even by extending trade protection policies in the teeth of the comparative advantage theorem. Public-choice analysis, as we shall now show, goes far to explain the particular choices among alternative instruments of trade protection that are registered in political markets. Just as political motives can underlie the determination of levels of protection, so such motives can influence the means of protection that are chosen (Hillman 1989).

During the last two decades, the world economy has witnessed a pronounced shift away from tariffs towards direct quantitative restrictions on trade (Vousden 1990). Economists explain this shift by reference to the success of GATT trade negotiation rounds in achieving widespread tariff reductions and by the relative ease of defining formulae for tariff as opposed to non-tariff reductions. Surely, these factors have played a role. Yet there remain numerous instances in which governments have chosen non-tariff forms of protection in circumstances where they were not prevented from using tariffs (Deardorff 1987). In this section, we shall seek to explain such behavior in terms of (a) non-equivalence of the instruments; (b) information asymmetries; (c) differential interest group pressures; and (d) institutional constraints.

The non-equivalence of trade protection instruments
There are many reasons why tariffs and quotas are not equivalent, some of which were explored earlier in this chapter. The two policies differ in their effects in the presence of uncertainty, in a large country context, in the presence of retaliation and when the protected industry is a monopoly. In circumstances such as these, political forces may favor selection of one policy in preference to another, even in the absence of any failure of the vote motive. Let us review an example of non-equivalence at work, based on the Stigler–Peltzman version of the political support process which avoids explicit modelling of voters, interest groups and political markets (Stigler 1971; Peltzman 1976).

Cassing and Hillman (1985) consider the political choice between tariffs and quotas in the presence of domestic monopoly. The choice between the two instruments is made by a policy-maker who maximizes political support by trading off the gains to the beneficiary of protection (the domestic pro-

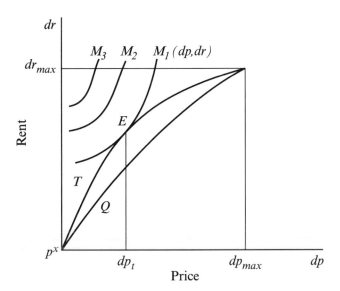

Figure 4.7   The regulator's choice between a tariff and a quota

ducer) against the penalty inflicted on the losers (the purchasers of the good). Figure 4.7 outlines the situation. Political support M is assumed to be an increasing function of the protection-induced increment in the monopolist's rent dr and a decreasing function of the increment in price dp. Suppose that the revenue derived by the government does not enter into the policy-maker's calculations. It is then possible to derive political iso-support curves as illustrated in Figure 4.7. Higher iso-support curves are associated with higher levels of political support.

The origin in Figure 4.7, p^x, corresponds to free trade. From there, as domestic price increases in response to either a tariff or a quota, producer rents also increase up to a maximum dr_{max} which occurs in the case either of a zero quota or a maximum usable tariff at a domestic price p_{max}. At any domestic price between p^x and p_{max} producer rents are higher under a tariff than a quota, and the curve relating dr to dp for a tariff, T, lies everywhere above the corresponding curve for a quota, Q. The policy-maker maximizes political support at point E where an iso-support curve is tangential to T. The policy chosen in this case is a tariff because, for any given penalty to the consumers, the tariff yields higher producer rents. The political equilibrium at point E also determines the level of the tariff at dp_t. Of course, this example does not help to explain the prevalence of quotas over tariffs in the real world, since it does not deploy information asymmetries or differential interest group lobbying power as the basis for its logic.

Asymmetric information
Another potential influence on instrument choice is information asymmetry. This argument rests on the proposition that some instruments are more transparent, or more conspicuous, in their protective effects than others. Specifically, it is argued that the protective effect of a quantitative restriction is not immediately discernible to the losers from protectionist policies, whereas a tariff provides an explicit expression of the increase in domestic price over the world price due to protection (Hillman 1989). By making the extent of the losses incurred by the losers from protection less transparent, a quantitative restriction facilitates provision of benefits to the gainers from protection in a politically less costly manner than a tariff.

Hillman (1989) illustrates the power of the asymmetry effect with the example of United States automobile imports. While the US government imposes only a low tariff on imports of automobiles, imports of Japanese automobiles are subject to strict quantitative restrictions in the form of voluntary export restraints (VERs). VERs have significantly increased domestic US prices of Japanese automobile imports and, by substitution in domestic consumption, they have raised US automobile prices generally. Simultaneously, the quantity constraint on Japanese imports has resulted in some quality upgrading of such imports. Consequently, the computation of the cost of the quantitative restrictions is complex, well beyond the capability of most US automobile consumers. Politicians who broker VER agreements are well aware of the political advantages of such obfuscation.

A similar transparency argument explains the politician's preference for tariffs over tax-subsidy instruments of trade protection. The domestic effects of a tariff can be duplicated precisely by the combination of an equal percentage subsidy to domestic producers of the good protected by the tariff and a tax on the domestic consumption of the same good. The tax-subsidy solution is more efficient than the tariff when lump-sum subsidies are feasible, in that the deadweight cost is avoided. However, tax-subsidy interventions are much less likely to escape voter attention than tariffs and, as such, are much less attractive to vote-seeking politicians.

This transparency explanation of instrument choice has been formalized by Steven Magee (1988). Magee suggests that instrument choice is governed by a *principle of optimal obfuscation* which leads tariffs to be chosen in preference to more efficient tax/subsidy means of intervention. Policy-makers optimize by choosing the degree of obfuscation to trade off political costs and benefits of instrument choice. Policy obfuscation yields a political gain by making income transfers less detectable by the losers from intervention. However, it carries some loss from decreased political support since the less-efficient policy instrument incurs higher deadweight costs. The optimal degree of obfuscation balances these countervailing influences at the margins of trade protection policy.

Differential interest group pressures
Trade protection is designed to protect domestic industries from international competition. If the domestic supply elasticities in political markets are less than infinite, such protection defines monopoly rights which give rise to future rents. In such circumstances, trade protection has a domestic rent-seeking constituency prepared to devote resources to lobbying in support of trade protection policies. In certain circumstances, trade protection may also have a foreign constituency. Rent-seeking outlays by these constituencies will determine the precise instruments of protection traded in the political market place (Rowley and Tollison 1986).

The rent-seeking constituency in support of tariff protection extends beyond that of the domestic industry exposed to foreign competition. It encompasses additionally those who seek to divert the revenues accruing from tariffs, including bureaucrats in the Department of the Treasury and those who perceive rents from illegal evasion of the tariff (smugglers). The interests of these separate constituencies are by no means identical since the revenue-maximizing tariff differs from the tariff required for total trade diversion. Following Olson (1965), the domestic industry influence is likely to be more effective than the general revenue lobbies, and the smuggling influence, for obvious reasons, must be especially covert in its lobbying.

The present value of the differential value is available as a rent to the domestic producer(s) only where that differential is not eroded or eliminated by subsequent domestic output expansion. In this sense, the tariff is *not* equivalent to an output restricting domestic monopoly right. Domestic producers can take full advantage of the tariff only where they are non-contestable, single-firm monopolies or non-contestable cartels shielded from new entry by government-imposed protection. Otherwise, output expansion will occur to the point where normal returns are achieved by the marginal firm, with rents available only to relatively low-cost suppliers. If free entry coincides with constant cost supply, there are no equilibrium rents available even from durable tariff protection.

In 1965, Jagdish Bhagwati identified circumstances in which a tariff and its quota counterpart could be considered to be equivalent. In essence, the equivalence criterion rests on the provision of identical levels of protection to some pre-designated domestic industry. For almost a decade thereafter, international trade theory centered attention on protection levels rather than on the nature of protection instruments.

In 1974, Krueger, utilizing Tullock's 1967 rent-seeking insight with respect to quotas rather than tariffs, disturbed Bhagwati's equivalence theorem, establishing that quantitative restrictions were always inferior to tariffs (because of rent-seeking resource loss) and that overall real equilibrium would differ under conditions of Bhagwati equivalence. In 1980, Bhagwati and Srinivasan responded by emphasizing the rent-seeking implications of tariff revenues as a counterpart to rent-seeking into quota licenses. They acknowledged, however, that the two outcomes might well differ as a consequence of different capital–labor ratios in the alternative rent-seeking scenarios.

In our view, the important debate between Krueger and Bhagwati and Srinivasan somewhat misses the point of the rent-seeking insight, namely the latter's contribution to understanding the public-choice mechanics of the market in trade protection (Rowley and Tollison 1986). The relevant issue is not whether Bhagwati-equivalent tariffs and quotas provide identical economy-wide equilibria in real resource allocations. Rather, it is whether the differential rent-seeking behavior in the trade protection market will influence the public-choice decision on the instrument of protection. Olson's logic of collective action suggests that such indeed will be the case, with rent-seeking predictably biasing intervention in favor of quota restrictions, since the latter offer rents to more narrowly based and better-organized special interests than is the case with tariffs, and do so with much less political transparency.

Quotas offer a number of potential advantages over tariffs that make them attractive to rent-seekers. To the domestic industry seeking out protection, they provide absolute limits on import penetration, secure against unforeseeable shifts in market conditions, whereas tariffs clearly do not. Given *ex ante* equivalence, risk-averse domestic producers predictably prefer the quota. Foreign suppliers who obtain quotas are protected against export expansion by rival foreign suppliers. To the secondary rent-seekers who market in import quota licenses, they provide for more specialized rents than are available to those who rent-seek into the generalized tariff revenues accruing to the US Department of the Treasury. To the relevant government bureau, the Department of Commerce or the ITC, they offer a more complex system of administration and, hence, a larger budget, especially where the import quotas are not simply auctioned off in sealed bid markets.

Voluntary export restraints, together with other kinds of bilateral quantitative restrictions, such as orderly marketing agreements (OMAs), differ from global import quotas in two important respects. First, they tend to discriminate between nations, in contravention of the most-favored-nation principle enshrined in Article I of the GATT as well as Article XIII, which governs the use of quantitative restrictions. Second, they render the exporting country responsible for administering the quota system through export licenses distributed to participating corporations.

Thus VERs offer monopoly rights to the protected domestic industry (assuming non-contestability) similar to but less comprehensive than those provided by global import quotas. The direct domestic rent-seeking implications, therefore, slightly favor the global quota. Like import quotas, VERs make no rents immediately available in the form of general government revenues. Unlike import quotas, however, VERs provide no secondary rents to domestic import agencies. In consequence, VERs would not dominate in a rent-seeking competition exclusive to domestic interests.

Once opportunities arise for foreign interests to lobby US political markets, however, the balance may shift decisively in favor of VERs. The quota rents available from such instruments are now appropriated either by foreign corporations or (in the case of competitive auctions) by foreign governments. In such circumstances, foreign interests have a direct incentive to lobby key committee members in the US Congress in favor of VERs. US congressmen are generally currency-blind with respect to campaign contributions and respond energetically to foreign lobbyists who payroll their way to re-election victory.

Institutional constraints
The form that trade protection takes is subject to the institutional arrangements which govern the conduct of a country's international trade policy

(Hillman 1989). In the US, national trade laws provide administrative tracks that can be taken by industries seeking protection. Protection can also be sought by appeal to the legislative branch, lobbying to win the support of majorities in both houses of Congress in conjunction with the significance of the president. In the event of a presidential veto, the lobbyists must secure a two-thirds Congressional majority in both houses for a veto override. Substantial lobbying effort is therefore required on this track. On the other hand, legislation is much more durable than administered protection.

The executive branch, acting on its own, can take action outside the reference frame of the national trade laws by negotiating bilateral voluntary trade restrictions or orderly marketing agreements with foreign governments representing the interests of foreign exporters. Substantial lobbying is necessary to evoke such intervention. Only a very few US industries have been successful on this track: automobiles, steel, textiles and apparel, semiconductors, beef, sugar and lumber are rare but important examples of such successful rent-seeking.

Choice of the instrument of protection is also influenced by international institutional arrangements. The GATT exhibits a preference for tariffs over import quotas and other non-tariff barriers on the ground that, unlike tariffs, the latter instruments do not permit expansion of trade in response to increases in domestic demand. However, because GATT negotiations have succeeded in securing significant multilateral tariff reductions, non-tariff barriers have come to replace tariffs as formidable barriers to free trade both in the US and elsewhere.

References

Anderson, G., Shughart, W.F. and Tollison, R.D. (1988) 'On the incentive of judges to enforce legislative wealth transfers', *Journal of Law and Economics*, 31: 215–28.

Arrow, K.J. (1950) 'A difficulty in the concept of social welfare', *Journal of Political Economy,* LVIII: 328–46.

Becker, G.S. (1983) 'A theory of competition among pressure groups for political influence', *Quarterly Journal of Economics,* 98: 371–400.

Bhagwati, J. (1965) 'On the equivalence of tariffs and quotas', in R. Caves (ed.), *Trade, Growth and the Balance of Payments* (Chicago: Rand-McNally), ch. 12.

Bhagwati, J. (1969) *Trade, Tariffs and Growth* (London: Weidenfeld & Nicolson).

Bhagwati, J. (1980) 'Lobbying and welfare', *Journal of Public Economics*, 14: 355–63.

Bhagwati, J. (1988) *Protectionism* (Cambridge, Mass.: MIT Press).

Bhagwati, J. and Srinivasan, T.N. (1984) *Lectures on International Trade* (Cambridge, Mass.: MIT Press).

Black, D. (1948) 'On the rationale of group decision-making', *Journal of Political Economy*, LVI: 23–34.

Brock, W.A. and Magee, S.P.C. (1978) 'The economics of special-interest politics: the case of the tariff', *American Economic Review*, 68: 246–50.

Buchanan, J.M. (1980) 'Rent-seeking and profit-seeking', in J.M. Buchanan, R.D. Tollison and G. Tullock (eds), *Towards a Theory of the Rent-seeking Society* (College Station: Texas A&M University Press), 3–15.

Buchanan, J.M. and Tullock, G. (1962) *The Calculus of Consent* (Ann Arbor: University of Michigan Press).

Cairnes, J.E. (1884) *Some Leading Principles of Political Economy* (London: Macmillan).

Cassing, J.H. and Hillman, A.L. (1985) 'Political influence motives and the choice between tariffs and quotas', *Journal of International Economics*, 19: 279–90.

Crain, W.M. and Tollison, R.D. (1979) 'The executive branch in the interest-group theory of government', *Journal of Legal Studies*, VIII: 555–67.

Deardorff, A.V. (1987) 'Current issues in trade policy: an overview', in R.M. Stein (ed.), *US Trade Policies in a Changing World Economy* (Cambridge, Mass.: The MIT Press).

Downs, A. (1957) *An Economic Theory of Democracy* (New York: Harper & Row).

Gwartney, J. and Wagner, R.E. (1988) *Public Choice and Constitutional Economics* (Greenwich: JAI Press).

Hamilton, A., Jay, J. and Madison, J. (1787) *The Federalist* (New York: The Modern Library, 1937).

Hillman, A.L. (1989) *The Political Economy of Protection* (New York: Harwood Academic Publishers).

Johnson, H.G. (1965) 'The theory of tariff structure with special reference to world trade and development', in H.G. Johnson and P. Kenen (eds), *Trade and Development* (Geneva: Librairia Droz), pp. 9–29.

Krueger, A. (1974) 'The political economy of the rent-seeking society', *American Economic Review*, 64: 291–303.

Landes, W.E. and Posner, R.A. (1975) 'The independent judiciary in an interest group perspective', *Journal of Law and Economics*, 18: 875–902.

Lee, D. (1987) 'Deficits, political myopia and the asymmetric dynamics of taxing and spending', in J.M. Buchanan, C.K. Rowley and R.D. Tollison (eds), *Deficits* (Oxford: Basil Blackwell).

Magee, S.P. (1988) 'Optimal obfuscation and the theory of the second-worst: a theory of public choice', in S.P. Magee, W.A. Brock and L. Young (eds), *Endogenous Policy Theory* (Cambridge: Cambridge University Press).

Magee, S.P., Brock, W.A. and Young, L. (1989) *Black Hole Tariffs and Endogenous Policy Theory* (Cambridge: Cambridge University Press).

Mayer, W. (1984) 'Endogenous tariff formation', *American Economic Review*, 74: 970–85.

McKelvey, R.D. (1979) 'General conditions for global intransitivities in formal voting models', *Econometrica*, 47: 1085–1112.

Olson, M. (1965) *The Logic of Collective Action* (Cambridge, Mass.: Harvard University Press).

Peltzman, S. (1976) 'Toward a more general theory of regulation', *Journal of Law and Economics*, 19: 3–21.

Plott, C. (1979) 'Path-independence, rationality and social choice', *Econometrica*, 41: 1075–91.

Riker, W.H. (1980) 'Implications from the disequilibrium of majority rule for the study of institutions', *American Political Science Review*, 74: 432–46.

Riker, W.H. and Ordeshook, P.C. (1973) *An Introduction to Positive Political Theory* (Englewood Cliffs, N.J.: Prentice-Hall).

Rodriguez, C.A. (1974) 'The non-equivalence of tariffs and quotas under retaliation', *Journal of International Economics*, 4: 295–8.

Rowley, C.K. (1984) 'The relevance of the median voter theorem', *Journal of Institutional and Theoretical Economics*, 140: 104–35.

Rowley, C.K. (1992) 'The supreme court and takings judgements: constitutional political economy versus public choice', in N. Mercuro (ed.), *Taking Property and Just Compensation: Law and Economics Perspectives of the Takings Issue* (Boston, Mass.: Kluwer Academic Publishers), pp. 79–124.

Rowley, C.K. (1993) *Public Choice Theory* (Brookfield: Edward Elgar Publishing), vol. 2, ix–xxix.

Rowley, C.K. and Thorbecke, W. (1993) 'The role of congress and the executive in US trade policy determinations: a public choice analysis', in M. Hilf and E.-U. Petersmann (eds),

National Constitutions and International Economic Law (Boston, Mass.: Kluwer Academic Publishers), 347–69.

Rowley, C.K. and Tollison, R.D. (1986) 'Rent-seeking and trade protection', *Swiss Journal of International Relations,* 41: 141–66.

Rowley, C.K. and Vachris, M.A. (1992) *Why Democracy in the United States May not Produce Efficient Results* (Fairfax: Center for Study of Public Choice).

Shepsle, K.A. and Weingast, B.R. (1987) 'The institutional foundations of committee power', *American Political Science Review,* 81: 85–104.

Stigler, G.J. (1971) 'The theory of economic regulation', *Bell Journal of Economics and Management Science,* 2: 3–21.

Stigler, G.J. (1974) 'Free riders and collective action: an appendix to theories of economic regulation', *Bell Journal of Economics and Management Science,* 5: 359–65.

Stigler, G.J. (1988) *Chicago Studies in Political Economy* (Chicago: University of Chicago Press).

Tollison, R.D. (1988) 'Public choice and legislation', *Virginia Law Review,* 74: 339–71.

Tullock, G. (1967a) *Toward a Mathematics of Politics* (Ann Arbor: University of Michigan Press).

Tullock, G. (1967b) 'The welfare costs of tariffs, monopolies and theft', *Western Economic Journal,* 5: 224–32.

Tullock, G. (1971) 'The cost of transfers', *Kyklos,* 24: 624–42.

Tullock, G. (1981) 'Why so much stability?', *Public Choice,* 37: 189–202.

Vousden, N. (1990) *The Economics of Trade Protection* (Cambridge: Cambridge University Press).

Wagner, R.E. (1987) 'Parchment versus guns', in J.M. Buchanan, C.K. Rowley and R.D. Tollison (eds), *Deficits* (Oxford: Basil Blackwell).

Weingast, B.R. and Marshall, W.J. (1988) 'Why legislatures, like firms, are not organized as markets', *Journal of Political Economy,* 96: 132–63.

Williamson, O.E. (1985) *The Economic Institutions of Capitalism* (New York: The Free Press).

Young, H.P. (1978) 'The allocation of funds in lobbying and campaigning', *Behavioral Science,* 23: 21–31.

PART II

INSTITUTIONS

5   The Congress

1   Introduction

The United States Constitution grants to Congress the power to regulate commerce with foreign nations. It also grants to Congress the power to levy duties as well as other forms of taxes, although it prohibits Congress from imposing any form of export tax (Article 1). The Constitution likewise provides the president with powers relating to international trade through his responsibility for conducting foreign relations (Article 2). In practice, with a typical deference to the legislature, the courts have held the authority of Congress to be pre-eminent whenever presidential actions have conflicted with congressional legislation (Baldwin 1985: 33). For this reason, it is appropriate to commence our study of trade protection in the United States with a detailed review of the legislative behavior of the United States Congress.

In many ways, Congress is a unique or unusual body (Mayhew 1974). It is the most professionalized of all legislatures in the sense that it promotes long-term careerism among its members, providing them with the salaries, staff and other resources to sustain themselves in office and to repel potential competition. Its individual members, working through committees and subcommittees, are exceptionally influential in specialized areas of policy. Its political parties are unusually diffuse and weak. Laboring, unlike most although not all European legislatures, with a separately elected executive branch, it is well-endowed to check executive power should its members be so inclined. Increasingly, since the early 1970s, they have been of such a mind with respect to the trade policies of the United States government.

In this chapter, the theory of legislative behavior outlined in Chapter 4 is extended to take account of the changing institutional arrangements of the United States Congress epitomized by the declining influence of party leadership and the associated advance in subcommittee powers. The nature of the relationship between the legislative and the executive branches of government is also evaluated. These and other external influences are then combined to identify the tilt to protectionism that characterizes Congressional trade politics in the late twentieth century.

2   Congress: keystone of the Washington establishment

The generative assumption of the public-choice theory of Congressional behavior is that United States congressmen are interested in achieving re-election, indeed that they are interested in little or nothing else (Fiorina 1988). The evidence inescapably suggests that they have been increasingly successful in achieving this objective. In the modern Congress, the congressional career is unmistakably upon us. Turnover figures show that over the past century increasing proportions of members in any given Congress have been holdovers from previous congresses – members who have sought and won re-election (Mayhew 1974).

Membership turnover in the United States Senate noticeably declined among the southern senators as early as the 1850s and among senators generally just after the Civil War. In the House, turnover began to dip in the late nineteenth century and continued to decline throughout the twentieth. By the early 1970s, 20 percent of House members had served at least ten terms. The modern Congress is an assembly of professional politicians spinning out lifetime careers in politics, with pay, perquisites and prestige of office well in excess of their opportunity wages. Since this incumbency effect has significant implications for congressional attitudes towards trade protection policy, it is worth describing in more detail at this stage.

The incumbency effect is the extra percentage of the vote that results simply from being an incumbent, and not from party membership, region, election year or any other factor. For the House of Representatives, Erickson (1971) estimated that during the 1950s and early 1960s the incumbency effect was statistically present but politically unimportant, amounting to somewhere between 1 and 2 percent of the congressional vote.

In the mid-1960s, however, Erickson's estimates jumped to 5 percent, implying that the typical marginal district congressman was no longer marginal when he ran for re-election after a term or more in office. This incumbency effect explains the emergence of continuous single-party government in the House of Representatives over a period of almost 40 years. Current House re-election rates are staggeringly high, ranging from 90 percent in 1982 to 98 percent in 1986, 1988, 1990, and 1992.

The Senate elections – only 30 to 35 every two years and subject to greater visibility and media attention than the House – predictably evidence more variability. Yet Kotroski (1973) estimated that the Senate had undergone much the same kind of change as that chronicled for the House. For Democratic senators, Kotroski estimated an incumbency advantage of 4 percent in 1948–52, increasing steadily to 12 percent in 1966–70. For Republicans, the increase was from 1 percent to 11 percent over the same period. This is especially noteworthy since senators' constituencies cannot be gerrymandered through redistricting, as is the case with the House (Erickson 1972). Since the late 1970s, however, the Senate elections have displayed greater variability, with 60 percent of Senate incumbents succeeding between 1976 and 1980; with 90 percent in 1982 and 1984; and with only 75 percent of senators re-elected in 1986 (Fiorina 1988). Nevertheless, incumbency advantages clearly exist in the Senate as well as the House.

Fiorina (1988) has suggested that the marginal constituencies disappeared in the United States in part because congressmen in such constituencies diverted their activities somewhat from lawmaking (which divided their districts) to casework and success in securing pork (which unified support within their districts). As Congress created a government ever larger and far-reaching, it simultaneously increased the opportunities for its members to build up political credit with their constituents. In so doing, it weakened the importance of party identification as increasing numbers of voters began to think of their congressmen less as policy-makers and more as ombudsmen and pork barrelers:

> In legislative matters he is merely one vote of 435. But in bureaucratic matters he is a benevolent, nonpartisan power. And if more and more citizens come to think of their congressman in this manner, then the basis of the incumbency effect is obvious. *Experience in Washington and congressional seniority count when dealing with the bureaucracy.* So long as the incumbent can elude a personal morality rap and refrain from casting outlandish votes, he is naturally preferred over a newcomer. *This incumbency effect is not only understandable; it is rational.* And it would grow over time as increasing numbers of citizens come to regard their congressman as a troubleshooter in the Washington bureaucracies. (Fiorina 1988: 49)

The decline of party importance created a context that encouraged constituency attentiveness and made it politically profitable in non-marginal as well as in marginal constituencies. As local party organizations withered, members of Congress had to replace the electoral resources that parties previously had supplied. They did so by augmenting their personal resources – staff, district offices, and travel – and by increasing their usage of such existing resources as the frank. This shift was accelerated in 1956 when the Republican Party failed to carry either the House or the Senate despite Eisenhower's sweeping presidential victory (the first such failure in 100 years) and was confirmed in 1960 when Kennedy lost in a majority of the nation's House districts and ran behind 243 of 265 winning Democratic representatives. By the mid-1960s, the writing was on the wall for the old party order, and officeholders were reconciled to a more individualistic future in which they would consolidate their own constituency loyalties.

One implication of officeholder independence has been a significant growth in the numbers of congressional staff, with more than 25,000 staffers now employed by congressmen, and with personal staff outnumbering committee staff by a ratio of four to one in each chamber. As Fiorina (1988) notes, each representative employs an average of eighteen staff and each senator twice as many. Subcommittee chairmanships, which are numerous and well-spread among the membership in both the House and the Senate, provide many congressmen with an added complement of staff. In excess of 40 percent of all staffers are assigned to district offices to work exclusively on constituency matters. A considerable volume of constituency work is also carried out in Washington. Overall, the proportion of staff resources devoted to constituency matters rather than to lawmaking is well in excess of 50 percent.

A second feature of officeholder independence is the proliferation of subcommittees and the devolution of collective power to component parts of the institution, which is characteristic of the late twentieth-century Congress. Curbs on the arbitrary powers of the congressional party leadership at the beginning of the twentieth century were a direct consequence of the increasing professionalization of congressmen (Fiorina 1988). The 1910 revolt against Speaker Joe Cannon completed the destruction of party leadership powers and introduced in its place the contemporary seniority system, rewarding lengthy service in the Congress, and depriving both local districts and states of any incentive to replace old, tired and corrupted representatives or senators with younger, better qualified and hopefully more honest alternatives.

Power was distributed away from the party leaders to a much larger group of standing committee chairmen (there were 60 standing committees in 1910), each of whom achieved the chairmanship through an automatic process of seniority. This reform endured until the end of the Second World War when it also was swept away by a new era of decentralization. The Legislative Reorganization Act of 1946 reduced the number of standing committees by more than a half. There followed a steady growth in the number of subcommittees catering to the specialized constituency interests of individual congressmen. In 1955, there were 83 subcommittees in the House and 79 in the Senate. By 1973, the number had risen to 125 in the House and 128 in the Senate in response to rising membership pressures for chairmanship privileges.

As the number of congressional subcommittees increased, their powers and autonomy also advanced, especially in the House, where individual members were restricted to a single chairmanship and where subcommittee jurisdictions were tightly drawn and rigidly enforced. Supported by sizeable budgets and adequate staffing, the subcommittees played a key role in the developing Washington establishment based on a series of subgovernments each composed of the standing subcommittee, the agencies under its jurisdiction and the special interests serviced by the agencies. By logrolling between the subcommittees, legislation designed to favor organized minorities is facilitated through both the House and Senate through majority votes, thus servicing the constituency interests of vote-conscious congressman. In their more extreme manifestations, these subcommittees are known as *iron triangles*, operating as fiefdoms all but autonomous from the main body of Congress itself:

The incentives that support such arrangements are not difficult to identify. Committee members enjoy the opportunity to exercise great influence in a particular policy area – given the pattern of committee assignments, often an area of considerable concern to their districts. The agency receives protection and support from the committee. The clientele benefits from the program and the circle closes when the clientele provides support for friendly committee members. (Fiorina 1988: 122)

The iron triangles are now less individually powerful than was the case during the 1970s, as a result of developments both internal and external to Congress. Among the external factors, the most important is the dramatic expansion in the range of interest groups that now lobby the federal government. Initially, subgovernment politics were based on a harmony of interests among a small number of concerned groups. With the expansion of interest groups and with the rise of effective public interest groups (in defiance of Olson's logic of collective action) whose principal purpose is to expose the iron triangles to public scrutiny, the particularist excesses of these subgovernments have been more costly to maintain.

Developments within Congress have also made subgovernment politics more difficult. As the number of subcommittees has increased, jurisdictional conflicts among them have become frequent. Such conflicts have been exacerbated by the behavior of credit-seeking staffers who do not hesitate to trespass on each other's turf. In consequence, relatively few agencies now answer to a single powerful committee. By playing one subcommittee against another, agencies may gain considerable discretion from their congressional overseers.

Subcommittee power has also been eroded by the increasing influence of floor amendments and by the growing significance of floor majorities in the United States Congress. In part, this reflects the rise in jurisdictional conflict, as aggrieved members of one committee attack the work of another (Fiorina 1988). In part, the greater openness of Congress makes it more difficult for congressmen to defend self-imposed limitations on their chamber involvement than was the case in the 1970s. In part, of course, the erosion of subcommittee power, especially in the House, is the consequence of twelve years of divided government, eight of which were presided over by a popular president (Reagan) who did not believe in politics-as-usual and who appointed agency chiefs who were opposed to their agencies' programs and sometimes even intent on dismantling them.

Finally, it would be remiss to close this discussion of changing subcommittee power without referring to the explosive rate of growth of political action committees (PACs) following the Federal Election Campaign Act amendments of 1974 and the Federal Election SUN-PAC decision of 1975. In 1974, individuals provided 79 percent of House campaign funds compared with 17 percent from PACs, and 83 percent of Senate campaign funds compared with 11 percent from PACs. By 1986, PAC contributions had risen to 36 percent for the House and to 22 percent for the senate. There is clearly an opportunity in this expansion for PAC monies to loosen the close link between congressmen and their geographic constituencies since virtually all PAC contributions come from out of district and more than four-fifths come from out-of-state sources.

To the extent that PAC contributions flow disproportionately to incumbents, they further intensify the incumbency effect, although, as the 1994 elections demonstrated, this may not withstand a major political sea-change. At the same time, they tempt members to vote for special interests that may be at odds with the special interests of their districts, thus weakening the iron triangles that are defined in geographic terms, while certainly not destroying them completely. PAC monies are still a minority of total campaign contributions and ultimately the voters vote for their congressman exclusively on the basis of the district and the state. However influenced they may be by campaign contributions, congressmen still must respond to constituency pressures if they are to secure the seniority benefits of continuous incumbency.

With only rare exceptions (Krehbiel 1992), public-choice scholars nevertheless continue to acknowledge the primacy of the strategic distributive roles of committees in both houses of Congress. There is a substantial consensus, in this respect, on a number of stylized facts (Shepsle and Weingast 1987):

1. committees are 'gate-keepers' in their respective jurisdictions;
2. committees are repositories of policy expertise;
3. committees are policy incubators;
4. committees possess disproportionate control over the agenda in their policy domains;
5. committees are deferred to, and that deference is reciprocated.

These foundations of committee influence appear to be well-grounded empirically and yet are not 'carved in granite' (Shepsle and Weingast 1987). Committees do act as veto groups that may choose to keep the gates closed on a particular bill. Yet parliamentary majorities have recourse to mechanisms by which to pry the gates open – the discharge petition is the most obvious. Yet they are rarely used.

Similarly, committees observably enjoy information advantages and proposal powers. Yet the Speaker of the House of Representatives is relatively free to break any monopoly of proposal power though his right of recognition in House proceedings, his referral powers, his control of the Rules Committee and his power to create *ad hoc* and select committees for specific purposes.

These powers are rarely deployed, presumably because of deference to the members of the standing committee.

The puzzle remains as to just how deference, as a form of self-enforcing *ex ante* institutional bargain among legislators, survives the manifest opportunities to renege that are available to determined majorities at each stage in the legislative process. Shepsle and Weingast (1987) explain the robustness of such deference as the consequence of three mechanisms employed by committees to bolster their institutional influence: (a) punishment; (b) *ex ante* defensive behavior; and (c) *ex post* defensive behavior.

A committee may discourage opposition to its actions (or non-actions) by developing a reputation for punishing those who oppose it. Such powers are evidently available to the Senate Finance Committee and to the House Ways and Means Committee, the two influential standing committees primarily responsible for trade policy legislation. Dan Rostenkowski, until recently Chairman of the House Ways and Means Committee, was especially feared for his ability to keep score and to take revenge on anyone who failed to supply deference to the policies supported by his committee.

A committee may also induce cooperative, deferential behavior by *ex ante* accommodation. It will surely attempt to anticipate, when formulating its proposals, what will pass in the parent chamber. Similarly, it will reflect on likely reactions before killing a bill within committee Yet, such *ex ante* accommodation is more appropriately voiced as a recognition of the influence of others, rather than as an influence mechanism of the committee. After all, majorities may veto committee bills by voting them down. The Rules Committee in the House may scuttle a committee bill by refusing to grant a rule. The Speaker may manipulate the agenda in ways detrimental to a committee bill. Small groups of senators may filibuster a bill or deny it expeditious passage. Why are these powers not more frequently invoked?

Shepsle and Weingast (1987) suggest that the most potent enforcement mechanism available to the committee, through which it maintains its dominance as a veto group and as the primary policy proposer in its jurisdiction, is *ex post* defensive behavior. Specifically, the *ex post* veto is sufficient to render gate-keeping and proposal power effective, even if that effectiveness appears to outside observers to be the product of nothing more than informal reciprocity arrangements. Suppose some legislative majority was tempted to pry the gates open. The *ex post* veto would ensure that changes in the status quo adverse to the interests of a decisive committee majority could be denied final passage. Suppose that a chamber majority contemplated a major amendment to a committee proposal. The threat of an *ex post* committee veto would weaken the resolve of that chamber majority.

Conference committees arguably institutionalize the *ex post* veto powers of legislative committees. In the United States Congress, a bill must pass through both chambers of the legislature in precisely the same form before it may be sent to the chief executive for his signature. Should a bill pass in different forms, a process is set in motion to reconcile differences. This process, known as *messaging between the chambers*, cannot continue indefinitely. Once a stage of disagreement is reached in which one chamber insists on its version of the bill and the other chamber disagrees, then one chamber requests a conference and the other chamber accepts. Almost all major bills end up in conference.

Conferees of each chamber are appointed by the presiding officer and are drawn principally from the committees of jurisdiction at the suggestion of the committees' respective chairmen. Even where additional conferees are appointed, the views of the committee chairman are dominant in such selections. The conferees from each chamber seek to resolve differences in the respective versions of the bill. An agreement is reached when a majority of each delegation signs the conference report. The agreement then is brought back to each chamber to be voted up or down under a closed rule.

The conference procedure described above institutionalizes the *ex post* veto and gives credibility to the committee during floor deliberations in its chamber. It also confers additional *ex post* adjustment powers on the committee to be exercised in the conference itself. Subcommittee power has been similarly reflected in conference committee membership following the decentralization of the United States Congress. To the extent that committee members are outliers with respect to their respective chambers on the policy issues under review, the conference may be less of an arena for conflict than one in which like-minded congressmen join forces to hammer out a mutually acceptable deal. In many instances, the members of the House and Senate subcommittees who control the conference have more in common with one another than either may have with their fellow chamber members.

In this interpretation, the distributive functions of the congressional subcommittees are fostered by the *ex post* enforcement powers conferred by conference rules. In the absence of enforcement powers, it is unlikely that individual members of Congress would invest institutional careers in the committees on which they serve. We are aware that this distributional theory has been challenged by Krehbiel (1992) who counter-asserts that majoritarian forces dominate Congress and utilize committees primarily for information cost reasons. We do not find Krehbiel's arguments convincing and proceed throughout this chapter with an uncompromising distributive theory of congressional politics that is strongly supported by empirical evidence of trade policy legislation.

3 1600 Pennsylvania Avenue

In parliamentary systems, the executive branch of government – the prime minister and the cabinet – is drawn from the elected legislature. There is no substantive separation of powers and the basis of representation essentially is identical. The executive branch is dependent for its continuation in office upon the majority support of the legislature. The prime minister can disband parliament and call for new elections if he cannot sustain majority support for his legislative program. In such circumstances, significant policy disagreements are unlikely to emerge between the prime minister and the majority, or at least to prevail for long. Agenda control powers provide the prime minister and his cabinet with significant policy discretion, especially if cycles occur that provide opportunities for policy manipulation.

In some of the public choice literature (Wittman 1989), there is an erroneous tendency to ignore the particular nature of the US Constitution and to play down the role of the president within a system characterized by separation of powers. The Virginia political economy program (Rowley 1993) recognizes that there is a fundamental difference between parliamentary democracy and constitutional republicanism. Two somewhat conflicting theories are derived from this point of recognition, each relevant to particular electoral conditions. Both differ sharply from the erroneous vision.

In one interpretation (Crain and Tollison 1979), which may apply where the president's political party controls both chambers of the legislature, the president is not accorded much of an independent role. Rather, he is viewed as exploiting the separation of powers to increase the returns to congressional policy brokerage, exercising his veto powers or the threat thereof to extend the perceived durability of legislation. In this interpretation, the US Constitution provides not a separation but a collusion of powers, offering a legislative–executive nexus analogous to a vertically integrated purveyor of long-term legislation to special interests. Such a nexus certainly was not favored by the Founding Fathers.

In the alternative view, which is particularly relevant when the president's party does not control both chambers of the legislature, the veto power enables the president to enter the legislative process effectively as a third chamber, either to logroll on policies in order to forge a legislative equilibrium or to destabilize an existing legislative equilibrium. As we show in Chapter 9, US presidents have successfully exercised independent leadership with respect to tariff legislation, while logrolling with legislative interests with respect to bureaucratic trade protection initiatives. Congress itself has devolved upon the president considerable executive authority with respect to trade policy.

Potential differences in the interest group constituencies of the Congress and its committees on the one hand, and of the president on the other, emanate in considerable part from their differing bases of representation, with the special interests much more effective in the specialized committees of Congress. Potential differences occur also with respect to time horizons, with myopia most apparent among House representatives as they walk their two-year treadmills, and with longer-term horizons usually most evident in the presidency, both for dynastic and for historical reputation motives. Potential differences also occur as a consequence of differences in the degree of transparency in the relevant political markets, with special interests more effective in opaque environments (Crew and Rowley 1988). Presidential politics usually are more transparent than congressional politics. For all these reasons, the president may be expected to exercise an independent role in trade policy, whether or not his own party controls the legislature.

Where the Congress and the Presidency are at odds with each other, it is by no means clear which branch will dominate. Madison (1786) envisaged the legislature as the dominant branch and worried about the power that this would offer to special interests. Powerful presidents, however, have influenced policy even when their parties have been in a legislative minority. Certainly, presidents are able to destabilize an existing legislative equilibrium when the policies at issue are high priority and can be pursued under conditions of relative transparency.

4   Is there a protectionist tilt to congressional trade politics?

The theory of endogenous protection advanced by Chicago-oriented political economists offers little or no scope for independent action on the part of congressional law-makers and views with more than a modicum of skepticism the notion that institutions matter at all in the determination of policy (Magee *et al.* 1989). By endogenous protection, such scholars mean that trade restrictions are set by maximizing, self-interested behavior on the part of all the economic agents, lobbies, political parties, and voters.

By the *powerless-politician effect*, such scholars mean that trade policies are largely outside the control of the policy-makers in a competitive political system, that protection can be explained by those exogenous variables that drive the behavior of special interests and general interests that favor or oppose protection. Magee *et al.* (1989) find empirical support for the powerless politician effect, claiming that approximately 75 percent of the variability in tariffs during the twentieth century is explained by endogenous policy considerations (factor endowments, terms of trade, unemployment and inflation). Even so, some 25 percent of the variability must be driven by other factors, leaving considerable scope for institutional influences.

Suppose that the variable to be explained is the average US *ad valorem* tariff, calculated as total US tariff revenue divided by the value of total US imports. Suppose further that Democratic congressmen favor more protection and Republican congressmen favor less protection (relatively). Endogenous protection theory, in its modelling, assumes that the Democratic Party supports a tariff and that the Republicans support an export subsidy. Given the lobbying resource flows, each party sets its policy to maximize its probability of election. Protectionism is a three-player game among protectionists, pro-export interests, and voters, with the political parties acting as intermediaries. Tariff levels are determined as the equilibrium of the political game, and are explained by variables that affect the protectionist lobby, the pro-export lobby, and the voters.

Suppose that economic behavior is described (in the long run) by the standard neoclassical Heckscher–Ohlin–Samuelson two-factor, two-commodity model. All actors maximize their utilities. Each factor of production receives its marginal product in competitive factor markets; each lobby maximizes the returns to the factor of production that it represents; each party maximizes its probability of election by its optimal choice of a redistributive policy variable; voters are rationally ignorant in that they under-invest in information; and the median voter, although generally opposed to protection, is malleable in response to advertising financed by lobby contributions (Magee *et al.* 1989). In such circumstances, variations in the equilibrium level of protection will be driven by exogenous forces – factor endowments, terms of trade, unemployment, and inflation – as they impact on the relevant margins of pressure to which both political parties respond.

If this indeed were the full nature of trade politics, there would be little point in analyzing the behavior of legislative institutions in the depth that is characteristic of this chapter. For a number of reasons, however, the black box model of Magee *et al.* (1989) is inappropriate with respect to trade protection legislation. As we relax the assumptions of the black box to interpolate institutional detail, the protectionist tilt of the US Congress becomes clearly apparent.

Let us first identify those assumptions of endogenous trade protection theory that are consistent with the Virginia political economy approach as outlined in Chapter 4. Most voters (although not all) are ignorant of trade protection policies. They are unaware of the average level of US *ad valorem* tariffs and of the variance associated with that average. They are unacquainted with the myriad of quantitative restrictions, voluntary or coercive, that tie up import markets and raise CIF prices of imported products on the US market. They are aware neither of the nature of the agencies responsible for administering the US fair trade laws nor of the practicalities of their interventions. They are indoctrinated by mercantilist media assertions that US corporations suffer from an uneven playing field. Otherwise, they are rationally ignorant of trade protection politics, given the extremely low probability that their votes individually will be decisive in any federal election.

Those voters who are well-informed about trade protection policies typically are associated with the relevant government bureaux, import agencies, import-competing industries or export industries. They have a considerable economic stake in trade policy and tend to affiliate themselves with interest groups that lobby on their behalf. They fuel such interest groups with membership dues that in turn are deployed to purchase legislative votes, particularly on the trade policy subcommittees but also within the two chambers of Congress at large. Such outlays may be viewed as rent-seeking or as rent-protective and, for the most part, are dissipative of the nation's wealth. For the most part, political brokers respond efficiently to the market signals that they perceive, given the institutional environment in which they operate.

However, the environment itself tilts the political market against the free trade option given the underlying preferences of all those directly concerned. In the first place, Olson's (1965) logic of collective action predicts that competition among interest groups introduces significant bias into political markets. Such bias is a consequence of unequal access to political influence, reflective of the differential impact of the free-rider problem on the formation and effective mobilization of various kinds of interest groups.

Special interests emerge to take advantage of rational ignorance within the electorate and limited information available to the legislature to obtain advantages for members more than commensurate with their relative combined voting strength. As we noted in Chapter 4, their success depends upon their ability to remunerate politicians (with votes and money) who broker policies favorable to their members. Business and labor interests that are directly or indirectly specialized in international trade are predictably much more active in trade politics than consumers, who confront only the diffused costs of trade protection policies. As Figure 4.1 suggests, import-competing groups have been much more active in lobbying the US government than export groups, although that situation is changing.

In the second place, lobbying does not follow the pattern dictated by Stolper–Samuelson (and emphasized by endogenous protection theory), but rather takes the form suggested by Ricardo–Viner. Given the greater geographic specificity of import-competing and export industries than capital and labor at large, the political party positions on trade protection policy are more ambiguous and political parties exert less influence over individual members of Congress than endogenous protection theory typically allows (Magee *et al.* 1989).

In the place of political parties, the committees and subcommittees of Congress with specific oversight authority over international trade attract the attention of interest groups in the distributive battle over trade laws. Although a growing number of congressional subcommittees now make jurisdictional claims to various aspects of trade policy – a reflection of the increasing influence of international trade on the US economy since the early 1970s – the key subcommittees empowered to oversee trade legislation are the *Trade Subcommittee* of the Ways and Means Committee in the House of Representatives and the *International Trade Subcommittee* of the Finance Committee in the Senate. Because these subcommittees are branches of extremely powerful revenue committees, their gate-keeping and enforcement powers tend to be greater than the average for their respective chambers.

Appointments to Ways and Means and to Finance are by no means easy to secure, given the influence that their members wield. Self-selection is much less feasible in such circumstances and the scope for outlier appointments reflecting constituencies with minority particularist preferences is narrower than for less-prestigious bodies. Moreover, there is some expectation that Ways and Means and Finance will pursue universalist goals in their dealings with other committees (Mayhew 1974). Nevertheless, particularist proclivities cannot be completely dampened in an interest-group-dominated legislature and the trade subcommittees are keystone players in brokering protectionist laws.

References

Baldwin, R.E. (1985) *The Political Economy of U.S. Import Policy* (Cambridge, Mass.: MIT Press).

Crain, W.M. and Tollison, R.D. (1979) 'The executive branch in the interest-group theory of government', *Journal of Legal Studies*, VIII: 555–67.

Crew, M.A. and Rowley, C.K. (1988) 'Toward a public choice theory of monopoly regulation', *Public Choice*, 57: 49–68.

Destler, I.M. (1986) *American Trade Politics: System Under Stress* (New York: Twentieth Century Fund).

Erickson, R.S. (1971) 'The advantage of incumbency in congressional elections', *Polity*, 3: 395–405.

Erickson, R.S. (1972) 'Malapportionment, gerrymandering and party fortunes in congressional elections', *American Political Science Review*, 66: 1234–1355.

Fiorina, M.P. (1988) *Congress: Keystone of the Washington Establishment* (New Haven, Conn.: Yale University Press).

Kotroski, W. (1973) 'Party incumbency in post-war senate elections', *American Political Science Review*, 68: 1213–34.

Krehbiel, K. (1992) *Information and Legislative Organization* (Ann Arbor, Mich.: University of Michigan Press).

Madison, J. (1786) *The Federalist, No. 53* (New York: The Modern Library, 1937).

Magee, S.P., Brock, W.A. and Young, L. (1989) *Black Hole Tariffs and Endogenous Policy Theory* (Cambridge: Cambridge University Press).

Mayhew, D.R. (1974) *Congress: The Electoral Connection* (New Haven, Conn.: Yale University Press).

Olson, M. (1965) *The Logic of Collective Action* (Cambridge, Mass.: Harvard University Press).

Rowley, C.K. (1993) 'Introduction', in C.K. Rowley (ed.), *Public Choice Theory*, vol. I (Aldershot, Hants., and Brookfield, Vt.: Edward Elgar).

Shepsle, K.A. and Weingast, B.R. (1987) 'The institutional foundations of committee power', *American Political Science Review*, 81: 85–104.

Wittman, D. (1989) 'Why democracies produce efficient results', *Journal of Political Economy*, 97 (6): 1395–1424.

6 The President

1 Introduction

The United States Constitution grants to the president powers relating to international trade through his responsibility for conducting foreign relations (Article 2). These powers are constrained, however, by Article 1, which grants to Congress the power to regulate commerce with foreign nations and the power to levy duties as well as other forms of taxes. For the most part, the courts have held the authority of Congress to be pre-eminent where presidential initiatives have conflicted with congressional legislation (Baldwin 1985: 33). To a considerable degree, therefore, the president's authority to shape US trade policy rests upon the discretion vested in him by Congress.

Although such discretion has shifted significantly over the period from 1930 to 1990, and in particular has been narrowed sharply since the early 1970s, the president's authority over trade policy is still enormous. It is the purpose of this chapter to outline the precise nature of such presidential authority, to analyze the pressures that direct presidential behavior in the trade policy arena and to review the implications of presidential interventions for the tilt between free trade and protectionism in the United States trade policy.

2 A public-choice theory of presidential behavior

A great deal of the public-choice literature focuses exclusively on the behavior of Congress and the relationship between Congress and the federal bureaux, ignoring the potential policy influence of the presidency and any relationship that may exist within the executive branch between the president and the federal bureaux and independent agencies. Yet a great deal of the political science literature focuses on the important policy role played by the president, and public opinion tends to allocate at least equal responsibility to the president as to Congress for the performance of the US economy.

Evidently, in the field of US trade policy, as section 2 of this chapter confirms, the presidency is vested with considerable discretionary authority. Why has this lacuna in the public-choice literature arisen? Why has the role of the presidency been so excessively de-emphasized, and with what implications for the predictive power of the public choice approach?

It has been forcefully argued (Moe 1990, 1991) that public choice has neglected an important aspect of political institutions. In this view, political institutions serve two very different purposes. On the one hand, they help to mitigate collective-action problems, especially the commitment and enforcement problems that potentially debilitate political exchange. In this manner, they facilitate the behavior of political actors as they cooperate to realize political gains from trade. On the other hand, political institutions are also weapons of coercion and redistribution. They are the structural means through which political winners pursue their own interests, often at the considerable expense of political losers. It is this latter side of the story that has been neglected in the public-choice approach.

The explanation of this comparative neglect lies in the social choice ancestry of the public-choice research program (Arrow 1950). The analytical world of social choice is a world of voting. Citizens vote on candidates and parties, legislators vote on public policies. In the typical scenario, voters are taken to be equals, each with the right to cast a single vote and with social choice determined by a pre-existing rule, usually majority rule. The basic theme running throughout the social-choice literature is one of instability. If voters are endowed with heterogeneous preferences, their efforts to pursue such preferences through majority rule voting generally fail to yield equilibrium social choices. Indeed, such efforts may well yield majority rule outcomes that cycle over the entire policy issue space.

Much of the recent public-choice literature on the Congress is best understood as a reaction to this basic theme, as an attempt to explain the political reality that social choices are not chaotic. Indeed, they are quite noticeably stable. The structure-induced equilibrium explanation is that social choices are not simply governed by majority rule, but rather by all kinds of institutions and protocols that constrain how majority rule operates: what alternatives succeed in being considered, in what order, and by whom. The public-choice role, in this perspective, is to understand what roles such institutions play, and, more fundamentally, where these institutions come from in the first place.

Legislatures have taken center stage in this institutional analysis, not only because of their substantive importance, but also because they are susceptible to vote analysis. Legislators vote, and their jobs and incentives are structured by their own electoral connection to voters in their home districts or states. They are also amenable to analysis based on the techniques of transaction-cost economies and agency theory that have recently swept through economics and positive political science (Moe 1990: 216). This new institutional economics, like the methodology of social choice, has left a somewhat skewed mark on the public-choice explanation of political institutions.

The new institutional economics is concerned with voluntary exchange among autonomous actors. It presumes an existing legal system that specifies and enforces property rights, authorizing each actor to make choices about the disposition of his own property and to claim legal possession of its proceeds. Within this secure legal context, actors seek to realize gains from trade by entering into exchanges with each other. Even in this relatively secure environment, the market does not always work well in a structure-free context.

This is especially the case when trades are contemplated by boundedly rational actors and depend on privately held information or specialized investments, when they entail future performance, or when they are contingent on future events. In a world of opportunism, all of these characteristics make agreements about exchange difficult to design and to enforce and call for special institutional arrangements that impose an appropriate structure on the actor's current and future behavior. In this literature, economic organizations are important. They emerge and take form as solutions to collective problems and as facilitators of gains from trade. They are good things. They make everybody better off (Moe 1990: 217).

Recent applications of transaction cost economics to politics (Weingast and Marshall 1988) attempt to explain the organization of Congress in the same way as the organization of business firms, while recognizing one important difference between politics and private markets. Political actors cannot simply engage in market exchange, as economic actors can, but must make decisions under majority rule, which is inherently unstable. This is reflected in the kinds of institutions that they ultimately adopt.

Cogent as it is, this analysis ignores an important part of the story, namely that politics fundamentally is about the exercise of public authority and the struggle to gain control over that authority (Moe 1990: 221). When two poor individuals and one rich individual make up a polity governed by majority rule, the rich person is in trouble. He is not in trouble, as Weingast and Shepsle might suppose, because majority rule is unstable. Nor is he in trouble because a prisoners' dilemma prevents the three participants from realizing gains from trade. He is in trouble because the poor participants will take advantage of the public authority to invade his wealth (Moe 1990). They win and he loses. In this sense, politics cannot be well-understood in terms of voluntary exchange and gains from trade.

Because property rights are never fully vested in a democratic political system, the issue of effective organization is of central importance in the politics of structural choice. Groups seek to ensure that their favored policies and programs are carried out as effectively as possible. This strongly influences the positions that they adopt and the strategies that they pursue in the political struggle. In democratic politics, public authority does not belong to any individual or group. It simply exists, attached to various public offices that are accessed by those who temporarily win the right to its exercise. Political uncertainty implies, moreover, that whatever today's winners create stands to be subverted or destroyed without compensation by tomorrow's winners.

Recognizing the dangers of political uncertainty, today's winners fashion structures designed to insulate their favored programs from the future exercise of public authority, albeit thus reducing their own as well as their opponents' opportunities. They want their organizations to be effective, and they also want to control them; however, they dare not design them for effectiveness and control, lest they later be turned against them (Moe 1990: 228).

For this reason, structure cannot always be viewed, in political markets, as a means to an end, since the link between structure and mandate is frequently severed as a response to political uncertainty. Moreover, the link may be severed not only by the winners but also by the losers. For the losers cannot simply exit the system. Trapped as they are, they participate also in the design of agencies and programs that they fundamentally oppose. They use such power as they have to design structures that will fail to achieve the goals for which they are explicitly designed.

The reality of public authority also conditions the nature of the principal–agent relationship that exists between the voters and interest groups on the one hand and the legislators and presidents whom they elect to office on the other. Although the voters and interest groups nominally are the superiors in this hierarchy, it is the legislators who actually hold public office and reserve the right to make the law. Although technically they are agents, legislators access the public authority with the full support of the police powers of the state. They are empowered for the duration of their term of office to tell their principals precisely what they must do. In this sense, the tables are turned on the principal–agent relationship that exists in the private sector. Even the authority to make laws governing the nature of elections rests with public officials and not with voters.

The situation is more complex in the US than in parliamentary systems of government because of the independent authority vested in the presidency. Presidents are not important solely because of the constraints that they impose on legislators through the use of the veto power. They are very powerful independent players in the politics of structural choice, far more to be feared in this aspect than any individual legislator; often more to be feared than Congress as a whole. The president after all is the chief executive and, as such, exercises a range of formal powers in managing and controlling the public bureaucracy from the Executive Office.

As chief executive, the president is empowered to make many structural choices on his own without going through the legislative process. If the legislature chooses to foreclose such options it must engage in the difficult process of legislation and run the gamut of the presidential veto. Even if such legislation succeeds, the president can utilize his considerable administrative discretion to qualify the impact of the new laws. After all, the public authority required to implement legislation resides within the executive branch of government.

The presidential impact on policy is not of consequence simply because presidents are powerful, but also because the interests that they pursue are often sharply divergent from those pursued in the legislature. In part, this divergence is due to differences in constituency. Legislators are tied to the relatively narrow interests of their districts or their states and must be highly responsive to the lobbying of special interest groups. Presidents deal with a more heterogeneous national constituency in which specialized lobbying is more exposed to the general will. In addition, presidents are only exposed to re-election considerations during their initial term. Thereafter, they tend to become more preoccupied with effective governance and with their historical legacy than with their dynasty.

In consequence, the president is the only actor on the political stage who is motivated to create a coordinated, centrally directed bureaucracy responsive to his agenda. His large, heterogeneous, competitive constituency, together with the lower priority accorded to re-election, provides him with substantial autonomy to pursue his own vision of the public agenda through a coherent bureaucratic machine that he can control from the top. Legislators, in contrast, are more than willing to build the bureaucracy piecemeal without any concern that it makes sense as an organizational whole.

The special interest groups that seek to control the political process thus have rational grounds for fearing the autonomy both of legislators and of presidents, the latter more than the former. One solution is to pressure current legislative majorities to embed in the statutes detailed restrictions on virtually every aspect of an agency's behavior. Such constraints are designed to limit the potential damage to the special interest agenda inherent in a future shift in the legislative majority or in the exercise of presidential prerogative. Presidents, in turn, impose their own bureaucratic mechanism to counteract those imposed upon them by an alien Congress.

This tension between interest groups, legislators and the president may create – has indeed created in the case of trade protection policy – what looks like an organizational mess. The mess is rational and not chaotic, driven by the peculiar characteristics of the separation of powers in a constitutional republic (Moe 1990: 238). There is even a sense (ignored by Moe) in which such an apparent mess may have been anticipated and accepted by the Founding Fathers as a necessary price for ensuring that no single branch of government (the legislature) could ever completely dominate the political process and thus destroy the checks and balances of the US Constitution.

If the president can indeed play an influential role in US trade politics it is important to evaluate the kind of role that predictably he will play, especially in so far as that role will diverge from that of Congress. Once again, public choice offers an invaluable lens through which to focus on presidential trade politics. We assume that a first-term president is interested in repaying election debts and in securing a second term and that a second-term president is interested in repaying election debts, providing effective governance and securing a dynasty.

Since his constituency is broader than that of members of Congress, the president tends to be responsive to interests that may not fare well in Congress because of the logic of collective action. Generally, the president will be less protectionist than Congress unless (as in the case of President Hoover) the specifics of the electoral college calculus dictate a protectionist stance. The more politically transparent the trade policy issue, the less protectionist will be the presidential position. On less transparent issues (notably VERs), however, the president may be as protectionist as any congressman, irrespective of his own political party affiliation, his campaign rhetoric, or even his personal political ideology.

3 The protectionist tilt of the executive branch

Public-choice theory suggests that United States presidents will adopt positions less favorable to trade protection than those favored by Congress but more favorable to protection than those advocated by the large majority of economists, irrespective of ideology (Rowley and Thorbecke 1993). This moderating influence of presidential interventions predictably will be more marked in the case of major legislation where public interest in the issue is aroused and where the presidential intervention is relatively transparent.

However, in the case of specific issues in administered protection, where public interest is dormant and where the presidential intervention is opaque and hidden, presidents will take a more protectionist position, sometimes even more protectionist than Congress itself.

References

Arrow, K.J. (1950) 'A difficulty in the concept of social welfare', *Journal of Political Economy* 58: 328–46.

Baldwin, R.E. (1985) *The Political Economy of US Import Policy* (Cambridge, Mass.: The MIT Press).

Baldwin, R.E. (1988) *Trade Policy in a Changing World Economy* (Chicago: University of Chicago Press).

Destler, I.M. (1986) *American Trade Politics: System under Stress* (New York: Twentieth Century Fund).

Heclo, H. (1977) *A Government of Strangers* (Washington, D.C.: The Brookings Institute).

Moe, T.M. (1990) 'Political institutions: the neglected side of the story', *Journal of Law, Economics and Organization*, 6: 213–54.

Moe, T.N. (1991) 'Politics and the theory of organization', *Journal of Law, Economics and Organization* 7: 106–29

Rowley, C.K. (1993) 'Introduction', in C.K. Rowley (ed.), *Public Choice Theory*, vol. I (Aldershot, Hants.: Edward Elgar) ix–xxix .

Rowley, C.K. and Thorbecke, W. (1993) 'The role of the Congress and the executive in US trade policy determination: a public choice analysis', in M. Hilf and E.-U. Petersman (eds), *National Constitutions and International Economic Law* (Boston, Mass.: Kluwer Academic Publishers), 347–69.

Weingast, B.R. (1981) 'Republican reregulation and deregulation', *Journal of Law and Contemporary Problems,* 44: 147–73.

Weingast, B.R. and Marshall, W.J. (1988) 'Why legislatures, like firms, are not organized as markets', *Journal of Political Economy*, 96: 132–63.

7   The Bureaucracy

1   Introduction

'Work expands so as to fill the time available for its completion' (Parkinson 1957). With these fateful words C. Northcote Parkinson launched the modern theory of bureaucracy and challenged at its roots the earlier theory of bureaucracy dominated by Weberian notions of impartial, efficient service by government officials concerned to serve the public interest as interpreted by their governments (Weber 1947). *Parkinson's Law* (as it became known) was a scientific statement derived from detailed statistical analysis first of British Admiralty data and subsequently of British Colonial Office data, each compiled over an extensive period of time.

The strength of the British Navy in 1914 could be shown to be 146,000 officers and men, 3,249 dockyard officials and clerks and 57,000 dockyard workmen. By 1928, there were only 100,000 officers and men, but the dockyard officials and clerks by then numbered 4,558. Yet the number of warships was a mere fraction of its 1914 strength: 20 capital ships in commission as compared with 62. Over the same period, the number of Admiralty officials had increased from 2,000 to 3,560, providing 'a magnificent navy on land'. The Navy had diminished by a third in men and by two-thirds in ships and its size was limited for the foreseeable future by the Washington Naval Agreement. Yet the number of Admiralty officials had grown at an annual rate of 5.6 percent throughout this period of significant decline.

The administrative staff at the British Colonial Office grew from 372 in 1932 to 1,661 in 1954, despite the major shrinkage of the British Empire as colonies successfully achieved self-government. The peacetime rate of increase averaged 5.24 percent per annum between 1935 and 1939, and 6.55 percent per annum between 1947 and 1954, percentages remarkably similar to those of the Admiralty staff as outlined above. Parkinson hypothesized on this basis that the staff in any public administrative department would grow at annual percentage rate (X) given by the formula

$$X = 100\frac{(2k^m + 1)}{yn} \tag{7.1}$$

where k represents the number of staff seeking promotion through the appointment of subordinates, 1 represents the difference between the ages of appointment and retirement, m represents the number of man-hours devoted to answering minutes within the departments, *n* represents the number of effective units being administered, and *y* represents the number of original staff.

According to *Parkinson's Law*, staff increase in any public bureau at an annual rate between 5.17 and 6.56 per cent, irrespective of any variation in the amount of work (if any) to be done (Parkinson 1957: 14).

If the publication of *Parkinson's Law* coincided with a rising undercurrent of popular criticism of bureaucrats on grounds of laziness and insensitivity to citizen's preferences ('busy loafers', as Nikita Krushchev contemptuously labelled them), economists intent on remedying alleged failures of private markets by government intervention continued to ignore the writing on the wall. Nevertheless, the work attracted the attention of a small group of scholars during the early 1960s as they laid the foundations of the new discipline of public choice.

In 1965, the first fruit of the public-choice revolution appeared with the publication by Gordon Tullock of *The Politics of Bureaucracy* (Tullock 1965), in which the utility-maximizing model for the first time was applied to *Homo bureaucraticus*. Tullock focused attention on the merit-based selection and promotion procedures of the US federal bureaucracy which tend (in his view) to favor intelligent, ambitious and somewhat unscrupulous individuals, thus providing a bias against moral behavior within the organizational hierarchy, the desire to get ahead typically outweighing the desire to promote the public interest.

Tullock consolidated the theoretical basis for Parkinson's law by emphasizing the role of unscrupulous behavior as an explanation of bureaucratic imperialism. He also identified the problem of information loss (whispering down the lane) as a chronic component of the over-centralized, hierarchial bureaucracy that is essential to effective career advancement on the part of *homo bureaucraticus*. This combination of unscrupulous behavior and information loss gives rise to a serious problem of control in which those formally responsible for the behavior of a bureau simply lose control over their subordinates, who then divert the organization to their own agendas.

Drawing upon Tullock's contribution, Anthony Downs (1967) in his book *Inside Bureaucracy* subjected *homo bureaucraticus* to rigorous scrutiny and derived a number of testable hypotheses (he elevates them to the status of laws), most of which have survived subsequent empirical testing:

Law of Increasing Conservatism: All generations tend to become more conservative as they become older, unless they experience periods of very rapid growth or internal turnover.

Law of Hierarchy: Coordination of large-scale activities without markets requires a hierarchical authority structure.

Law of Imperfect Control: No one can fully control the behavior of a large organization.

Law of Diminishing Control: The larger any organization becomes, the weaker is the control over its actions exercised by those at the top.

Law of Increasing Coordination: The larger any organization becomes, the poorer is the coordination among its actions.

Law of Counter-control: The greater the effort made by a top-level official to control the behavior of subordinate officials, the greater the efforts made by those subordinates to evade or counteract such control.

Law of Self-serving Loyalty: All officials exhibit relatively strong loyalty to the organization controlling their job security and promotion.

Law of Interorganizational Conflict: Every large organization is in partial conflict with every other social agent that it deals with.

The implementation of US trade policy is significantly dependent upon the performance of federal bureaux and independent agencies, notably the Office of the United States Trade Representative, the *Department of Commerce* (the *International Trade Administration*) and the *International Trade Commission*, but also many others. The early public-choice analysis above outlined cast serious doubts on the ability and willingness of such bureaux and agencies to carry out the explicit responsibilities defined by the laws and regulations that define their respective mission. The remainder of this chapter reviews subsequent contributions to the economics of bureaucracy in an attempt to assess the precise relationship between Congress, the executive branch and the federal bureaucracy that shapes the implementation of trade protection policies in the United States.

2 The budget-maximizing bureaucrat

The early public-choice critiques of bureaucracy focused attention on the self-interested behavior of senior bureaucrats, on the chronic inefficiency of internal bureaucratic organization and on the inevitable loss of information and control associated with hierarchical command structures. Each of these critiques of the public-interest model centered attention on the internal organization of bureaucracy and ignored the external environment against which bureaucratic behavior occurs. All this changed in 1971 with William Niskanen's book *Bureaucracy and Representative Government*.

Niskanen defined a bureau as a non-profit organization, financed primarily by an appropriation or grant from a sponsor, in which no individual can appropriate legally any part of the difference between revenues and costs as direct personal income. In such circumstances, self-seeking senior bureaucrats will evidence an interest in any budget surplus only to the extent that such a surplus can be utilized in ways that augment their individual utilities and only to the extent that such a surplus is not subject to mandatory confiscation by the sponsor.

If bureaucrats are not the neutered eunuchs of Max Weber's vision, attention shifts to their personal motivations as an indispensable prerequisite for predicting their responses to the reward–cost structure that confronts them. Niskanen (1971) suggested that the principal components of a senior bureaucrat's utility function – power, money income, security, perquisites of office and patronage – are all positive monotonic functions of budget size, and that an additional component – the easy life – is a positive monotonic function of budget growth. In such circumstances, senior bureaucrats would coalesce in favor of policies predicted to result in large and growing budgets, irrespective of the dictates of laws and regulations defining their mission or of ideological differences concerning the appropriate direction of the bureau's policies.

Given that bureaucrats seek to maximize the size of their budgets, the constraint that ultimately limits the size of it is the requirement that it must supply the output expected by its sponsor at the time the bureau's budget appropriation was determined. The necessary condition for achieving the

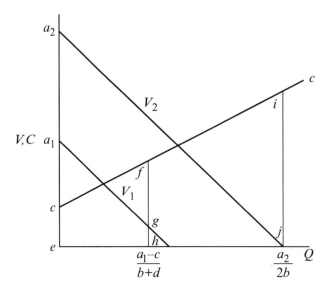

Figure 7.1   Equilibrium output of a bureau

expected output is that the budget must be equal to or greater than the minimum total expected cost of supplying this level of output. This constraint is a critical element from which Niskanen develops a theory of bureaucratic non-market equilibrium.

In Figure 7.1 a one-period relationship is depicted between a bureau, considered to be a monopoly supplier of the service but a competitive purchaser of factor imputs, and a legislative committee sponsor that is assumed not to exercise its potential monopoly power as a single buyer of the service, either because of lack of incentive or lack of opportunity. The total potential budget available to the bureau is represented by the budget-output function, let us say:

$$B = aQ - bQ^2 \quad 0 < Q < \frac{a}{2b} \tag{7.2}$$

The minimal total cost is represented by the cost function, let us say:

$$TC = cQ + dQ^2, \quad 0 < Q \tag{7.3}$$

The budget constraint is represented as:

$$B \geq TC \tag{7.4}$$

In Figure 7.1, V_1 represents a situation in which the sponsor's demand function for the bureau's services is relatively low, as represented by the marginal valuation function of the sponsor (legislative subcommittee). The marginal cost function of the bureau is given by cC. The equilibrium output of the bureau, in this case, is *budget-constrained* at output $a_1 - c/b + d$ where the area of the polygon ea_1gh is equal to the area of the polygon $ecfh$. At this output, the bureau must be technically efficient since its total budget just equals its minimum total cost. The output of the bureau is higher than politically optimal, assuming that the sponsor's marginal valuation function somehow reflects the preferences of the median voter. This is evidenced by the fact that marginal cost, hf, exceeds marginal value, hg, at the output equilibrium.

For higher sponsor demand conditions, however, represented in Figure 7.1 by the marginal valuation function V_2, the equilibrium output of the bureau is *demand-constrained*, with the marginal value of output equal to zero at output $a_2/2b$. The total budget at this output, given by the area of the triangle ea_2j, exceeds minimum total cost given by the polygon $ecij$. At the equilibrium output, therefore, the bureau is technically inefficient, with surplus budget wasted on unnecessary outlays. Output is much higher than the politically optimal level (twice as high in the linear case depicted in Figure 7.1, with marginal cost at ji and with the marginal value of the service at zero).

To obtain these results, Niskanen assumes that the bureau typically operates like a price-discriminating monopolist securing for itself the total surplus by offering a total output in return for a total budget appropriation. Bureaux are assumed to benefit from asymmetric information, being better informed than their sponsors regarding production costs. The asymmetry gives rise, in high-demand conditions, to overmanning, excessive on-the-job leisure, gold-plating of offices, excessive travel and entertainment and cost-inefficient input purchases, all despite periodic oversight reviews and repeated media exposures.

The early confidence expressed by Niskanen in 1971 that bureaucrats would always pursue budget-maximizing goals waned somewhat following criticisms by reviewers who sensed that alternative behavior patterns were compatible with utility maximization by senior bureaucrats (Migue and Belanger 1974). At issue in this tension over budget objectives is the precise balance struck among members of the top-level bureaucracy between those working primarily for money income, security and the easy life, which rest predominantly on budget size and rate of growth, and those seeking power, perquisites of office and patronage, which rest predominantly on the size of the discretionary budget that remains once the total cost of the bureau's output has been accounted for. Furthermore, since all bureaucrats are rational, the balance between budget size and budget discretion ultimately pursued by the bureau will depend not only upon the distribution of underlying preferences but also upon the particular reward–cost environment within which bureaucrats pursue their goals.

To illustrate, let us suppose that the utility function of each senior bureaucrat takes the form

$$U = aY^{w1}p^{v1} \qquad (7.5)$$

where Y is the present value of expected personal income, security and the easy life, P is the present value of power, perquisites of office and patronage, and w_1 and v_1 differ according to individual predisposition.

Further let us suppose that the reward structure confronting such bureaucrats takes the form

$$Y = a_2 Q^{w2} (B - C)^{v2} \qquad (7.6)$$

and

$$P = a_3 Q^{w3} (B - C)^{v3} \qquad (7.7)$$

where Q is the output of the bureau, B is the maximum budget that would be approved by the legislature, C is the minimum cost of producing the output of the bureau, and $B-C$ is the discretionary budget.

A specific theory of budgetary behavior must be based on the characteristics of equations (7.5)–(7.7). For example, a bureaucrat's reward structure is characterized by a relatively low value of v_2 since the budget residual cannot be diverted into personal income. The parameters w_2, w_3 and v_3, however, tend to be relatively high. If the w terms are low throughout the three equations and the v terms are relatively high, the senior bureaucrats will opt for a budget size that maximizes the discretionary budget and that falls well short of the maximum budget technically available. If the w terms are high and the v terms are low, the maximum budget will be pursued, in the limit, at the cost of all budgetary discretion.

In the case of a demand-constrained bureau, bureaucrats face a genuine choice between budget size and budgetary discretion, with their choices determined by the precise nature of equations (7.5)–(7.7). In the case of the budget-constrained bureau, there is no ultimate choice available since the feasible budget excludes discretion and imposes a bureau output at which total revenue equals minimum total cost. Predictably, bureaucrats will lobby the legislature to avoid budget-constrained scenarios.

3 Why the worst get on top

Surely, it might be argued against the economic theory of bureaucracy, that individuals engage in public service because they are highly motivated to serve the public interest and because they are especially immune to the temptations of narrow self-seeking. In such circumstances, might not the economic theory of bureaucracy ignore unjustifiably the ability of the 'great and the good' to contain *Homo bureaucraticus* and to direct their bureaux much along the lines outlined by Max Weber (1947)? Not so, according to Friedrich Hayek in his 1944 book *The Road to Serfdom*.

In Hayek's view, there are strong reasons for believing that what may appear to be the worst features of such totalitarian regimes as Hitler's Germany, Stalin's Russia and Franco's Spain are not accidental byproducts but phenomena that all organizations based on command structures are certain sooner or later to produce. The key questions to be answered, he suggests, are what moral views will be produced by a collectivist organization and what views are likely to rule it.

In Hayek's opinion, the two central features of every collectivist system – and here we are viewing bureaus as collectivist systems – are the need for a commonly accepted system of ends of the group and the all-overriding desire to give to the group the maximum power to achieve these ends. From these two central features grows a definite system of morals that does not leave the

individual conscience free to apply its own rules but rather promulgates the
principle that the end justifies the means:

> The *raison d'état* in which collectivist ethics has found its most explicit formula-
> tion, knows no other limit than that set by expediency – the suitability of the
> particular act for the end in view. ... There can be no limit to what its citizen must
> be prepared to do, no act which his conscience must prevent him from commit-
> ting, if it is necessary for an end which the community has set itself or which his
> superiors order him to achieve. (Hayek 1944: 147)

Once it is admitted that the individual is merely a means to serve the ends
of some higher entity (in this case the bureau leader), most of those factors of
totalitarian regimes which horrify us follow of necessity. From the collectivist
standpoint, intolerance and brutal suppression of dissent are essential and
unavoidable consequences of this basic premise. Where there is one common, overriding end, there is no room for any general morals or rules. To be a
useful assistant in the running of such an institution, it is not enough that a
man should be prepared to accept specious justification of vile deeds; he must
himself be prepared actively to break every moral rule he has ever known if
this seems necessary to achieve the end set for him.

Since in any command structure it is the supreme leader who alone determines the ends, his instruments must have no moral convictions of their own.
In itself, this will discourage men of good morals from aspiring to leading
positions, while offering special opportunities for the ruthless and unscrupulous. There will be jobs to be done the badness of which, taken by themselves, is beyond doubt, positions in which it is necessary to practice cruelty
and intimidation, deliberate deception and spying. Yet it is through such jobs
and positions that the road to the highest positions in any bureaucratic system
leads.

4   The theory of bureau dominance

If senior bureaucrats are not motivated to serve the public interest, and if
their incentive structure encourages them to seek either maximum budgets or
maximum budgetary discretion, what checks, if any, exist against the potential abuses of power that might occur? In this section, the role of the legislature as overseer of bureaucratic behavior is analyzed through the lens of
public choice (Niskanen 1971, 1975).

In his 1971 model, Niskanen noted that bureaux typically are financed by a
single or dominant collective organization, which in turn is financed by tax
revenues or by compulsory contributions. In the case of federal bureaux and
agencies, oversight and appropriations authority is vested in the relevant
subcommittees of Congress. The relationship between bureau and legislative
subcommittee is analyzed by Niskanen as one of bilateral monopoly, and is

characterized by both threats and deference, by both gaming and appeals to a common objective (Niskanen 1971).

Because the members of the legislative subcommittees typically are more concerned with re-election issues than with bureau-monitoring and because their electoral constituents tend to be rationally ignorant concerning their subcommittee activities, Niskanen argues that they tend to be easily diverted from their oversight and appropriations responsibilities. Given the asymmetric access to relevant budget information available to bureau heads, the bureau is provided with 'overwhelmingly dominant monopoly power' (Niskanen 1971: 30).

Under such conditions, the committee review process is a farce. The bureaux estimate the largest budget that will be approved by Congress and add a few percent based on the historical record of reductions made by the subcommittee. The review committees oblige by making the expected reductions. Congress dutifully approves the budget recommended by the committee.

Even though the interests of the review committee and the bureau may not be identical, Niskanen argues that they are often consistent, not least because the review committee tends to be manned by high-demand congressmen concerned to service constituents who stand to benefit directly from the bureau's output. Even when the interests diverge, the low incremental benefits to the review committee and the high cost of an effective review typically will induce the subcommittee to endorse the bureau's budget appeal.

In 1975, Niskanen extended his model to incorporate more formally the predicted behavior of the government officials who establish the demand for government service and who monitor the behavior of the bureaux. The four characteristics of the legislature deemed to be central to this analysis are: majority rule decision-making; committee review; vote-maximizing behavior by legislators; and legislator discretion in the use of his own time and resources. These characteristics are combined with the specific institutions of the review process to analyze the likely nature and impact of legislative oversight.

Niskanen noted that, at least in the United States, most review committees are dominated by legislators who have higher demands for the services reviewed than the median demand in the whole legislature Committee decisions are very seldom amended or reversed by the whole legislature. Most legislators receive the committee assignments that they request; and the requests tend to be correlated with services that are most important to their regional constituencies. For these reasons, the output preferred by a bureau will be much closer to that of a high-demand review committee than to that preferred by the median legislator. However, a high-demand committee has the same incentives to control production in efficiency as would a randomly selected committee. In Niskanen's view, a high-demand committee is 'in the bureau's pocket' only with respect to the output decision.

Because legislators are endowed with substantial discretion in the use of their time and staff resources, and because the monitoring function is a public good within the legislature, there exists a substantial free-rider problem internal to legislatures and the expectation that monitoring activities will be undersupplied, especially where it might upset influential interest groups. Predictably, legislators from districts that pay only a small share of the total taxes appropriated to federal bureaux will spend most of their time on activities specific to their respective districts. In the case of the United States legislature, where the party leadership cannot effectively sanction individual legislators to enforce activities that are beneficial to the group, the free-rider problem is substantial.

For these reasons, Niskanen (1975) confirms his earlier predictions that there will be overspending by government bureaux and that such overspending will take the form both of inefficiency in producing a given set of outputs and a higher than optimal level of some outputs. Niskanen does not address the equally important question whether or not legislative oversight is capable of biassing the nature of a bureau's output. Given his emphasis on bureau independence, however, his predictable answer to that question must be that it will only rarely do so.

5   The theory of congressional dominance

The congressional dominance approach assumes that congressmen – or more specifically, particular congressmen on the relevant committees – possess sufficient rewards and sanctions to create an incentive system for agencies (Weingast and Moran 1983). Notwithstanding agency mandates, rewards go to those agencies that pursue policies of interest to current committee members. Those agencies that fail to do so are confronted with sanctions. It follows that if the incentive system works effectively, then agencies will pursue congressional goals even though they receive little direct guidance from their overseers.

Congressmen on the relevant committees may appear ignorant of agency proceedings because they evaluate the success of programs indirectly through constituents' reactions rather than through detailed study. Since public hearings and investigations are costly of staff time, congressmen will use them sparingly in the case of bureaux that smoothly benefit congressional clientele. Significant use of such instruments will be reserved for bureaux that fail to take care of such considerations. Indeed, the threat of such *ex post* sanctions will be deployed to create *ex ante* incentives for a bureau to serve its congressional clientele. The more effective this incentive system, the less often we should observe sanctions in the form of congressional hearings and investigations (Weingast and Moran 1983).

A number of factors jointly make up the congressional incentive system. First, in the budgeting process, each agency competes with many others for budgetary support. Within the federal system, some 2,000 agencies confront only thirteen subcommittees of the Appropriations Committee. Each subcommittee develops only one bill that (as amended) becomes the actual federal budget allocation. Congressmen pursuing their own electoral goals predictably will favor those bureaux that best service their constituents. This factor is largely ignored by Niskanen in his theory of bureau dominance.

Second, oversight plays a significant role in sanctioning aberrant bureaux. Congressional subcommittees wield a number of such sticks, including threatened or actual new legislation, specific prohibitions on bureau activities, and other interventions designed to embarrass senior bureaucrats, to hurt their future career opportunities or to obstruct their pet projects. A compliant bureau will escape such costly oversight.

Third, Congress ultimately controls who gets appointed and reappointed to senior bureau positions. In some instances, the battle over such appointments manifests itself in lengthy confirmation hearings. More usual is the somewhat perfunctory hearing preceded by active congressional participation in the selection of nominees or in the careful accounting by the executive branch of congressional preferences on this matter. Even if a congressional subcommittee often fails to secure its ideal appointment to an agency headship, it can always guarantee that it will not confirm a nominee that it really dislikes, however much that nominee is favored by the president.

For these reasons, evidence of a lack of direct and continuous congressional action in ongoing bureau matters does not necessarily support the theory of bureau dominance over the theory of congressional dominance. With this in mind, advocates of the theory of congressional dominance (Weingast and Moran 1983; Rowley and Elgin 1985) turned to the development of a more specific model and more appropriate tests. In this analysis, it is assumed that each congressmen responds to the interests within his state or district, choosing actions so as to maximize his political support function, i.e. that he votes his district.

Because interests are not distributed uniformly across districts, the groups that are important for one legislator's electoral fortunes differ from those that are important for another's. This implies that there are gains to legislators from devising a means of regularizing the provision of benefits to a variety of groups and of avoiding intergroup conflict. The institutional mechanism deployed for this purpose by Congress is the committee system, which allocates influence over policy-making in a manner designed to make all legislators better off. In stylized form, the system works as follows.

First, committees have near-monopoly jurisdiction over a small set of policy issues. This includes the power to make proposals that alter the *status quo* (subject to majority rule approved by the legislature and presidential signature) as well as effective veto power over proposals made by others. In this way, committees provide members with extraordinary influence over a small set of policy issues in return for sacrificing influence over other policies.

Second, members are assigned to committees to a considerable extent on the basis of self-selection (Shepsle 1978). The advantage to each member is that he gains greater leverage over precisely those issues that are relevant for his own political support and hence his re-election. Congressmen therefore tend to specialize in a small portfolio of policy issues that are not easily divested without a significant sacrifice in terms of committee seniority. In such circumstances, congressmen have powerful inclinations, as principals, to monitor the behavior and performance of their bureaucratic agents, despite Niskanen's arguments to the contrary.

This approach yields two testable implications for policy-making: (a) specific oversight committees should be observed to have more influence than the rest of Congress over a particular agency; (b) the following comparative statics result should hold: if the interests represented on the committee change, then so too should agency policy. These implications are evaluated with respect to the empirical evidence concerning the behavior of the International Trade Commission in Chapter 10 of this book. The available evidence strongly supports the theory of congressional dominance as above outlined.

The thrust of this theory is bold and clear (Moe 1987): Congress successfully controls the bureaucracy through fire-alarm oversight backed by powerful rewards and sanctions. Because Congress is in the driver's seat, it is appropriate to explain and to predict bureaucratic performance simply by modelling the determinants of subcommittee members' preferences within the legislature. As it is presented by Weingast and Moran (1983), this is a very strong claim that, in our view, significantly overstates the nature of the principal–agent relationship that exists between Congress and the federal bureaux and agencies. The claim merits close consideration at two levels, namely (a) institutional complexities, and (b) property right limitations.

Institutional complexities
The hub of the efficient-governance hypothesis is the assumption that congressional committees exercise near-monopoly jurisdiction rights over specific federal bureaux and agencies, thus defining property rights that encourage effective downward monitoring designed to eliminate adverse agency discretion. However, the institutional problems of monitoring bureaux are much more serious than those of monitoring corporations (Rowley and Elgin 1985; Rowley and Vachris 1993).

First, there is no capital market mechanism in the public sector capable of signalling adverse performance by marking down stock values. The absence of this mechanism implies that stock option schemes cannot be utilized by principals to reward bureaucrats who improve the economic performance of their respective bureaux. Closely associated with this weakness is the absence of an effective outside labor market for bureaucrats comparable to that for senior corporate executives, further weakening incentives for upward and downward monitoring by individual bureaucrats to moderate shirking within a team production environment (Alchian and Demsetz 1972; Fama 1980).

Second, the concept of output is much more nebulous in the case of bureaux than in that of corporate enterprise, with evident implications for monitoring effective performance. Even where physical output itself can be unambiguously identified, legislative goals tend to be less clear cut and consistent than is the profit yardstick for corporate enterprise. Even when legislative goals are clearly defined, the monopoly nature of most federal bureaux implies that principals have no outside benchmark against which to review bureaucratic performance.

Third, to the extent that fire-alarm oversight works successfully to constrain agency behavior, it does so because it is backed by the strategic use of legislative resources (Moe 1987). It is open to question just how effective these resources really are. It is well known, for example, that most agencies seek larger budgets most of the time and thus that budgets can be used as rewards and sanctions. It is also evident that agency activity is a function of how much money it receives and how that money is distributed across programs. No doubt subcommittees can play on these facts to constrain agency behavior. It is less than easy, however, to generate desired results.

A fundamental problem arises because the budget plays two roles: one that shapes bureaucratic incentives, and one that provides a financial foundation for programmatic behavior. In the case of a deviant bureau, these often work at cross-purposes. As Moe (1987) indicates, if the subcommittee throws money at the bureau it rewards it for non-compliance. If the subcommittee slashes the budget as a punishment, it denies the bureau the resources it needs to comply with its wishes. There is no clear solution.

Use of the budget as a control mechanism is also problematic because a lot of players care about the outcome. Suppose, for example, that a House appropriations subcommittee threatens to slash a bureau's budget. It cannot do so unilaterally. The Senate Appropriations Committee may determine otherwise, as may the president, and both will make a mark upon the final budget. Even within the House, the subcommittee may fail to have its way. The authorizing committees (in both Houses) may object and if the House appropriations committee forces the issue it will then pay a price with respect to other potential initiatives. As Moe (1987) remarks, it is easy to exaggerate the power of the purse.

New laws can be designed to impact significantly on budgets, personnel, jurisdictions, and other matters about which bureaucrats care a great deal. Therefore, the potential for new legislation itself is a control mechanism available within the legislature. Like the budget, the threat of new legislation is clearly a useful but not a perfect instrument of control. First, it is far from easy to pass new legislation.

For example, a Senate subcommittee may threaten to narrow the jurisdiction of a deviant bureau. However, its proposal must work its way through the full committee, the full Senate, the corresponding House subcommittee, the full committee of the House, the full House, a Senate–House conference committee, the full House and the Senate once again, and then be signed by the president. The eventual outcome, if the law passes, may bear little resemblance to the initial threat and may have taken several years to come to pass. Most such threats fail, falling victim to one of the many veto points in the legislative process. As Moe (1987) notes, the reality of politics is that most threats are empty and this is known to all concerned.

Suppose, however, that the threatened legislation actually passes in some form. The subcommittee then confronts a new statutory context in which the old problems may reassert themselves. The conflict between the legislative subcommittee and its agency is not simply washed away by new laws. This is known to both parties at the outset and dilutes further the *ex ante* value of the subcommittee's threat even before the lengthy legislative process is set in motion. New laws, therefore, tend to be a desperate solution to serious principal–agent conflicts only occasionally, and then not always successfully, utilized to assert legislative control.

Weingast and Moran (1983: 769) suggest that 'perhaps the most effective means of influence is that Congress controls who gets appointed and re-appointed'. Moe (1987) correctly challenges this assertion on the ground that the power of appointment is fundamentally presidential. The House plays no role whatsoever in the appointments process. The Senate constitutionally is empowered to play a significant role through its responsibility for approving most important appointments. To the extent that it pursues this role aggressively, the Senate oversight committee will be more effective than its counterpart in controlling the behavior of its federal bureau.

In practice, Senate committees traditionally have adopted the view that, except in sensitive areas, the president has a right to build his own administrative teams in his own way. This deference is stronger when the same party controls the Senate and the presidency. It is weaker when a president pursues a mandate directly hostile to Senate committee agendas. Nevertheless, the norm of deference is strong and is widely adhered to. Moreover, even when differences emerge, the president can deploy his unique power and patronage to fragment opposition and to logroll in favor of his nominees. As we noted in Chapter 6, the president is by far the most powerful player on the political stage. There is really no basis for believing that the power of appointment offers Congress an effective means for the systematic control of bureaucratic behavior.

Property right limitations

Untruncated property rights provide individuals with clearly defined authority to use their resources as they wish and to transfer their resources to whomsoever they wish, whenever they so choose. Such rights, to be fully effective, must be enforceable through a well-functioning legal order. In such circumstances, it is predictable that the unambiguous determination of property rights will lead to efficient outcomes, regardless of the initial assignment of such rights, at least when transaction costs are low (Coase 1960).

The best example of such a right in capitalist economies is that of stock ownership in a publicly quoted corporation (Jensen and Meckling 1976; Fama 1980), for such stocks are highly divisible, clearly define rights of exclusive ownership, and are freely transferrable through an efficient market. In consequence, one of the most widely supported hypotheses in financial economics is that of the efficient capital market, in which stock prices are viewed as reflecting all publicly available information economically relevant to the performance of each quoted corporation. In such circumstances, rational behavior ensures that resources move to their highest-valued uses. The marketability of stock enables risk-averse stockholders to diversify their stock portfolios and to rely upon market specialists to monitor and to control the behavior of corporate management.

Property rights in political markets are much more attenuated than those in corporate stock (Rowley and Vachris 1993, 1994). Nowhere is this more clear than in the case of the committee structure of Congress. Rights in policy brokerage are strictly non-transferrable – though policy logrolling is endemic – since committee seats are not openly marketed. Nor do such seats readily capitalize the flow of future income, since periodic elections represent a threat to committee composition. Nor can risk-averse committee members diversify their portfolios of political rights in the manner of the corporate stockholder. For all these reasons, the congressional monitoring of federal bureaux will be less effective than capital market monitoring of corporate enterprise.

The hub of the efficient governance hypothesis is the assumption that congressional committees enjoy near-monopoly jurisdictions over well-defined sets of policy issues and that specialization in such jurisdictions provides strong incentives to ensure that the relevant bureaux efficiently service constituency interests. This hypothesis has merit, but must not be exaggerated. A significant weakness lies in the multiplicity of principals involved in agency governance (Rowley and Vachris 1993, 1994).

Multiplicity of principals arises from at least four sources: (a) the jurisdictional overlap of many oversight committees within each chamber of the legislature; (b) the duality of oversight inherent in a bicameral legislature; (c) jurisdictional conflicts between oversight and appropriations committees within each chamber; and (d) competition between Congress and the presidency. As we noted in Chapter 5, Shepsle and Weingast (1987) resolve the problem posed by jurisdictional conflicts within Congress in terms of the *ex post* veto powers of conference committees. Such powers are not to be exaggerated. Any weakening of committee power implicit in multi-principal bargaining opens up windows of discretionary opportunity that will be exploited by experienced bureaucrats, diluting the political efficiency of the committee system.

6   The impact of presidential politics

Because of the close interconnection between the special interests that invade political systems characterized by rational voter ignorance, the congressional committees that parlay special interest politics into law, and the federal bureaux that parlay the laws into policy, the combination of actors involved is referred to in political parlance as the iron triangles. Most of the literature of public choice exaggerates the tightness of such iron triangles, not just because it ignores the problems of institutional complexity and the attenuation of property rights within Congress, but also because it ignores the impact of the most important individual actor in US politics (Rowley and Vachris 1993, 1994; Rowley and Thorbecke 1993).

Weingast (1981) is almost alone among the major proponents of congressional dominance in recognizing the destabilizing influence over the iron triangles potentially available to an effective president when a combination of propitious circumstances occurs. First, the intervention must be a high presidential priority, especially when it is directed at an ongoing program rather than at a new program initiative. Second, the policy change must reflect a significant shift in broadly based public opinion, or in the relative balance between competing special interests. Third, the presidential constituency must be resilient to powerful counterpressures from the iron triangles exerted through the Washington establishment.

If these conditions hold, and if the president is popular within the broadly based electorate and is skilled in policy-making, even a robust iron triangle is vulnerable to destabilization. Inevitably, however, the process of attempted destabilization, especially if it involves a protracted conflict across the separation of powers, opens up opportunities for discretionary behavior by bureaucrats of the kind outlined in the theory of bureaucratic dominance.

References

Alchian, A.A. and Demsetz, H. (1972) 'Production, information costs and economic organization', *American Economic Review*, 62 (5): 777–95.

Coase, R.H. (1960) 'The problem of social cost', *Journal of Law and Economics*, III, 1–44.

Downs, A. (1967) *Inside Bureaucracy* (Boston, Mass.: Little, Brown).

Fama, E.F. (1980) 'Agency problems and the theory of the firm', *Journal of Political Economy*, 8: 288–307.

Hayek, F.A. (1944) *The Road to Serfdom* (Chicago: University of Chicago Press).

Jensen, M. and Meckling, W.H. (1976) 'The theory of the firm: managerial behavior, agency costs and ownership structure', *Journal of Financial Economics*, 3: 305–60.

Migue, J.L. and Belanger, G. (1974) 'Toward a general theory of managerial discretion', *Public Choice* 17: 27–42.

Moe, T.M. (1987) 'An assessment of the positive theory of congressional dominance', *Legislative Studies Quarterly*, XII (4): 475–520.

Niskanen, W.A. (1971) *Bureaucracy and Representative Government*, (Chicago: Aldine Press); reprinted in *Bureaucracy and Public Economics* (Aldershot, Hants and Brookfield, Vt.: Edward Elgar Publishing, 1994), 3–230.

Niskanen, W.A. (1975) 'Bureaucrats and politicians', *Journal of Law and Economics*, XVIII (3): 617–44; reprinted in *Bureaucracy and Public Economics* (Aldershot, Hants and Brookfield, Vt.: Edward Elgar Publishing, 1994), 243–67.

Parkinson, C.N. (1957) *Parkinson's Law and Other Studies in Administration* (New York: Ballantyne Books).

Rowley, C.K. and Elgin, R.S. (1985) 'Towards a theory of bureaucratic behavior', in D. Greenaway and G.K. Shaw (eds), *Public Choice, Public Finance and Public Policy* (Oxford: Basil Blackwell), 31–50.

Rowley, C.K. and Thorbecke, W. (1993) 'The role of the congress and the executive in US trade policy determination: a public choice policy analysis', in M. Hilf and E.-U. Petersmann (eds), *National Constitutions and International Law* (Boston, Mass.: Kluwer Academic Publishers).

Rowley, C.K. and Vachris, M.A. (1993) 'Snake oil economics versus public choice', in C.K. Rowley (ed.), *Public Choice Theory*, vol. III, (Aldershot, Hants and Brookfield, Vt.: Edward Elgar Publishing), 573–84.

Rowley, C.K. and Vachris, M.A. (1994) 'Why democracy in the United States does not produce efficient results', Locke Institute Working Paper, Fairfax.

Shepsle, K.A. (1978) *The Giant Jigsaw Puzzle* (Chicago: University of Chicago Press).

Shepsle, K.A. and Weingast, B.R. (1987) 'The institutional foundations of committee power', *American Political Science Review*, 81(1): 85–104.

Tullock, G. (1965) *The Politics of Bureaucracy* (Washington, D.C.: Public Affairs Press).

Weber, M. (1947) The *Theory of Social and Economic Organization* (New York: The Free Press).

Weingast, B.R. (1981) 'Republican reregulation and deregulation: the political foundation of agency–clientele relationships', *Journal of Law and Contemporary Problems*, 44: 147–73.

Weingast, B.R. and Moran, M.J. (1983) 'Bureaucratic discretion or congressional control: regulatory policy making by the Federal Trade Commission', *Journal of Political Economy*, 91: 765–800.

PART III

THE MARKET IN TRADE PROTECTION

8   Trade politics in the legislative branch

1   Introduction

The quantity of trade protection provided within an economy and the instruments used to provide it are determined in the political market place. Demanders of protection (import-competing firms, and labor unions and associated interests, as well as bureaucrats in relevant government departments and agencies) interact through brokers (Congress, the president and bureaucrats) with suppliers (export firms, and labor unions and associated interests, as well as consumers) to determine a trade protection equilibrium. The public-choice model yields specific predictions concerning how each of these actors will behave.

Interest groups

We assume that these are most effective when they represent small, well-organized segments of society. Firms and labor unions are both good examples of successful interest groups, capable of offering concentrated benefits to their members and of inducing a supply of pressure from members by coercion as well as by privatized benefits. We assume that firms and unions in import-competing industries will lobby for trade protection and that firms and unions in export industries will lobby for free trade. We further assume that multinational firms will lobby for free trade. We assume that large, diffuse interest groups that offer members only small benefits and that cannot exclude individuals from such benefits when they fail to supply pressure will be politically unsuccessful. Free-riding will erode lobbying effectiveness in such circumstances. In general, consumers' groups that favor free trade will be weakened by the free-rider problem. In general, competition among interest groups does not lead to economically efficient loss-minimizing policy outcomes.

Voters

We assume that all voters seek to maximize their expected utilities. Voters who stand to gain or to lose significantly from trade policy will be rationally well-informed about such matters. They will be immune to persuasive advertising on such issues by interest groups or by politicians. Such voters typically will be members of effective interest groups. The large majority of voters, who do not stand to gain or to lose significantly from trade policy on an individual basis, will be rationally ignorant about such matters. This category of voters will be vulnerable to persuasive advertising on trade policy issues by interest groups or by politicians, in some cases voting in favor of protection even though such policies actually harm them. If the costs of protection become egregious, the median voter will become rationally well-informed and will vote against it, typically securing less protectionist legislation and/or driving protectionism into opaque channels.

Bureaucrats

Senior bureaucrats are assumed to be expected utility maximizers pursuing such rewards as salary, perquisites, power, patronage, ease of management, and the quiet life. Each of these rewards is monotonic, increasing with the bureau's budget. Bureaux overseeing trade policy depend on the existence of trade protection to fuel large or growing budgets. Senior bureaucrats typically will lobby in favor of protectionist policies, whether or not they consider such policies to be wealth-maximizing for society.

Members of Congress

We assume that they seek to secure re-election and that they broker trade policies to this end. In doing so, they need to be sensitive to their geographic constituencies as well as to the political action committees that bankroll their campaigns. If their constituencies are dominated by specific industries, they will reflect the trade preferences of those industries. They will use committee and subcommittee agenda power to seek favor with their own constituencies. In trying to obtain trade protection benefits for their districts, they will logroll with colleagues, ignoring party differences. Committee and subcommittee chairmen, in particular, will manipulate agenda power to secure benefits for their districts and for those other special interests that support them. We also assume that on highly visible issues they will tend to vote with the opinion polls (especially those drawn from their own constituencies) in order to avoid disaffecting voters. On obscure issues, they will vote or maneuver to please the special interests that support them financially, even at some cost to more general constituency interests.

The President

We assume that a first-term president is interested in securing re-election and that a second-term president is interested in securing a dynasty and a place in history. Since his constituency is broader than that of members of Congress, the president tends to be responsive to interests that may not fare well in Congress because of the logic of collective action. Generally, therefore, the president will be less protectionist than Congress unless the specifics of the electoral college calculus dictate a protectionist stance. The more open the trade policy issue, the less protectionist will be the presidential position. On obscure issues, the president may be as protectionist as any congressional trade committee chairman, irrespective of political party affiliation or campaign rhetoric.

On the basis of such self-seeking motivations, the major actors behave in a highly predictable manner in the political market for trade protection. If the economy enters into recession, the demand for protection increases as import-competing industries confront declining sales and falling profits and contemplate labor layoffs. Simultaneously, the supply of export subsidies increases as constituency-conscious politicians seek to expand labor hirings through export-led economic expansion. Rationally ignorant voters predictably facilitate the brokering of increased protection in such circumstances in response to persuasive advertising by special interests that capitalizes on ephemeral trade-cycle factors to pursue mercantilist objectives.

Similar behavior follows any significant appreciation in the value of the dollar or any increase in the size of the trade deficit even when the latter is clearly a consequence of domestic budget imbalances. If politicians are able to develop ways to broker protection that are hidden from voters, predictably the equilibrium level of protection will rise, as they mine new margins of rent-seeking outlays available from import-competing special interests.

On the other hand, if inflation increases sharply, voters may become rationally well-informed and strike down tariff barriers (if not non-tariff barriers) in an attempt to restore price competition within the domestic economy. Similarly, sharp improvements in the terms of trade or in the trade balance tend to abate the demand for protection.

In section 2 of this chapter, we provide a brief overview of changing trade politics within the United States Congress over the period 1900–88. In section 3, we present a sequence of case studies of trade politics with respect to each major attempt at US trade legislation, 1930–88. In section 4, we review the overall evidence relevant to our thesis that US trade policy is driven by public choice and not by public interest considerations. The public-choice approach stands up remarkably well to this analysis.

2   Changing trade politics in the United States Congress

A number of generalizations can be drawn concerning trade policy in the United States during the twentieth century. First, Democratic presidents in this century have favored freer trade than Republican presidents, who have favored greater protection (Table 8.1). Even recent Republican presidents (Eisenhower, Nixon, Reagan, and Bush) have been somewhat more protectionist than Democrat presidents (Kennedy, Johnson, Carter). Second, the House of Representatives is generally more protectionist than the Senate or the president. Third, the focus of protectionist pressure in the House of

Table 8.1   Major United States trade legislation

Act	Year	Trade effect	President
Dingley	1897	Protectionist	R. McKinley
Payne–Aldrich	1909	Marginally freer trade	R. Taft
Underwood–Simmons	1913	Freer trade	D. Wilson
Fordney–McCumber	1922	Very protectionist	R. Harding
Smoot–Hawley	1930	Very protectionist	R. Hoover
Reciprocal Trade Agreement Act	1934[a]	Freer trade	D. Roosevelt
International trade negotiations			
Geneva	1947		
Annecy	1949		
Torquay	1950–51		
Dillon Round	1956–61		
Trade Expansion Act	1962	Freer trade	J. Kennedy
Kennedy Round negotiations	1964–7		
Burke-Hartlee Bill[b]	1970	Very protectionist	R. Nixon
Trade Act	1974	Freer trade	R. Nixon/G. Ford
Tokyo Round trade negotiations	1974–9		
Trade Act	1979	Freer trade	D. Carter
Trade Act	1988	Somewhat protectionist	R. Reagan

Notes:
[a]   Renewed by Congress eleven times, 1934–62
[b]   Did not pass.

Source: S.P. Magee, W.A. Brock and L. Young (1989) *Black Hole Tariffs and Endogenous Policy Theory* (Cambridge: Cambridge University Press), p. 182.

Representatives has switched from the Republican party (in 1900) to the Democratic party (today).

Fourth, prior to 1934 Congress largely controlled tariff levels, but after 1934 the executive branch was the dominant force. Fifth, as US tariff barriers have fallen since 1930, so US trade protection policy has shifted towards non-tariff barriers, notably in the form of voluntary export restraints (VERs). Sixth, the influence of political parties over US trading policy has waned during the second half of the twentieth century, eroded by the emergence of committee and subcommittee agenda powers, especially in the House of Representatives.

All the early protectionist tariff acts were passed during Republican administrations (McKinley, Taft, Harding, and Hoover). Similarly, major non-tariff barriers such as the oil import quota and VER agreements have been negotiated or imposed by Republican presidents (Eisenhower, Nixon, and Reagan). In contrast, trade liberalizing acts have tended to occur under Democratic presidents (Wilson, Roosevelt, Kennedy, and Carter). If one were to accept the Stolper–Samuelson hypothesis, this behavior would present a paradox: why should pro-labor Democratic presidents support freer trade than pro-capital Republican party presidents, who support protection, in an economy where labor is the relatively scarce factor input?

The answer to this apparent paradox, of course, is that the conditions underlying the Stolper–Samuelson hypothesis do not hold in the myopic environment of US trade politics. Lobbying with respect to trade policy in the United States follows the path of the Ricardo–Viner hypothesis, with labor and capital grouping in accordance with short-run import-competing or export goals and not on the basis of relative factor scarcity.

3   A public-choice analysis of US trade legislation: 1930–88

In this section, we shall demonstrate that the public choice model is a powerful lens through which to analyse specific trade laws enacted during the last 60 years in the United States. We consider the legislative histories of the Smoot–Hawley Tariff Act of 1930, the Reciprocal Trade Act of 1934, the Trade Expansion Act of 1962, the Trade Act of 1974, the Trade Agreements Act of 1979, the Trade and Tariff Act of 1984, and the Omnibus Trade Act of 1988. In each case, we show that the public-choice model, carefully articulated in terms of the specific characteristics of the political market, is invaluable in explaining the behavior of the major players and the actual policies enacted.

The Tariff Act of 1930

According to endogenous policy theory, circumstances were ideal in 1930 for an upward adjustment in the equilibrium rate of the average US *ad valorem* tariff. The rate of unemployment had risen from 3.6 percent in 1926 to 12.8 percent; inflation was running at a negative rate of 9.4 percent; US terms of trade had improved from 91.2 in 1926 to 97.8; the amount of labor used per $100,000 of capital had increased from 14.75 in 1926 to 15.15; and the amount of capital employed per unit of labor had declined from $6.778 in 1926 to $6.600. In the absence of any protectionist tilt from the political process, such conditions were auspicious for a tariff hike (Magee *et al.* 1989).

The protectionist tilt was provided by the 1928 elections which swept a Republican president, Herbert Hoover, into the White House and which resulted in landslide victories for the Republican party in both the House of

Representatives and the Senate. Both Hoover and the Republican party had campaigned on a trade protection platform, strongly endorsing the protectionist Fordney–McCumbar Act of 1922 (Schattschneider 1935: 7). Indeed, their stands in favor of protection were so unequivocal that the *New York Times* (10 Feb. 1929: 3) characterized high levels of trade protection as a tenet of Republican religious dogma. On October 27 1928, during the presidential campaign, Hoover called for a *'limited revision'* of tariffs on agricultural products (*New York Times*, 28 Oct. 1928: 1). Once the ballots were counted, the victorious Republicans immediately set out to raise the US tariff structure.

House action on the bill   The House Ways and Means Committee, dominated by Northeasterners, did not limit the revision to agriculture. On December 5 1928 they circulated a notice of upcoming tariff revisions and invited all interested parties to attend hearings. As Schattschneider (1935: 165) documents, the notice produced 'highly selective' responses, with well-organized interest groups responding and many other producers remaining unaware of the hearings. The notice attracted 1,100 respondents, who were heard with dispatch – 177 witnesses were heard in one four-day period, for example (Schattschneider 1935). The hearings were non-adversarial, and little attempt was made to verify whether data supplied to justify higher tariffs were accurate. The hearings ended on February 27, 1929, and the Republican majority of the committee then met to decide what tariffs to recommend.

This meeting among the Republican Committee members was in Taussig's (1931: 491) words, 'ideal for logrolling'. Each of the fifteen Republicans was assigned to several subcommittees, each consisting of a chairman and two other members. Each chairman was selected from a district which had an interest in the items under review. Each chairman supported benefits for the other members' districts in exchange for their support of benefits for his district. All fifteen members then met and used the recommendations of the subcommittees to draft a final bill. This bill, which was favorably reported to the House on May 7, raised duties substantially on agricultural products, clothing, chemicals, shingles, and other products. Containing 83,000 words, it failed to fulfil Hoover's wish for a *limited revision of agricultural tariffs*.

During debate in the House, as the *New York Times* reported (23 May 1929: 28), disappointed and angry members obtained higher tariffs to keep them in line on the final vote. A good example of the attempt to placate lobbyists and Congressmen came after cattle hides were granted a 10 percent duty. Leathermakers then complained that the cost of an input had gone up. They thus demanded a 10 percent duty to offset this, plus a little more for themselves. They received a 15 percent duty. Shoemakers then complained that the cost of one of their inputs had gone up. They demanded a 15 percent duty plus a little extra for themselves. They received a 20 percent duty (ibid). Taussig summarizes the outcome in the House by saying, 'everybody pretty much got what they wanted' (Taussig 1931: 495).

The increases in tariffs on non-agricultural items displeased farmers and their representatives. Representative Nelson from Missouri argued that the bill would hurt farmers because it did not increase the price of what they sold by enough but did increase the price of what they bought (*New York Times*, 23 May 1929: 28). Democrats from farm states were also displeased with the transfer of power to the president implied by the flexible tariff provision which gave the president broad powers to raise and lower tariffs unilaterally.

The bill, including the flexible tariff provision and tariff increases for a large number of goods such as construction items, clothing, shoes, and food, passed the House on May 27 1929 by a 264–147 vote. The vote was along party lines, except for twenty Democrats and twelve Republicans who crossed over. The Republican crossovers were mainly from the farmbelt, which was dissatisfied with the farm schedule.

Senate action on the bill   The bill next proceeded to the Senate Finance Committee, which announced public hearings on June 7 1929 and began them on June 14. The Chairman of the Senate Finance Committee was Reed Smoot (Republican, Utah). Smoot, according to the *New York Times* (23 May 1929: 28), never met a tariff wall which was too high. He was restrained, however, by the fact that the administration was concerned that the tariffs passed by the House were too high and were creating voter dissatisfaction.

By the end of August, the Republican members on the committee had agreed on a bill. It contained more rate decreases than increases from the House bill, probably due to Hoover's influence (see *New York Times*, 5 Feb. 1929: 12). The problem with the bill was, as Taussig (1931: 496) stated, that 'the changes were haphazard, a bit more here, a bit less there'. The *New York Times* (20 Aug. 1929: 18), speaking somewhat prophetically, said that they expected one of the bitterest contests ever on the Senate floor.

On the Senate floor, the worst fears of the party leaders were realized, as the GOP leaders completely lost control of the proceedings (Schattschneider 1935: 34). An open fight broke out between Senators from the Western and Mountain agricultural states (the insurgents) and those from Eastern manufacturing states. The insurgents were unhappy with the large tariff increases that import-competing industries were scheduled to receive. The debate was acrimonious, with Senator Moses from New Hampshire calling the Western senators 'sons of wild jackasses' (*New York Times*, 9 Nov. 1929: 5). Senator Boran from Idaho sought, but failed, to eliminate all tariffs on non-agricultural items (ibid., 31 May 1929: 20). The insurgents did succeed in passing an amendment giving aid to farmers in the form of export debentures. They also formed a coalition with the Democrats which for a while succeeded in voting down any tariff increases proposed for manufacturing items.

Then, at the beginning of March, several tariff increases were passed. Senator Smoot's amendment for a higher sugar tariff passed on March 4 1930. An amendment for a higher tariff on cement passed on March 7. One for a duty on soft wood passed on March 20. The *New York Times* (6 March 1930: 1) argued that this 'progress' was the result of trades made between different tariff schedules.

The story of Smoot's pursuit of sugar protection is particularly informative. Smoot, whose native state of Utah had a large sugar beet industry, originally sought to obtain a tariff against sugar from the Philippines. However, since the Philippines was a US territory, imposing a tariff on its exports was difficult. So Smoot first obtained an amendment on March 4 that applied to sugar imported from foreign countries. Then he and other Senators such as Boran began seeking independence for the Philippines (*New York Times*, 19 Jan. 1930: 6). At the end of the legislative year, a bill authorizing independence for the Philippines had been reported favorably to both Houses (McMahon 1930: 940).

Consumers were much less vocal than import-competing industries concerning tariff hikes. Some of the few complaints heard were from women, who complained that the tariffs on clothing would increase the price of dresses (*New York Times*, 3 Oct. 1929: 2). There was no indication, however, that Congress responded to their complaints. As the New *York Times* argued (23 May 1929: 28), consumers did not receive any benefits from the bill because they organized no lobbies to testify before Congress.

The Senate passed the bill on March 24 1930. It included the highest tariff rates in US history, the export debenture plan for agriculture, and a modified flexible tariff which took some of the proposed power away from the president. The bill then proceeded to the House–Senate Conference.

The House–Senate Conference and final passage   Further conflict ensued in conference. Agriculture interests wanted the export debenture plan retained, but Hoover intimated that he would veto the bill if it was. Democrats wanted to limit Hoover's power under the flexible tariff, but again Hoover indicated that he would veto the bill if this happened. The president of the National Association of Manufacturers urged that the bill should be speedily passed to help the nation with its unemployment problem (*New York Times*, 24 March 1930: 2). The auto industry, fearing tariff retaliation from Germany and France, urged that the bill should be abandoned (ibid., 2 June 1930: 1). The American Bottlers of Carbonated Beverages lobbied for a limit on the sugar tariff (ibid., 27 April 1930: 5).

These conflicts were settled hastily. Taussig (1931: 499) suggests that these important decisions were made by a process which was incomprehensible to those not directly involved. The final bill revised tariffs on 20,000 items, most revisions being upward. It dropped the export debenture plan and gave the president the authority to use the flexible tariff. It was passed by the Senate on June 12 1930 and by the House on June 14. In the Senate, support for the bill was mainly from the Northeast (11–1), Middle Atlantic (9–3), and Great Lake states (8–0) and opposition was mainly from the South (5–21) and Midwest (3–13) (*New York Times*, 24 June 1930: 1, 2, 15).

The bill next went to Hoover, who had received several indications that he should veto it. More than 30 countries had threatened to retaliate; 1,028 economists, headed by Irving Fisher, Frank Taussig and Wesley Mitchell, had sent him a letter urging him to veto it (ibid., 5 May 1930: 1). The stock market, seeking to recover from the crash, had declined once again on news that the Senate had passed the bill.

Hoover, however, ignored these warnings and announced on June 15 1930 that he would sign the bill. His justification was that foreigners would not need to retaliate because he, using the flexible tariff, could adjust rates downward. However, since the Tariff Commission and the president had succeeded in lowering fewer than a hundred duties since 1922, this justification was not very convincing. It is more likely that he was responding to two facts. First, protectionist interests had largely been responsible for his getting elected, and he was being responsive to their desires.[1] Second, his party had invested so much time and energy in getting the bill passed that he felt unable to go before the American people with nothing to show for their efforts (see Taussig 1931: 500).

A public-choice interpretation   Several aspects of this legislative history correspond to the public-choice model presented above. One of the most striking is the influence of interest groups. Well-organized interest groups representing various industries exerted disproportionate influences on the outcome. Not only did they learn about the hearings (whereas less-organized groups did not), but they had the political influence to convince politicians from their districts to defend their interests. Consumer groups, on the other hand, were either non-existent or almost without influence. When interest groups sought protection, they sometimes couched it in the national interest, as when the president of the National Association of Manufacturers argued that the tariff bill should be passed soon to alleviate the unemployment problem.

The tendency of members of Congress to represent narrow constituency interests for protection at the expense of the general interest was seen by the tendency of Northeastern members to seek protection for manufacturing,

Western members to seek protection for sugar, and agricultural state members to seek protection for agriculture. The tendency to logroll was then seen at every stage from the House Ways and Means Hearings until the final House–Senate Conference. The disproportionate influence of key congressional leaders was seen in the ability of Smoot to pass the sugar tariff even at a time when the insurgents were blocking tariff increases and to advance legislation on independence for the Philippines.

President Hoover did not seek to advance freer trade (this is the only case examined where the president failed to do so), but it can still be argued that he was seeking to secure re-election by representing his constituency. He had run on a platform that tariffs were desirable, and was strongly supported by groups such as the American Tariff League and the National Association of Manufacturers. They had given large sums to his campaign and influenced many to vote for him. His election by millions of votes could be viewed as a mandate for protectionism (see Schattschneider 1935: ch. 1). Thus, when brokering or allowing protection, one could argue that he was responding to his constituency with a keen eye on the Electoral College, and seeking to get re-elected.

Firms were seeking to use the government to advance their interests. Those in import competing industries such as sugar were seeking tariffs to hinder foreign competition. Those who used imports as inputs either sought free trade, as in the case of the American Bottlers of Carbonated Beverages, or sought higher tariffs on their products to offset the higher tariffs on inputs, as in the case of the leather and shoe industries. Those in export industries such as automobiles were seeking free trade to avoid the risk of retaliation. Evidently Hoover and the Congress were concerned for import-competing firms, for they were unresponsive to complaints about the international effects of tariffs.

The Reciprocal Trade Agreements Act of 1934

The Smoot–Hawley Tariff Act of 1930 contributed to an economic disaster. Real US net national product fell by over 30 percent from 1929 to 1933. US exports over this period fell from $5.2 billion to $1.7 billion and imports from $4.4 billion to $1.5 billion.

This economic collapse persuaded many throughout the country that change was necessary. The *Saint Louis Globe Democrat* argued that high barriers to imports were a grave economic mistake (quoted in *New York Times*, 6 May 1934: 4). The *Kansas City Star* argued that open markets abroad were essential for farmers (quoted ibid.). One government official estimated that 75 percent of the people wanted lower import duties (ibid., 16 Dec. 1933: 6).

Roosevelt won 90 percent of the electoral vote in 1932 on a platform which advocated free trade, although ambiguously. Hawkins and Norwood

(1963: 69) report that although Roosevelt's platform had 'condemned the Hawley–Smoot Tariff Act and had advocated a policy of freer international trade', he also 'straddled the issue, at times calling for protectionism and... at other times advocating the lowering of tariffs'. Roosevelt's reticence was understandable, for the tariff had come to be regarded as 'untouchable (unless to raise it) by anyone who valued his political life' (ibid.: 73).

Roosevelt's ambivalence on the trade protection issue is well-explained by endogenous protection theory (Magee, Brock and Young 1989: 191). Unemployment climbed from 12.8 percent in 1930 to 20.8 percent in 1934. The terms of trade improved from 97.8 to 111.2. The amount of labor employed per $100.000 of capital increased from 15.15 in 1930 to 18.25 in 1934. The amount of capital employed over labor unit declined from $6,600 in 1930 to $5,479 in 1934. All these changes presaged a further protectionist hike in tariff rates. However, average US tariff rates had already hiked from 15.1 percent in 1930 to 16.7 percent in 1934 and the inflation rate had surged from minus 9.4 percent in 1930 to 6 percent in 1934. US protectionism had also rendered the United States a pariah within the international community. The 1932 elections had ushered in a Democratic president supported by a Democratic Congress. These latter factors would tilt the political market against renewed protectionism.

In the winter of 1933–4, Roosevelt ordered Secretary of State Cordell Hull, a relative free-trader, to begin drafting trade legislation, Hull faced several choices. One was to seek unilateral, bilateral, or multilateral tariff reductions. Another was to seek selective tariff cuts on some industries or horizontal cuts on all industries. On the first issue, Hull favored multilateral cuts, but realized that the Congress would not accept it (ibid.). He decided therefore to seek bilateral agreements combined with a most-favored-nation clause (Hawkins and Norwood 1963: 75). Hull also favored the horizontal approach to tariff-making, because the selective approach produced 'a strong tendency to see the tariff problem narrowly through the eyes of the particular producers concerned rather than broadly from the standpoint of the national interest' (ibid.: 74). Here again, to please Congress he accepted the selective approach.

Congressional action on the bill and final passage   On March 2 1934, Roosevelt transmitted the bill to the House. He desired to negotiate agreements to lower tariffs whenever he found US tariffs to be 'unduly ... restricting the foreign trade of the United States'. He sought the authority to negotiate bilateral tariff reductions on selective items of up to 50 percent. He also sought to repeal the cost-equalization provision of the Smoot–Hawley Act.

Representative R.L. Doughton, the Democratic chairman of the Ways and Means Committee, began hearings on March 8 1934. He scheduled only seventeen witnesses, seven from the administration. The administration witnesses argued that the president needed broad powers to expand 'foreign markets for the products of the United States'. Republicans countered with a 'statement of the necessity for a protective tariff' which they had presented earlier in 1930. The Committee added a few amendments and reported the bill favorably on March 17 1934. These amendments left the principal thrust of the bill unchanged, although the Committee did include one protectionist clause designed to help millers.

On the House floor, Republican opposition centered around objections raised by Representative Treadway. He claimed that the proposed delegation of power to the president was unconstitutional and that the interests of small and middle-sized (import-competing) businesses were being sacrificed for large exporting industries. The Republican party since Hoover had typically been the party of small and medium-sized business, and Treadway was thus representing his constituency. Treadway also complained that the president was given indefinite powers to deal with a transitory crisis. Republicans also advanced several blatantly protectionist amendments.

The Democrats compromised on Treadway's complaints, but fought off the protectionist amendments. They agreed that the Act should terminate after three years. Amendments to protect industries such as sugar, however, were rejected. This altered bill was passed by a party-line vote.

The Senate Finance Committee began hearings on April 2 1934. It modified the requirement stipulating termination of the Act after three years to state that the president's authority to enter new agreements should expire after three years. This implied that negotiated tariff agreements would still hold after the pact expired. Also, under pressure from the protectionist American Tariff League, they accepted an amendment stipulating that any interested group should be able to present its case to the executive branch before any agreement was negotiated (ibid.: 37). The Finance Committee favorably reported the bill to the Senate on May 2.

On the Senate floor, Democratic leaders fought off many protectionist amendments. They even repealed a provision of the Smoot–Hawley Act governing duty litigation because it had become a source of low track protection (ibid.: 38). The Senate passed the bill on June 4 1934. Two days later the House agreed to the Senate changes, and the president signed the bill on June 12. R.L. O'Brien, chairman of the Tariff Commission, discussed how this change improved national welfare. He said: 'it substitutes the national welfare for special favors. It offers a fair hearing to every interest but permits no single one to be guiding'.

A public-choice interpretation   The behavior of the actors corresponds to the public-choice prediction. The president sought to advance the national interest by advancing free trade. Congressional Republicans sought to respond to import-competing pressure groups by opposing the bill. Export industries such as automobiles favored free trade. To forestall protectionist pressures the administration had to compromise, agreeing to bilateral rather than to multilateral negotiations and accepting selective rather then horizontal tariffs. The Act granted protection to millers and imposed time limits on the president's authority to reduce tariffs. The power of key congressional leaders was also evident. Ways and Means Chairman Doughton helped prevent the protectionist disaster of Smoot–Hawley by limiting the number of witnesses to seventeen, most of whom favored free trade. Democratic leaders in the House and Senate then defeated protectionist amendments that arose on the floor.

Most important of all, from the public-choice perspective, was the recognition by Secretary of State Cordell Hull and by senior members of the Democratic party that Congress must change the way it handled trade issues in order to protect against any repetition of Smoot–Hawley protectionism if the Republican party once more gained control of Congress. The 1934 Act deliberately channelled product-specific trade decisions out of the committees of Congress and off the House and Senate floors to other governmental institutions. There was no bipartisan consensus for such a policy in the 1930s (Destler 1986: 29). In 1934, 1937, and 1940, no more than five Republican votes were cast in favor of reciprocal trade in either house.

In order to rationalize such a delegation of congressional power, the Act linked tariff-setting to international negotiations, a clear executive branch prerogative. The United States moved decisively from an inflexible, statutory tariff to a *bargaining tariff*. The president was empowered to reduce tariff rates by up to 50 percent, but only after negotiating bilateral agreements in which the United States received as well as provided tariff concessions. The bargaining tariff shifted the balance of trade politics by engaging the interests of export producers, since tariff reductions henceforth could be defended as a direct means of winning new markets for American exports.

In 1934, despite strong pressuring by Cordell Hull to provide the new authority to the executive branch on an indefinite basis, the overwhelmingly Democratic Congress proved willing to cede its powers only tentatively for an initial period of three years. However, Congress did not insist on approving the specific agreements that were negotiated. In the event, the new authority would remain in effect indefinitely, with presidents employing tariff-negotiating authority ever more ambitiously – to negotiate multilaterally after the Second World War and to bargain on general tariff levels rather than item by item as part of the Kennedy Round.

Congress would later grant new authority for the executive branch to negotiate agreements on non-tariff trade barriers (1974) although such negotiations would require subsequent congressional approval. The 1934 Act,

therefore, should be viewed as a landmark event in which Congress acknowledged the protectionist tilt within the legislature and attempted to protect
itself from excessive group pressures. Until the late 1960s, this 'old system'
worked effectively to protect the US economy from the ravages of protectionism despite the continuing protectionist powers within the legislative
market place.

The era of trade liberalization: 1934–62

If the 'old system' was to work effectively, Congress needed to locate a focal
point of trade policy management within the executive branch, an official
motivated to balance foreign and domestic concerns in the formulation of
trade policy, resistant to overtly protectionist pressures and yet sensitive to
the less myopic concerns of the congressional leadership. Given such a
hinge, individual congressmen would be free to give vent to protectionist
rhetoric on the chamber floor, even to articulate protectionist policies within
the trade policy committees, secure in the knowledge that executive branch
leadership would undercut their initiatives by pursuing export-oriented trade
negotiations with other nations. This 'bicycle theory' of continuous trade
liberalization led by the executive branch was the only viable route towards
freer trade policy, given the protectionist tilt of Congress epitomized by the
Smoot–Hawley fiasco.

For the first decade under the 'old system' the position of trusted executive
agent was admirably occupied by Secretary of State Cordell Hull, a former
congressman who tilted trade policy in the freer trade direction as much as
was politically feasible (Destler 1986: 16), while never forgetting that Congress was the continuing source of his trade policy authority. When Hull
resigned in 1944, the trade policy hinge between Congress and the White
House all but disappeared and was not effectively replaced until 1962.

In the immediate postwar years, this lacuna simply did not matter, given
the devastation of Western European and Japanese economies, the hegemonic
position of the United States with respect to international trade, and the onset
of the Cold War. The most important reason underlying the success of the
Democratic leadership in subordinating US trade policy to a foreign policy
unequivocally dedicated to shoring up and reconstructing a classical liberal
economic order among free world countries was the dominant trade and
payments position that the United States assumed in the immediate postwar
period (Baldwin 1984).

As late as 1952, the US share of total exports of the ten most important
industrial countries was 35 percent (up from 26 percent in 1938) and the US
export share of manufactures was also 35 percent (up from 21 percent in
1938). There was an export surplus in every major industrial group except
metals. The vigorous postwar domestic economy recovery served to mask

protectionist pressures from industries whose underlying comparative cost position was deteriorating and to build support for freer trade policies on the part of those sectors whose international competitive position was strong.

The ability of government leaders to broker domestic support for trade liberalization was enhanced by the commencement of the Cold War in the late 1940s. There was a widespread public recognition that the USSR and its allies represented a serious political and economic threat to the free world and general US support for the mounting of a program to offset this threat based on military aid to friendly nations and assistance in the form of economic aid and of lowered US tariffs. In such circumstances, domestic protectionist pressures (with the notable exception of agriculture) were easily deflected by the State Department on the ground of overriding foreign policy prerogatives. Throughout the 1940s and 1950s, over 80 percent of the Democrats in the House of Representatives supported their party's position on extending the trade agreements program.

Trade liberalization did not flow without opposition, however, even under such favorable conditions. Many industries testified during the 1940s and the 1950s against extending the power of the president to cut duties on imports competing with domestically produced goods. Baldwin (1984) lists textiles and apparel, coal, petroleum, watches, bicycles, pottery and tiles, toys, cutlery, ball bearings, glass, cheese, lead and zinc, copper, leather, and umbrellas as industries whose representatives failed to share the trade liberalization objectives of the US government. Such special interests found ready support among many Republicans who continued to support protectionism on the erroneous but doctrinaire grounds that this policy promoted domestic economic development and high living standards.

To reassure domestic interests that duty cuts would not be made where serious injury might result to any US industry, President Truman agreed in 1945 to include in all future trade agreements an escape clause permitting the modification or withdrawal of tariff reductions if increased imports from such a concession caused or threatened to cause serious injury to an industry. In 1947, President Truman responded to Republican pressure by issuing an executive order establishing formal procedures whereby the Tariff Commission would advise the president whether any such modification was warranted.

The 1948 extension of the trade agreements program, enacted at a time when both houses of Congress were controlled by the Republican party, introduced the *peril-point provision* directing the president to submit to the Tariff Commission a list of all articles under consideration for tariff negotiations and requiring the Commission to determine the limits to which each duty could be reduced without causing or threatening serious injury to import-competing domestic industries. The peril-point provision was repealed in 1949 when the Democratic party regained control of Congress but was reintroduced in 1951 even though the Democratic party enjoyed majorities in both houses of Congress. The escape clause was also formally enacted into law in 1951.

Even during the early 1950s, therefore, US policy was by no means one of free trade. Rather, it was dedicated to maintaining a classical liberal world order that allowed scope for domestic protectionism where political pressures so dictated. The failure of the US Congress to ratify the International Trade Organization, or even to approve the GATT as an executive agreement, is further evidence of the protectionist tilt that masqueraded behind the free trade rhetoric of most congressional members.

The year 1951 marked a significant shift in political party positions on trade policy, with the Democrats voting in favor of the peril-point provision and the escape clause and a large number of Republicans supporting freer trade. Thereafter, the Democratic party gradually became the party of protection and the Republican party gradually became the party of free trade, a sea-change that has continued to the present time.

In 1952, the Republicans gained the presidency and secured control of Congress without returning to the protectionist policies that many observers had expected. President Eisenhower adopted trade liberalization as an important instrument of foreign policy, echoing the position of his Democratic predecessor. 'Republican business leaders, especially those representing large corporations, also concluded that a classical liberal trading system was desirable from their own economic perspectives' (Baldwin 1984b: 26). Even so, protectionist-oriented Republicans in the House blocked tariff-cutting in 1953 and 1954, whereas Democratic majorities in 1955 and 1958 assisted the president by granting him additional tariff-reducing authority. Nevertheless, the Republican party shift was persistently in the direction of freer trade.

Simultaneously, Democrats began to press for exceptions to the free trade position as their constituents increasingly began to lobby for import protection. During the 1940s, the industries lobbying for import protection typically were small and politically unimportant. By the mid-1950s, however politically influential industries, such as cotton textiles, coal and petroleum, whose employees tended to vote Democrat, were besieging Capitol Hill pleading for protection. In 1954, the determination of injury in fair trade law cases was removed from the Treasury Department to the Tariff Commission in a tilt towards protectionism. In 1955, the coal and oil industries were rewarded in the Trade Act with a national security clause permitting quantitative import restrictions if imports of a product threatened to impair national security. In the same year, President Eisenhower pressured the Japanese government into 'voluntarily' restricting exports of cotton textiles to the United States. In 1958, 'voluntary' oil quotas were introduced on national security grounds, and these became mandatory in 1959. Evidently, the era of consensual freer trade was drawing to a close.

As protectionist lobbying increasingly made its impact on Capitol Hill, the trade negotiating role of the Department of State came under growing criticism. The Department was charged with favoring foreign interests over US interests and with bargaining away US commercial advantages in the interest of good political relations or other diplomatic goals (Destler 1986: 17). In 1953, President Eisenhower was pressured into joining with Congress in setting up a commission chaired by Clarence B. Randall to develop recommendations for his overall trade policy. Subsequently, Randall was brought into the White House as a special trade advisor to implement the commission's report.

Clearly, the era of relative presidential autonomy on trade liberalization policy was drawing to an end. During the 1950s Congress slowed the momentum of trade liberalization by grudging, often single-year extensions of presidential negotiating authority, by escape clause criteria that made it relatively easy for industries to qualify for a relief, by a 1958 provision allowing Congress, with a two-thirds veto in both houses, to compel the president to implement a Tariff Commission escape clause recommendation, and by limiting the range of future tariff reductions. For example, in the Dillon Round negotiations of 1960, authority to cut tariffs was restricted to 20 percent and only a 10 percent reduction was achieved.

The Trade Expansion Act of 1962
From the early beginnings of the trade agreements program, many members of Congress felt that the president was too eager to reduce tariffs in import-sensitive sectors and – together with the Tariff Commission – too reluctant to raise tariffs in favor of import-injured industries (Destler 1986: 19). More generally, such congressmen continued to complain that Congress had given the president too much of its own constitutional authority to regulate commerce with foreign nations and to levy import duties. On each occasion of the program's renewal, therefore, Congress would introduce provisions designed to force the president and the Tariff Commission to comply more closely with such congressional views.

Endogenous protection theory suggests the presence of some political ambivalence on the trade protection issue when President Kennedy launched a trade-liberalizing initiative in December 1961 (Magee, Brock and Young 1989: 191). Tariff rates had drifted upwards from 6.4 percent to 7.1 percent from 1958, and inflation had fallen from 1.6 percent to 0.1 percent. The terms of trade had improved from 89.6 to 93.8. Each of these adjustments was modestly favorable to freer trade. However, unemployment had risen slightly from 5.4 percent to 5.6 percent, the amount of labor employed per $100.000

of capital had fallen from 13.23 to 12.41, and the amount of capital employed per unit of labor had risen from $7,557 to $8,061. Each of these adjustments was modestly favorable to greater protectionism. The Democratic presidency tilted the balance towards freer trade. Democratic party control of Congress was a neutral factor, given the shift towards protectionism within the Democratic party at that time.

With the recently formed European Economic Community (EEC) threatening US exports by its common tariff barriers, President Kennedy on December 6 1961 called for new powers to lower tariffs in order to negotiate reciprocal reductions from the EEC. He contended that reducing tariffs would help 'meet the Communist economic threat to the West', demonstrate 'the virtues of free competitive enterprise', and give consumers a 'wider choice of products at competitive prices'. He was thus seeking to advance the broader public interest at the expense of protectionist interests. Protectionist sentiment at this time was running high due to 'the current recession and the balance of payments difficulties'.

Kennedy's plan was threatened by this sentiment, and to forestall protectionists he offered concessions to the most powerful of the special interests. On March 27 1961, Representative Carl Vinson (Democrat, Georgia), head of the 128-member textile group in the House, warned Kennedy: 'Unless quotas are imposed that will provide the necessary protection to the textile industry in the United States, I think I can safely predict that at least some of the members who voted to extend the Trade Agreement Act of 1958 will have second thoughts if a bill to extend the Act is presented on the floor in 1962' (*CQ Almanac* 1962: 287). In response, Kennedy negotiated the Long Term Agreement (LTA) with seventeen other nations, allowing the US to contain textile imports at the same level for the next two years. This satisfied the cotton textile industry, and on March 31 1962 its pressure group, the American Cotton Manufacturers Institute, endorsed the president's bill (see Pastor 1978: 105). The labor movement was also concerned by Kennedy's free trade initiative. To placate labor, he offered trade adjustment assistance of 65 percent of a worker's wage for 52 weeks to those displaced by increased imports from the Act. This satisfied the American Federation of Labor and Congress of Industrial Organizations (AFL–CIO) and on March 19 1962 president George Meany endorsed the bill.

When President Kennedy sent his bill to the House Ways and Means Committee on January 25 1962, he had thus already eliminated much of the opposition. The main provisions were: authority to lower tariffs by up to 50 percent in reciprocal negotiations; authority to eliminate tariffs on items where the US and the EEC together accounted for 80 percent of world trade; and authority to assist workers and firms the Tariff Commission ruled had been injured by trade liberalization. The 80 percent rule was an incentive for the EEC to allow Britain to join because, with Britain, the EEC and the US would make up 80 percent of the market on many goods. Kennedy's bill did not contain the peril point of the 1934 Trade Agreements Act, which authorized the Commerce Department to determine the minimum point below which tariff reductions would damage domestic industries. Instead it authorized the Tariff Commission to report the likely effect of tariff cuts on specific industries without specifying a minimum point beyond which tariff cuts would injure those industries.

Voters surveyed about the trade bill exhibited 'ignorance about the mechanisms of international commerce' (see *Wall Street Journal*, 9 Feb. 1962: 14). Although the interviewer did acknowledge that oil producers could talk intelligently about oil quotas and wheat farmers about the export-expanding policies, he found most respondents to be totally ignorant. Responses included the claims that only shipbuilders benefited from foreign trade, that America should not import anything that could be produced domestically, and that the best strategy was to sell US goods abroad but not to buy any foreign goods. The interviewer concluded, 'the man on the street responds to a question about trade much as he might to a question about the mating habits of the domesticated yak'.

House action on the bill   The bill initially went to the House Ways and Means Committee, chaired by the influential Wilbur Mills. His ability to influence legislation was such that one presidential aide said, 'Our success or failure hinges pretty much on what he does' (*Wall Street Journal*, 5 Jan. 1962: 5). Unlike many other representatives, Mills was a relative free trader. He was able to support trade liberalization more than other representatives because his popularity with the voters in his district made him almost unbeatable (ibid.).

Several groups testified before the committee, export interests generally favoring the bill and import-competing industries often opposing it. Carl Gilbert, chairman of a pressure group representing export interests, the Committee for a National Trade Policy, favored the bill. Couching his argument in terms of the national interest, he argued that 'competition ... without our borders is ... a major stimulant to domestic progress' (*CQ Almanac* 1962: 269). Similarly, the president of Parker Pen Corporation argued that the best means of preventing prolonged injury to certain US producers is to force them to learn to compete efficiently (ibid.: 270). The master of the National Grange recommended passage but advocated that the president offset European protection of agriculture (ibid.).

Import-competing firms often opposed the bill. Sometimes they sought relief from competition on national interest grounds, as when the president of the National Machine Toolmakers Association argued that the bill should contain a list of industries (including his own) which 'are vital to national security and whose continued strength and prosperity ... must be assured by whatever means' (ibid.: 280). Others, such as the United Mine Workers, and makers of hats, glass, carpets, copper and brass argued for protection to preserve their industries. The United Mine Workers, for instance, argued for a restraint on residual oil imports to prevent the loss of markets in the US for 44 million tons of domestic coal.

The administration was politically expedient, responding to some of these claims but not to others. President Kennedy, for the first time, accepted a Tariff Commission injury ruling and granted protection to glass and carpets. He did not change oil quotas at all, although there were suspicions that he had made private commitments (ibid.: 250). One group to which the president did not respond, and which almost cost him the bill, was the farm lobby.

The farm lobby induced Representative Harrison (Democrat, Virginia) to introduce an amendment after the hearings were over that would bar the president from lowering tariffs with the EEC if the EEC retained its variable tariff on agriculture. This caused tariffs on imported agricultural products to be adjusted to ensure that their prices were always higher than domestic prices. This amendment attracted support from all Republicans on the committee and from four Democrats with agricultural constituents (Harrison, Virginia; Herlong, Florida; Watts, Kentucky; Ullman, Oregon). The administration rejected the amendment, claiming that it would halt trade negotiations. Mills delayed voting and sought a compromise. Finally, on May 11 1962, it was agreed that the Harrison amendment would be adopted but that the president still should be permitted to negotiate reductions if this would help achieve the goal of the bill. Since the goal of the bill was to expand trade, this effectively left the president unrestrained in cutting tariffs.

On other issues, Mills exhibited skill in defeating protectionist outcomes, using proxy votes from absent members of Congress to defeat one protectionist amendment after another. These included:

- a provision by Alger (Republican, Texas) to restore the peril point provision;
- another by Alger to allow Congress to override a tariff cut by a majority vote of the House;
- an amendment prohibiting further reductions in shoe tariffs by Burke (Democrat, Massachusetts);
- an amendment by Baker (Republican, Tennessee) helping coal miners by reducing the quota on oil imports.

To avert protectionist outcomes Mills would sometimes use lunch breaks to try to persuade members to change their votes. The *Wall Street Journal* (19

June 1962: 7) reports how at one time 13 out of 25 committee members favored reducing the size of payments to workers. However, since this would stop labor's support of the bill, it made its passage doubtful. Mills managed the voting so that this coalition could never vote together (ibid.).

Because President Kennedy was seeking broad new authority to reduce tariff rates across the board rather than item by item, Mills faced especially forceful resistance within his committee. To weaken such resistance, he proposed that the President designate a Special Representative for Trade Negotiations (STR). Such a presidential negotiator could balance domestic with foreign concerns in trade negotiations. President Kennedy reluctantly accepted Mills' proposal allowing Congress to create its own agent, albeit under White House control.

Mills' skilful maneuvering was invaluable for furthering freer trade since House rules prohibited the offering of amendments once the bill reached the House floor. Thus, by preserving the bill in the form that Kennedy had presented it, he greatly increased the chance that a trade-liberalizing bill would be passed. On June 4 1962, the Ways and Means Committee favored a bill very close to the one Kennedy had offered. One of the few difficulties was that the Committee included a provision allowing Congress to override a presidential decision against the use of the escape clause by a simple majority vote.

Since House rules prohibited the offering of any amendments, the Republicans' only option was to offer a substitute bill. Representative Mason (Republican, Illinois), senior minority member of the Ways and Means Committee, decided that this should be a motion to recommit the bill to the Ways and Means Committee and to extend existing trade authority for one year. Those opposing the original bill sought to establish a coalition of Republicans and conservative Democrats to oppose the bill. They failed, and the bill passed the House on June 28 1962 by a 298–125 vote. Representative Vinson and others from the southern textile-producing states voted for it.

Senate action and final passage   The Senate Finance Committee began hearings on the bill on July 16 1962, and received testimony from many of the same witnesses who had addressed the Ways and Means Committee in the House. Kennedy's bill faced many challenges in the committee.

One major objection was to adjust assistance to workers. It was argued that by providing more for workers displaced by trade liberalization than for other workers the government was creating a double standard. Further, there was concern that the tax burdens on firms to support this unemployment insurance would be heavy. The administration sought to placate the opposition by agreeing that the Federal government should pick up the extra expense. This succeeded, and on September 14 the administration succeeded in defeating a motion to eliminate the adjustment assistance.

Protectionist forces sought to emasculate the bill. Senator Bush (Republican, Connecticut) sought to deny the president the right to make five-year 50 percent cuts. He also sought to restore the peril point provisions. Senator Muskie (Democrat, Maine) argued that the US shoe industry should receive quota relief similar to that provided to US textiles. The administration succeeded in fighting off the Bush amendments. On September 14 the committee rejected these and other protectionist clauses. There was an agreement that the shoe industry should receive assistance.

One interesting exchange occurred between Senator Douglas (Democrat, Illinois) and the administration (see Pastor 1978: 115). Douglas argued that the rule that the president could eliminate tariffs when the EEC and the US produced 80 percent of world production of that good should be amended. He argued that it would be more in the interest of free trade if the president were allowed to eliminate tariffs when the US, the EEC, and the European Free Trade Association (including Britain) produced 80 percent of world output. Under-Secretary of State George Ball argued that it would be difficult to negotiate agreements with so many countries.[2] Nevertheless the committee voted to include Douglas's amendment. It also passed another Douglas amendment giving the administration authority to raise tariffs in retaliation against foreign restrictions.

The Senate Finance Committee favorably reported the bill on September 14, and the whole Senate began debate. An amendment by Bush to restore the peril-point provision was narrowly defeated 38–40. Other amendments to decrease the president's tariff-cutting authority and to eliminate adjustment assistance were also defeated. The Senate passed the bill on September 19 by a 78–8 vote. The bill then went to conference, where a few minor changes were made. Under pressure from Under-Secretary Ball, Senator Douglas's proposal to include the United Kingdom when calculating the 80 percent world trade was eliminated. The final bill, in a form very close to the one Kennedy had originally submitted, was passed by the conference, confirmed by the House and the Senate, and signed into law by the president on October 11 1962.

A public-choice interpretation   Several aspects of this history accord with the public-choice model. The president sought to represent his broader constituency by seeking freer trade. Narrow special interests, such as textiles, labor, and glass, then demanded exceptions. They were supported by members of Congress from their districts, who were more responsive to constituency interests than to the public interest. To win the support of these legislators and to pass his trade liberalization bill, Kennedy had to offer protection to these interests and relinquish some of his trade negotiating powers to a Special Representative. Voters, as demonstrated by the *Wall Street Journal* survey, were largely ignorant of what was happening unless it concerned their own industry. Bureaucrats, such as Under-Secretary of State Ball, sought not only the public interest but also to eliminate Douglas's proposal to further free trade because trade negotiations would be more difficult.

The legislative history also demonstrates how export-oriented industries often seek free trade and import-competing industries seek protection. Further, both sides often use national interest arguments when pursuing their respective policies. The export-oriented Committee for a National Trade Policy sought to open trade because it would lead to 'domestic progress'. The National Machine Tool Builders Association argued that import protection should be granted to ensure the prosperity of member firms because it was 'vital to national security'.

The paradoxes of majority voting, discussed by authors such as Black (1948) and Arrow (1951) are also illustrated in this history. At one point a majority of the House Ways and Means Committee favored the elimination of adjustment assistance. However, its chairman, Wilbur Mills, ordered the voting in such a way that they could never form a majority. This incident also demonstrates the disproportionate influence that key committee chairmen possess in the form of agenda control

The rising tide of protectionism: 1962–74

The policies of successive postwar United States governments, aimed at maintaining the liberal international framework against European communism, succeeded extremely well (Baldwin 1986a: 82). By 1960, the export market shares of France, Germany, Italy, and Japan either exceeded or came close to their prewar levels. Among the industrial nations only the United Kingdom, burdened by postwar socialism and an incentive-deadening welfare state, failed to regain its prewar position by that year. This recovery was reflected in a corresponding decline in the exceptionally high market share of the United States, from 35.2 percent in 1952 to 29.9 percent in 1960 (still higher than its 1938 share of 25.6 percent).

For manufactured products alone, the situation was much the same. The US world export share declined from 29.4 percent in 1953 to 18.7 percent in 1959, while the shares of Western Europe and Japan rose from 49 percent to 53.7 percent, and from 2.8 percent to 4.2 percent respectively (Branson 1979). The export market share for Western Europe remained unchanged through the 1960s. Significantly, however, that of Japan continued to rise, reaching 10 percent by 1971. By 1971, the US share of world exports of manufacturers had declined to 13.4 percent.

By the late 1960s the era without significant import pressures on politically important US industries was drawing to a close. The new protectionism would emerge within the context of a much more open US economy, with exports increasing from 6.3 percent of gross domestic product in 1950 to 9.2 percent in 1970, and with imports rising from 5.6 percent to 8.7 percent. Predictably, in such circumstances the protectionist tilt of the US Congress once again would raise its ugly head, as import protection lobbying became the norm within such industries as wool, man-made textiles and apparel, footwear, automobiles, steel, and electrical goods such as television sets, radios and phonographs.

The most significant change in the support for protectionism occurred in the late 1960s when the American Federation of Labor and Congress of Industrial Organization (AFL–CIO) abandoned its long-held belief in the desirability of a liberal US trade policy and supported a general quota bill. This shift in labor's position was directly related to the rapid rise in import penetration ratios across many manufacturing sectors during the late 1960s. Labor also complained that domestic jobs were being sacrificed because of extensive direct investment abroad by US manufacturing firms.

The shift in labor's position was also triggered by the manner in which the Trade Adjustment Assistance (TAA) program of the 1962 Trade Expansion Act had been implemented. The AFL–CIO had supported this legislation primarily because its leaders believed that the extended unemployment benefits and retraining positions of the TAA program would ease any adverse employment effects of the Kennedy Round tariff cuts and any job displacement effects of the changing structure of comparative advantage in the free world economy (Baldwin 1984a). They were deceived in this expectation. Not a single decision providing adjustment assistance to workers was made under the TAA program until November 1969. In 1970, the AFL–CIO testified in favor of protectionist legislation.

This change in the trade policy position of organized labor was reflected in the trade policy votes of Democratic members of Congress, and accentuated the shift to protectionism within the Democratic party. In 1970, Wilbur Mills, chairman of the Ways and Means Committee and a long-time supporter of trade liberalization, responded to the pressures of his committee and sponsored a bill establishing import quotas for textiles and footwear and requiring the president to accept affirmative import-relief decisions of the Tariff Commission if certain conditions governing the extent of import penetration were fulfilled.

In the House of Representatives, 137 Democrats voted in favor of the bill and only 82 against it. Republicans opposed the bill 82–78. Further protectionist clauses were added in the Senate Finance Committee, and the bill looked well-placed to pass through Congress with President Nixon likely to sign it into law. However, the Finance Committee shackled the bill by adding it on to a social security bill that was strongly opposed by members of the Senate, thus exposing the bill to twin filibusters: by liberal traders and by critics of welfare reform. The threat of a filibuster by a small group of Democratic senators who strongly supported trade liberalization forced recommittal of the trade features of the bill to the Finance Committee, where they were suppressed. The bill died as the Ninety-first Congress adjourned.

Early in 1971, sensing the sea-change in Congress, Wilbur Mills avoided further protectionist legislation by persuading the Japanese textile industry to develop its own unilateral plan to restrain exports. Although the limits achieved were far less stringent than those sought by the administration, Mills endorsed the plan immediately upon its announcement, thus sheltering Congress from the temptation to launch a new trade bill.

The view that gradually gained support within Congress during the late 1960s and early 1970s was that much of the increased competitive pressure experienced by United States industries was due to unfair trade practices by foreign companies and their governments. Beginning in the late 1960s, Senator Russell Long, the chairman of the Senate Finance Committee, and his Democratic colleagues, began to argue forcefully that 'it is to the Congress, not the Executive, that the Tariff Commission is expected to be responsive' (Baldwin 1984a: 30). Henceforth, the Committee became extremely wary of consenting to Tariff Commission nominees whose professional background was largely in the executive branch.

This reduced accommodation made its impact on Tariff Commission appointments. In the period from 1953 to 1967, five of the thirteen commissioners appointed had extensive prior employment experience in the executive branch, and another two had worked for the Commission itself. Between 1968 and 1980, none of the newly appointed commissioners had such backgrounds. Instead, seven of the approved nominees had significant congressional experience, either as a member of Congress or as congressional staffers. Already, the uneven playing field argument was making its deceitful passage into the congressional litany and shaping the protectionist tilt that was to dominate the United States Congress over the following quarter century and beyond.

The new era was ushered in by a United States policy action as dramatic as it was unexpected (Destler 1986: 37). On August 15 1971, at the urging of Treasury Secretary John B. Connally, President Nixon took several related steps aimed at reducing the value of the US dollar. He suspended the US commitment to support its currency by selling gold reserves on demand; he called upon other advanced nations to raise the value of their currencies against the dollar; and he imposed a temporary 10 percent 'additional tax' on imports. The combined package was designed to ensure that American products would not be disadvantaged because of unfair exchange rates.

This luckless president, who earlier had embraced Keynesianism just as it was dying throughout the academy, now embraced protectionism just as trade liberalization policies were beginning to reap significant benefits throughout the Western world. Devaluations of 10 percent apiece followed in December 1971 and February 1973, following which, in March 1973, a floating-rate regime emerged that held the real value of the dollar at or below the March 1973 level throughout the Nixon, Ford and Carter administrations. Hiding behind a 'dirty float', United States governments could now manipulate exchange rates as an opaque instrument of trade protection, instead of binding themselves to gold, much as Ulysses had bound himself to the mast of his ship to avoid the temptations of the Sirens as his vessel plowed its passage across the Mediterranean Sea.

Until 1974, congressional trade restraint had depended, to a considerable degree, on the capacity of legislative leaders to control legislation by preventing floor votes on product-specific restrictions (Destler 1986). The chairman of the House Ways and Means Committee, Wilbur Mills, in particular, was a past-master at putting a damper on particularism in tariff matters. Powerful trade committees were the twin cantilevers on which the 'old system' of US trade liberalization were made to rest. The tragedy of one man came to symbolize the demise of this order and to serve as the harbinger of renewed protectionism in the congressional theater (Destler 1986), as it brought with it the decentralization of committee power within the US Congress.

In October 1974, Wilbur Mills became the central figure in a scandal which exposed his heavy drinking and an extra-marital relationship with an Argentine strip-tease artiste. In November 1974, he won re-election, but with a much reduced majority of 59 percent. In December 1974, he declared himself to be an alcoholic and announced that he would not serve as chairman of Ways and Means in the new Congress.

In 1975, egged on by a freshman class of post-Watergate reforms, the House stripped Ways and Means of its most formidable power base, namely its responsibility for committee assignments. The Ways and Means chairman was further weakened by expanding the size of the committee from 25 to 37 members and by decentralizing its trade responsibilities to the Trade Subcommittee, making close management in the Mills mode virtually impossible. The new chairman of Ways and Means, Al Ullman (Democrat, Oregon) was a congressional nonentity, who was eventually to be swept from office in Ronald Reagan's 1980 landslide victory, but who presided first over the diminution of the House Committee's influence over US trade policy.

The Trade Act of 1974
Endogenous protection theory suggests the presence of some political ambivalence on the trade protection issue when President Nixon launched a trade liberalizing initiative in Spring 1973 (Magee, Brock and Young 1989: 191). The inflation rate had sharply escalated from 3.3 percent in 1970 to 9.9

percent; the amount of labor employed per $100,000 of capital had fallen from 9.90 in 1970 to 9.58, and the amount of capital employed per unit of labor had risen from $10,104 in 1970 to $10,435. Each of these adjustments was moderately favorable to freer trade.

However, tariff rates had drifted downwards from 6.1 percent in 1970 to 4.1 percent, unemployment had increased from 4.9 percent in 1970 to 6.6 percent and the terms of trade had deteriorated sharply from 100 in 1970 to 84.7 percent. Each of these adjustments was moderately favorable to greater protectionism (Magee, Brock and Young 1989: 191). The Republican presidency, though to a lesser extent than most Democratic presidencies, tilted the balance towards freer trade. Democratic party control of Congress tilted the balance towards protectionism.

On April 10 1973, President Nixon, still basking in his landslide re-election victory, and seeking to 'negotiate for a more open ... world trading system (*Congressional Quarterly* 1973: A-42), asked Congress to give him the power to raise and lower tariffs and non-tariff barriers. He was concerned about the 'wide variety of barriers to trade' that acted to 'distort the world economy' (ibid.). To remedy these, he asked for greater trade liberalizing authority when engaged in multilateral negotiations. These multilateral negotiations had been requested earlier by then Treasury Secretary John Connally as a precondition for devaluing the dollar in 1971. Nixon, in addition to asking Congress for the ability to adjust trade barriers, also requested the option of whether or not to submit these actions to Congress. If he submitted them, he asked that they be enacted if neither chamber voted to reject them within 90 days. Treasury Secretary George Schultz argued that these powers were essential for the administration to have credibility in multilateral negotiations (ibid.: 838)

In presenting the bill, the administration was seeking to support freer trade, which benefited the broader interests of society. The *Wall Street Journal* (12 April 1973: 18) reported that the bill was carefully designed and politically balanced to preserve the world's momentum towards freer trade. Nixon himself defended the bill, using the language of comparative advantage and arguing that 'it is in the best interest of every nation to sell to others the goods it produces more efficiently and to purchase the goods which others produce more efficiently' (*Congressional Quarterly* 1973: A-43).

The administration did include several provisions designed to make the bill attractive to special interests. To please labor, assistance for workers who had been displaced by imports would be granted if imports 'contributed substantially' to unemployment, rather than being 'the major factor', as the previous trade act stipulated. Also to please labor, there was a provision to increase the taxes of firms which moved their plants overseas, out of reach of American workers. To placate import-competing firms, import relief would

be granted when increased imports, whether due to previous trade liberalization acts or not, were 'the primary cause' rather than 'the major factor'
injuring the firm. Also to please such firms, time limits were fixed on rulings
in antidumping and countervailing-duty cases. To gain support from farmers,
who were upset about closed markets in Europe, there was a section allowing
the president to retaliate against countries which discriminated against US
products. The administration hoped that these provisions would make the bill
sufficiently acceptable to special interests so that the Congress would pass it
without major alteration.

House action on the bill   The bill initially went to the House Ways and
Means Committee, which was chaired by the pro-trade representative Wilbur
Mills. Mills wanted to see the president's bill passed, but was concerned that,
unless it included tough measures to trim the trade deficit, Congress might
not approve it. Part of the pressure for action came from the fact that the 1972
trade deficit, running at $6.8 billion, was only the second the country had run
since 1888.

Many lobbyists testified before the Ways and Means Committee during the
month of May 1973. The chemical industry, led by lobbyist Fletcher Byrom,
said that the American Selling Price (ASP) system and other non-tariff barriers should be subject to veto by Congress (*Congressional Quarterly* 1973:
840). The industry was concerned by administration suggestions that they
might unilaterally eliminate the ASP system under which duty on imported
chemicals was assessed based on US prices. The multinational corporations,
represented by Donald Kendall, argued that a tax on firms abroad was 'unacceptable' (ibid.: 839). Also, fearing retaliation which could close markets for
US products abroad, they requested that a limit be set on the president's
ability to raise tariffs. The textile industry demanded protection from 'unfair'
competition from abroad.

These lobbies substantially influenced the policies enacted. The Ways and
Means Committee rejected the president's ability to eliminate the ASP, unilaterally requiring instead that it be treated as any other non-tariff barrier and
made subject to congressional veto. The final act deleted higher taxes for
firms operating abroad and placed limits on the president's ability to raise
tariffs. The president himself provided protection for the textile industry by
negotiating the Multifiber Agreement, which allowed quotas to be placed on
textile and apparel products.

Organized labor was very unhappy with the president's bill. Couching
their arguments in terms of the national interest, they argued that it would
'increase the damage to American employment and industrial production'
(ibid.: 835) and that it was 'unacceptable in a democracy' (ibid.: 840) for the
president to negotiate trade issues with only token congressional control.

They also argued that traditional arguments for free trade were 'passé' and that the adjustment assistance proposed by the president did not go far enough. Labor favored instead the Burke–Hartke measure, which would impose across-the-board import quotas.

On July 16 1973, the Ways and Means Committee defeated by 7–17 an amendment closely related to Burke–Hartke which would have imposed quotas without exception where imports accounted for at least 15 percent of the US market. Five of the seven committee members voting in favor of this amendment were Democrats from northern states where labor was strong.[3]

On October 4 1973, a bill close to the one Nixon proposed passed the Ways and Means Committee. It contained some restrictions on the president's ability to change tariffs and subjected any reduction in non-tariff barriers to a 90-day period during which either House could veto it by a majority vote.[4] It also gave the president power to cut tariffs or quotas to supplement his anti-inflation program. The administration was pleased with the final bill.

It passed the full house by a 272–140 vote on December 11 1973, despite a struggle from organized labor. The AFL–CIO tried to kill or delay the bill once it reached the House floor (*Wall Street Journal*, 26 Sept. 1973: 23). When they were unable to do so, they lobbied Congressmen heavily to vote against it. Northern Democrats, who were most responsive to organized labor, did vote 39–103 against the bill. On the other hand, all but two representatives from the southern textile states[5] voted in favor of the bill.

Baldwin (1985: 61–9), using a multivariate probit analysis, provides more formal evidence concerning the factors that influenced this vote; he found three which had a statistically significant effect. First, members of Congress were more likely to vote against the bill the greater the proportion of their constituents who were employed in import-sensitive industries. Second, they were more likely to vote against the bill the larger the contributions they received from unions. Third, they were more likely to vote against the bill if they were Democrats. A fourth factor, the proportion of constituents in export industries, did not have a significant effect.

Senate action on the bill and final passage   The bill next went to the Senate Finance Committee, where the chairman, Russell Long, was clearly a protectionist. Long had argued in 1973 that quotas or surcharges should be applied against nations that ran trade surpluses with the US (*Wall Street Journal*, 23 Feb. 1973: 2). He was also instrumental in obtaining a quota for the sugar industry. Further, as Baldwin (1985) describes, Long for many years had been involved in seeking to wrest control of the Tariff Commission from the executive branch, presumably so that he could manipulate it for protectionist purposes. Starting in 1968, he and other members of the Senate Finance

Committee began to confirm as commissioners only those candidates who were sympathetic to the Congress and not the executive branch (Baldwin 1986b: 97–101, gives a lucid discussion). Between 1953 and 1967 only one out of thirteen appointees had congressional experience whereas between 1968 and 1983, the proportion had increased to eight out of sixteen.

The Finance Committee approved an altered version of the House bill on November 26 1973 by a 17–0 vote. Like the House bill, the Senate version gave the president significant but not total freedom to raise and lower tariffs.[6] It also required that agreements on non-tariff barriers be submitted to Congress for review. The Senate committee required that the president consult with congressional committees on non-tariff barriers and receive positive congressional approval before any agreement could be implemented.

The bill contained several provisions designed to make the International Trade Commission (ITC) more independent of the executive branch. First, it increased from six to seven the number of commissioners, with no more than four from one political party. It also required the president to report to Congress whenever he failed to follow an ITC ruling, and it authorized Congress to compel the president by a concurrent resolution to follow any such ruling. The bill also sought to 'assure a swift and certain response to foreign import restrictions, export subsidies, and dumping (*Congressional Quarterly* 1974: 557), making it more mechanical and less subject to human judgement. It further made import relief and assistance to dislocated workers easier to obtain.[7]

When the bill reached the Senate floor, the footwear industry lobbied hard for protection. They induced New England senators to propose the McIntyre amendment, which would prohibit the president from lowering the protection on any good for which imports exceeded 33.3 percent of the market (imports of footwear were currently at about 40 percent). After this failed, the Senate did pass several amendments which favored the footwear industry. One was John Pastore's amendment excluding footwear and other items imported from developing countries from duty-free treatment. Another was the McIntyre amendment authorizing the President to negotiate an agreement on footwear within the GATT. A third was Hathaway's amendment which denied the Treasury secretary any freedom to waive countervailing duties on footwear. A fourth was Ribicoff's amendment which held that the government should provide relief to industries like footwear if that industry was hurting in one geographic region even though it was not hurting in the country as a whole.

The Senate passed the trade bill with these amendments on December 13 1974, and the whole Congress approved a final version on December 20 1974. This Trade Act of 1974 authorized the president to enter into trade agreements with other countries to reduce tariff and non-tariff barriers. It authorized him to eliminate tariffs on goods carrying duty of 5 percent or less and to reduce tariffs up to 60 percent on goods carrying higher duty. It also authorized him to enter into agreements to reduce non-tariff barriers. He had to notify Congress 90 days before the agreement, consult with appropriate committees, and receive positive congressional approval. It authorized him to take retaliatory action against unjustifiable practices carried out by foreign firms or governments. It also provided a method for constructing the fair price in dumping cases, basing this price on the requirement that firms earn at least 8 percent profit and pay 10 percent overhead.

The US Tariff Commission was renamed the US International Trade Commission (ITC). The ITC would submit its budget directly to Congress, making it independent of the executive branch. The ITC also acquired the discretion to initiate investigations under the fair trade laws.

The Act also made it easier for firms and workers to obtain relief from injuries due to increased imports. Firms under the escape clause could get relief if imports were a 'substantial cause' of serious injury, rather than a 'major cause' as before. Further, the increase in imports did not have to be due to previous trade liberalization. Similarly, workers displaced by imports could receive assistance if imports contributed importantly to their displacement rather then being the major cause. The benefits workers would receive in such circumstances were raised to 70 percent of their wages for 52 weeks.

A public-choice interpretation   Several aspects of this legislative history are consistent with the public-choice approach presented above. The president, who represents a broad constituency, sought to liberalize world trade. Narrow special interests, including textiles, footwear, and chemicals, succeeded in obtaining protectionist clauses which benefited them. Organized labor, in seeking quotas, couched their arguments in public-interest terms such as preventing damage to American employment and industrial production, and opposing practices unacceptable in a democracy. They also sought to obtain protection by arguing that the theories which held that free trade was in the public interest were no longer relevant.

Although labor did not succeed in obtaining all the protection it desired, the tendency for members of Congress to support narrow constituency interests over the national interest was seen by the fact that Democrats in districts where labor was strong voted overwhelmingly against the free trade bill, and by the evidence that those who received larger contributions from unions tended to vote against it. This tendency was also seen by the fact that representatives from Southern textile states, who before the Multifiber Agreement had opposed the act, voted almost unanimously in favor of it.

The public-choice prediction that politicians will broker more protection when it is hidden from the public eye was also confirmed by this episode. Senator Long, in quietly gaining control of the ITC for Congress, increased the quantity of protection provided. For example, under the 1974 Trade Act, 60 percent of the import injury rulings would eventually result in positive findings, as opposed to 28 percent under the 1962 Trade Act. Although not conclusive evidence, this significant increase in positive determinations suggests that US industries obtained more protection. Similarly, the number of countervailing duty petitions filed rose from 5 in 1974 to 36 in 1975. This suggests that the new legislation encouraged more rent-seeking.

A third example concerns the way in which the steel industry used the new antidumping rules contained in the Act. The new rules stated that there is dumping when a firm sells its products in the US below a fair price, where this fair price is determined from an artificially 'constructed value'. In 1977, the Gilmore Corporation charged the Japanese with selling steel below this fair price. When the Japanese balked at supplying sensitive information needed to determine the constructed value, the data supplied by the Gilmore Corporation were used. This resulted in the imports of Japanese steel being declared 'unfair' and the Gilmore Corporation obtaining substantial relief (Stallings 1990 provides a thorough discussion of steel industry protection under the Act). Thus, the US steel industry, based on a questionable ruling, received massive protection while rationally ignorant voters only learned that Japanese imports had been 'unfair'. Congress under this new law was able to broker much more protection without risking the displeasure of voters.

The effect of macroeconomic factors on rent-seeking is also evident. The initial impetus for a new round of trade liberalizing negotiations came with the devaluation of the dollar in 1972. With a lower dollar, US exporting firms would benefit from increased trade abroad since their goods could be priced more competitively. One reason given for passing the bill was to increase the president's ability to fight inflation. As inflation increases, one would expect voters to be less complacent about policies which keep domestic prices high. The 1973–4 economic boom also contributed to the government's ability to lower protection, as both the demand for protection from unemployed workers and unprofitable firms and, perhaps, the supply of protection from voters decreased. On the other hand, the large 1972 trade deficit, which contributed to protectionist pressures in Congress, probably made it easier for the textile industry and the chemical industry to obtain protection.

The consistent macroeconomic effects are indicative of the power of endogenous protection theory, which, taken together with public-choice theory, offers such a powerful explanation of trade protection policy in the United States. The passage of a fairly liberal trade bill through a protectionist-tilted Congress owed a great deal to aggressive presidential support together with the making of a few key concessions to protectionist interests (Baldwin 1986: 61). Crucial to the administration's success was its prior renewal of the quota arrangement on steel in 1971, and its negotiation of the multilateral agreement in 1974 covering all textile products manufactured from man-made materials, wool and cotton.

A less-protected Congress: 1974–9

The period from 1974 to 1979 was marked by significant changes within the US Congress that left it much less protected against special interest lobbying. It was marked also, fortuitously, by a rise in anti-protection political activity that undoubtedly averted a repetition of Smoot–Hawley protectionist legislation in response to the continued opening up of US markets to import penetration (Destler 1986: 57–86).

By 1974, as Chapter 5 indicates, the influence of party machines over congressional elections had already sharply declined and been replaced by personal entrepreneurship in nurturing constituency interests. In such changed circumstances, congressmen simply could no longer afford to serve 'quietly as apprentices for the twenty or thirty years it might take to move up the ranks to chair a major committee' (Destler 1986: 59). The Watergate election, with its replacement of one-third of the House of Representatives, offered an opportunity for institutional reform that was not missed.

Reactivating the long-moribund Democratic caucus, the reformers exploited a recently adopted requirement for caucus votes on all House committee chairs to oust three chairmen and to serve notice on several others. The Ways and Means Committee was stripped of its role of committee on committees and was severely weakened by a 50 percent increase in the number of its members. It narrowly avoided a complete loss of its jurisdiction over trade and tariffs following a recommendation by the Bolling Committee to shift authority for these issues to Foreign Affairs. It was forced to establish legislative subcommittees, each with its separate staff. The committee was also subjected to new House rules making markups of bills open to the public. Its bills were also subjected to procedural changes that made open rules (allowing floor amendments) the norm, so that on-the-record roll-call votes on such amendments were now far easier to obtain.

Although the congressional reform movement itself was not directed at the issue of trade policy, the pressures for decentralization of power and for openness of procedures both challenged the 'old system' of US trade policy formation. Postwar trade liberalization policies had been grounded on closed politics and had prospered under a system of powerful committee chairmen (Wilbur Mills most notably but not alone), who could protect their colleagues from up-or-down roll-call votes that dictated protectionist constituency-orientated behavior (Destler 1986: 59). More open-floor procedures also offered opportunities for special interests to press their proposals; opportunities that largely countered the tendency for policy transparency to weaken pressure group effectiveness.

This weakness was exposed in 1978 when Senator Ernest Hollings, an ultra-protectionist from South Carolina, attempted to subvert all the textile tariff reductions offered by the United States in the almost completed Tokyo Round. Hollings attached his proposal to a bill supported by the administration – renewing the lending authority of the Export–Import Bank – and won Senate approval despite the fact that the volume of textile imports had declined some 6 percent below its 1973 peak.

The weakened Ways and Means Committee could not protect the Tokyo Round by preventing a floor vote in the House of Representatives (Destler 1986: 62). Instead, the Export–Import Bank measure had to be formally abandoned and its provisions attached to another bill, leaving the textile-tariff proposal to pass through Congress as an amendment to a bill that President Carter could afford to veto – one authorizing the sale of Carson City silver dollars. Even this amended bill was delayed so that the presidential veto fell after the mid-term elections. This was a farcical way for a supposedly great nation to conduct its trade policy.

In the conventional public-choice view, US trade policy is a running battle between special interests which favor protection and the general interest which favors free trade. As we have demonstrated, much US experience accords with this view. As US political institutions have become more and more vulnerable to special interest rent-seeking, therefore, a much more protectionist trade policy is predictable. Fortunately, a countervailing pressure began to make itself felt during the late 1970s as special interests that suffer from trade restrictions began to mount more vigorous and increasingly overt political efforts to oppose campaigns for new import restrictions (Destler and Odell 1987: 23).

Several types of anti-protection groups were particularly active: highly dependent exporters, highly dependent import-using industries, retailers (when a consumer good was at issue), and governments and companies of targeted exporting countries. Multinational companies, banks and broad commercial organizations such as the Chamber of Commerce maintained general trade liberalization pressures while typically avoiding involvement in product-specific protection battles. Most consumer organizations, following the logic of collective action, avoided making even minor commitments in international trade politics.

Anti-protection lobbying was mostly reactive and episodic, and not as powerful as might have been predicted on economic grounds. It was particularly directed against increases in trade restrictions on automobiles, copper, footwear, steel, sugar and textile imports. It was much less evident in opposition to generic trade-restrictive proposals such as amendments to trade remedy laws (Destler and Odell 1987: 110). Nevertheless, the emergence of anti-protection lobbying proved to be a significant factor preventing a less-protected Congress from lurching back to Smoot–Hawley protectionism during the late 1970s and the 1980s.

The Trade Agreements Act of 1979

In 1978, President Carter, while in the process of completing the Tokyo Round of trade liberalization, realized that he must seek an extension from Congress of his authority to waive countervailing duty (CVD) rulings made by the International Trade Commission. Unless he did so, the Tokyo Round itself would be jeopardized by a sequence of high tariff impositions on specific imports into the United States (Baldwin 1985: 70, estimates $47 million in duties would have been imposed). In addition, congressional approval was required to implement exchanges in non-tariff barriers agreed in the Tokyo Round negotiations. The president submitted a trade liberalizing bill to Congress late in the 1978 session to achieve these interrelated objectives.

Endogenous protection theory suggests the presence of some political ambivalence on the trade protection issue at this time (Magee, Brock and Young 1989: 191). The stagnant economy and large trade deficits of the late 1970s undoubtedly increased protectionist pressures, as did the relatively high rates of inflation (9.7 percent) and unemployment (6.4 percent), and the declining level of the average tariff (down to 3.6 percent from 6.1 percent in 1970 and 4.1 percent in 1974). On the other hand, the terms of trade were improving (up from 84.7 in 1974 to 87.0), the amount of labor per $100,000 of capital was falling (from 9.58 in 1974 to 8.92) and the amount of capital per unit of labor was increasing (from $10,435 in 1974 to $11,215). The Democratic presidency, albeit a weak one, tilted the balance towards freer trade. Conversely, the Democratic Congress tilted the balance sharply towards protectionism. The scene was set for a serious battle over the direction of US trade policy.

The minimum requirement of the president was legislation to implement the non-tariff barrier codes agreed earlier in 1978 as part of the Tokyo Round. Since the principal countries were unable to resolve differences on escape clause issues, there was no request for changes in Section 201 of the US laws governing escape clause relief. In addition, as noted above, President Carter chose to use the bill to seek an extension of his waiver authority on CVD rulings.

Senator Russell Long, chairman of the Senate Finance Committee, linked Carter's request to a bill which would fix the price of sugar at 16 cents per pound. Long was from Louisiana, where sugar-growing and -refining was prominent. To gain further support for the bill, Long agreed with Frank Church to tie the bill to a proposal to sell 30,000 tons of government tin. Tin was used as an input by the steel industry, and selling this stockpile would lower tin prices and help steel. In return for these benefits, they agreed to lobby in favor of President Carter's requests.

The Senate passed the bill on October 12 1978 and sent it to a House–Senate Conference. The Conference reached an agreement on October 15 1978 and referred the bill back to the two chambers. At this stage, however, the corn lobby and sugar users such as Coca-Cola began lobbying against the bill. The corn lobby was unhappy that corn sweeteners would not benefit. Sugar users were concerned about higher prices. Together these two lobbies prevailed, and the House voted by 17 votes to kill the bill. The 1978 Congress thus ended without Carter extending his authority to waive CVDs.

As the 1979 Congress began, President Carter placed high priority on obtaining this authority. The House Ways and Means Committee agreed to give it to him if he could work out an acceptable compromise with the textile industry. At the end of the 1978 session, he had vetoed a bill sponsored by Senator Ernest Hollings which would have prevented the US from making any concessions on textiles at the GATT negotiation. Although he was concerned about the inflationary impact of protecting textiles, he reached an agreement with the industry on February 15 1979 concerning a package of protectionist measures.[8] The House Ways and Means Committee one week later approved a bill restoring the Treasury's authority to waive CVD rulings. The full House passed the bill on March 1 1979 and the Senate Finance Committee and full Senate soon followed. This provision was a 'key step to the Geneva trade agreements' (*Wall Street Journal*, 2 March 1979: 3). To secure passage through the Senate the president apparently had to make concessions to the sugar industry. He agreed to use quotas and other mechanisms to keep the price of sugar at 15.8 cents per pound, 7.3 cents above the world price.

The major purpose of this bill was to ratify agreements on non-tariff barriers that had been accepted by GATT negotiators. One of the controversial agreements to emerge out of these negotiations was the injury code, which required firms to show that they had suffered 'material injury' by a subsidy before a CVD could be imposed.

Lobbies pressured Congress to weaken the force of this agreement. As Baldwin (1985b: 76) discusses, the steel industry sought to define subsidies strictly to protect them from growing competition. The final definition included government loans at below-market rates, government compensation for losses, and goods and services sold below market prices. Baldwin further discusses how the Senate Finance Committee sought to delete the word 'material' from this clause. The final bill, in a victory for the president and House Ways and Means, retained the word 'material', but emasculated it by defining it as 'not inconsequential, immaterial, and unimportant'. As the *Congressional Quarterly* (1979: 297) discusses, the administration sought to placate business displeasure by 'expediting investigations, imposing penalties earlier in the process, and providing more opportunities for judicial review'.

These changes in the bill were sharply criticized by importers. They argued that the 'shorter deadlines to make preliminary decisions would tend to produce arbitrary decisions that tend to favor domestic industries' (ibid.). The lobbyist for the Automobile Importers of America complained: 'I deplore the fact that as the product of an international effort to liberalize trade, we now see these two statutes turned into protectionist measures. I think it's appalling, a testament to the excessive price (US trade representative) Strauss paid to get the bill through' (ibid.). Importers also complained that material injury ought to have been defined as 'important, substantial, and significant', rather than as 'not inconsequential, immaterial, and unimportant'.

Neutral observers agreed that the law had taken on protectionist tendencies in passing Congress. Richard Self, director of the Office of Tariff Affairs in the Treasury Department, stated: 'There's a distinct possibility that the preliminary determination will favor the complainants more often' (ibid.: 298). Similarly, Harald Malmgren, a former deputy trade negotiator, stated of the law: 'Critics ... are pessimistic regarding its future application, because of their feeling that protectionist sentiments are strong in the Congress, and because of their feeling that the ITC is sensitive to Congressional attitudes in making injury determinations' (ibid.).

By far the most important single change in the 1979 Act was organizational, a protectionist shift of administrative responsibility for the unfair-trade-remedies laws from the Secretary of the Treasury (deemed to be too prone to freer trade) to the Secretary of Commerce (deemed to be a prisoner of trade protection special interests). The Senate Finance Committee declined to bring the legislation to the floor until the president had submitted a trade reorganization plan endorsing this shift of power.

A public-choice interpretation   Several aspects of this history correspond to the public-choice model. The president was seeking to advance the broader public interest by passing the GATT trade liberalizing agreements. The sugar, textile, and steel lobbies then succeeded in obtaining protectionist provisions which benefited them. The power of key congressional leaders was seen in Senator Long's ability to persuade the president to agree to help the sugar industry.

The importance of logrolling trades was also apparent. Long, in seeking passage for the sugar quota, agreed to help the steel industry by selling stockpiled tin. The administration, in order to receive authority to waive CVDs, had to agree to provide protection to the textile industry.

The Act also shows how Congress seeks to provide protection in hidden ways. The changes in the CVD and anti-dumping laws appeared minor, setting stricter time limits on the rulings and transferring authority for rulings from the Treasury to the Commerce Department. However, the net effect, as documented by Destler (1985: 125), was a flood of antidumping and countervailing duty petitions. Under these new laws many firms obtained protection, but voters only learned that 'unfair' practices were being stopped.

There is also some evidence that macroeconomic factors affected the supply and demand for protection. The high inflation of 1978 and 1979 made President Carter less generous in offering protection to textiles. The stagnant economy and large trade deficits of the late 1970s increased protectionist pressures, contributing to the protectionist clauses of the final act.

Congressional trade politics in the 1980s
The electoral victory of President Ronald Reagan in 1980, together with the Republican party majority in the Senate and the increased conservatism of the Democratic party majority in the House of Representatives, opened up the prospect of a significant shift towards freer trade politics within the United States Congress. President Reagan had campaigned successfully with an exceptionally well-defined and internally consistent set of domestic and international policy objectives and had made vigorous initial efforts to implement them as a means of reforming the US economy.

As Baldwin (1984b: 10) notes, three policy aims of the president were especially important in shaping trade policy: (a) to curtail the role of the government in economic affairs and to rely instead to a greater degree upon the private free-market mechanism to allocate economic resources and to distribute income; (b) to restore non-inflationary growth; and (c) to increase the military strength of the United States relative to the Soviet Union. Unfortunately, various political pressures and unforeseen economic and political events were to combine to produce a set of trade policies during his two terms of office that directly conflicted with his campaign rhetoric and his repeated free trade enunciations from the Oval Office.

The administration's stance on trade issues was set forth officially by the United States Trade Representative, William Brock, before the Senate Finance Committee in July 1981. In his statement, Ambassador Brock maintained that free trade is essential to the pursuit of a strong US economy. Surprisingly, even at this early stage in the first term, Brock emphasized that the Reagan administration would strictly enforce US laws and international agreements relating to such unfair practices as foreign dumping and government subsidization. With respect to export-credit subsidies, the international objective was 'to substantially reduce, if not eliminate, the subsidy element, and to conform credit rates to market rates'.

A major import implication of the free market approach is that when other countries possess 'a natural competitive advantage, US industry must either find a way of upgrading its own capabilities or shift its resources to other activities'. The language of comparative advantage could not have been clearer in this early statement of the administration's philosophy. Sadly, language was about as far as the administration's commitment to free trade ever actually advanced. In large part, endogenous protection theory explains the total failure of President Reagan's trade pretensions. Specifically, the macroeconomic policies of his administration had the reverse effect on his trade policy initiatives to that originally anticipated.

When the new administration assumed office in 1981, interest rates and inflation rates were running very high, the result of early macroeconomic incompetence on the part of the Carter administration. By the final quarter of 1981, tight monetary policies by the Federal Reserve System produced a slackening in the rate of inflation as predicted.

The tight monetary policies and slack fiscal policies also initiated a significant upward movement in the international value of the dollar (up 26 percent by the end of 1982 compared with the first quarter of 1981). This combination of a monetary refrigerator and a fiscal furnace continued throughout Reagan's first term and had a very adverse effect on both US export- and import-competing industries, not least because domestic interest rates remained at high levels relative to those in most other countries. Inevitably, this adverse effect worked its way into congressional politics in the form of accelerated rent-seeking by those inadequates who look to import protection and export subsidies as substitutes for free enterprise capitalism.

An early example of congressional ambivalence concerned the provision of trade adjustment assistance for workers affected by import substitution. In 1981, the Congress responded to a Reagan initiative with legislation that sharply curtailed the Trade Adjustment Assistance (TAA) program by introducing more-stringent qualifying requirements and by reducing financial benefits. Yet only a year later, in 1982, it reversed itself (with support from the administration), with legislation restoring the qualifying requirements of the 1974 Trade Act.

Again, early in 1981 Congress held hearings to publicize the plight of the US automobile industry (largely of the industry's own making as a consequence of appalling mismanagement, overmanning, and miscalculation of the implications for optimal vehicle design of the escalation in gasoline prices). Representative Richard Gephart (Democrat, Missouri), the Hawley of the House of Representatives, suggested that the House should pass protectionist legislation because it was the easiest way for congressmen to demonstrate that they were doing something about unemployment (*Wall Street Journal*, 8 Feb. 1982: 1). The *Wall Street Journal* of 24 March 1982 stated that 'many lawmakers, frustrated by high unemployment in ailing domestic industries, are turning to trade legislation as a remedy' (p. 12). It also stated that Congress felt 'growing frustration over the nation's $18 billion trade deficit with Japan' (ibid., 8 Feb. 1982: 1).

This pressure produced two specific bills, the first of which was blatantly protectionist: the Domestic Content Rule for automobiles. Pushed by the United Autoworkers and the AFL–CIO, the bill required Japanese automakers to use a certain percentage of domestic parts and labor, where the fraction used depended on the number of cars sold. Toyota would be required to use 75 percent domestic content, while Mazda and Honda would be required to use 30 percent. The United Autoworkers and the AFL–CIO lobbied hard for the bill, securing the support of 200 lawmakers who were 'straining to come up with a Congressional response to the high unemployment rate' (ibid., 17 June 1982: 5).

The second bill began as only potentially protectionist. It was the Trade Reciprocity bill. Pushed by Senator Danforth (Republican, Missouri), the Chairman of the Senate Subcommittee on International Trade, the bill would have closed domestic markets to those countries which failed to allow 'substantially equivalent market access'. This policy, unlike the GATT approach of getting others to open their markets by offering to open yours, sought to force others to open their markets by threatening retaliation. The *Wall Street Journal* (4 Feb. 1982: 30) complained that the bill would put on automatic pilot a policy that protectionists could use at will. Even lobbyists pushing for the bill conceded that 'it would take skillful management for reciprocity not to lead to a protectionist spree' (ibid., 8 Feb. 1982: 1).

Free trade forces opposed the protectionist provisions of both bills. Representative Dannemeyer (Republican, California) sought to ridicule the domestic-content bill by presenting an amendment calling it the Smoot–Hawley Tariff Barriers Act of 1982. President Reagan's trade representative William Brock called the bill 'the worst piece of economic legislation since the 1930s' (*Congressional Quarterly* 1982: 56). President Reagan opposed the original reciprocity bill by contending that it would violate GATT (*Wall Street Journal*, 17 June 1982: 2).

Pro-trade forces succeeded in deflecting the protectionist pressure. Although the Domestic Content bill passed Congress on December 15 1982, it contained an amendment stating the law would not supersede any 'treaty, international convention, or agreement on trade and tariffs'. This meant that courts could invalidate the measure for violating GATT. Similarly, the Senate Finance Committee on June 17 1982 passed a compromise reciprocity bill that the administration accepted. This bill required the government to demand 'fair and equitable market opportunities' rather than the much stronger 'substantially equivalent market access' (ibid.). The bill eliminated non-reciprocity as an independent cause for retaliation, instructed the government to seek international agreements on services, high technology, and investment, and required the government to report annually to Congress all barriers to US exports and any actions taken to ease such barriers.

Protectionism barriers remained strong as 1983 began. High unemployment was putting pressure on Congress (ibid., 17 Nov. 1982: 56; 1 Dec. 1982: 4). Farmers were in financial trouble, largely as a consequence of excessive debt, and frustrated by competition against subsidized European agriculture. Labor was upset about the one million jobs that had been lost in automobile and related industries since 1978 (ibid., 9 Feb. 1984: 1).

This protectionist pressure showed itself in the House, which again passed, on November 3 1983, the Domestic Content Bill. The bill passed with the support of industrial state Democrats and over Reagan's strong objection that the bill was a 'cruel hoax' which would raise the cost of cars and invite retaliation. This time the protectionist forces also prevailed by rejecting 219–199 an amendment which required that the bill be void if it was found to violate GATT.

The protectionist forces in the Senate, on the other hand, were not successful. The entire Senate passed a reciprocity bill similar to the one the Senate Finance Committee had passed the previous year. The Senate fought off an amendment by Arlen Specter (Republican, Pennsylvania) which would have helped the steel industry by allowing foreign courts to issue injunctions against imports if they were dumped. William Brock had argued that such a policy would invite retaliation abroad.

A sideshow to trade policy in 1983 was the struggle by Commerce Secretary Malcolm Baldridge to combine the trade functions of the Commerce Department, the Office of the Special Trade Representative, and the Department of Agriculture into one agency. To bring this about he curried support from business executives, the textile industry, and farmers (who strongly opposed this). He offered the textile industry a permanent representative on the new agency if they supported the plan. Trade Representative Brock opposed the plan, arguing that his office currently provided an 'honest broker' to coordinate the views of those with a legitimate interest in trade.

The Trade and Tariff Act of 1984

As 1984 began, trade policies were influenced by the up-coming elections. The *Wall Street Journal* reported that steel, footwear, tuna copper, and uranium were all trying to force the administration to rule on protection just before the election. Both President Reagan and Democratic candidate Mondale were trying to portray themselves as 'tough' on trade. The administration was also pushing a free trade pact with Israel, which they thought would win votes in the election.

Several of these groups seeking protection were denied. On June 7 1984, the ITC denied a request of the footwear industry for relief from imports from

Taiwan, South Korea, and Brazil. On September 6, the President rejected the ITC's recommendation to grant relief to the copper industry. He also refused on the same day to accede to the steel industry's request for quotas.

The administration was trying to renew the General System of Preferences (GSP), which allowed certain exports from developing countries to enter the US duty-free. In 1983, the administration 'was unable to find a single House member to sponsor it' (Destler 1986: 79). This bill was appealing to the administration, both because it accorded with their liberal intentions, and because it gave them leverage when trying to open markets abroad.

In seeking to get GSP passed, the bill was linked in the Senate with the US–Israel free trade pact and with Senator Danforth's trade reciprocity bill. Majority Leader Baker was reluctant to introduce the bill on the Senate floor because he was afraid it would become, in Danforth's words, 'a Christmas tree for really bad trade policy' (ibid.). The bill was released, however, on September 17 1984, and amendments were immediately passed calling for a voluntary export restraint for copper, a new chance for footwear to petition the ITC, and an effort by the president to lower barriers to wine abroad. While the protectionist amendments were being passed, Reagan offered to negotiate VERs with foreign steel producers.

A similar bill cleared the House Ways and Means committee on September 26 1984, and the whole House on October 3. In addition to containing measures for US–Israel free trade and extending GSP for five years, it contained many protectionist items. Steel imports were to be limited to 17 percent, less than the 20 percent that President Reagan had offered to seek. Grape growers were authorized to file unfair trade petitions over wine imports. The US would assess countervailing duties on goods made in one country with inputs dumped in that country from a third country (downstream dumping).

In discussing this Omnibus Trade bill which had passed both houses, the *Wall Street Journal* (4 Oct. 1984: 32) said: 'It's "omnibus" in the sense that all the wacko trade ideas in Washington climbed on'. The *Washington Post* (28 Sept. 1984: A21) called it the 'Anti-Trade Bill' and said it was a 'classic of special interest politics'. President Reagan threatened to veto it, and trade representative Brock worked assiduously during the conference to remove the protectionist provisions (as a former Senator, Brock could obtain access to the floor during these negotiations).

Brock and Reagan succeeded, and many protectionist clauses were dropped. The downstream dumping laws were excluded. The wine stipulation was amended to read that the trade representative should consult with foreign wine producers to help the wine industry. The GSP provisions were extended for 8.5 years. The *Washington Post* (18 Oct. 1984: A1) withdrew its criticism, calling the final bill 'pretty respectable legislation'.

A public-choice interpretation   Several aspects of this history correspond with the public-choice approach. The administration again sought free trade, which is in the broader national interest. Special interests fought hard for provisions benefiting them. The United Auto Workers succeeded in getting the Domestic Content Bill through the House, although it implied much higher prices for consumers and possible retaliation from abroad. The grape growers won the right to petition against imported wine. Footwear won the chance to again petition the ITC. The steel industry received a voluntary export restraint protecting it from foreign competition.

In seeking protection, these interests received help from members of Congress who were sensitive to constituent interests. Democrats elected from industrial constituencies, who had many constituents belonging to the United Auto Workers Union and the AFL–CIO, strongly supported the Domestic Content Bill. Senator Domenici (Republican, New Mexico), who had a large copper constituency in his state, added the amendment that the copper industry be granted a voluntary export restraint. Arlen Specter (Republican, Pennsylvania), who had many steelworkers in his district, proposed an amendment seeking to allow the steel industry to obtain court injunctions against imports.

The administration fought effectively against the protectionist forces. In 1982, it succeeded in stripping the Reciprocity Bill of its protectionist provisions. In 1984, it used the threat of veto to cause House–Senate conferees to drop downstream dumping and other protectionist clauses. Sometimes it needed to allow some protectionist policies to avert worse outcomes, as when it agreed to negotiate a VER with foreign steel in 1984, just as the Senate was debating many protectionist provisions. The political strength of President Reagan, as seen by the landslide election he won one month later, probably explains his success in fighting off protectionist amendments.

The tendency of bureaucrats to maximize their own (rather than the nation's) preference functions was seen in the attempts by Baldridge to establish a new agency (which he would presumably head). It is hard to reconcile his offers to give textiles and other industries offices in the White House with the broader public interest. It is easier to view this as an attempt by a bureaucrat to advance his own interests by increasing his power base.

The relevance of endogenous protection theory is also clear (Magee *et al.*, 1989: 191). With unemployment hovering in 1982 at 8.5 percent, with tariff rates at an all-time low of 3.4 percent, with the strong dollar crowding out net exports and contributing to a record trade deficit, protectionist pressures on Congress were intense. For the president to hold the line with a modest piece of protectionist legislation in an election year, under such circumstances, he must be credited with powerful freer trade ideals despite the somewhat disappointing outcome.

The Omnibus Trade Act of 1988

In 1985, representatives of a wide spectrum of industries, from steel to mining to textiles, came to Washington seeking protection. The 40 percent appreciation of the dollar and resulting triple-digit trade deficit in 1984, they claimed, was threatening their survival. As Bhagwati (1989: 442), noted, the situation differed from past episodes of protection-seeking in that it involved so many firms in so many industries.

Although many believed that the strong dollar was due to President Reagan's budget deficits, the administration during the first eight months of the year was unresponsive to requests for help. Business leaders were told that 'they were crybabies and should stop asking the government for help against the workings of the marketplace' (Destler 1986: 104). One high-ranking administration official was even reported to have said, when asked to work together with the Japanese to lower the dollar–yen exchange rate, that the Japanese should worry about their exchange rate and that we would worry about ours. The administration allowed the voluntary restraint agreement with Japan to lapse in March. The request of the troubled shoe industry for escape clause protection, championed by Senate Finance Committee chairman Danforth (Republican, Missouri), was rejected by Reagan in August.

Congressional initiative   Danforth and others in Congress, besieged with requests for protection, were angry with the administration's inaction. Congress perceived that the trade deficit would be a major issue in the upcoming mid-term elections. This perception was heightened when a Democrat in a special House election in Texas defeated a heavily funded Republican candidate who said he did not know what trade policies had to do with bringing jobs to East Texas (*CQ Almanac* 1985: 254). Danforth was especially angry at the $37 billion trade deficit with Japan, and with the fact that the Reagan administration was not using the retaliatory powers provided under Section 301 of the 1974 Trade Act to open Japan's markets up. Danforth succeeded in passing, by a 92–0 vote, a non-binding resolution asking the president to retaliate against Japan if it did not buy more US imports. The House passed a similar bill on April 2 1985. These bills demonstrate the strength of the sentiment generated by the trade deficit. This sentiment was also demonstrated by the fact that over 300 trade bills were introduced in Congress in 1985, of which '99 were directly and seriously protectionist, and 77 more were potentially so' (Destler 1986: 84).

One bill that was particularly protectionist was introduced by Representative Jenkins (Democrat, Georgia), whose district had been badly damaged by imported textiles. He proposed a 30 percent cutback in textile imports from countries which currently provided 10 percent of the market (South Korea and Taiwan). Representatives from textile states overwhelmingly supported the bill, while those from Northwestern export states opposed it. The bill was approved by the House Ways and Means Subcommittee on Trade on September 14 1985, and at this time had nearly 300 cosponsors (*CQ Almanac* 1985: 256). The bill passed the full House on October 10 1985 by a 262–159 vote. Many representatives who did not have textile interests in their states voted for it out of 'frustration with the administration's overall trade policy' (ibid.: 257). The bill next went to the Senate, where Republican Strom Thurmond and Democrat Ernest Hollings, both from the textile state of South Carolina, co-sponsored it. To win support from Northern states they agreed to add a provision to cut shoe imports. To win support from copper states they accepted the proposal from Domenici (Republican, New Mexico) that a voluntary export restraint be negotiated with copper producers. On November 13 1985, the Senate voted to approve the bill 60–39. The House accepted the Senate version without conference, and the President vetoed the bill on December 17. Congress attempted to override the veto the next year. The final override vote on August 6 1986 failed by eight votes: 276 to 149.

This volume of trade activity, and especially the passage of the Jenkins bill by the trade subcommittee on September 19 1985 with 300 co-sponsors, jarred the administration into action. In the famous Plaza Accord of September 22 1985, Treasury Secretary James Baker agreed with the other G-5 countries (France, Germany, Japan and the UK) to attempt to lower the dollar's value. He hoped that this would help import-competing and exporting firms to compete. On the next day, President Reagan declared that he would fight for fair trade for US producers, and seek to oppose unfair practices in Japan, Korea, the European Community, and elsewhere. Destler (1986: 106) argues that these actions were intended to diffuse the protectionist threat. During the next year, President Reagan imposed limits on imports from Taiwan, Hong Kong and Korea. The *Wall Street Journal* (17 July 1986: 24) suggested that President Reagan was 'imposing a little protection to forestall the truly awful Jenkins bill'. He also sought to defeat the bill by inviting lawmakers to the White House, calling eighteen of them personally, and using the last radio address before the veto vote to warn of the dangers of the bill (ibid., 7 Aug. 1986: 5).

The Omnibus Trade bill   The administration's inaction during the first eight months, however, had done a lot to weaken the pro-trade agenda. As Destler (1986: 106) argues, 'during the eight month leadership vacuum, many legislators had gotten deeper into trade questions, invested their time and reputations in them, and moved Congress toward trade action'. These included the chairman of the House Ways and Means Committee Dan Rostenkowski (Democrat, Illinois) and committee member Richard Gephardt (Democrat, Missouri). Motivated by a trade deficit approaching $140 billion, they introduced an Omnibus Trade Bill. They hoped this bill would demonstrate that Democrats were in favor of trade protection and thus would gain votes in the 1986 election.

The primary focus of the bill was a provision forcing the president to retaliate against countries that did not open their markets. The president already had this power, and the aim of the bill was to take away his discretion. It also sought to limit the president's ability to deny relief to industries and workers hurt by foreign competition. Further, it included a controversial amendment by Gephardt that would require the US to negotiate a 10 percent reduction in the trade deficit the US was running with Japan, Taiwan and West Germany. If the reductions failed to materialize, the president would be required to impose quotas to reach this goal. The bill also sought to transfer the authority to make unfair trade determinations from the president to the US Trade Representative (USTR). The bill passed the Ways and Means Committee on May 1 1986. The *Wall Street Journal* (15 May 1986: 28) characterized the bill as 'outrageously protectionist' and stated that 'no president with any regard for the health of the international economy could sign it'.

President Reagan concurred, saying it was kamikaze legislation that would spark further retaliation (*CQ Almanac* 1986: 341). White House Press Secretary Larry Speakes said it was 'pure protectionism' and 'trade destroying' (Destler 1986: 84). The president argued that the 528 anti-dumping and countervailing-duty cases the administration had initiated demonstrated that they were already seriously pursuing fair trade. These investigations, were mainly in response to pressure from Congress (see *Wall Street Journal*, 30 May 1986).

In spite of the administration's strenuous objections, the bill passed the House on May 22 1986, by a 295–115 vote. Support was especially strong in regions hurt by imports. As the *Congressional Quarterly* noted, all but two House members from New England, where imports were damaging shoemakers, potato farmers, and fisherman, voted for the bill (*CQ Almanac* 1986: 344). Many Southern representatives, whose districts contained languishing textile and lumber firms, supported the bill. This even included the Republican Whip, Trent Lott (Republican, Mississippi). Representative Bill Frenzel (Republican, Minnesota) said that the Republicans were supporting the protectionist bill in such large numbers because 'they are reflecting what their constituents feel' (ibid.).

The Senate passed an Omnibus bill in 1987, which differed from the House bill (which was repassed in 1987) in a few major points. The Senate bill replaced the Gephardt amendment with more moderate legislation. The bill was aimed largely at opening up markets which were closed to US firms. The new legislation required the USTR to target countries with consistent patterns of import barriers. The Representative would then enter into negotiations. If these negotiations failed, sanctions were not automatic but were to be pursued according to existing laws. The Senate bill also had a provision that the president could no longer modify an ITC request for relief. The new bill generally gave the USTR a larger role and diminished the discretion of the president. The Senate passed the bill on July 21 1987 by a vote of 71–27. Many Republicans ignored the administration's objections and voted for the bill.

The House and Senate engaged in a seven-month conference, the main goal of which was to produce a bill, that President Reagan would be prepared to sign. The Gephardt bill was eliminated. The bill transferred authority to decide whether practices hindering trade were unfair from the president to the USTR. It required the USTR to retaliate against 'unjustifiable acts' but gave the representative discretion in dealing with 'unreasonable' or 'distortionary' acts. The final bill included the so-called 'super 301' provisions which required the USTR to identify acts the elimination of which would increase exports. The USTR would be required to negotiate changes and, if these failed, perhaps to retaliate. The bill specified criteria to decide what constituted dumping and subsidized production by non-market economies. President Reagan signed the bill into law on August 23 1988.

A public-choice interpretation   The behavior of the major actors is consistent with the public-choice approach. Congress supported narrow constituent interests in several ways. The egregiously protectionist textile bill, for instance, was overwhelmingly supported by members of Congress from textile states. Members of Congress also engaged in pork-barrel trades. Thus, to get the textile bill passed the sponsors added provisions for Northern shoemakers and Western copper-miners. The president represented the national interest by vetoing the bill. Those seeking protection couched their arguments in terms of the public interest. Thus the Gephardt amendment, which most economists considered absurd, was justified as necessary to obtain fair trade.

During the course of the debate, the administration fought to remove this and other protectionist items (sugar subsidies, tightening of steel quotas, a lamb quota) from the 1988 trade bill. Sometimes, to avert a more protectionist outcome the president had to offer some protection, as he did by restricting textile imports from Asian countries and by pursuing 527 antidumping and countervailing-duty investigations largely at the insistence of Congress.

The bill's progress demonstrates how Congress will broker more protection if it is hidden from the public. The antidumping and countervailing-duty laws, for instance, were tightened. Congress reported to the public that procedures to penalize unfair traders were strengthened. However, as Bhagwati (1988: 50) and Finger (1993: 3) have argued persuasively, these laws had already been captured and misused by protectionists.[9] Thus, strengthening these laws made it easier for protectionists to obtain benefits. The transfer of authority to the USTR, although justified as necessary to ensure that trade policy goals were not subordinated to other goals, probably biased the policy process towards protection. As Representative Jim Kolbe (Republican, Arizona) said: 'it would be easier for Congress to browbeat [the Trade Representative] with our parochial concerns than it would be to browbeat the president'. (Bello and Holmer 1988: 9). Similarly, Representative Jack Kemp (Republican, New York) argued that the transfer makes 'it easier for protectionist interests to maneuver the United States into a self-defeating cycle of retaliatory measures' (ibid.).

A final example of how the bill allows Congress to broker protection in hidden ways is evident in the so-called 'Super 301' provisions. While the public learns that these help to expand exports into unfairly closed markets, knowledgeable observers shudder. As Bhagwati (1988: 53) has documented, threats of retaliation by the US towards weaker trading partners, even before the 1988 bills, caused these countries to substitute imports from the US for imports from more competitive countries.

For instance, Bhagwati (1988: 53) describes how South Korea responded to pressure from the US by switching agricultural imports from Argentina and China to the US and industrial parts from Japan to the US. If the 1988 provisions sparked similar outcomes, where political power rather than comparative advantage determine the flow of trade, the world would move even further from an efficient allocation of its resources.

The importance of macroeconomic factors for trade policy is also seen in this legislative history. The strong dollar and huge trade deficit of 1985 induced trade protection rent-seeking. Steel, textiles, mining, shoemaking, and many other industries which were languishing due to foreign competition, diverted resources from production to seeking protection. In response to this massive constituency pressure, members of Congress introduced 176 protectionist bills in 1985. Sympathy with these industries and low inflation could have made voters more willing to supply protection (inflation was below 2 percent). The willingness of voters was illustrated by the fact that in legislation such as the textile bill, many members of Congress whose districts did not directly benefit still voted for it.

4   Conclusion

It is easy to discern that actors in many of these cases were acting as the public-choice model predicts. The president, in every case except the Smoot–Hawley Act, sought to obtain freer trade. Sometimes, to obtain this he had to offer protectionist provisions. For example, this happened when President Carter offered protection to the textile industry in 1979, or when President

Reagan offered to negotiate a VER for steel in 1984. Members of Congress often voted protection for their districts. To ensure that their districts received this protection, they often engaged in logrolling trades. This was seen at each stage of the Smoot–Hawley Act, and in the agreement between shoes, textiles, and copper in 1988.

The disproportionate influence of key Senators was seen in Smoot's ability to obtain the sugar amendment in 1930 and Long's ability to cause the president to help sugar in 1979. The power of lobbyists to obtain favors was evident throughout. Two notable examples were the ability of the footwear, chemical, and textile interests to obtain protectionist clauses in 1974 and the ability of the steel industry to redefine subsidies in the 1979 bill. These special interests were much more successful at influencing legislation in their own interests than consumers were in influencing it in theirs. Indeed, apart from complaints by women about higher dress prices in 1930, consumers played hardly any direct role in these legislative battles.

Firms sought different outcomes depending on whether they were export-orientated or import-competing. For instance, in 1930 automakers fought to lower tariffs to avoid retaliation, whereas in the 1980s they sought increased protection to maintain their domestic market shares. Firms using imports as inputs often sought to lower protection; for example, the Coca-Cola company in 1979, when they sought to lower sugar prices.

The importance of macroeconomic factors, especially the dollar and the trade deficit, was clear throughout. The strong dollar and the triple-digit trade deficit in 1984 sparked 176 protectionist bills in 1985. High unemployment in 1930 and the early 1980s probably made consumers more willing to supply protection. High inflation in 1974 and 1979 probably made them less willing to supply it.

It is also clear that members of Congress prefer brokering protection in ways that are hidden from the public. Thus the takeover of the ITC by Congress in 1974, the tightening of the antidumping laws in 1979, and the delegation of Super 301 powers to the US Trade Representative in 1988, all increased the quantity of protection offered. However, voters, the true suppliers, remained ignorant of this or were even glad when they heard that 'unfair' practices were being stopped. Thus, by offering hidden protection, Congress was able to serve special interests without displeasing voters.

Notes

1　For a discussion of how Northeastern manufacturing lobbyists had financed his campaign, see *New York Times* 27 April 1930.

2　He also argued that this would not give the EEC an incentive to include Britain. However, this was probably not as strong a reason because there were already signs that the Common Market would not let Britain in.

3　The Democrats voting for it were Burke (Massachusetts), Vanik (Ohio), Green (Pennsyl-

vania), Karth (Minnesota), Rostenkowski (Illinois), Fulton (Tennessee), and Duncan (Tennessee).
4   The House bill allowed the president to eliminate tariffs on goods carrying duties of less than 5 percent, reduce tariffs 60 percent on goods carrying duty between 5 and 25 percent, and reduce tariffs 75 percent on goods carrying duty greater than 25 percent.
5   Alabama, Georgia, Mississippi, North Carolina, South Carolina, Tennessee, and Virginia.
6   The Senate bill allowed the president to eliminate tariffs on goods carrying duty of 10 percent or less and to reduce by 50 percent tariffs on goods carrying duty greater than 10 percent.
7   Import relief was to be provided if imports were a 'substantial cause' of injury, rather than the 'primary cause' as the Nixon proposal stated. Similarly, assistance for workers would be provided if imports 'contributed importantly' to their unemployment, rather than being the 'primary cause'.
8   See *Wall Street Journal*, 12 Feb. 1979: 5, for a discussion of Carter's dilemma between fighting inflation with anti-protectionist measures or placating the textile industry with protection.
9   Bhagwati discusses how the procedures are unfair because the plaintiff and the judge in an antidumping procedure are both American. Further, he argues, there is no penalty for frivolous complaints, so a US firm has an incentive to tie up foreign rivals in expensive litigation. Palmeter adds that the concept of fair value is nebulous and often results in ridiculous outcomes. For instance, if a foreign firm sold a product one month for $200 in the US and its country, and the next month at $100 in both places, the price used to determine fair value would be the average foreign price ($150). Since this is below the price charged at one time in the US ($200), the firm would be guilty of dumping. Thus firms have been able to use these laws to obtain protection.

References

Arrow, K. (1951) *Social Choices and Individual Values* (New York: John Wiley).
Baldwin, R.E. (1976) 'The political economy of postwar US trade policy', *The Bulletin, New York University Graduate School of Business Administration*, 5–37.
Baldwin, R.E. (1984a) 'The changing nature of US trade since World War II' in R.E. Baldwin and A.O. Krueger (eds), *The Structure and Evaluation of Recent US Trade Policy* (Chicago: University of Chicago Press), pp. 5–27.
Baldwin, R.E. (1984b) 'Trade policies under the Reagan administration', in R.E. Baldwin (ed.), *Recent Issues and Initiatives in US Trade Policy* (Cambridge: National Bureau of Economic Research), pp. 10–32.
Baldwin, R.E. (1986a) 'Changes in the global trading system: a response to shifts in national economic power', in D. Salvatore (ed.), *The New Protectionist Threat to World Welfare* (Amsterdam: North-Holland).
Baldwin, R.E. (1986b) *The Political Economy of US Import Policy* (Cambridge, Mass.: MIT Press).
Bello, J. and Holmer, A. (1988) 'The heart of the 1988 Trade Act: a legislative history of the amendments to Section 301', *Stanford Journal of International Law*, 1–44.
Bhagwati, J. (1988) *Protectionism*, (Cambridge, Mass.: MIT Press).
Bhagwati, J. (1989) 'US trade policy at the crossroads', *World Economy*, 12: 439–79.
Black, D. (1948) 'The decisions of a special majority', *Econometrica*, 16: 245–61.
Branson, W. (1979) *Trends in US International Trade and Investment since WWII* (Princeton: Princeton University Press).
CQ Almanac (various issues), USGPO.
Destler, I.M. (1986) *American Trade Politics: System under Stress* (Washington, D.C.: Institute for International Economics).
Destler, I.M. and Odell, J.S. (1987) *Anti-Protection: Changing Forces in United States Trade Politics* (Washington, D.C.: Institute for International Economics).
Finger, J.M. (1993) 'Antidumping is where the action is' in J.M. Finger (ed.) *Antidumping: How it Works and Who Gets Hurt* (Ann Arbor: University of Michigan Press).

Hawkins and Norwood (1963) 'The legislative basis of US commercial policy'.

MacMahon, A.W. (1930) 'Recent legislative acts', *American Political Science Review,* 24: 915–39.

Magee, S.P., Brock, W.A. and Young, L. (1989) *Black Hole Tariffs and Endogenous Policy Theory* (Cambridge: Cambridge University Press).

New York Times, various issues.

Palmeter, D. (1989) 'The capture of the Antidumping Law', *Yale Journal of International Law,* 182–98.

Pastor, (1978) *US Trade Policies, 1929–76.*

Schattsneider, E.E. (1935) *Politics, Pressures and the Tariff* (New York: Prentice-Hall).

Stallings (1990) 'Flexible exchange rates and administered protection', unpublished Ph.D. dissertation, George Mason University, Fairfax, Virginia.

Tasca, Henry (1970) *Reciprocal Trade Policy of the United States*

Taussig, Frank W. (1931) *The Tariff History of the United States* (New York: G.P. Putnam).

Wall Street Journal, various issues.

Washington Post, various issues.

9 Trade politics in the executive branch

1 Introduction

The Founding Fathers who wrote the US Constitution were profoundly concerned about potential concentrations of power. In consequence, they relied heavily upon the principle of distributing power among three branches of the federal government – the executive branch, Congress and the courts – and between the federal and state governments. One consequence of this structure is a continuous tension between Congress and the executive branch, a power struggle fully anticipated by the Founding Fathers, indeed welcomed by them as part of a system of checks and balances designed to prevent any one branch becoming too powerful.

Although the president is viewed as endowed with the 'foreign affairs power' the US Constitution does not include the phrase 'foreign affairs'. Nor does it enumerate many specific grants of authority with regard to foreign affairs. With respect to military affairs and national security matters, specific powers are granted to Congress (the power to declare war: Article I, Section 8) and to the president (the Commander-in-Chief power: Article II, Section 2) without any specification of the relationship between these powers.

The situation with respect to foreign economic affairs is somewhat more precise. The Constitution grants to Congress the power 'to regulate commerce with foreign nations' and 'to lay and collect Taxes, Duties, Imports and Excises' (Article I, Section 8). In consequence, Congress has strong textual support for claiming pre-eminence in this field. However, the Constitution grants to the president powers to conduct relations with foreign nations (for example, the power to 'make treatises: Article II, Section 2; and the power to 'receive Ambassadors': Article II, Section 3).

These grants give the president some authority in foreign trade and in economic negotiations. Legislative history (see Chapter 8) and practical exigencies (the entire Congress cannot negotiate with a foreign nation) further weaken the arguable pre-eminence of Congress in foreign economic relations (Jackson 1993: 67–8).

During recent decades, beginning with the crisis induced by the Smoot–Hawley Tariff Act of 1930, the powers of the US presidency have grown considerably. A Supreme Court case in 1936, *United States* v *Curtiss Wright Export Co.*, even propounded the theory that the president possesses certain inherent powers over foreign affairs that do not depend on the Constitution. Most scholars reject this judgement as induced by New Deal pressures; but their skepticism has not prevented the presidency from exercising a pre-eminent role in the conduct of US foreign affairs.

The presidential powers in this area are indeed formidable (Jackson 1993: 69). The president has authority to negotiate international agreements and to conduct international diplomacy. In consequence, he may enter into executive agreements on his own constitutional authority. More significantly, Congress has delegated to the president a wide variety of powers relating to international affairs. Since the president is the chief actor in international affairs, he may sometimes interpret these delegations expansively. The limits on such presidential powers are far from clear.

A number of significant court cases have addressed the issue of the president's power to enter into international agreements. In 1953, in *United States* v *Guy Capps, Inc.*, the Fourth Circuit US Court of Appeals held that the president's officials had exceeded presidential authority by entering into an agreement with Canada concerning the importation of potatoes to the United States. There was no explicit statutory authority for such an agreement. The judgement was affirmed by the Supreme Court, but on other grounds. The Court declined to take a position on the presidential power issue (Schwartz 1983: 165–6).

During the late 1960s and early 1970s, US government officials promoted an informal understanding whereby steel producers in Japan and in Europe despatched unilateral letters to the United States government containing assurances that steel shipments to the US market would not exceed specified quantities. In *Consumers Union* v *Kissinger* (1974), this voluntary restraint was challenged as a violation of US antitrust laws and as exceeding the president's power. The antitrust portion of the suit was dismissed because of lack of investigative resources by the complainant. On the *ultra vires* issue, however, the Court of Appeals for the District of Columbia circuit ruled in favor of the president, noting that the arrangement did not involve any formal agreement on behalf of the United States. The Supreme Court refused to take the case.

The president and his officers clearly have the authority to negotiate on any foreign affairs matter at any time. This does not necessarily imply any authority to accept as binding the results of the negotiation. Indeed, negotiations will often be *ad referendum* with the understanding that the president must obtain authority to accept any agreement resulting from the negotiation. The negotiating power itself has not often been probed (and never successfully) by the Courts or by Congress (Jackson 1993: 71).

The president and his agents have the power to sign international agreements on behalf of the United States. The signature of an international agreement is not equivalent to acceptance; rather, it certifies that the language of the agreement is in accord with what has been negotiated. The power to accept an international agreement and the method of acceptance depends on whether the international agreement is a *treaty* under US law or an *executive agreement*. The US Constitution requires that treaties be submitted to the US Senate for 'advise and consent', requiring a two-thirds affirmative vote, before the president can enter into them on behalf of the United States. During the two centuries of constitutional history, however, alternative forms of approval of international agreements have developed. Practice divides international treaty agreements into treaties which must be submitted to the Senate, and executive agreements which may be approved in several ways.

Executive agreements may be submitted to Congress for approval by the passage of a statute which grants authority to the president to accept the international agreement. Many trade agreements are approved in this manner; prime examples are the Tokyo Round GATT agreements by the 1979 Trade Agreements Act and the North American Free Trade Agreement (NAFTA) by the NAFTA Act of 1993. Alternatively, Congress may enact a statute which authorizes the president in advance to negotiate, enter into, and accept an international agreement on behalf of the United States. Yet again, a treaty may give the president advance delegated authority within limits to enter into an executive agreement designed to implement the treaty. Finally, there are some executive agreements which the president may enter into on his own inherent authority under the US Constitution, notably under his authority as commander-in-chief of the armed forces, or which are implied by the Constitution as falling under presidential authority.

2   US trade negotiations and the US Constitution
Following the Tariff Act of 1930, the Roosevelt administration proposed, and Congress adopted, a statute, the Reciprocal Trade Agreements Act of 1934, which was designed to allow the executive branch to negotiate with foreign nations for the mutual reduction of tariffs. The 1934 Act was of limited duration but, until the mid-1960s, renewals were regularly re-enacted: in 1937, 1940, 1943, 1945, 1948, 1951, 1953, 1954, 1955, 1958 and 1962. The tariff-negotiating authority has always been limited in duration. The authority granted for the Tokyo Round expired in January 1980, but the 1988 Omnibus Trade and Competitiveness Act renewed that authority for the Uruguay Round until June 1 1993.

The basic negotiating authority of this series of trade acts has provided a two-part presidential power. First, it authorizes the president to negotiate and accept an international agreement on the reduction of tariffs – an executive agreement pursuant to congressional authority granted in advance. Second, these statutes authorize the president to proclaim such agreements on tariffs, so that they become part of the domestic law. A Senate report stated in 1943: 'Under the Trade Agreements Act changes in our tariff rates are made, so far as our domestic law is concerned, by the President's proclamation under the authority of the Trade Agreement Act' (Jackson 1993: 83).

The 1962 renewal of the trade agreements authority was marked by a shift in emphasis away from simple renewal or date-extension toward more elaborate legislation. The 1962 Trade Expansion Act established the framework for US participation in the sixth GATT trade-negotiating round, the Kennedy Round, and explicitly referred to the goal of reducing non-tariff barriers.

From 1967 to 1975 there was a hiatus in the trade agreements authority that was eventually corrected in the Trade Act of 1974 which established the framework for US participation in the seventh GATT trade-negotiating round, the Tokyo (Nixon) Round. The 1974 Act renewed the advance authority for the president to enter into tariff agreements until January 1980. It also made prominent changes in the escape clause and in certain other legislative provisions. More significantly, it introduced major titles of law concerning non-tariff measures, provisions for industry group liaison, treatment of communist or non-market economies and provisions for preferential treatment of under-developed countries.

The next important US trade legislation was the Trade Agreements Act of 1979 which approved the agreements concluded in the Tokyo Round negotiations under the so-called 'fast-track' procedure. This was followed in 1984 by the Trade and Tariffs Act which renewed the preference title concerning underdeveloped countries and provided authority to negotiate a bilateral free trade area with Israel. In 1986, the eighth GATT trade-negotiating round, the Uruguay Round, was launched, triggering the Omnibus Trade and Competitiveness Act of 1988 which, as with the 1984 Act, continued a considerable shift away from the traditional trade legislation since 1934 (see Chapter 8), while renewing until June 1993 the trade-negotiating authority for the Uruguay Round.

As the multiple rounds of GATT negotiations slowly but inexorably moved to extinguish the tariff problem, attention shifted within the US executive branch to negotiations with foreign nations designed to reduce non-tariff barriers to international trade. Presidents naturally sought advance authority for such negotiations comparable to those that had been granted by Congress for tariff negotiations. Their requests were met by stiff congressional resistance. Non-tariff measures typically 'reach deeply into interstices of domestic policy and regulations' (Jackson 1993: 85) and for this reason Congress is reluctant to allow the executive branch *ex ante* authority to change its laws through the devise of international agreements without *ex post* congressional approval.

A compromise was forged during the early 1970s and was introduced as part of the Trade Act of 1974 in the form of the *fast-track procedure*. This procedure basically requires the president to establish an order, regulation or international draft agreement and to submit it to Congress for consultation. In addition to the consultation requirement, the fast track provided three essential rules: (a) a bill, when introduced, would not be amendable; (b) committees to which the bill was referred would be required to report on the bill within a short period of time; and (c) debate over the bill in both houses would be limited. These rules, however, had no statutory authority. They were incorporated into the rules of each house of Congress and were amenable to change through parliamentary procedure, from which the president, of course, was excluded. The fast-track procedure worked well during the 1979 enactment of approval and implementation of the Tokyo Round agreements and was extended to January 1988. The procedure was used to implement the US and Canada free-trade area agreement and also the NAFTA agreement. It was available to implement the 1994 Uruguay Round agreements.

In 1983, the US Supreme Court, in the case of *INS* v *Chadha,* held that a legislative veto procedure was not permissible under the US Constitution. The fast-track procedure was not threatened by this judgment since the president must finally sign into law any statute enacted by Congress under this rubric. Certain other trade act veto procedures were subsequently changed because of that judgment (Jackson 1993: 86).

The authority of the executive branch in US trade policy derives substantially from enactments by Congress; a number of these are enactments which the executive has sought specifically. Typically, where Congress grants authority it extracts a *quid pro quo* in the form of certain specific procedural or judicial restraints on executive action or by mandating trade-policy activities with import-restricting consequences. In dealing with such *quid pro quo*s, the federal courts have played a relatively cautious role. With respect to foreign affairs, they have displayed a great deal of deference to the president. This deference has carried over into matters of trade policy, noting that Congress, in giving the executive authority in foreign affairs, 'of necessity must paint with a brush broader than it customarily wields in domestic areas' (Jackson 1993: 88).

However, the courts are markedly less deferential in situations where Congress itself has delegated powers of judicial review over executive branch administrative decisions. This has been particularly the case with respect to anti-dumping and countervailing duty cases where the Court of International Trade has intruded deeply into the decisions of the US Department of Commerce and the International Trade Commission.

3   The Office of the United States Trade Representative
In preparing the Smoot–Hawley tariff bill in 1930, the House Ways and Means Committee accumulated 11,000 pages of testimony and briefs over a period of 43 days of hearings. Not a single page of testimony was contributed

by the executive branch. The Hoover administration was seemingly paralysed by its protectionist campaign rhetoric and failed to exert the trade-liberalizing influence expected of the executive branch (Destler 1986: 16).

The lesson was not lost on Hoover's successor, President Roosevelt, who provided seven of the seventeen witnesses who presented testimony on the trade liberalizing 1934 Act. If Congress was not to lapse into repeated protectionism, the executive branch evidently must provide a focal point for trade policy-making capable of balancing foreign and domestic concerns in a broadly trade-liberalizing direction (Destler 1986: 16).

From 1934 to 1944, this focal point was provided by a former member of Congress, Cordell Hull, Secretary of State in the three Roosevelt administrations, who systematically tilted trade policy in a trade-liberalizing direction while always cultivating the goodwill of Congress. Hull resigned in 1944, leaving a gap in the executive branch with respect to trade policy that would not be closed in any durable way for almost twenty years. This gap became a problem in the 1950s as international competition re-emerged to challenge US domestic industries, and as members of Congress increasingly charged the State Department with favoring foreign over US interests.

In 1953, President Eisenhower 'found it prudent to join with Congress in setting up a commission chaired by Clarence B. Randall to develop recommendations for his administration's overall trade policy' (Destler 1986: 17). Randall was then brought into the White House as a special trade advisor to implement the commission's report. Following this initiative, President Kennedy developed his major trade expansion in the White House under the direction of Howard C. Petersen. Evidently, the State Department was being systematically bypassed on trade policy initiatives within the executive branch.

In 1961, the Kennedy administration went to Congress to seek broad new authority to reduce tariff rates across the board in an initiative designed to meet the protectionist challenge posed by the establishment in 1958 of the European Economic Community. House Ways and Means Chairman Wilbur D. Mills questioned whether the State Department could be trusted with this new authority, given its tilt toward foreign interests. Because of the technical incompetence of the Department of Commerce, and its perceived unresponsiveness to US agricultural interests, Mills suggested that a new presidential negotiator, capable of balancing domestic and foreign concerns, should be appointed to assume the new authority (Destler 1986: 17).

Mills proposed that the president designate a Special Representative for Trade Negotiations (STR). President Kennedy reluctantly acceded to the proposal as an acceptable price to pay for the broad new negotiating authority sought by his administration. The Trade Expansion Act of 1962 created the STR and established two roles for this new trade official: the STR was to be 'the chief representative of the United States' during the authorized negotiations and also chairman of the 'interagency trade organization' that was to manage the negotiations on behalf of the president (Section 241).

The 1962 Act was silent concerning the staffing and location of the STR, since President Kennedy had insisted on retaining authority over these issues. By Executive Order 11075, issued on January 15 1963, the President placed the new unit within the Executive Office of the President. The STR was clearly designed to play the executive broker role required by the US trade policy-making system – between domestic interests and foreign governments, between the executive branch and Congress, and among the concerned government agencies (Destler 1988: 89).

Organizationally, the STR was an anomaly (Destler 1986: 18). Although housed in the Executive Office of the President, few of its administrators would ever have close personal contact with presidents who, for political reasons, would wish to limit their direct responsibility for decisions that ran counter to influential trade constituencies. In a government of strangers (Heclo 1977), the STR often was the most lonely stranger of all. Nevertheless, the White House location provided the STR with flexibility and power in forging an executive branch trade policy.

President Kennedy appointed as STR a prominent Republican, former Secretary of State and Massachusetts Governor, Christian A. Herter, who conducted the Kennedy Round negotiations with a small staff including one deputy for Washington management, William M. Roth, and one for Geneva bargaining, W. Michael Blumenthal. When Herter died in December 1966, President Johnson designated Roth as his replacement (Destler 1986: 89). Neither trade executive spent much time with the president. President Johnson wrapped up the Kennedy Round negotiations in the spring of 1987 mainly through his Deputy Special Assistant for National Security Affairs, Francis M. Bator. From that point until 1971, STR went into eclipse (Destler 1988: 90), with the multinational trade negotiations over and its role in bilateral and product-specific negotiations far from well-established.

In 1969, President Nixon's Secretary of Commerce, Maurice H. Stans, made an unsuccessful bid to have trade coordinating responsibilities transferred to his office. Supported by the president, Stans' bid was frustrated by congressional and interest-group opposition. However, Stans gained the right to control the appointment of the STR, and also the lead role in the first trade action of the Nixon administration, the textile wrangle with Japan, which he proceeded to bungle, provoking fierce Japanese resistance. Recognizing the importance of restoring central trade policy leadership, President Nixon in 1971 named a new STR, William B. Eberle, who organized a strong staff to handle trade policy legislation. Notwithstanding this re-emergence of the STR, President Nixon also established in 1971 a Council for International Economic Policy (CIEP) headed by an Assistant to the

President for International Affairs, first Peter G. Peterson, and then, in 1972, Peter M. Flanigan. Flanigan moved, with President Nixon's support, to have the STR formally incorporated in CIEP under his direction (Destler 1986: 90).

This move was thwarted by Congress. House Ways and Means responded in 1973 by adding to the bill authorizing a new trade round, a section making STR a statutory office. The Senate went further, placing STR in the Executive Office of the President by law, and giving cabinet rank and salary to its chief. President Ford signed this amendment into law in the Trade Act of 1974. Meanwhile, STR was asserting *de facto* leadership in lobbying the Trade Act through Congress and in successfully concluding trade concession negotiations with the European Community designed to offset the trade-diverting effects of British entry. By the time that the multinational trade negotiations bill was in Congress in 1979, Robert S. Strauss, President Carter's extremely effective STR, had strengthened the position of STR in the executive branch and had forged close relationships with a number of senior senators, including the relatively protectionist chairman of the Senate Finance Committee, Russell B. Long (Destler 1986: 92). The successful completion of the Tokyo Round negotiations was perhaps the only major economic policy success of the Carter administration.

Strauss deployed his talents as STR to keep the overall US trade regime moving in a broadly trade-expanding direction while tolerating modest trade protection initiatives to dampen special interest pressures. His White House location enabled him to deploy in trade negotiations the dependably antiprotectionist departments of Treasury and State to counterbalance protectionist pressures elsewhere in the executive branch and, especially, in Congress (Destler 1986: 97). Despite Strauss's skills in this area, however, the political weakness of President Carter resulted in Congress-dominated reorganization of STR which became effective in January 1980.

The Carter reforms created a two-tier executive branch structure. The upper tier consisted of an enlarged and renamed Office of the United States Trade Representative (USTR). This Office was assigned international trade policy development, coordination and negotiation functions, including responsibilities previously handled by the State Department regarding GATT, bilateral, commodity and East–West trade matters, as well as policy responsibility for overseeing trade remedy cases. The lower tier, which was assigned trade administration responsibilities, was assigned to the highly protectionist Commerce Department, thus removing from the orbit of the relatively trade-liberating Treasury Department all authority over countervailing duty and antidumping cases (Destler 1986: 99).

As a consequence of this reorganization, Strauss resigned his position, to be replaced as USTR by former Florida governor Reubin Askew, a man of little experience in trade policy matters. He was not in office long enough for any challenge to be mounted against his leadership on trade issues.

Askey's successor, in the first Reagan administration, was William E. Brock, a man, like Strauss, of considerable political talent and also well networked with Congress, having served in both chambers. The appointment of a committed trade liberalizer by a president deploying free-trade rhetoric, augured well for anti-protection policy. Unfortunately, as with so many of President Reagan's policies, rhetoric ran well ahead of action and, in the case of trade policy, actually ran counter to presidential policy-making.

Brock's appointment was counterbalanced by President Reagan's choice as Secretary of Commerce of the more-protectionist minded Malcolm Baldridge, who would vie with Brock throughout Reagan's first term for control over trade policy and who would aggressively seek to tie up import competition through a network of voluntary export restraints. The outcome of this conflict, which was not to be resolved by President Reagan, was that the executive branch endorsed liberal trade in principle but tightened protection in practice throughout the first Reagan term.

In March 1985, Brock was transferred from USTR to the Department of Labor, in a move designed to forge new relationships with the labor movement, apparently with little or no thought to the implications for trade policy. There followed a critical three-month vacuum before Clayton Yeutter was confirmed to USTR, during which the executive branch lost agenda control of trade policy to Congress at a time of rising protectionist hysteria. The number of protectionist trade bills increased dramatically and progressed through the trade committees on to the House and Senate floors (Destler 1988: 105).

In late September 1985, the administration finally moved to ease the pressures on Congress, announcing the *New York Plaza Accord* negotiated between the finance ministers of the United States, France, Germany, Japan and the United Kingdom, and designed to ease import penetration by driving down the value of the dollar through intervention in the foreign exchange markets. Simultaneously, President Reagan announced his intention to press a range of fair trade practice cases against Japan, the European Economic Community, Korea and Brazil. As a direct consequence of policy ineptitude, President Reagan would be openly committed to a protectionist trade policy for the remainder of his second term.

The ambivalence between USTR and all presidents, which goes back to President Kennedy's initial reluctance to create a trade representative in the executive office, is understandable though shortsighted. Presidents do not take kindly to the establishment of offices designed to serve the purposes of Congress in the White House. Furthermore, presidents do not relish association with an office dedicated to aggressive trade liberalization because, rhetoric notwithstanding, they also like to establish working relationships with protectionist constituencies. Yet in the absence of some such fulcrum as USTR that can bridge across the separation of powers, Smoot–Hawley will always beckon from the shades and the bicycle theory of US trade policy will always be vulnerable. In a dramatically narrowing and overtly protectionist world economy, US presidents need a degree of protection from protectionism that they do not always, or even usually, appreciate.

4 The routes to special protection

Since the end of the Second World War, the US government has relied heavily on special protection for individual industries confronted by severe import competition (Hufbauer and Rosen 1986). By special protection is meant exceptional restraints on imports, implemented through high tariffs, quota, or other limitations, that go well beyond normal tariff or border restrictions. The costs to consumers of special protection tend to be very high; for example, in 1984, they amounted, approximately, to \$56 billion (ibid.: 5). Public choice accurately predicts the way in which such costly intervention comes to pass and how, subsequently, it is rationalized.

Hufbauer and Rosen (1986: 5–6) summarise the route to special protection as follows: in Act One, the president customarily resists the request from some troubled industry for protection, pointing to the cost of protection, America's international commitments, and (in some cases) to the virtues of self-help. Where industry is politically ineffective as a consequence of the logic of collective action, or where it quickly recovers its domestic market, the play usually ends. However, where the industry is politically effective but seemingly incapable of holding its own in a competitive market, congressional pressure predictably builds for some form of relief.

In Act Two, key senators and congressmen, often members of the trade subcommittees or elected from geographic districts in which the troubled industry can make waves, urge the industry's case to the executive branch. To underline their concern, the lawmakers attach protectionist riders to legislation perceived as having high priority within the executive branch. The vulnerable departments within the executive branch (notably Commerce) also are lobbied both by the special interests and by members of Congress and, in return, exert protectionist pressure on USTR and the president.

In Act Three, the president sees priority political goals endangered and, grudgingly, comes to accept the case for some kind of trade restraint. In supplying some form of protection, the executive branch is guided by the need to obfuscate as much as possible, minimizing the transparency of the intervention to limit political damage. The president is also concerned to build maximum flexibility into the regime so that restrictions can be removed as the demand for special protection declines.

In the final act of the play, the president defends his program against its critics by emphasizing the horrors that might have arisen if he had not headed off the much more protectionist designs of Congress. Hopefully for the president, a thick curtain then falls upon the play.

High tariffs

One legal path to special protection takes the form of exceptionally high tariffs. Those that remain on the statute books are largely a legacy of the Fordney–McCumber Tariff Act of 1922 and the Smoot–Hawley Tariff Act of 1930 (Hufbauer and Rosen 1986: 6). They are retained by industries with sufficient political strength to protect themselves against the erosion of rounds of trade liberalization under the auspices of GATT. Prior to each round of tariff cuts, these industries persuade Congress that they cannot compete without the tariff protection to which they have become addicted. Congress responds by specifically excluding them from the president's tariff-cutting authority, by designating them as peril-point cases (prior to 1962) or as import-sensitive industries (thereafter), or by persuading the president to use his own constitutional powers to protect them from tariff cuts.

The average US tariff on dutiable imports has fallen to 5 percent from the 60 percent imposed by Smoot–Hawley. The tariff-based instances of special protection involve tariffs of 15 percent and higher. The recipients of such tariff protection include benzenoid chemicals, rubber footwear, ceramic articles and tiles, glassware, canned tuna, textiles and apparel, and orange juice (Hufbauer and Rosen 1986: 10). Both textiles and apparel and ceramic articles and tiles also receive additional forms of protection.

The escape clause

The second legal path to special protection, the escape clause, was initially viewed as *the* major discretionary route. This route was introduced as an industry consultation provision in the Reciprocal Trade Agreements Act of 1934. A formal escape clause was included in the 1942 bilateral trade agreement with Mexico. President Truman issued an executive order in 1945 requiring that an escape clause be included in all future trade agreements.

A legislative escape clause was included in the Trade Agreements Extension Act of 1951; and a revised escape clause was included in section 301 of the Trade Expansion Act of 1962. The 1962 Act required that trade concessions be the major cause of increased imports and that rising imports be a *major factor* in causing or threatening injury. The escape clause route is now granted under section 201 of the Trade Act of 1974, which dropped the linkage to trade concessions and relaxed the causation test to *substantial cause*.

In practice, escape clause relief has become a secondary road to special protection. The award is highly discretionary and has been granted only infrequently. Moreover, the escape clause contains features that are uncomfortable for any industry that is (or wishes to become) dependent on protection. It contemplates the decline of protection from year to year and a corresponding adjustment of the petitioning industry to the realities of international competition. This has all the attraction to the addict of a shift from heroin to methadone.

An industry seeking escape clause relief must satisfy two conditions (Hufbauer and Rosen 1986: 11). First, it must persuade the International Trade Commission (ITC) that the industry has been seriously injured or threatened with serious injury, and that rising imports are the most important cause of such injury. Second, once half or more of the commissioners who review the case recommend trade relief, the industry must persuade the president that trade relief is justified as serving the national interest.

From 1975 to 1984, 53 import petitions were brought to the ITC under sections 201 and 203. The ITC found favorably in 31 cases. Of these, the president granted trade relief in only 13 cases, several of which involved insignificant levels of trade. Significant instances of escape clause relief included ball bearings, specialty steel, nonrubber footwear, color television, mushrooms, motorcycles, CB radios, bolts, nuts and large screws, and ceramic articles (Hufbauer and Rosen 1986: 11). Between 1984 and the end of 1993, only one industry, cedar shakes and shingles, successfully pursued an escape clause case (Hufbauer and Elliott 1994: 16).

Presidents are reluctant to utilize the GATT escape clause because, although Article xix of GATT allowed members to impose temporary import barriers for the products of trade-injured industries, they were supposed to do so on a nondiscriminatory basis. In practice, therefore, Article xix was increasingly circumvented by voluntary export restraints (VERs) or orderly marketing agreements (OMAs) by which specific exporting nations agree to limit their sales.

The most recent flurry in escape clause cases came during the re-election campaign of President Reagan in January 1984. In that month, the carbon steel, shoe, copper, and table flatware industries all submitted petitions in order to pressure the White House at a time of maximum political vulnerability. Section 201 had been transformed suddenly from a means of diverting political pressure to a device for asserting it (Destler 1988: 123). In two important cases, steel and copper, the ITC recommended protection, forcing presidential decisions in September, only two months before the general election. President Reagan denied relief to the copper industry but ordered negotiation of export restraint agreements for steel.

Constitutional powers

The third legal path to special protection involves the use by the president of his inherent constitutional powers for the conduct of foreign policy to persuade foreign governments to limit their exports to the United States, using administrative means. For reasons of public choice, this low-visibility, high-flexibility form of protection has become a favored means of helping troubled industries (Haufbauer and Rosen 1986: 11–12).

These arrangements pose a serious threat to the maintenance of a liberal trading order. Many of them are secret. They are rarely subjected to the scrutiny of domestic or international proceedings. They usually result from crude political favors rendered to specific pressure groups. In most cases, they have dubious international legal status. They appear to violate the requirements of GATT Article XI (regarding export restraints) and they are not sanctioned in GATT Article XIX (most-favored-nation clause).

Since 1970, whenever the US government has chosen to assist a troubled domestic industry, the most common prescription has been a peculiar form of non-tariff barrier known by such names as voluntary export restraints (VERs), orderly marketing agreements (OMAs) and voluntary restraint agreements (VRAs). VERs are complicated, negotiated agreements, not covered by any set of international rules. To implement a VER, the United States must negotiate with an exporting government to limit the exporter's shipment of some particular good, usually for three to five years. VERs are rarely airtight agreements. Frequently, they are circumvented by exporters. Periodic renegotiations over terms, definitions and duration are often necessary.

If protection is to be granted, most economists agree that traditional forms of protection, such as quotas and tariffs, are preferable to an equivalent VER. Tariffs, in particular, are simple tools, economically more efficient and subject to relatively clear international rules. Yet the United States has negotiated VERs in industries ranging from textiles and apparel to footwear, automobiles, steel, and machine tools, at very high cost to consumers and, indeed, to the US economy (Coleman and Yoffie 1990: 137).

There are two conventional but conflicting views of why the US government has flirted so extensively with VERs despite their high cost. The first, which is public-interest orientated, suggests that the executive branch utilizes VERs to satisfy a protectionist legislature while actually promoting trade liberalization. In this perspective, the executive branch recognizes that, with VERs, it can appear to provide protection while in fact providing a weak porous form of trade restriction that will exert little positive impact on the domestic industry while assuaging the legislative critics of liberal trade policy. Implicit in this view is the notion that the protected industry does not fully appreciate the porous nature of the VER. *A priori*, this is an unconvincing theory, at least from a long-run perspective.

The alternative, rent-seeking view assumes that VERs are preferred to tariffs by troubled industries in the belief that they offer more protection than would the price increases associated with tariffs; that they are preferred by foreign exporters because the enforced reduction in sales is recompensed by higher profits; and that they are preferred by the US government because they are relatively opaque in nature and this gives rise to reduced consumer resistance.

Traditional political science analyses do not help to resolve the differences between these competing perspectives (Coleman and Yoffie 1990: 138). Variables such as the party in power and election cycles provide no help in explaining the spread of VERs over the past two decades. Democratic presidents have chosen VERs as often as Republicans, and VERs have been utilized before, during and after election years. The type of industry also provides little guidance. The United States has employed VERs to protect capital-intensive (automobile) and labor-intensive (apparel) business, differentiated products (machine tools) and homogeneous products (steel), and concentrated industries (automobiles) as well as fragmented industries (machine tools).

Only by drawing upon the institutional characteristics of the Congress, the executive branch and the bureaucracy, is it possible to explain the explosion of VERs in rational terms. Rather than assuming that government is a rational actor maximizing a specific utility function or that it is simply the vector of interest group pressures, it is important to recognize that the US government is composed of a wide range of individuals and institutions imbued with a range of motives. Some government officials, notably the president and USTR have preferences for free trade and consumer welfare. Others, notably Congress and Departments of Commerce, Energy and the Environment, have preferences for trade protection and are deeply responsive to the special interests. Inevitably, policy outcomes in such circumstances reflect an interaction between competing interests.

With this kind of mixed-motive model, VERs become a highly desirable protectionist tool precisely because they skirt around policy incoherence, addressing powerful political demands without inflicting high political or economic costs. Although the welfare losses associated with queueing and unpredictable price increases are potentially high, most VERs in practice tend to be leaky. Typically, they are so complicated that deft foreign exporters are often able to find loopholes which they then exploit to maintain or even to increase the volume of their exports. Such leakiness also appeases domestic consumers by alleviating the potential market disruption that a VER otherwise must entail. Such leakiness also appeals to the trade liberalizing policymakers within the executive branch because it allows more imports into the US economy than would a comparable tariff.

The foreign-policy cost of a VER is lower than that of a comparable tariff. VERs are negotiated by the importing and exporting governments whereas tariffs are imposed unilaterally by the government of the importing economy. In the case of a tariff, the importing government imposes a tax and collects revenue. Foreign firms typically must cut prices or lose export volume. VERs, by contrast, are implemented by the government of the exporting economy. In consequence, foreign exporters usually are able to raise their own prices, lower the contestability of their own domestic markets and collect the rents generated by protectionism.

The domestic political cost of a VER is also lower than that of a comparable tariff. The protected industry typically prefers a quantitative restriction to a tariff rate increase, to the extent at least that leakiness is not anticipated. Moreover, while both tariffs and VERs predictably will cause domestic prices to rise and will impose deadweight welfare losses on consumers, the effect of the tariff is much more transparent, and the government for that reason is much more vulnerable to voter alienation.

Empirically, the most important variable distinguishing industries that receive tariffs from those that receive VERs is *size*. Of the ten industries provided with protection between 1977 and 1984, for example, the six that received VERs or OMAs were all large, as defined by sales and employment, whereas the four that received tariffs were all small (Coleman and Yoffie 1990: 143).

Size is an important proxy for domestic political and foreign policy costs. The larger the domestic industry, the higher the political costs of transparent tariffs. Similarly, tariffs and quotas on the products of large domestic industries necessitate higher compensation and/or more friction with trading partners. Thus, if the industry is large, the benefits of VERs outweigh the transaction costs of bargaining with foreign governments. Tariffs on small industries, by contrast, are less likely to provoke a domestic political backlash or to induce foreign retaliation.

The analysis so far suggests that institutional incentives create a stable political equilibrium that should contrive to produce somewhat leaky VERs for large industries in distress. For such an equilibrium suits the varied interests of Congress, of the president and of other players in the executive branch. However, it does not suit the interests of the troubled industries that mistakenly rely upon it for substantive relief.

Assuming that industries learn not only from experience but also from each other, two things occur. Common patterns emerge, producing a diffusion of knowledge about an effective VER. Industries that come to believe that their own VERs are inadequate repeatedly return to the executive branch to request additional protection. In this sense, VERs promote political learning and protectionist recidivism. During the 1960s, textiles was the lone recidivist; by the mid-1970s, it was textiles and steel; by the late 1970s, it was textiles, steel, television, and footwear. By 1985, more than 60 separate industry groups had filed petitions on two or more occasions (Coleman and Yoffie 1990: 145). Indeed, most of the increase in demand for protection during the Reagan administration can be traced to recidivists.

Recidivism is important for the future of VERs in the United States, since it creates players that learn ever more sophisticated means to exploit the system. Recidivists tend to have strong common interests and common complaints. Unlike newcomers to Washington, they are likely to know each other. They will have testified before the ITC on many occasions, utilized the same specialized set of Washington lawyers, and lobbied the same committees on Capitol Hill. The VERs that they insist on having negotiated will be less and less leaky and less and less palatable to the governments of the exporting economies.

As political learning increases and sophistication grows, the willingness on the part of a troubled industry to accept VERs diminishes. The US–Japan semiconductor industry experience clearly marks the shape of things to come. In 1985, the US semiconductor industry filed an unfair trade petition against Japan under section 301 of the Trade Expansion Act of 1974, claiming discriminatory access to the Japanese market. Subsequently, three US companies and the Department of Commerce filed antidumping suits.

To alleviate the impact of dumping duties, the Japanese government offered a voluntary export agreement on dynamic random access memories (DRAMs). Fearing a leaky VER, the US Semiconductor Industry Association rejected the Japanese offer. Instead, it insisted on a formula of 'foreign market values' that Japan would have to apply to such products in all markets. The Reagan administration acceded to this request, supplying significant protection to the US semiconductor industry.

As domestic industries become ever more sophisticated in VER negotiations, so the governments of exporting economies respond in kind (Coleman and Yoffie 1990: 147). For example, when Japan first negotiated a VER in textiles with the United States, it failed to consider the possibility that other countries would fill the gap created by the volume restraint on Japanese products. Hong Kong and others gained market share at Japan's expense. By the mid-1960s, whenever Japan negotiated a deal with the United States, it insisted that its exporting firms should not be disadvantaged *vis-à-vis* other countries. The US was required to negotiate additional VERs with other countries.

In this manner, VER protectionism has progressively tightened and the mixed-motive equilibrium model outlined above has increasingly been placed in jeopardy If damage control of diplomatic consequences is a major reason why presidents use their constitutional powers to negotiate VERs, as the cost of such protectionism rises predictably they will search for substitutes that reintroduce those elements of leakiness on which the entire political equilibrium initially was made to rest.

Statutory frameworks for discretionary protection
A fourth legal route to special protection is found in statutory frameworks that give the president latitude in deciding how to answer the trade problems of affected industries. Examples are section 204 of the Agricultural Act of 1956, used as the statutory vehicle for restraining textile and apparel imports, and section 22 of the Agricultural Adjustment Act of 1933, currently used to limit dairy, peanut, cotton, and sugar imports. 'In deploying both these statutes, presidents pay close attention to congressional sentiment' (Hufbauer and Rosen 1986: 12).

Another statute, section 232 of the Trade Expansion Act of 1962, permits trade restrictions for purposes of national security. Section 232 was deployed to restrain petroleum imports between 1962 and 1973. During the 1980s, the bolts, nuts and large screws industry and the machine tool industry tried to make use of section 232, albeit without success in the face of Reagan administration intransigence (Hufbauer and Rosen 1986: 12).

Unusual quantitative relief in countervailing-duty and antidumping-duty cases is a recent example of extraordinary restraint within a statutory framework. The approach was first used by the Carter administration in 1978 in the form of the trigger-price mechanism for carbon steel products. The same approach was used by the Reagan administration in settling subsidy complaints against Chinese textiles in 1983. In 1984 and 1985, President Reagan used this approach to impose import quotas on steel from virtually all countries except Japan and Korea. In 1986, he used the same approach to restrict imports of Japanese semiconductors (Hufbauer and Rosen 1986: 13).

In essence, the aggressive pursuit of the antidumping and countervailing duty remedies is now deployed by US industries to drive foreign producers to the quota bargaining table. Once foreign producers are subject to such a quota regime, they lobby hard to expand the regime to cover third-country competitors. In this way, the protectionist noose is tightened around the necks of unsuspecting US consumers.

Statutory quotas
The fifth legal route to special protection is that based on statutory quotas. These quotas represent the most decisive exercise of congressional power. Typically, they establish a rigid limit on imports. Alternatively, they bar foreign suppliers from the US market. Examples include the manufacturing clause of the copyright law, the Jones Act, the Meat Act and the Magnusan Fisheries Act (Hufbauer and Rosen 1986: 13).

Each of these laws strictly limits foreign entry, allowing presidential discretion only with respect to details of implementation. Presidents predictably attempt to head off such statutory quotas either by logrolling with Congress or by exercising the veto power. A recent setback to this form of trade restraint was President Reagan's veto of the Textile Trade and Enforcement Act of 1985.

5 Aggressive unilateralism

Throughout the period 1934–88, the United States government followed a principle of broadly balanced reciprocity, based on the practice of unconditional most-favored-nation status. Unconditional MFN guaranteed the diffusion of the benefits of trade liberalization to all economies practicing this principle. It helped to limit the striking of bilateral agreements and other discriminatory practices, all of which promoted the politicization of trade. This kind of reciprocity provided the basis for the post-Second World War international trading system. It constituted a central norm of the GATT. With its use, global trade flourished (Milner 1992: 163).

MFN PRINCIPLE

Despite this success, US trade law seems to be turning away from unconditional MFN and towards aggressive unilateralism in pursuit of narrow and ultimately short-sighted trade objectives (Bhagwati 1992). This shift of direction can be traced back at least to 1962. The Trade Expansion Act of 1962 empowered the president to retaliate against foreign practices that discriminated against US exports. According to section 252 of the Act, if *unreasonable* or *unjustifiable* foreign import restrictions were found in the case of manufactured goods, the president could withhold trade agreement concessions from that country. For agricultural goods, the president could go even further and impose duties or other import restrictions. Section 252 was designed as a threat of retaliation to press the European Economic Community and the European Free Trade Association to keep their markets open to US exports.

AGGRESSIVE UNILATERALISM

(RULE)

In the early 1970s, section 252 was revised to provide the president with expanded discretion in combating unfair trade practices abroad. Section 301 of the Trade and Tariff Act of 1974 provided the shorthand for the current US policy of aggressive unilateralism. Amended repeatedly, its main transformations and elaborations have occurred in sections 301 to 306 in 1984 and, most notably, in sections 301–310 of the Omnibus Trade and Competitiveness Act of 1988.

'The section 301 legislation of 1974 was directed broadly at foreign restrictions on US trade and used to enforce trade rights conferred by GATT and by bilateral treaties, if necessary through retaliation against those judged to have violated such rights. In the case of GATT-defined rights, or the nullification and impairment of GATT-negotiated benefits, section 301

SECT. 301

complaints were to be pursued by first invoking GATT's dispute settlement machinery' (Bhagwati 1990: 2).

In essence, the 301 procedures, at least in principle, were GATT-consistent. Section 301 enabled the president to deploy a wide range of retaliatory actions against any country that applied *unjustifiable* or *unreasonable* import restrictions or any export subsidies that reduced the sales of US goods abroad. The statute left a great deal of discretion to the president concerning how the section was to be used, how foreign countries were to be dealt with, and when and how retaliation was to be employed.

In practice, section 301 (as well as section 252) was hardly ever used. Between 1975 and 1979, only eighteen petitions under section 301 were filed; on none of these petitions did the president take retaliatory action. Following minor revisions in the 1979 Act, section 301 was invoked more frequently: 35 times between 1980 and 1985. Once again, however, the successful removal of trade barriers and/or retaliations simply did not occur. Predictably, such presidential reluctance to employ aggressive unilateralism induced Congress to revise the statute.

SUPER 301

In 1985, against a background of large US trade deficits and mounting protectionist pressures, Congress initiated a new trade bill targeting Japan as an unfair trader and threatening retaliation in the form of across-the-board import duties on its products. This legislative threat shook the Reagan administration out of its (admirable) five-year policy of benign neglect on the trade policy front. The administration announced its support for fair rather than free trade. It coordinated with foreign governments to lower the value of the dollar. It pledged itself to work with Congress in writing a new trade bill that would deal specifically with unfair trade practices.

A congressional majority moved to seek remedies by rewriting the US trade laws, especially section 301. Specifically, they maneuvered to make this statute a more credible weapon with which to negotiate trade barrier reductions. 'Super 301' was born in late 1988 as part of the Omnibus Trade and Competitiveness Act after more than three years of sustained congressional activity.

Super 301 orders a *National Trade Estimate*, showing foreign barriers to US trade and their costs. On this basis, USTR is required to investigate countries with consistent patterns of unfair trade practices. If these practices are found to be unjustifiable or unreasonable, USTR must attempt to persuade the countries in question to halt them within a specified period of time. If these practices continue, then the president must retaliate against an equivalent value of the foreign country's goods. The president can decide not to retaliate when either the adverse impact of retaliation for the US economy would be extreme, or retaliation would cause serious harm to US security. If he chooses not to retaliate, he must explain his reasons in detail to Congress.

Special 301 is similar to Super 301 but is addressed specifically to the issue of intellectual property rights.

Super (and Special) 301 is thus targeted against whole countries, not particular products. It limits presidential discretion through stricter provisions, tight deadlines and the use of USTR. Finally, it mandates retaliation unless the president can show, on specific grounds, that this would hurt the United States. It puts in place all the machinery necessary for the United States to manifest the bully-on-the-block syndrome that rent-seeking US industries and their congressional brokers have worked hard to promote.

Public-choice theory once again performs well in explaining the inclusion of Super 301 provisions in the 1988 Act, and especially in explaining the tensions between Congress and the executive branch during the lengthy negotiations that preceded the legislation. The president was confronted with the termination of his negotiating authority in 1988 and with the initiation of the Uruguay Round of multilateral trade negotiations. In these circumstances, he needed new authority to sustain certain priority foreign policy goals.

The executive branch did not want a trade bill considered in 1985 or 1986, since these were years of powerful protectionist sentiment associated with record-breaking US trade deficits. Any deal struck with Congress in such circumstances predictably would extract a high price for providing presidential negotiating authority (Milner 1992: 174). As the deficit figures improved and US exports increased after 1986, a better deal could be struck. Congress needed to satisfy its constituents – especially such powerful Democratic lobbyists as organized labor – and section 301 amendments would help to do this.

By delegating authority for the administration of Super 301 to USTR and by allowing significant executive branch discretion, Congress would also avoid recriminations for any undesired retaliations that might occur. By shifting some authority from the president to USTR, Congress also sent a signal to the president and to the voters that he should be more responsive to domestic pressures. By accepting the bill, President Reagan signaled his and his Republican successor's concern for domestic interests without sacrificing his ability to pursue broader foreign policy goals. There was little or no concern for the public interest in the deal that was eventually cut.

The shift from section 301 to Super 301 carried with it significant implications for the GATT. Section 301 complaints were expected to be pursued by first invoking GATT's dispute-settlement machinery. At least in principle, section 301 procedures were supposed to be GATT-consistent. Following a favorable finding, the GATT itself must authorize section 301 retaliation for the latter to be unambiguously GATT-legal. Yet, of the six Gatt-based section 301 cases implemented by the United States during the period 1975–9, retaliation was never authorized by the GATT (Bhagwati 1992: 2).

Only one of these six retaliations was GATT-legal, although others involved legal breakdowns on which it would have been difficult to rule. None of these six cases triggered a legal crisis. GATT complaints were filed against three of the six retaliations. Two of the complaints – European wheat and flour and Japanese semiconductors – were not pursued to adjudication. The third – European hormones – was blocked from prosecution by the United States. The 1988 Act, however, imposed timetables to be followed in these regular 301 cases that almost inevitably must conflict with the more leisurely GATT procedures. This greatly increased the probability of GATT-illegal 301 retaliations on the part of the United States.

The real threat of aggressive unilateralism, however, arises not from the regular section 301 retaliations but from the Super (and Special) 301 retaliations authorized by the protectionist 1988 Act. For these categories contemplate, indeed require, retaliation against other countries' trade practices that do not violate any legal obligation. For example, among the list of unreasonable practices supplied by the 1988 Act are such items as inadequate workers' rights and insufficient anticompetitive policy measures, which are not matters traditionally dealt with in trade negotiations.

The actions taken by USTR Carla Hills on behalf of the Bush administration on June 16 1989 against Japan, India and Brazil are good examples of Super 301 aggressive unilateralism. 'The United States chose five priority practices among the three countries: quantitative restrictions, citing Brazil for its balance of payment restrictions; government procurement restrictions, citing Japanese restrictions on supercomputers and satellites; technical barriers to trade, citing Japanese standards on forest products; trade-related investment measures (TRIMs), citing India for export performance requirements imposed on foreign investors; and barriers to trade in services, citing India for restrictions on foreign insurance' (Bhagwati 1990: 3).

These cases were all resolved in one way or another (Destler 1992: 428). In December 1989, after formal consultations were initiated under GATT, Article xxiii, Brazil indicated its intent to reduce the prohibited import list and expand quotas. After USTR notified Brazil that it would pursue dispute settlement, Brazil abolished the import list and removed all quotas. USTR terminated investigations on May 21 1990.

After bilateral consultations the United States and Japan reached an understanding to provide open access to the Japanese public satellite market and to ensure market opportunities for US supercomputer supplies. After extensive consultations, the US and Japan also reached an agreement on a package of tariff concessions and construction standards designed to expand market opportunities for US forest products supplies. USTR suspended its 301 investigations of Japan on June 15 1990.

After unsuccessful talks with the government of India, USTR renewed its designation of India as a *priority country* and its investment barriers and lack of trade insurance market access as priority practices under Super 301. USTR determined that India's practices were unreasonable and burdened US commerce. However, it took no action and terminated its investigation, putting the Indian government on notice that it would review India's practices following the completion of the Uruguay Round.

'Carla Hills, US Trade Representative appointed by President Bush, is credited with the metaphor of using a crowbar to pry open foreign markets' (Bhagwati 1991: 49) by applying Section 301 and Super 301 actions. Although she skillfully minimized the damage that such policies inflict on the GATT multilateral system, her actions epitomized export politics pursued 'by exceptionally aggressive means' (Destler 1992: 127). Although for political reasons the Bush administration targeted a number of countries with 301 actions, its most important target was Japan.

There was no doubt whatsoever, anywhere in the executive branch, about which specific country Congress had uppermost in mind when drafting the mandatory retaliation clauses into the 1988 Act (Destler 1992: 127). President Bush, throughout his term of office, was anxious to appease Congress on matters of economic policy. USTR, reflecting this policy, proposed to Japan a separate negotiation outside the 301 framework on *structural impediments* to trade. The resulting *Structural Impediments Initiative* talks aimed at the sort of broader import resistance that Congress had in mind, avoiding further resort to Super 301 actions.

The wielding of the executive branch crowbar against Japan would eventually take President Bush to Tokyo in his abortive attempt to open up the Japanese automobile market to US producers. This fateful mission, in which he was joined by the failed chief executives of the three major US auto producers, justly culminated in an embarrassing episode in which the President of the United States vomited at the banquet table of his stunned Japanese hosts. Notwithstanding this awesome message from above, the Clinton administration, through USTR Mickey Kantor, continues to use the crowbar on the Japanese government in pursuit of aggressive unilateral objectives.

6   Multilateral trade negotiations

The Reciprocal Trade Agreements Act of 1934 addressed the question of how to avoid unbalanced trade pressures of the kind that had culminated in the Smoot–Hawley Tariff Act of 1930. Its solution was to delegate authority for trade negotiations to the executive branch. In the process of trade negotiation, 'getting' and 'giving' predictably were defined in terms of producers, not consumers. However, the concept of the 'bargaining tariff shifted the balance of trade politics by engaging the interests of export producers, since tariff reductions henceforth could be justified as a direct means of winning new markets for US products overseas' (Destler 1992: 16).

The bargaining tariff was to become an 'essential ingredient in the emerging US trade policy-making system' (Destler 1992: 16). Initially, it was utilized on a bilateral basis, with Congress content to allow the president full authority to approve the specific agreements. After the Second World War, however, presidents would deploy tariff-negotiating authority much more ambitiously, to bargain on general tariff levels rather than item by item, and would seek new authority to negotiate agreements on non-tariff trade distortions. In the case of such latter negotiations, Congress would always insist on requiring subsequent legislative approval.

The first multilateral tariff negotiations occurred in 1947, while international discussions were still continuing over the specific provisions to be included in the ultimately doomed International Trade Organization. The choice of negotiating technique was far from easy. A multilateral approach in which the participants would follow a simple tariff-reducing rule was rejected on the ground that it paid insufficient attention to the problems of individual import-sensitive industries (Baldwin 1988: 190). A multilateral approach based on item-by-item negotiations was also ruled out as impracticable. The negotiating procedure adopted must be consistent with the most-favored nation (MFN) principle adopted by the United States in 1923.

The solution devised, to minimize the free-rider problem that would arise if two countries reciprocally cut their duties on many items and extended these cuts to all other countries, was one utilizing the principal-supplier rule. Under this rule, two countries exchange offer and request lists on tariff items for which each is the (or at least a) principal export supplier of the other country. This enabled the MFN principle to be followed by all countries. Countries that failed to make major concessions would not receive concessions on their major products.

Even so, a small country that was heavily reliant on a few items for most of its export earnings from large countries, but was not itself a principal supplier of these items, would have little incentive to open up its own markets to the large countries. To counter such free-riding, the large countries would cut their duties somewhat in negotiations with principal suppliers, but then cut these duties further in negotiations with non-principal suppliers for whom concessions on the item were important. The cuts would be extended to all countries each time. Another technique, to be followed when there were distinguishable country differences in the quality of a product covered by a single tariff rate, was 'to establish separate tariff lines for each variety and then to negotiate with the principal supplier of each' (Baldwin 1988: 191).

Following the principal–supplier rule, while simultaneously requiring a rough balance of concessions bilaterally, inevitably limited the scope of such negotiations. Mutual concessions would typically be forthcoming on lists of items whose total export values were approximately equal. Where the export values of principally supplied items differed significantly, the countries involved would usually not negotiate. If they did negotiate, the larger exporter in value terms would cut its duties by a smaller percentage.

The five multilateral negotiations from 1947 until the Kennedy Round in 1962 were essentially a series of simultaneous bilateral negotiations. Country teams were formed to exchange offer and request lists and to conduct reciprocal negotiations. Participants were expected to take into consideration the indirect benefits they received from the negotiations between other governments in determining when a balance of concessions with their trading partners had been reached. This was effected only after a series of tentative pairwise agreements had already been reached and therefore did not alter the essentially bilateral nature of the negotiations.

Predictably, the increase in world trade generated by such bilateral bargains, even though the MFN principle was scrupulously honored, fell far short of what might have been achieved by truly multilateral bargains. To test this hypothesis, Baldwin and Lage (1971) compared the trade-expansionary effects of a maximum 50 percent cut from a bilateral versus a multilateral balancing requirement for a group of six major participants in the Kennedy Round, namely, the United States, the EEC, the United Kingdom, the European Free Trade Association, Japan and Canada. They used a linear programming approach applied to actual 1964 trade and tariff data for dutiable imports of non-agricultural goods, assuming a reasonable set of import-demand elasticities.

They determined that if a multilateral approach had been followed, using the constraint that the change in a group's total imports from the others could not exceed its change in total exports to the others by more than 20 percent, the maximum possible increase in world trade would have been $5.91 billion. In contrast, using the constraint that no group's change in imports from any other group could exceed its change in exports to that group by more than 20 percent, Baldwin and Lage (1971) determined that the maximum possible increase in world trade would be no more than a miserly $0.35 billion. A bilateral balancing requirement limited the permissible increase in world trade to less than 6 percent of that achievable via constrained multilateral negotiations, at least in the circumstances depicted.

The extent of duty cuts in the four GATT tariff-reducing rounds that followed the 1947 negotiations clearly illustrated the difficulty in going much beyond duty-cutting in industries not faced with significant import competition. In most industrial countries, the end of the Second World War found many high-duty sectors that had received protection as a consequence of the general protectionist trend of the 1930s and not because they faced severe import competition. It was not difficult to lower tariffs in such cases. The average cut in all US tariffs in the 1947 negotiations, therefore, was 21.1 percent. It was extremely difficult to continue this pace of trade liberalization. In the next four rounds, between 1949 and 1962, the average US tariff cuts amounted only to 1.9, 3.0, 3.5 and 2.4 percent respectively.

The Kennedy Round

The Kennedy Round is the popular name for the sixth round of trade negotiations under the aegis of the GATT, conducted during 1963–7, which produced major cuts in tariffs. In the case of the United States, cuts in protective tariffs resulting from the Kennedy Round averaged 35 percent.

The immediate stimulus in favor of a major round of multilateral trade bargaining was the establishment in 1958 of the European Economic Community and the perceived threat to the bicycle theory of trade liberalization posed by a potential Fortress Europe. Evidently, the early postwar series of multilateral bargaining had encountered severely diminishing returns by the late 1950s. Furthermore, with the re-emergence of international competition, protectionist pressures were beginning to regain their prewar vigor within the United States. The threat to trade liberalization implicit in these developments galvanized President Kennedy to initiate a new, ambitious round of trade negotiations.

First, however, the president had to purchase the support of Congress for an initiative opposed by powerful protectionist lobbies, though fortuitously supported by organized labor. One concession was the establishment of STR within the executive branch as a congressional watchdog over potential presidential excesses. The second concession, to buy off the US textile industry, was a multilateral trade-restricting arrangement in 1961 which took shape as the Short-term Arrangement Regarding International Trade in Textiles. The Short-term Arrangement (STA) embodied a network of restrictions involving sixteen countries and over sixty product categories. The STA was succeeded by the Long-term Arrangement (LTA) in 1962. The LTA lasted, with two extensions, until 1974, restricting cotton textile exports to the United States from seventeen countries.

After the EEC adopted a common external tariff schedule by averaging the tariffs of its six members, 'Community trade officials became increasingly concerned about the difference between their industry profile of tariffs and the duty profiles of the United States, Japan and the United Kingdom' (Baldwin 1988: 193). The averaging process tended to yield a pattern of EEC tariff rates predominantly in the 10–20 percent range, whereas many US, Japanese and UK tariffs remained above 30 percent. There was concern that this divergent structure would cause a significant volume of trade to be diverted from these other important import markets to the EEC. To counter this prospect, Community trade officials favored a negotiating approach that would bring about significant cuts in high-duty items of the United States, Japan and the United Kingdom.

To implement this objective, the EEC had proposed an across-the-board tariff cut of 20 percent at the outset of the fifth round of negotiations (the Dillon Round) in 1960. This proposal had been rejected by the United States, with damaging consequences for the tariff-cutting exercise (an average cut of only 2.4 percent). Therefore, for the Kennedy Round United States officials moved to a position favoring a general tariff-cutting rule rather than an item-by-item approach.

President Kennedy wanted a deep average cut in tariffs for both international political and domestic economic reasons. He believed that such a cut would strengthen political ties among the non-communist nations and that it would reduce the degree of trade diversion away from US suppliers in favor of EEC suppliers threatened by the elimination of tariff barriers within the EEC. Congress responded in 1962 by authorizing negotiations to cut tariffs across the board.

In granting such broad tariff-reducing authority, however, Congress protected itself from any special interest group backlash. The president was required to exclude certain products from any duty cuts, to obtain advice from the Tariff Commission, appropriate agencies and private groups prior to entering into tariff-cutting negotiations, and to seek information and advice from the Departments of Agriculture, Commerce, Defense, Interior, Labor, State and Treasury as well as from the STR prior to entering into any trade agreement.

The EEC negotiators pressed for a cutting rule that would bring about a larger reduction in high-duty items than in low-duty items. They proposed a rule based on the concept of *écrêtement* (depeaking) that would reduce tariffs on manufactured goods by 50 percent of the difference between their existing levels and 10 percent. Duties on semi-manufacturers and raw materials would be cut 50 percent of the difference between their existing rates and 5 percent and zero respectively. The United States opposed this rule, ostensibly on the ground that there would be an average cut of only 15 percent even before any exceptions were made.

The US proposal for a 50 percent cutting rule was eventually accepted with the qualification that 'special rules of general and automatic application' would be deployed where significant disparities existed in tariff levels. In fact, because of opposition from third countries, a general disparities rule was never adopted. Instead, the EEC dealt with major disparities on a case-by-case basis. An important feature of the Kennedy Round was an agreement at the outset that only 'a bare minimum' of exceptions to the cutting rule would be allowed. The exceptions were quite modest, and were mostly confined to declining industries or to industries where national security considerations were deemed to be important. The United States tabled a smaller exception list than either the EEC or Japan (Baldwin 1988: 195).

Once each country had tabled its exceptions, the process of achieving reciprocity proceeded in a manner similar to the earlier item-by-item method. Each of the participants prepared request lists of products on which they asked for greater tariff reductions from various other participants. They prepared and circulated *indicative lists* of items on which they would withdraw their initial offers, either in whole or in part, if their requests for concessions were not forthcoming. The United States negotiators, because of their smaller exceptions list, felt that the EEC and Japan must be much more forthcoming for a satisfactory balance of concessions to be attained (Baldwin 1988: 195).

However, further significant liberalization failed to materialize. In November 1966, the United States presented its indicative withdrawal list. In March 1967, it formally withdrew many items from its list of products subject to the full 50 percent cutting rule. After other countries had responded to such US withdrawals, the United States removed still more items from its offer list in May 1967. In fact, about 10 percent of all dutiable items were withdrawn from the US offer list during the final stages of the negotiations (Baldwin 1988: 195).

Although the Kennedy Round was widely considered to be a success, with negotiated nominal tariff reductions averaging 35 percent, many congressmen were displeased with the executive branch and dissatisfied with the outcome. In part, their displeasure focused on the lack of progress in opening up international markets to US agriculture and on the failure to address the issue of non-tariff measures. More important, however, was the widespread belief in Congress that 'the executive branch had exceeded its negotiating authority by subscribing to an antidumping agreement' (Low 1993: 174). In addition, the administration had negotiated away the American Selling Price (ASP) method of customs valuation, 'whereby the valuation basis calculating import duties was taken to be the price in the home market of the same article produced domestically' (Low 1993: 174). Evidently, Congress was rethinking its role on trade policy at a time when the US economy was viewed as increasingly vulnerable to international competition. It began this rethinking by refusing to implement the antidumping code and the ASP revisions of the Kennedy Round.

Baldwin (1985: 161) analysed the pattern of tariff cut exclusions in the Kennedy Round to determine the importance of public choice pressures. Using probit analysis, he compared the characteristics of those US industries in which at least 5 percent of the tariff line items were not reduced at all with the characteristics of those industries in which less than 5 percent of the tariff line were excluded from cuts. This crude comparison suggested that the exclusions tended to be concentrated in sectors where skill levels were low, employment was high, labor's share of value added was high and the import penetration ratio was high. Baldwin concluded from this study that a short-run self-interest framework was 'insufficient to account fully for the variations in tariff cuts and tariff levels across US industries' (Baldwin 1985: 165).

The Tokyo Round
The Tokyo Round is the popular name for the seventh round of trade negotiations under the aegis of the GATT initiated formally by the Tokyo Declaration in 1973 and completed in 1979. The Tokyo Round, also called the Multilateral Trade Negotiations (MTN), differed from previous GATT rounds in its primary focus, which was to reduce and regulate non-tariff barriers (NTBs). It yielded a number of multilateral codes covering, among other subjects, subsidies and countervailing measures, antidumping, customs valuation, government procurement and technical barriers to trade. Participating nations also agreed to a substantial further reduction in tariff rates (Destler 1992: 442). With varying degrees of success, the Tokyo Round addressed tariffs, agriculture, and a range of trade practices, most of them covered by the GATT but thought to be in need of clearer or stricter regulation.

The immediate backcloth to the new trade negotiations was a dramatic and unexpected policy initiative by the United States. On August 15 1971, President Nixon took several related steps aimed at reducing the foreign exchange value of the dollar, thus terminating the fixed exchange rate system known as the Bretton Woods System. This decision was made to revise a significant decline in the US export–import surplus that had occurred since 1968 and that was widely attributed to an overvalued dollar. Within four months, the dollar was effectively devalued by 10 percent against other major currencies. Within two years, its value would decline substantially further, triggering an improvement in the US trade balance in early 1973, just as legislation to authorize the Tokyo Round made its way through the House of Representatives.

By February 1972, the United States, the European Community and Japan had all declared themselves in favor of a new round of multilateral trade negotiations. In the United States, the immediate issue confronting the Nixon administration was the kind of negotiating authority that should be sought. The president could reasonably expect to be granted tariff-cutting authority along the lines established by the Reciprocal Trade Agreements program in 1934. Authority to negotiate non-tariff measures, however, was much more problematic, given the sharp lesson delivered by Congress on the antidumping code and the ASP at the end of the Kennedy Round. The executive branch was determined not to be placed again in the embarrassing position of allowing Congress to unravel the administration's international commitments.

The final compromise between President Nixon and Congress was the *fast-track authority*. Under this arrangement, the president negotiates on non-tariff matters and, 90 days before entering into any agreements, notifies Congress of his intentions. The president then consults with relevant congressional committees and finalizes the international agreements for presentation to Congress. Congress then must consider the legislation and vote up or down, with no possibility of amendment. The system has worked well and Congress has continued to extend fast-track negotiating authority (Low 1993: 177).

Two other mechanisms were also introduced to ensure that international commitments entered into by the executive branch would have adequate domestic support (Low 1993: 178). First, arrangements were made for congressional representation on delegations to international negotiations. Certain congressional representatives would be entitled to full and regular progress briefings. Second, private-sector committees were established to supply advice and information regarding priorities and strategies in the negotiation. An Advisory Committee for Trade and Policy Negotiations (ACTPN) was created, supported by a network of 27 advisory committees, to provide advisory opinions on the results of the negotiations. Although cumbersome in administrative terms, ACTPN ensured smooth US adoption procedures at the end of the Tokyo Round.

The trade bill presented by President Nixon in April 1973 was not passed by Congress until December 1974, after President Gerald Ford had assumed office. This meant that the United States was negotiating without authority for the early part of the Tokyo Round. Congress dragged its heels in part because of Watergate and in part because some of its members opposed the proposal to extend MFN treatment to the USSR. Eventually, the legislation passed with an amendment tying MFN treatment for communist countries to their emigration policies (Low 1993: 178).

The Tokyo Round of tariff negotiations differed in a number of ways from the Kennedy Round (Baldwin 1988: 195). First, the United States agreed to a duty-cutting rule that reduced higher-duty rates by a greater percentage than lower rates. Under a formula proposed by the Swiss negotiators, each duty rate would be cut by a rate equal to $x/(x + 0.14)$ where x was the existing rate of duty. A 14 percent duty under this rule would be cut by 50 percent.

Second, the duty-cutting formula was negotiated primarily by the trade ministers from the participating countries and did not involve detailed high-level political decisions concerning the exceptions to the tariff reductions process. This meant that, for the United States, the internal negotiations over the cutting rule were quite separate from those over the nature of the exceptions list (Baldwin 1988: 196). The United States included a large number of exceptions in its original offer and expressed a willingness to provide many greater-than-formula cuts to obtain the overall average cut of 40 percent that had been agreed by some participants. However, the US demanded reciprocity for this concession. The EEC declined to give credit in its reciprocity calculations for cuts that worked against the harmonization objective.

In consequence, in April 1978 the EEC announced a list of tentative withdrawals designed to yield a better balance of concessions and, in July 1979, it made these withdrawals part of its formal offer list. Approximately 20 percent of its tariff items were withdrawn from formula cuts at this time. In response, the United States withdrew almost all of its greater-than-formula cuts. In its final offer, in March 1979, the EEC exempted another 15 percent of its tariff items from full formula cuts. The United States pulled back still more in its final offers announced in April 1979 (Baldwin 1988: 197).

In any event, despite the product exemptions, the formula succeeded in reducing tariff escalation. The formula was applied by the major industrial countries and the reductions were supplemented by tariff line negotiations between countries on a product-by-product basis. This bilateral negotiation, with subsequent multilateralization of exchanges, is the traditional GATT negotiating technique.

The weighted average tariff reductions made on manufactured products by nine major industrial countries in the Tokyo Round amounted to 34 percent, leaving an actual weighted average tariff of 4.7 percent. The corresponding figures for the United States were 31 percent and 6.4 percent. The annual value of international trade affected by such tariff cuts was of the order of $155 billion (Low 1993: 182).

In contrast to the Kennedy Round, negotiations over non-tariff barriers were a major part of the Tokyo Round. Committees were established to negotiate new codes of good international behavior with regard to subsidies, government procurement, procedures, safeguards, customs valuation practices and technical barriers to trade. Six such agreements (codes) were established as a consequence of Tokyo Round negotiations.

- *The Government Procurement Code* sought to narrow the scope of any government to deploy procurement as a means of giving domestic producers additional protection. The terms of the code applied only to purchasing entities located in signatory countries and listed in an annex to the agreement. The code obliged signatory countries to extend national and nondiscriminatory treatment to fellow signatories in procurement matters. This code was not rooted in the GATT (Low 1993: 183).
- *The Code on Technical Barriers to Trade* sought to prevent the establishment of unnecessary obstacles to trade, and to ensure non-discrimination and national treatment with respect to standards, technical

regulations, testing methods and certification systems. It also encouraged the adoption of international standards and outlined procedural obligations designed to ensure maximum transparency in such matters.

• One major objective of the United States was to curtail the use of government subsidies with respect to international trade. This objective was challenged by EEC trade negotiators. *The Code on Subsidies and Countervailing Duties*, in consequence, was 'broadly worded and ambiguous' (Baldwin 1988: 198). It sought 'to clarify, but not significantly to modify, pre-existing rules on subsidies' (Low 1993: 183), to define procedures for using countervailing duties and to provide a dispute-settlement mechanism.

• *The Customs on Valuation Code* sought to establish a single, more precise system of customs valuation than that described in Article VII of the GATT. The code set out five methods of valuation, to be applied sequentially when a method in the hierarchy could not be applied. Undeveloped countries were permitted certain leeway with respect to this code.

• *The Code on Import Licensing Procedures* established the principal that licensing procedures should be neutral in application and equitably administered.

• *The Antidumping Code* required proof of injury to domestic producers before antidumping duties could be imposed. It also required that duties imposed must be sufficiently high to remedy the injury. Price undertakings might be accepted from exporters as an alternative to antidumping duties.

• *The Code on Trade in Civil Aircraft* eliminated tariffs on all civil aircraft and their parts, directed that the provisions of the standards code and subsidies code apply to that sector, provided that the application of any non-tariff measures be consistent with GATT practice and prevented signatories from obliging domestic airlines to purchase domestically manufactured aircraft.

The overall outcome of the Tokyo Round was somewhat mixed. Most observers deemed the tariff cuts to be successful from a trade-liberalizing perspective. 'Negotiations over non-tariff barriers were most successful when they went beyond general declarations of good intentions and resulted in specific trade-liberalizing concessions by the participants' (Baldwin 1988: 198). Negotiations on unfair trading practices led to vaguely worded rules that were subject to weak dispute settlement procedures and ineffective enforcement mechanisms, especially with regard to the subsidies issue. Despite two sectoral agreements on agriculture, the Tokyo Round failed ignominiously to deal effectively with the problem of agricultural protection, arguably the single most intransigent obstacle to trade liberalization facing the GATT. Failure was a direct consequence of special interest lobbying.

By April 1979, most of the Tokyo Round results had been virtually finalized, although discussions vainly continued on agriculture and infant-industry safeguards, and a few outstanding matters were left to be resolved in the field of customs valuation and antidumping. Between April and November 1979, domestic ratification processes took place. The United States negotiators had granted long-sought concessions – the abandonment of the American Selling Price (ASP) system of customs valuation and an injury test for the imposition of countervailing duties – in exchange for commitments on a range of trade-distorting foreign practices. In view of the Kennedy Round experience, the executive branch awaited congressional responses with a degree of nervousness, relying upon STR Robert Strauss to negotiate across the separation of powers.

A mixture of factors ensured a much more cooperative legislative response on this occasion. The executive branch had carefully courted Congress and kept its members fully informed at all stages in the Tokyo Round, throughout the Nixon, Ford and Carter administrations. The private sector had also been carefully courted. In consequence, there were no surprises. Congress only modified one small aspect of the procurement code to protect some minority interests.

However, some difficult problems persisted when it came to adopting the results of the negotiations, stemming from the juridical status of the codes (Low 1993: 186). In particular, the legal rights of non-signatories that did not subscribe to the discipline of the codes remained uncertain. In November 1979, the contracting parties incorporated the codes into the GATT system through a Decision while noting that existing GATT rights and benefits of those countries that were not parties to the Decision would not be affected.

Baldwin (1985) subjected the Tokyo Round tariff to public-choice analysis. Using probit analysis, he determined that the industries receiving low duty cuts were characterized by relatively unskilled and low-paid workers, by large labor forces, slow employment growth, high and rising import-penetration ratios and high levels of protection. As with the Kennedy Round analysis, Baldwin recognized some force in the public-choice explanation, while arguing that short-run self-interest alone was insufficient to account for the variations in tariff and tariff levels across industries.

The Uruguay Round
The Uruguay Round is the popular name for the eighth round of trade negotiations under the aegis of the GATT, initiated by the Punte del Este agreement of September 1986 and completed in April 1994. The talks were designed to reduce barriers and strengthen international rules affecting gen-

eral market access, agriculture, services, textiles trade, intellectual property rights, dispute settlement, safeguards and enforcement measures under the GATT.

As ratified, the Uruguay Round agreement will lower average tariffs by 30 percent; eliminate tariffs on pharmaceuticals, construction equipment, medical equipment, paper, and steel; eliminate over a ten-year transition period a system of textile and apparel quotas that limits imports into developed countries; provide twenty-year protection of patents, trademarks and copyrights; and reduce the volume of subsidized agricultural exports by 21 percent over six years. Japan and Korea will lift bans on rice imports. The ratified agreement will also replace GATT with a new World Trade Organization (WTO) as the arbiter of world trade.

The inter-round years between Tokyo and Uruguay, 1980–6, were inauspicious for the GATT system. The problems carried over from the Tokyo Round, most notably agriculture and safeguards, but also textiles, subsidies, remedies against unfair trade practices, and the role and responsibility of developing countries in the trading system, repeatedly threatened the survival of the liberal system during a period of worldwide recession and growing trade imbalances.

The US and other countries encountered continuing European intransigence against reductions in domestic protection levels and export subsidies in agriculture and against new safeguard rules that would prohibit all selective import controls. The underdeveloped countries refused to budge on non-discrimination, which they rightly viewed as the basic pillar of GATT. As discussions continued, industrial countries ignored their Article XIX obligations and took more and more selective safeguard actions in sensitive industries (Low 1993: 190).

In 1982, the situation had become so serious that a Ministerial Declaration was issued noting that the multilateral trading system was seriously endangered and committing members to a standstill and rollback undertaking which promised not to behave in a GATT-illegal fashion and which tacitly admitted past wrongdoings. Why governments considered it necessary thus to recommit themselves to upholding their solemn international treaty obligations can only be explained in terms of the near-collapse of the GATT system at that time.

Despite the 1982 Declaration, the period 1983–5 was one of the most stressful in the history of the GATT (Low 1993: 206). A new surge of protectionism fueled in the United States by the undervaluation of the dollar, once again tested the resilience of the liberal trading system. In mid-1983, the idea of preparing for a new round of negotiations was first floated. In June 1984, at the London Summit meeting, Prime Minister Nakasone of Japan persuaded the seven major industrial nations to consult with their trading partners about the objectives and timing of a new round. Despite reservations from many underdeveloped countries, the Contracting Partners managed to establish a preparatory committee by consensus in November 1985 and to prepare recommendations for adoption at a ministerial meeting in September 1986.

'As with all the earlier GATT rounds of negotiations, the United States was the prime mover behind the Uruguay Round' (Low 1993: 233), which the executive branch viewed as indispensable to the bicycle theory of export-driven trade liberalization in an exceptionally severe climate of domestic protectionism. The Reagan administration was particularly anxious to broaden the range of GATT multilateral negotiations to include mandates on trade in services, intellectual property rights (TRIPS) and trade-related investment measures (TRIMS) (all feared by the underdeveloped countries) and to include a mandate on trade in agriculture (feared by the European Community). President Reagan was also anxious to regain the trade agenda authority that he had lost to Congress in the first half of 1985, in part because of his preoccupation with his own personal problem of colon cancer, in part because of the vacuum in USTR following Brock's resignation in March 1985.

USTR Clayton Yeutter spearheaded the new, more activist policy of the executive branch towards trade, following his confirmation by the Senate in September 1985. He chaired the cabinet-level US delegation to the September 1986 GATT ministerial talks at Punte del Este which inaugurated the Uruguay Round. He won agreement that the new round's agenda would include trade in agricultural products and services. He demonstrated how the USTR leadership role can be made to work even in the most protectionist domestic environment.

The administration had resisted trade legislation throughout 1986, fearing protectionist pressures from Congress. In 1987, such legislation was accepted as inevitable, despite the loss of the Senate to the Democrats, because USTR would need an extension of fast-track authority to complete the Uruguay Round. Yeutter did not possess in 1988 the congressional ties that Strauss (in 1979) and Brock (in 1984) had used to such advantage (Destler 1992: 130). He and his aides were persistently excluded from key conference-related meetings. Nevertheless, in the 1988 Act Yeutter managed to secure the necessary negotiating authority for the Uruguay Round while neutralizing the most restrictive trade proposals of Congress. In so doing, he managed to save the liberal trade order from the idiosyncrasies of an increasingly unfocused presidency.

The Uruguay Round negotiations were scheduled to be completed in December 1990. In fact, they did not commence in earnest until the inconclusive Montreal mid-term review in December 1988. The first phase of the negotiations had dissolved in wrangles over organizational questions, as the various contracting parties maneuvered for political advantage over the most contentious agenda issues. In Montreal all results were put on hold and the Director-General of the GATT, Arthur Dunkel, was authorized to pursue agreements on the five outstanding issues – TRIPS, TRIMS, agriculture, textiles and clothing, and safeguards – and to report on progress in April 1989. The Director-General, in April 1989, successfully re-established the basis for continuing negotiations, still scheduled for completion in December 1990.

There then intervened a major upheaval in the world order, signalled by the collapse of the Soviet Empire and the end of the Cold War, leaving the United States as the only military superpower after 40 years of global confrontation. Uncomfortably, this new unparalleled military supremacy of the United States was coupled with a significant decline in the US economic position that weakened its bargaining power in the GATT relative to that of the European Community and of Japan. The USTR in the Bush administration, Carla A. Hills, competent though she proved herself to be, fell foul of this lost economic hegemony, predictably on the controversial issue of agricultural policy.

President Bush accorded the Uruguay Round negotiations a high priority – higher by far than NAFTA – and pressed for a breakthrough on agriculture at the seven-nation Houston economic summit in July 1990, recognizing that two of his counterparts, the French President, François Mitterand, and Germany's Chancellor, Helmut Kohl, held the keys to an agricultural breakthrough. Despite the earnest efforts promised at that meeting, there was no significant movement in the EEC position in Fall 1990. For the first time, there was open speculation whether the Uruguay Round would finish on schedule.

The Trade Negotiations Committee (TNC) sent to Brussels for the December 1990 meeting a 392-page document entitled the *Draft Final Act Embodying the Results of the Uruguay Round of Multilateral Trade Negotiations.* 'It contained little that could be described as final' (Low 1993: 219). In the case of textiles, safeguards, some MTN codes, some GATT articles, dispute settlement, and TRIPS, the text offered a reasonable basis for negotiations. Other texts contained numerous formulations of alternative language. The text on subsidies was accompanied by dissenting statements from the European Community, Brazil, Mexico, and Pakistan. Four major areas were without any text – antidumping, TRIMS, agriculture, and the GATT's balance-of-payments provisions.

'USTR Carla Hills flew to Europe, accompanied by a large US negotiating team, observers from Congress and a powerful delegation of US private-sector representatives' (Destler 1992: 134). She was met in the European capital by thousands of angry European farmers. Chancellor Kohl arrived victorious in the all-German elections, but up to his neck in commitments to backward German agriculture. So the talks failed. 'The agricultural negotiators could not even reach consensus on the framework for an agreement' (Destler 1992: 135). The final attempt at reconciliation collapsed three days into the meeting when the EC, Japan and Korea rejected a compromise proposal and when representatives of several underdeveloped countries walked out of the negotiations. 'When Carla Hills announced that, without progress in agriculture, the United States would not bargain on other issues, she drew cheers from the assembled US private-sector representatives' (Destler 1992: 135).

Still the negotiations dragged on, although GATT's credibility was badly shaken, and participants talked openly about the prospect of its imminent demise. Fast-track authority would lapse if President Bush failed to secure an extension from Congress by March 1 1991. A two-year extension was eventually granted by Congress, but more with NAFTA than with Uruguay in mind, and only after considerable lobbying by the administration and by business interests. Agreement continued to elude the contracting parties throughout 1992 and the Clinton administration showed little interest in trade issues.

Finally, on April 15 1994, the Uruguay Round negotiations were concluded at an official signing in Marrakech, Morocco, with the specific compromises that were outlined at the outset of this section. The final outcome was favorable for trade liberalization, lowering world tariffs, protecting copyrights, encompassing trade in services, reducing agricultural subsidies, and opening up markets formerly closed to the advanced nations.

7   Conclusions

The public-choice model has proved to be extremely helpful in explaining trade politics in the executive branch. Almost always, the president and USTR are less protectionist than Congress, irrespective of party affiliation. On the trade-liberalizing front, USTR typically is more effective than the president, because US presidents usually do not attach a high political priority to matters of trade.

The more transparent the trade policy issue, the more pronounced is the trade-liberalizing thrust of the executive branch. In particular, multilateral trade negotiations, where the bicycle theory is most relevant, manifests the greatest spatial distance between the executive branch and Congress. However, where protection is opaque, as is the case with most categories of special protection, presidents tend to be more protectionist than Congress, whatever the freer trade rhetoric put out by their respective administrations.

Where the managed-trade crowbar can be wielded to open up export markets for US suppliers, US presidents and USTRs appear increasingly to enjoy their bully-boy status and meddle with the property rights of others, cheered on by a Congress that long since has lost sight of the words of the Declaration of Independence concerning the value of freedom from foreign tyranny. This perhaps is the most sinister of all the recent developments in the managed-trade syndrome that has overwhelmed US executive branch thinking in the post-communist world order.

References

Baldwin, R.E. (1985) *The Political Economy of U.S. Import Policy* (Cambridge, Mass.: MIT Press).

Baldwin, R.E. (1988) *Trade Policy in a Changing World Economy* (Chicago: University of Chicago Press).

Baldwin, R.E. and Lage, G.M. (1971) 'A multilateral model of trade-balancing tariff concessions', *Review of Economics and Statistics*, 53: 237–45.

Bhagwati, J. (1989) *Protectionism* (Cambridge, Mass.: MIT Press).

Bhagwati, J. (1991) *The World Trading System at Risk* (Princeton, N.J.: Princeton University Press).

Bhagwati, J. (1992) 'Aggressive unilateralism' in J. Bhagwati and H.T. Patrick (eds) *Aggressive Unilateralism: America's 301 Trade Policy and the World Trading System* (Ann Arbor: University of Michigan Press), 1–45.

Bhagwati, J. and Patrick, H.T. (eds) (1992) *Aggressive Unilateralism: America's 301 Trade Policy and the World Trading System* (Ann Arbor: University of Michigan Press).

Coleman, J.J. and Yoffie, D.B. (1990) 'Institutional incentives for protection: the American use of voluntary export restraints', in F.A. Macchiarola (ed.), *International Trade: The Changing Role of the United States* (Montpelier: Academy of Political Science), 137–50.

Destler, I.M. (1986) *American Trade Politics: System under Stress* (New York: Twentieth Century Fund).

Destler, I.M. (1992) *American Trade Politics*, 2nd edn (New York: Twentieth Century Fund).

Heclo, H. (1977) *A Government of Strangers* (Washington, D.C.: Brookings Institution).

Hufbauer, G.C. and Elliott, K.A. (1994) *Measuring the Cost of Protection in the United States* (Washington, D.C.: Institute for International Economics).

Hufbauer, G.C. and Rosen, H.F. (1986) *Trade Policy for Troubled Industries* (Washington, D.C.: Institute for International Economics).

Jackson, J. (1993) 'U.S. constitutional law principles and foreign trade law and policy', in M. Hilf and E.-U. Petersmann (eds), *National Constitutions and International Economic Law* (Boston, Mass.: Kluwer Law and Taxation Publishing).

Low, P.C. (1993) *Trading Free: The GATT and US Trade Policy* (New York: Twentieth Century Fund).

Milner, H. (1992) 'The political economy of U.S. trade policy: a study of the Super 301 provision', in J. Bhagwati and H.T. Patrick (eds), *Aggressive Unilateralism* (Ann Arbor: University of Michigan Press), pp. 163–80.

Schwartz, B. (1983) *Super Chief: Earl Warren and his Supreme Court: Judicial Biography* (New York: New York University Press).

10 Trade politics and the fair-trade laws

1 Introduction

From the outset, this book has stressed that only individuals trade, and not nation states, and that the well-being of individuals, not of any organic entity, should be the rationale of trade policy. Whether the individuals under consideration should be just the members of one nation-state, or whether consideration should be extended to the worldwide population itself is an open question, though we recognize that nation-states matter and that trade policy evolves in nationalistic rather than in cosmopolitan terms, notwithstanding the General Agreement on Tariffs and Trade. In any event, as we note in Chapter 2, individual well-being is to be evaluated in this book in terms of liberty as well as expected wealth.

For the most part, the economic theory of free trade focuses on trade from the perspective of the nation-state rather than on free trade for all. As such, it offers no direct guidance for the design of an international trading system, though there is indeed a cosmopolitan, as opposed to a nationalistic, version of the theory of free trade. As Bhagwati (1988: 33) notes, 'if one applies the logic of efficiency to the allocation of activity among all nations, and not merely to one's own nation-state, it is easy enough to see that it yields the prescription of free trade everywhere'. That alone can ensure that goods and services will be produced where it can be done most cheaply. Equally, if individuals anywhere in the world are prohibited from trading freely with others by the imposition of arbitrary barriers, their natural rights to property, if not to life and liberty, inevitably are invaded.

From the cosmopolitan perspective, the notion that prices reflect true social costs is crucial, at least for the utilitarian conclusion, just as it is in the case for free trade for one nation alone. If any national government employs tariffs or subsidies 'to drive a wedge between market prices and social costs, rather than to close a gap arising from market failures, then surely that is not consonant with an efficient world allocation of activity' (Bhagwati 1988: 34). At the cosmopolitan level, therefore, the rule thus emerges 'that free trade must apply to all' (Bhagwati 1988: 34).

Herein lies an apparent contradiction that must be confronted in any discussion of the fair trade laws. The nationalist theory of free trade correctly ignores the use of tariffs, quotas and subsidies by other countries, urging individuals in any single nation to pursue free-trade policies regardless of the behavior of others. Yet the cosmopolitan theory requires adherence to free trade everywhere, ruling out artificial comparative advantage arising from subsidies and dumping, in so far as it is a technique used to secure an otherwise untenable foothold in world markets.

From this apparent contradiction, Bhagwati himself, despite his otherwise impeccable stance in the free-trade corner, constructs a defense of nationalistic fair trade laws. 'Think of the issue', he suggests, 'not in terms of other countries using protection while one's own country maintains free trade (the question that nineteenth-century Britain extensively debated) but in terms of other countries using export subsidies while one's own country keeps its markets open' (Bhagwati 1988: 34). It is hard enough to cope with the demise of one's own company or one's current job in pursuit of generalized gains from trade when another country has a market-determined advantage. But if the successful foreign competitor is backed by artificial support from its own government, then the pill is a bitter one to swallow. Angry questions inevitably arise concerning the fairness of unilateral free trade in the absence of a level playing-field.

The salve of the free-trade economist that such subsidies benefit individuals in the recipient country by providing them with cheap commodities is unlikely to sooth inflamed demands for countervailing protection which predictably will imperil broader free-trade policies where they presently exist. In Bhagwati's judgement, a free-trade regime that does not rein in or seek to regulate artificial subventions of this kind will probably help to trigger its own demise. In his view, this line of thought supports the cosmopolitan economist's position that the world trading order ought to reflect the essence of the principle of free-trade for all – if necessary by permitting the appropriate use of countervailing duties and antidumping actions to maintain fair, competitive trade.

2   The case against fair trade laws

Let us temporarily set aside Bhagwati's (1988) public-choice arguments and focus attention on the economic arguments advanced in defense of fair trade laws at the level of the nation-state. Both with respect to foreign subsidies and to foreign dumping, the central issue concerns predatory pricing and its consequences for domestic markets. Recent developments in the theory of non-cooperative strategic behavior and in the theory of contestable markets strongly suggest that there is no serious predatory pricing problem even when foreign governments are involved.

In predatory pricing, a firm initially lowers its price to drive rivals out of business and to scare off potential entrants. When rivals disappear, the firm raises its price, perhaps to the monopoly level, scaring off potential entrants or re-entrants because of their belief in its willingness instantaneously to re-engage in predatory pricing behavior should re-entry occur. When predatory pricing occurs across national frontiers, it is referred to as dumping and falls foul of antidumping laws, rather than the standard antitrust laws of the nation whose markets have been so invaded. In whatever form, predatory pricing is difficult to explain as a rational strategy.

During the period of predation the predator will lose much more income than its equally efficient rivals since it must satisfy all demands at the low price whereas its rivals are free to contract in order to minimize losses. Even if the predator succeeds in forcing its rivals into bankruptcy, relying itself upon its own protected domestic market sales to avoid bankruptcy, it must be sure that its rival's assets are permanently withdrawn from the industry or fall under its own control at knock-down prices; otherwise someone else could buy the assets and compete even if the assets were deployed elsewhere during the period of price predation.

In the case of contestable markets, characterized by complete freedom of entry and exit, the predator is never free from the prospect of potential competition if it raises its prices even temporarily above the competitive level. In such circumstances, predatory pricing is not a credible threat, nor does it constitute rational behavior, since the predator's rivals would simply redeploy capital elsewhere during the predation phase and re-enter immediately the predator raised its prices. In the absence of sunk costs, therefore, predatory strategies have no hope of succeeding, even when they are payrolled by foreign governments in the form of export subsidies.

Let us acknowledge that some industries – steel and automobiles perhaps, though certainly not computers, agricultural produce or textiles – exhibit sunk-cost characteristics that render their markets less than fully contestable. Let us further acknowledge that some foreign governments may have larger purses than some domestic companies, thus rendering the latter vulnerable to subsidized competition. Let us even acknowledge that some foreign companies may have larger purses than their US counterparts and that dumping just occasionally might result in some distortion in comparative advantage that would lead to some curtailment of domestic production. Even in this worst-case scenario, antidumping and countervailing-duty laws are not justified on strictly economic grounds in any realistic comparative institutions assessment.

First, there exists a serious risk that fair-trade laws weaken rather than promote competition by raising the cost of entry into US markets. Antidumping lawsuits are expensive, and US producers pay none of the costs of the lawsuits that they initiate simply by filing for relief. Foreign companies must factor in the expected cost of antidumping lawsuits prior to entering US markets. They also must anticipate difficulties in contracting with US importers who may themselves be hit with dumping penalties in the event of successful litigation. Antidumping liability is difficult to assess *ex ante* not least because the US antidumping laws are exempt from the Administrative Procedures Act and thus are not subject to due process guarantees. Antidumping lawsuits usually require foreign suppliers to disclose confidential cost information which, despite confidentiality guarantees, not infrequently are divulged to their US competitors.

Second, there is a serious risk that fair trade laws will result in higher domestic prices for reasons other than the reduction of foreign entry into US markets. In order to avoid antidumping suits, foreign producers will tend to raise their prices above the market optimum, thus enabling domestic producers to follow suit. Immediately after initiating an antidumping action, domestic producers may raise prices in order to accentuate the antidumping penalty applied to their foreign rivals. If the price rises impact on intermediate goods, US final-goods producers may hike their prices in response to increases in marginal cost. In all such cases, domestic consumers suffer as consumers' surplus declines in markets impacted by the fair-trade laws.

Third, the number of domestic jobs saved by the fair-trade laws may well be fewer than those that are lost when all the dislocations are factored in, including the impact on import-using domestic industries. A number of studies suggest that the cost of saving a single US job is extremely high; for example, $113,622 per annum for each steel job, $134,686 per annum for each textile job, and $220,000 per annum for each dairy job. If such sums were invested wisely elsewhere, many more high-value jobs would be created than those lost to foreign competition. Consumers benefiting from prices lowered as a consequence of foreign competition would have reserve spending power to attract new entrepreneurial initiatives that would open up attractive new job opportunities.

Fourth, the fair-trade laws are far from costless both inside and outside the USA. They offer government-supported wealth-transfer opportunities that attract rent-seeking outlays and that induce countervailing rent-protecting responses, all of which waste scarce resources in non-value-adding endeavors. The cost of filing an antidumping claim itself may involve little more than postage and stationery outlays for the protection-seeking domestic industry. The marshalling of the petition, however, and the lobbying of relevant participants is much more costly, diverting resources that might otherwise be available for cost reductions, product-enhancements or market research.

Once the petition is filed, the ITA and the ITC must be sweetened and Congress must be lobbied, activities that are pregnant with high attorney fees and very costly in senior management time. Foreign competitors, who must carry the full burden of their own legal responses and who must also counter-lobby the ITA, the ITC and the Congress, must factor such costs into their US market prices. In the efficient rent-seeking limit (Tullock 1980), the combination of rent-seeking and rent-protecting outlays will equal the expected value of the rent transfer that has been made available, severely diminishing the wealth of nations, both domestic and foreign.

Finally, it should not be thought that the fair trade laws will be administered efficiently in political markets characterized by asymmetric information and distorted by rational voter ignorance and the logic of collective choice. Predictably, in such markets the Congress and its agencies will broker outcomes favorable to the relatively small concentrated interests of protection-seeking domestic industries and harmful to the large diffused interests of the domestic consumers whether or not such outcomes reflect the economic rationale of the fair trade laws. By purporting to protect a tiny minority of US domestic industries from a small but real threat of predatory pricing, the antidumping laws actually provide opportunities for wealth transfers from consumers to producers and thus promote rent-seeking waste in a very large majority of instances where the fair-trade laws have no legitimate reach.

Complaining about the unfairness of foreigners has become the most popular and effective way for US producers who seek protection from imports to make their case to government (Finger 1993: 3). In the 1980s alone, almost 1,000 cases were processed in the United States under the fair-trade laws and many others were dealt with directly by executive branch intervention. Industries in a position to benefit from import restrictions have learned to use them more and more effectively, adopting multi-case strategies that involve the filing of a large number of petitions against a long list of imports, spanning the entire spectrum of an industry's products. A large number of lawyers and lobbyists now specialize in this rent-seeking exercise, impervious to the damage that they impose on comparative advantage in international trade and the losses that ultimately manifest themselves on consumers both domestic and worldwide.

The rent-seekers behave rationally, if at high cost to others, in pursuing wealth transfers via the instrument of government. Professional economists who have no axe to grind should not give weight to such nefarious activities by allowing hard cases to seduce them, contrary to their natural instincts, into endorsing bad laws. Categorically, we refuse to join with Jagdish Bhagwati (1988) and others in defending fair-trade laws that impose significant net costs on the United States economy and that threaten the economic liberties of United States citizens and foreign nationals.

3   The fair-trade laws and their impact on foreign competition

Article I of the United States Constitution grants to Congress the exclusive power to regulate commerce with foreign nations and to lay and collect duties. Until 1930, Congress jealously guarded this authority. Thereafter, it enacted a sequence of fair-trade laws that are jointly administered quasi-judicially by the International Trade Administration (ITA) of the Department of Commerce and by the International Trade Commission (ITC). The fair-trade laws encompass the antidumping and countervailing-duty laws enacted under Title VII of the Tariff Act of 1930 as amended and the general 'escape clause' provision incorporated into the Trade Act of 1951 as amended. The Trade Agreements Act of 1979, as amended, currently governs fair-trade investigations in the United States and regulates the relationship between the ITA and the ITC.

According to US law, discriminatory duties may be imposed on products that have been 'dumped' on the US market, but only if these imports 'harm' a US industry. Dumping is defined as selling in the US market below production cost or below export-country domestic prices. The ITA evaluates whether dumping has occurred. The ITC determines whether 'an industry in the United States is materially injured ... by reason of imports of [the dumped] merchandise'. Both agencies must make preliminary and final determinations, with stricter requirements for the latter. If both agencies rule affirmatively at the final stage, then duties equal to the dumping margin are placed on the 'unfairly priced' imports.

Instructions in the enabling legislation guide the decisions of the ITA and the ITC (Horlick 1993). The Congress devoted 247 lines in the Trade Agreements Act of 1979 to instructions about the calculation of dumping margins. The Act included only 40 lines on 'material injury', defining it vaguely as harm 'which is not immaterial, insignificant or inconsequential'. The ITC is instructed to consider the volume of dumped imports, the effect of the imports on prices and the impact of such merchandise on the domestic producers. In evaluating the impact on a domestic industry, the ITC should consider 'decline ... in output, sales, market share, profits, productivity, return on investment, and utilization of capacity ... and factors affecting domestic prices, and actual and potential negative effects on cash flow, inventories, employment, wages, growth, ability to raise capital and investment'.

It is clear from the legislative history of the Trade Agreements Act of 1979 that antidumping procedures are aimed narrowly at the effects of dumped imports on the domestic industry that produces the 'like product'. Antidumping duties are clearly not viewed as protection *per se*, but rather as a remedial action against unfair pricing. Nevertheless, the incentives are obvious for domestic firms to use the antidumping process as a means to limit competition.

Dumping, at least in the sense that it is employed in the US fair-trade laws, must be distinguished from export subsidies. The latter involve some benefit or subvention, usually derived from government sources, which accrue to the seller or producer of goods, provided that the goods are exported. The current rules regarding dumping and subsidies sharply distinguish the two practices, although older descriptions, including those of Adam Smith and even Jacob Viner, sometimes tend to lump the practices together.

Export subsidies, of course, can (but do not always) result in export prices lower than those on the domestic market, and thus dumping laws may sometimes apply to situations that have been engendered by subsidies. In such circumstances, US rules prohibit a double reaction. There are other important differences. Dumping is generally considered to be an activity of a particular firm or enterprise, although it may be sufficiently prevalent in a country to activate duties applied to all imports from the dumping country. Subsidies, on the other hand, are generally the actions of governments themselves. In consequence, a response to subsidies, in the form of countervailing duties, often involves a much higher level of diplomatic visibility, since it directly challenges the government of a sovereign state. Dumping issues, especially in large-scale cases such as semiconductors, steel or automobile products, occasionally may reach similar dimensions, but usually do not.

In accordance with a statute dating from 1897, if another government gave a 'bounty or grant' to a particular industry or firm, the US government, on the petition of the American interests affected, was supposed to impose a countervailing duty (CVD) equivalent to the size of the foreign subsidy. The basic law was mandatory: if a subsidy is found, a duty 'shall be imposed'. Yet the Department of the Treasury was always reluctant to apply the law, often dragging out investigations over several years only to reject the application. By the mid-1970s there was a widespread conviction that the current rules on subsidies and countervailing duties were inadequate to cope with the myriad of subtle governmental aids to export.

The Trade Agreements Act of 1979 shifted administrative responsibility for the CVD laws from the Secretary to the Treasury to the Secretary of Commerce, who was regarded as more receptive to trade protection pleas. It also introduced a 'material injury' test for all CVDs on products of countries adhering to the newly negotiated GATT code. Henceforth, the ITC must determine that 'material injury', defined as 'harm which is not inconsequential, immaterial or unimportant', was involved before countervailing duties could be imposed. As with antidumping petitions, the ITA and the ITC henceforth would work in tandem in dealing with CVD petitions.

The third prong of the US unfair-trade laws, the 'escape clause' provision, is a response to the problem of industries injured by import competition that cannot be claimed to be 'unfair'. If, for example, a US tariff reduction leads to an unexpectedly large influx of imports, should not competing domestic producers have the right to seek at least temporary trade relief? As early as 1943, the United States included just such an 'escape clause' in a trade agreement with Mexico. This approach was also incorporated in Article XIX of GATT. In an attempt to retain executive discretion, State Department officials proposed to include an escape clause in all future trade agreements. In 1947, President Truman issued an executive order setting forth procedures by which injured firms could seek relief. In 1951, Congress incorporated a general escape clause provision in an act extending presidential trade-negotiating authority.

The Trade Expansion Act of 1962 brought major revision and codification of the escape clause. An interest seeking relief henceforth had to demonstrate serious injury, the major cause of which was an increase in imports due to US tariff concessions. If the Tariff Commission (later the ITC) found that a particular interest met this test, the president had a choice of whether to accept the Commission's recommendation for tariff or quota relief. If he rejected the recommendation, Congress could override his negative decision by a majority veto in both houses.

The 1962 Act also imposed a major handicap on escape clause petitions by defining 'major cause' as 'a cause greater than all other factors combined'. Section 201 of The Trade Act of 1974, subsequently lowered that threshold by requiring that imports be only 'a substantial cause of serious injury, or the threat thereof'. 'Substantial cause' was defined as 'not less than any other cause'. Section 201 also removed the proviso that such an injury had to result from specific US tariff concessions.

The pattern of unfair trade-law petitions and of trade protection successes and failures closely mirrored the legislative changes. Until the early 1970s the laws provided little effective protection whichever the chosen route of petition. Out of 371 antidumping cases processed between 1955 and 1968, only 12 resulted in findings of dumping. Out of 191 investigations under the countervailing-duty law between 1934 and 1968, only 30 resulted in the imposition of CVD. Out of 143 escape clause investigations between 1948 and 1974, the Tariff Commission recommended relief in only 45 cases and the president provided relief in only 18 of these.

The immediate response to the rules changes initiated in 1974 was for firms to file many more cases and for the government to move more expeditiously in reviewing them (Anderson 1992: 916). In terms of relief granted, however, the petitioners once again were to be disappointed. Between 1975 and 1985, for example, the ITC conducted 59 investigations under the new escape clause criteria established by section 201, and made 30 affirmative determinations. However, presidents repeatedly rejected or modified the Commission's recommendations, ordering tariffs or quotas in only ten instances and denying all relief in twelve. Congress never voted to override the president with respect to these denials.

From 1976 through 1978, the Treasury made 35 affirmative CVD decisions, a marked increase over previous years. The Secretary then exercised a waiver in nineteen of these cases, operating under a special waiver authority added for the multilateral trade negotiations of the 1970s (the Tokyo Round). The number of antidumping cases during this period remained at about the level of previous years. Dissatisfaction with these outcomes manifested itself in protectionist lobbying, which gave rise to the Trade Agreements Act of 1979.

Since 1979 there has been a significant increase in trade protection filed under Title VII of the Tariff Act of 1930 as amended (antidumping and countervailing-duty cases). These statutes are increasingly being used to protect US industry (Anderson 1992: 917). As Table 10.1 shows, the number of outstanding Title VII orders more than doubled between 1983 and 1990: from 137 to 283. This must be compared with only 25 outstanding orders in 1968. Escape clause petitions are now much less important because industries petition instead for voluntary expert restraint 'agreements' to be negotiated directly on their behalf by the executive branch.

Table 10.1   Outstanding Title VII orders

	1983	1986	1990
All Title VII orders			
Number	137	193	283
Products	93	122	143
Countries	36	43	49
Antidumping orders			
Number	95	122	202
Products	70	90	111
Countries	26	32	40
Countervailing-duty orders			
Number	42	71	81
Products	28	48	54
Countries	22	31	35

Source: K.B. Anderson, 'Agency discretion or statutory direction: decision-making at the US International Trade Commission', *Journal of Law Economics* 36 (2): 917.

By 1990, imports of one or more products from 49 countries were subject to Title VII duties. Orders covered imports of 143 products from one or more countries. The products ranged from such basic consumer items as aspirin, candles, cookware, and flowers to such high-technology items as computer chips, cellular telephones, and laser light-scattering instruments. Many steel products – nails, wire rod, pipes and tubes – were covered, as were such food products as orange juice, rice, and raspberries. Japanese products were subject to by far the largest number of Title VII orders – 51 by the end of 1990. All of these were antidumping orders. Canadian products were subject to 21 orders: fifteen antidumping and six CVD. Other countries burdened with twelve or more such orders were Argentina, Brazil, France, Italy, and Taiwan (Anderson 1992: 916).

The increasing protection currently provided by Title VII is accentuated by the semi-permanent status of such orders. Although the Commerce Department will upon request periodically review the level of the duties collected under antidumping or CVD orders, the orders themselves do not expire after a fixed period of time. The oldest outstanding antidumping order, covering the import of cement from the Dominican Republic, dates from May 1963. The oldest outstanding CVD order, covering the import of certain castor oil products from Brazil, dates from March 1976. Almost one-quarter of all outstanding orders have been in place for over ten years.

4   The nature and role of the International Trade Administration

Until 1954, the Department of the Treasury was fully responsible for the implementation of the antidumping laws and the countervailing-duty laws. In the case of the antidumping laws, Congress then moved the responsibility for injury determination to the ITC (known as the Tariff Commission), on the theory that the ITC was better equipped to deal with injury because of its studies of US industries. In 1979, Congress shifted administrative responsibility for the antidumping and countervailing-duty laws from Treasury to Commerce in response to petitions that Treasury was devoting insufficient resources to the program and that its international orientation rendered it excessively vulnerable to foreign consideration. Simultaneously, Congress introduced a material-injury test for countervailing duty petitions and allocated responsibility for administering this test to the ITC.

The Department of Commerce was reorganized to handle its new fair-trade law responsibilities. A new position of Under-Secretary for Trade was established to oversee the department's renamed and expanded International Trade Administration (ITA) which now has no fewer than seventeen officials at or above the deputy assistant secretary level. The ITA has responded much more quickly and much more favorably to both antidumping and countervailing-duty law petitions than was the case with the Treasury, no doubt reflecting the expressed concerns of Congress and the specific wording of the 1979 statute.

An antidumping or countervailing-duty investigation begins when the government receives a petition from a domestic industry alleging that imports are being dumped or are benefiting from a subsidy. The government must determine within twenty days whether the petition meets the standards of law. If not, the petition is dismissed. Once a petition is accepted, the ITA begins an investigation to determine whether the imported goods in question are dumped or receive a subsidy. All antidumping and most countervailing-duty cases include a simultaneous but formally separate investigation by the ITC to determine whether the competing domestic industry is experiencing or is threatened by material injury from these imports. The ITC has 45 days from the receipt of a petition to determine whether 'the best available information' provides 'a reasonable indication' of such material injury. A negative preliminary determination at this stage terminates the case.

Trade law charges the ITA to determine at the preliminary level whether there is a 'reasonable basis to believe or suspect' that imports benefit from an unfair trade practice. However, unlike the ITC, a negative preliminary determination on subsidies or dumping does not end the case. In each instance, the investigation proceeds to a final determination. However, an affirmative preliminary determination triggers immediate 'suspension of liquidation', whereas a negative preliminary determination does not. Under a suspension of liquidation, the importer must post a bond to guarantee the payment of antidumping or countervailing duties if the final determination is also positive. The size of the bond is based on the preliminary estimate of the effect of the subsidy on the exporter's price, or on the margin of dumping. In effect, a suspension of liquidation imposes an import deposit requirement.

Positive determinations are necessary at the final stage from the ITA on subsidization or dumping and from the ITC on injury before an antidumping duty or countervailing-duty order is issued. Before such a final determination is reached, there are several possible avenues to a negotiated settlement, a qualitative export restraint agreement or an agreement to cease dumping or to eliminate the export subsidy. The foreign action must be monitored and a case may be quickly reopened if the US government concludes that the terms of the agreement have not been honored. Over the period 1980–8, almost 50 percent of all antidumping and countervailing-duty law petitions were superseded by negotiated export restraints.

In cases that reach an affirmative or a negative determination, dumping or subsidization is almost always found. Of the 774 petitions filed between 1980 and 1988 (385 antidumping and 389 countervailing-duty), 169 were superseded by a negotiated restraint agreement or a suspension agreement within the fair-trade laws. Another 48 cases were withdrawn or terminated without an announced capitulation or adjustment by the exporter. Of these, 25 were withdrawn or terminated by the ITA and the remainder by the ITC (Finger and Murray 1993: 245).

Table 10.2 reports the outcome of cases that reached a determination, affirmative or negative, on the questions of subsidy, dumping and injury. Clearly, the injury test bears the burden of rejecting petitions for protection. Of an initial basket of 100 cases, only five would be dismissed by a negative

Table 10.2   Negative and affirmative determinations in subsidy, dumping and injury tests, 1980–88

	Affirmative	Negative
Subsidy and dumping tests		
Preliminary	403	50
Final	484	60
Injury tests		
Preliminary	444	129
Final	190	113

Source: J.R. Finger and T. Murray, 'Antidumping and countervailing duty enforcement in the Unites States', in J.M. Finger (ed.), *Antidumping: How it Works and Who Gets Hurt* (Ann Arbor: University of Michigan Press, 1993), p. 247.

subsidy or dumping determination – fewer than one-fifth of the number that would be dismissed by a negative injury determination.

The core concept of dumping, as described in GATT and in US law, is expressed as the sale of products for export at a price less than 'normal value'. Normal value is defined as the price at which those same products are sold in the home or domestic market of the exporting firm. In principle, this is a relatively unambiguous concept. In practice, however, the process of calculating dumping or dumping margins is more complex and much more open to bureaucratic abuse, even with tightly drawn statutory instructions. Since the calculated dumping margin determines the level of protection provided in the case of successful petitions, any scope for administrative discretion is a potential rent-seeking margin to be exploited by domestic special interests.

A range of computational problems confront the ITA in its assessment of the dumping margin. A threshold question concerns the level of trade that should be used for price determinations, wholesale or retail. It might be thought that whatever level is used should be the same for home market and export sales. Yet it is not unknown for the ITA to compare US wholesale prices with foreign retail prices, thus providing an appearance of dumping when none exists. Such discrepancies can only be the result of vulnerability to domestic lobbying.

Another threshold question concerns the nature of the product at issue in the investigation. It might be thought that, whatever the product definition, it would always be the same for the foreign and the domestic producers. Not so. The ITA more than occasionally compares the prices of higher-quality products with those of lower-quality foreign imports. Since this error never occurs in the reverse direction, systematic error can be ruled out, but not rent-seeking. Similarly, the ITA ignores differences in volume, in packaging, in advertising costs and in warranty services when such differences would be helpful to foreign competition.

Where foreign competitors do not sell their products in their own domestic markets, the ITA sometimes makes third-country comparisons, even including non-market economies where prices cannot be accurately determined. In so doing, it ignores comparative cost advantages that might justifiably explain price differentials, even as between market economies. Such third-party price comparisons are fairly systematically unfavorable to foreign competitors, and often are based on a quite ridiculous choice of surrogate, as a former ITA official has explained:

> Gary Horlick, who was Deputy Assistant Secretary of Commerce for Import Administration from 1981 to 1983, described the process to the Senate Finance Committee: I can tell humor stories about how one goes about choosing a surrogate; it is usually done about 10 at night when one has run out of any reasonable alternative. Just to take an example, for Chinese shop towels we went through in order: Pakistan, Thailand, Malaysia, Hong Kong, the Dominican Republic, Colombia, and wound up with a hypothetical Chinese factory in India. It just doesn't make any sense. (Bovard 1991, p. 132)

Even where price data exist for like products in both markets, the ITA uses a method of comparison that is tilted against the foreign competitor. One common abuse is for the ITA to calculate an average price in the foreign market over a six-month period and to compare this against a strategically chosen price in the US market. If the foreign competitor sells any output in the US market at a price below the computed average price in its own market, the ITA uses this discrepancy to determine a dumping margin, irrespective of the volume of sales involved. Even the US General Accounting Office has criticized this practice. The Court of International Trade has condemned it outright.

Most important of all, however, is the misuse made by the ITA of the concept of 'sales below cost of production' as a means of resolving dumping petitions. This criterion was introduced by Congress in the Antidumping Act of 1921 as a fall-back in cases where all foreign merchandise was produced solely for export. It became a normal benchmark for the ITA as a consequence of a little-noted amendment to the Trade Act of 1974 that allowed for constructed value complete with an 8 percent minimum profit. Sales at prices below this 'fully allocated' cost of production now constitute prima facie evidence of dumping, despite a large body of US antitrust decisions that require prices to be less than average variable cost, if not marginal cost, as acceptable evidence of predatory pricing. Since 1980, about 60 percent of all

US dumping cases have been based at least in part on allegations of sales below cost. Since the ITA is not bound by any cost-accounting criteria it is free to manipulate cost calculations and profit margins as a means of finding dumping in domestic markets where US producers can exert political pressure.

For all these reasons, plausible economic definitions of dumping play little or no role in influencing the behavior of the ITA with respect to dumping determinations. If the politics of the situation tilts against foreign competition, as is almost always the case, then the legal definition of dumping can be stretched to accommodate an affirmative determination. Malfeasance at the ITA in such circumstances is a predictable outcome of rent-seeking pressures and will occur irrespective of the personal views of ITA bureaucrats concerning the issue of free trade.

The ITA must complete its investigations within a very short period of time (160 days for the preliminary determination plus 75 days for the final determination). It might be thought that information required of foreign competitors in such circumstances would be correspondingly simple and brief. Not so. The ITA investigation is essentially adversarial and is initiated with a very detailed questionnaire sent out to foreign respondents, who are given a tight deadline for completion. Petitioners' counsel have full access to the entire response, notwithstanding the confidential information that is often requested, and have full opportunity to critique the response (Horlick 1993: 158).

The ITA then 'verifies' the information in the response on-site, usually after the preliminary determination, typically in the presence of the respondent's counsel, and prepares a verification report containing all the data to be ruled upon. This report, once again, is critiqued by both sides' counsel. After the final determination, the ITA provides another disclosure to both sides. At any stage, the ITA may consult outside experts without notifying the respondents and without making available to them any information gathered from such outside sources. The cost of the ITA investigation alone is clearly a weapon employed by unscrupulous domestic producers to drive foreign competitors out of US markets.

5   The nature and role of the International Trade Commission

The early origins of the ITC are to be found in the rise in anti-German sentiment during the First World War and a widespread popular conviction that German corporations were dumping products on the US market. To divert pressures in favor of increasing US tariffs, President Woodrow Wilson proposed legislation targeted specifically against foreign dumping. In 1916, sections 800 and 801 of the Revenue Act made it illegal to import goods at prices substantially below market value in the producing country or in countries to which they commonly were exported, provided that there was an intent to injure, destroy or prevent the establishment of an industry in the United States, or to restrain competition. Although this law is still on the books, and despite triple-damage provisions for successful petitioners, only one suit has ever been brought, and that unsuccessfully: *Zenith Radio Corporation* v *Matsushita Electrical Industry Company* in 1970.

Again in 1916, in response to a recommendation by President Wilson, Congress established the Tariff Commission (now the ITC) to provide both it and the president with expert and impartial information for the formulation and implementation of US import policy. In his congressional message proposing the Commission, the president stressed that the objective was to create a body that would be 'as much as possible, free from any strong prepossession in favor of any political party and capable of looking at the whole economic situation of the country with dispassionate and disinterested scrutiny'.

To this end, the 1916 Act specified that the Tariff Commission should be composed of six commissioners, each appointed by the president, subject to advise and consent by the Senate, for a single term of twelve years. No more than three commissioners were to be members of the same political party. The Commission's role with respect to import policy was exclusively advisory and was extremely limited, given political reluctance at that time to adjust tariffs.

The Tariff Act of 1922 expanded the Commission's role by authorizing the president to vary import duties by up to 50 percent to ensure that US tariffs equalized the difference in production costs for specific goods in the United States and in the principal exporting country. The Commission was directed to assist the president by calculating such differences in production costs and by determining instances of unfair import competition and unreasonable or discriminatory practices by foreign companies.

The Tariff Act of 1930 reorganized the Tariff Commission but left its basic functions unchanged. In response to allegations that the Commission had allowed itself to become politicized, the Act terminated the unserved terms of office of all commissioners and shortened the term of office for all new appointees from twelve to six years. Although the 1930 Act required the president to approve tariff rate recommendations by the Commission 'if in his judgement they are necessary to equalize differences in costs', subsequent court decisions confirmed the authority of the president to set rates other than those recommended by the Commission.

The Trade Agreements Act of 1934 further expanded the authority of the president to negotiate tariff adjustments with other countries without taking account of comparative costs of production. Once again the president was required to seek advice from the Tariff Commission. The Commission exercised only a limited role in trade policy until 1947, when President Harry Truman issued an executive order formalizing procedures for escape clause petitions. The Commission replaced the Trade Agreements Committee as the responsible organization for investigating escape clause petitions and advising the president. In 1951, the escape clause route to trade protection was formalized by legislation. In 1955, this protection was extended by legislation that eased the requirement for serious injury and defined an industry more narrowly.

In 1954, the Tariff Commission's responsibilities were significantly extended by legislation making it responsible for determining whether injury had been inflicted on a domestic industry in cases where the Treasury Department had made a positive finding of dumping under the Antidumping Act of 1921. A majority vote of its commissioners was necessary for a positive determination. In 1958, Congress stipulated that evenly divided votes with respect to injury should be treated as a positive determination. Notwithstanding this tilt in favor of protection, there followed sixteen years of minimal trade protection via the antidumping statute.

Such passivity disappeared in 1974 in large part as a consequence of the Trade Act of that year which constituted the Tariff Commission as the International Trade Commission (ITC). The Act made it much easier for a domestic industry to obtain import relief, and many more cases began to come before the ITC. In the first four years of the new legislation, the ITC issued 37 decisions, compared with only 26 in the previous twelve years. Furthermore, the ITC tilted sharply in favor of trade protection in its antidumping determinations, finding in favor of the petitioner in 68 percent of the 48 cases decided between 1975 and 1983. This contrasted with a figure of only 28 percent for cases decided in the previous twelve years.

Although the ITC had played a role since 1922 in cases alleging unfair import practices, its activities had been confined to making recommendations to the president after conducting an investigation. In amending section 337 of the 1930 Tariff Act, the 1974 Act empowered the ITC to order the exclusion of unfairly traded goods or to issue cease and desist orders with respect to unfair practices. For policy reasons, the president may override either of these orders within 60 days of issuance. Between 1962 and 1974, only twelve section 337 cases had been dealt with by the commission. Between 1975 and 1982, 124 such cases were completed.

The ITC was also assigned a role in carrying out the broad new powers given to the president by section 301 of the 1974 Act, which dealt with unfair foreign import restrictions, including unreasonable or discriminatory policies and foreign export subsidies. In taking steps to counteract such policies, the president could request the ITC to present its views on the probable economic impact on the United States of any proposed action. Furthermore, before the president could act against subsidized exports to the United States, it was necessary both for the Treasury Department to find the existence of such a subsidy and for the ITC to determine that the imports had substantially reduced sales of a competitive US product.

The 1974 Act once again reorganized the ITC, increasing the non-renewable term of its commissioners from six to nine years. An automatic system based on seniority was established for determining the chairman and vice-chairman (although this was changed in 1977 to permit the president to appoint the chairman). Significantly, the 1974 Act removed the president from any control over the budget of the ITC.

The Trade Agreements Act of 1979 implemented the non-tariff barrier codes completed earlier that year in the multinational trade negotiations of the Tokyo Round. The Act introduced a 'material injury' test for all CVDs on products of countries adhering to the new code. Henceforth, duties aimed at offsetting the adverse effects of foreign subsidies could be imposed only if the ITC determined that the subsidized exports had caused material injury to a domestic industry. This test had the formal effect of tightening the criteria relief-seeking petitioners must meet in order to secure trade protection. Lobbyists for the European Community actively supported this tougher standard.

In order to expedite the handling of dumping and subsidization complaints, the ITC was directed to make preliminary as well as final determinations of injury. If the preliminary determination was negative, the investigation was terminated. Tighter time limits were mandated not only for CVD cases taken as a whole, but for each specific stage in the investigation. For example, investigations had to be initiated within twenty days and only clearly frivolous petitions were to be dismissed without any formal investigation. The overall timetable from initiation to final determination was compressed in normal cases, from twelve to seven months. These administrative changes favored petitioners, since foreign governments and firms now had less time to rebut the data of those seeking relief. Moreover, if there was a preliminary finding of injury, importers would now have to post a deposit just three months instead of a year after a petition was submitted. Similar changes were made to section 301, the authority granted in 1974 to presidents to retaliate against 'unjustifiable or unreasonable' foreign trade actions.

In deciding whether a US industry has suffered or is likely to suffer from material injury, the ITC is precluded from taking into account the impact on consumers, national welfare, or indeed any other general public interest indicator. Instead, its attention is restricted to a range of industry-specific criteria. In principle, such criteria of material injury should be relatively unambiguous, presumably implying a reduction in the present or future profitability of an industry, measured by stock market valuations, and (possibly) also a reduction in employment opportunities. As long as employment, factor incomes and share prices remain healthy, it should be inconceivable in almost all instances to find material injury or the threat thereof. Otherwise, the judgement of bureaucrats will be substituted for that of the market place.

In practice, the statutory listing of factors to be taken into account is more lengthy and, in some instances, completely bizarre, including output, sales, market shares, cash flow, inventories, and capacity utilization; measures that are only peripherally and intermittently associated with profitability. Because measures associated with profitability are notoriously difficult to calculate for single product lines in multi-product corporations, more easily identified but economically less relevant indicators are typically relied upon.

This procedural weakness is intensified by the statutory requirement that injury must affect an industry rather than individual corporations. Typically, an antidumping or a CVD complaint is registered by a few corporations, predictably the worst performers in the industry. The more successful corporations tend to be neutral or even hostile to the petition. The worst performers are also the most likely to respond to ITC questionnaires. Inevitably, the material injury investigation is thus biased in favor of a positive determination. Inevitably, the wide range of criteria that the ITC must take into account provides it with considerable discretion in its material injury assessments.

The investigative procedures employed by the ITC are much less adversarial and much more bureaucratic than those utilized by the ITA. Until 1988, the ITC was also more secretive with respect to information obtained. Thus, while ITC sent out questionnaires to all parties in both preliminary and final investigations, neither side's counsel was allowed to review the other side's responses, except with respect to extremely limited summary information. The questionnaires were not sent to a scientific sample of corporations nor were they verified scientifically. ITC staff also made *ex parte* telephone calls to purchasers, customers, industry experts and the like, the results of which were not made available in detail to either party. The only information to which counsel were allowed access was that presented in a summary report prior to the submission of pre-hearing briefs in the final investigation. There was no external check on the accuracy of the information so presented.

In section 1332 of the 1988 Trade Act, Congress required the ITC to make available under protective order virtually all information in an investigation for both sides, thus abruptly ending an investigation mechanism that had become as byzantine in its secrecy and as Kafkaesque in its disregard for due process as the worst horrors described in *The Trial*.

6   The relationship between the agencies and the courts

It was assumed by Congress in 1979 that the relationship between the ITA and the ITC would be formal, with little substantive overlap. The ITA would initiate cases within twenty days of filing and would notify the ITC of any dismissals. The ITC would determine whether there was a preliminary indication of material injury and notify the ITA of its determinations within 45 days. The ITA would make a preliminary and then a final determination of whether there was dumping and notify the ITC of the amount, if any. The ITC would determine whether there was final injury and notify the ITA, which would issue an order where appropriate. In practice, this arrangement has created two sets of problems (Horlick 1993: 106).

First, the procedural arrangements waste resources, both public and private. Upon receipt of a petition, the ITC must proceed immediately with its investigation without waiting to see if the investigation is initiated by the ITA. Where cases are not initiated, some twenty days of ITC preparatory work is wasted. Equally, the ITA must start its investigations, which involve heavy outlays within its office and for both parties, shortly after day 20, and cannot wait for the ITC preliminary determination vote, which usually occurs on about day 37. If the ITC vote is negative, all these resources are wasted.

Such waste can be much more serious towards the end of an investigation. In a case where the ITA makes an affirmative preliminary determination, the ITC begins its final investigation at once and typically has devoted as much as 183 days by the time the ITA makes its final determination – all wasted if that determination is negative. In practice, this problem is relatively minor while ITA determinations remain so uniformly positive. It would become much more costly if the ITA were ever to take its duties seriously.

The substantive problems in the relationship between the ITA and the ITC are less frequent but much more serious and arise because the ITC ignores information gathered by the ITA in making its final determination. The statute requires the ITC to determine whether material injury has been caused 'by reason of dumped imports'. Normally, the ITA determines whether each import sale during a six-month investigation period is made at fair value or not. Typically, it finds that only a certain percentage of imports (say 60 percent) are sold at less than fair value (say by 20 percent) and issues a determination on the weighted average dumping margin (say 11 percent). The ITC then often assumes that *all* imports are sold at 11 percent less than fair value (Horlicks 1993: 107), when in reality it should look only at the impact of the 60 percent of imports found to be dumped at the 20 percent margin. This problem is accentuated when the ITA only examines a portion of the total imports because of the high cost of investigating thousands of foreign exporters.

Congress provided for full judicial review of ITA and ITC decisions only in 1979. The initial review is by the US Court of International Trade (CIT). Although the CIT is expected to defer to the administrative expertise of the two agencies, in practice it has upheld the ITA and the ITC in only 50 percent of cases. The appellate court, the Court of Appeals for the Federal Circuit

(CAFC), demonstrated a higher degree of deference to government positions, upholding ITA and ITC decisions in 83 percent of its reviews. Many of the early cases brought before both courts were designed to flesh out possible ambiguities in the wording of the 1979 Act.

7   The relationship between Congress and the ITC

Of the two agencies responsible for implementing the US fair trade-laws, the ITC is much the more interesting, given the consistent willingness of the ITA to make almost universally positive determinations. In this section, we explore the question: what motivates decision-making at the ITC?

We confront the widespread judgement that the ITC is immune from special interest pressures in administering the fair-trade laws and that it meticulously implements the intent of the 1979 Trade Agreements Act as supplemented by the 1979 GATT code of conduct. We make use of public-choice theory, outlined in Chapter 7, which suggests that the ITC is influenced in its decision-making by the US Congress. We hypothesize that this influence diverts the ITC from fulfilling its statutory commitments; specifically, that it renders the ITC more protectionist than otherwise would be the case.

The modern public-choice approach emphasizes that special interests influence the behavior of government agencies through the relevant congressional oversight subcommittees (Weingast and Moran 1983: 132). The hub of the congressional influence theory is the assumption that congressional oversight subcommittees exercise a near-monopoly jurisdiction over their respective agencies; that they alone control all relevant legislative initiatives within their respective chamber of the legislature; and that they act as an effective buffer against outside congressional initiatives directed at their agencies. Members of Congress are assigned to oversight subcommittees largely on the basis of self-selection and seniority, and assume positions of influence on these subcommittees largely on the basis of time served. In such circumstances, members secure subcommittee assignments compatible with the interests of their electoral constituencies (which are not always identical to their geographical constituencies) and specialize in the policy issues serviced by these subcommittees. They secure near-monopoly powers over proposals within their jurisdictions and they use agenda-setting powers to impose outcomes that they prefer and to veto those that they find undesirable.

If this theory is correct, there are two implications that should survive empirical evaluation, namely (a) that specific oversight subcommittees exercise more influence than Congress as a whole over the behavior of particular agencies; and (b) that if the political complexion of a recent oversight subcommittee should shift (as reflected in the recent vote behavior of its chairman and members) then so will the policy-relevant behavior of the associated agency (Rowley and Thorbecke 1993).

US trade policy has long been the province of the two most powerful committees of Congress, namely the Senate Finance Committee and the House Ways and Means Committee. These are the tax committees whose jurisdiction over foreign commerce derives from the early revenue function of the tariff. These are the committees ultimately and primarily responsible for overseeing the ITC. As tax committees, they have broad authority and a reputation for being somewhat conservative. Prior to 1974, their respective chairmen were appointed in no small measure to put a damper on particularism in tax and tariff matters and to maintain centralized majority party control over trade policy (Destler 1986: 26).

Particularly pivotal in this respect, prior to 1974, was the House Ways and Means Committee. The House of Representatives had been subjected to single-party rule (the Democrats) for a period of twenty years and was organized by a strict set of rules and procedures promulgated by the Democratic majority. Secure in his position, and protected from the House leadership following the revolt against Speaker Joe Cannon in 1910 (Destler 1986: 26), the chairman of the Ways and Means Committee could virtually guarantee that the House of Representatives would consider only those trade proposals that his committee placed before it. Given his seniority and his powers of agenda control, the chairman could also ensure that his own personal policy imprint lay heavily on committee policy recommendations.

Wilbur D. Mills (Democrat, Arkansas), who chaired the Ways and Means Committee from 1958 to 1974, was a particularly skilled exponent of agenda control (Destler 1986: 27). While not by any means a free-trader by personal conviction, Mills was by no means an extreme protectionist. He became extremely skilled at protecting his congressional colleagues from special interests by diverting protectionist pressures away from Congress to the executive branch and by maneuvering to choke off statutory protection for specific domestic industries.

In overseeing the ITC, Mills had no difficulty in signalling to the agency the unequivocal support of the Ways and Means Committee for a minimalist approach to enforcing the fair trade laws. By effectively limiting the size of the committee, and by resisting the formation of subcommittees, by his superior grasp of both substance and politics and by his assiduous attention to detail Mills completely dominated the committee.

Unfortunately, Wilbur Mills was unable to control an appetite for hard liquor and, as a married man, for dallying with women of low repute (Destler 1986: 58). In October 1974, nemesis struck when a car in which Mills was riding was stopped (for speeding without lights) by a National Park Service police cruiser, at which point his flimsily clad female companion (a local strip-tease artiste) ran from the vehicle and leaped into the nearby Washington Tidal Basin. Within two months, Mills declared himself an alcoholic and, following an unusually narrow re-election victory, announced that he would not continue as chairman of the Ways and Means Committee in the new Congress. Two years later, he retired from public life.

The post-Watergate Congress comprised 75 freshman Democrats who joined veteran would-be reformers to activate the moribund Democratic caucus. The caucus moved quickly to diffuse power within the House of Representatives and to weaken the power of the Ways and Means Committee, stripping it of its role as the 'committee on committees' that decided who would fill vacancies on all other committees. The Ways and Means Committee itself was expanded from 25 to 37 members, making agenda control of the kind exercised by Mills much less feasible. The committee was decentralized into a number of legislative subcommittees, each with its separate staff. The main responsibility for overseeing the ITC henceforth would rest with the thirteen-member Trade Subcommittee whose chairman inevitably lacked the stature and chamber-leadership powers of Wilbur Mills. New House rules also opened up the Ways and Means Committee and all its subcommittees to public scrutiny (Destler 1986: 59).

The combination of congressional reforms and Mills' disgraced departure undoubtedly opened up the Ways and Means Committee to trade-protection pressures and exposed the ITC to protectionist incentives and sanctions from the Trade Subcommittee. Simultaneously, however, changes in the content of trade policy loosened the grip of the revenue committee over trade policy matters, thereby downgrading its ability to monitor downward. The rise of non-tariff trade issues during the late 1970s inevitably brought other House committees, such as Foreign Affairs into the substance of trade policy.

This multiplicity of principals provided incentives for individual members of any one subcommittee to shirk their responsibilities and often provided ambiguous or conflicting signals to the ITC concerning important industry petitions. In such circumstances, the House oversight subcommittee projected a more protectionist image but provided much weaker governance than earlier had been the case. Put bluntly, the Ways and Means Committee is no longer the major congressional player in overseeing the ITC.

By comparison with the House of Representatives, the Senate is much smaller, more informal and less rule-bound in its mode of operation (Baldwin 1985: 17). It is a much more individualistic institution in which committee chairmen possess less authority and in which an unlimited number of amendments typically are permitted after bills are sent from committee to the Senate as a whole. However, senators generally represent more populous and industrially diversified political units than the House members. It is less likely (Michigan excepted) that the proportion of workers employed in import-injured industries will be sufficiently high to allow a vote-conscious senator to adopt a protectionist posture. Thus, on balance, senators have less incentive but greater ability to provide import protection to particular industries than do congressmen.

Until 1974, the Senate Finance Committee relied heavily on Wilbur Mills in the House to deflect trade-protection pressures away from Congress. After 1974, trade oversight authority in the Senate was delegated to the fourteen-member International Trade Subcommittee, allowing increased influence to protectionist pressures. Since this subcommittee was spared the turf battles over trade policy that eroded the influence of its House counterpart, its incentives and ability to monitor the ITC were unimpaired. In addition, under the protectionist influence of Senator Russell Long, the subcommittee displayed much greater interest after 1974 in its advise and consent responsibilities with respect to presidential appointments of ITC commissioners. In combination these factors have catapulted the International Trade Subcommittee into the pre-eminent role as congressional monitor of the ITC.

Indeed, in recent years, the International Trade Subcommittee has competed openly and aggressively with the White House for the favors of the ITC commissioners. In this battle for influence, the subcommittee has the advantage of purse-string controls, given that the president is precluded from playing any role in ITC budget appropriations. In 1983, when Commissioner Eccles was testifying before the subcommittee about the ITC's desire for a new building, Senator Russell Long responded by emphasizing how important it was for the ITC to be responsive to Congress and not to the executive branch. Senator Long then added: 'the executive branch is not looking out for you very well as far as your building goes so I think that we had better arrange and try to take care of it.' Not long after, the ITC moved into a beautiful new building.

The conventional wisdom of the international trade literature has it that the ITC is immune to congressional pressure and that it faithfully adheres to statutory criteria when making material injury determinations with respect to antidumping and CVD petitions. Investigations based predominantly on pre-1980s data offer modest support for this viewpoint, although none of the studies focuses upon the *electoral* constituencies of the congressional oversight committees, and several of them do not incorporate congressional oversight committee preferences at all.

For example, Baldwin (1985: 43) analyzed the significance of party affiliation in explaining the voting pattern of individual ITC commissioners on import injury cases over the period 1949–83. He separated the study into three periods, namely 1949–62, 1963–74 and 1974–83. Despite the fact that the Republican Party shifted its position from strong to relatively weak protectionism during the 1950s, Baldwin surprisingly determined that Republican ITC commissioners almost always voted in a more protectionist manner than their Democratic or independent counterparts in each period under review.

However, in both negative and affirmative determinations by the ITC, the majority of the members of each party typically voted the same way. He further concluded that party affiliation was of declining significance after 1974 in explaining the voting pattern of the ITC. Since 1975, both Democratic and Republican members of the ITC have been more protectionist in import injury cases than before.

Baldwin (1985: 96) noted a significant change in the employment experience of ITC appointees in the period 1953–67 compared with 1968–83. In the earlier period a majority of the commissioners came from the academy and the executive branch, with only one out of thirteen drawn from a congressional background. In the later period, eight out of sixteen appointees were drawn from Congress, none from the academy and only one from the executive branch. Baldwin acknowledged that this increase in direct congressional influence was associated with greater protectionism, at least with respect to the escape clause cases that he subjected to review.

Goldstein (1986: 161) analyzed the ITC to determine whether the agency had become more or less protectionist over time. By examining the *acceptance rate* of ITC petitions from 1950 to the mid-1980s, she concluded that this rate had not changed significantly over time. Lenway (1985) came to a similar conclusion, namely that pressure groups exert little influence on trade policy. In her view, the GATT is the constraining force that stands between the pressure groups and rampant protectionism on the part of the ITC.

Hansen (1990: 21) challenged the validity of both these studies, claiming that they had ignored the demand side of the trade protection equation. She demonstrated that industries self-select themselves in applying for protection from the ITC, by comparing the benefits from tariff protection against the costs of applying and lobbying for protection.

On the supply side of her analysis Hansen determined that the political factors that appeared best to explain ITC decisions were: (a) location of the industry in a district whose representative was a Democratic member of the Trade Subcommittee of the Ways and Means Committee, and (b) location of the industry in a district whose representative was the chair of the Ways and Means Committee. Among the economic variables examined, the most significant were: (a) the US trade deficit; (b) industry size measured by employment; and (c) the industry's percentage change in employment. These results indicated some degree of support for a pressure-group model of regulation, especially one implying congressional dominance. It is important to note that Hansen employed a geographical constituency variable (plants located in relevant congressional districts) as the basis for her analysis.

Two more recent studies that analyse post-1979 ITC decision-making strongly support the congressional influence reported by Hansen. The first, by Moore (1992), analysed the final antidumping final determinations of the ITC over the period 1980 to 1986. His empirical results indicated that ITC commissioners were influenced by economic criteria consistent with their legislative mandate. Falling production and increased volumes of imports were important factors in ITC decisions. His results indicated, however, that the ITC was also influenced positively by economic variables that are not part of its statutory mandate, namely (a) where imports are from less-developed countries, and (b) where the domestic industry is characterized by low-wage employees or by low profitability.

Most significantly, Moore found evidence that petitions involving the constituencies of the Senate Trade Subcommittee members were systematically favored by the ITC. This led him to conclude that the institutional power of the Senate oversight committee over the ITC was sufficiently strong to affect its adjudication of antidumping petitions,

None of the studies referred to above attempted to identify the electoral constituencies of the ITC oversight committee members as critical influences over ITC decision-making. To remedy this omission, Rowley and Thorbecke (1995a) analysed all antidumping and CVD preliminary determinations by the ITC over the period 1980 to 1990 to test the hypothesis that ITC decisions were influenced by electoral pressures.

Rowley and Thorbecke utilized the Americans for Democratic Action (ADA) liberal quotient as a relevant measure of a senator's or a congressman's electoral constituency, relying upon evidence by Nollen and Iglarsh (1990) that this measure was the most important factor determining individual congressional votes in the 1984 trade vote on Unfair Trade Practices and the 1987 trade vote on the Omnibus Trade Bill, and on evidence by Coughlin (1985) that the measure was highly significant in explaining protectionist votes by members of Congress on the 1982 Automotive Products Act.

The higher the ADA rating of a congressman, the more protectionist is his electoral constituency in this interpretation. The ADA rating is a normalized variable with a range from 100 to 0 and a mean approximately of 50; this does not imply that congressmen with ADA ratings below 50 are pro-free trade, only that they are relatively less protectionist.

Rowley and Thorbecke, after experimenting with several economic variables, found (like Moore 1992) that the change in the volume of dumped imports as a ratio to domestic output and the change in domestic production, lagged one year were statistically significant and of the *a priori* expected signs. They determined that the ADA ratings of the Senate International Trade Subcommittee members were highly significant and of the predicted *a priori* sign in explaining preliminary ITC antidumping and CVD determinations. The level of unemployment in a subcommittee member's state also exerted a significant positive influence, whereas the level of export employment in the state exerted a significant negative influence, further confirming the existence of effective electoral pressure.

It is interesting to note from the Rowley and Thorbecke study that the ADA ratings for the Senate as a whole were insignificant influences on ITC behavior and that the ADA ratings of the House Trade Subcommittee were also insignificant. The ADA ratings of the president were of the correct sign, but only barely significant, as theory would suggest. Each of these results strongly conforms with the public choice approach.

In a yet more telling result, Rowley *et al.* (1995b) evaluated the final determinations over the period 1980–1989 of the ITC in antidumping petitions and found that the ADA ratings of the Senate International Trade Subcommittee members were highly significant determinants of ITC decisions and of the predicted *a priori* sign. Once again, the ADA ratings for the Senate as a whole were insignificant. At least for the period under review, this evidence supports the public-choice approach.

8   The rising tide of administrative trade remedies

The rise in the number of fair-trade petitions since 1979 makes it clear that Congress succeeded in the 1979 Act just as it had failed in 1974 (Destler 1992: 153). In response to industry petitions, the ITA initiated 345 CVD investigations and 438 antidumping investigations between 1980 and 1989. More often than not the petitioners obtained relief. Of the 258 CVD petitions carried through the full statutory process, 135 won either imposition of duties or suspension of the offending foreign practice. The remaining 87 were withdrawn by petitioners, almost always because the source nation promised to limit exports. Of the 327 antidumping petitions carried through the full statutory process, 173 resulted in duties or suspension agreements; 111 were withdrawn, largely after agreement on voluntary export restraints.

Relief granted in CVD and antidumping petitions continues unless and until the ITA determines that circumstances no longer justify it. Thus, by end 1990, there were 72 countervailing duties still in effect and 202 antidumping duties. This compared with 57 and 137 respectively in effect in mid-1983 (Destler 1992: 154). With such evident success rates, US firms increasingly exploit the fair-trade laws to create an intolerable situation for foreign competitors, forcing them to enter into voluntary export restraints as a precondition for withdrawal of the fair-trade petitions..

An illustration of the way in which such petitioning pressure works is to be found in the steel cases of 1982 (Destler 1986: 128). There is no doubt that steel producers in France and Britain were shipping subsidized steel to the US market at that time, offering a justifiable case for a CVD petition under the US fair-trade laws. In January 1982, seven US steel producers delivered 494 boxes containing three million pages of documentation for 132 countervailing and antidumping petitions, largely against European Community suppliers (Destler 1992: 157). The purpose of this flood of litigation was not to enforce the free trade laws but to intimidate foreign governments into trade protection negotiations.

The protectionist US Secretary of Commerce, Malcolm Baldrige, readily brokered a trade-restricting arrangement between foreign governments and domestic steelmakers entirely outside established procedures. Under this arrangement, the EC voluntarily restricted carbon steel exports to the United States to 5.44 percent of the US market.

Encouraged by the easy victory, the US steel industry moved again in 1984, deploying the same tactics as in 1982. With European imports fixed at 5.4 percent of US consumption and with imports from Japan informally pegged at the same amount, the remaining competitive threat came from Brazil, Mexico and South Korea. Once again there were multiple submissions of CVD and antidumping petitions supported by an enormous volume of paper. The real objective was openly expressed by Roderick of US Steel, namely to make the impact so burdensome that 'all players of substance in the import game ... would be very pleased to enter into quotas in a negotiated manner' (Destler 1992: 158).

A decision was forced by an escape clause petition, filed jointly by Bethlehem Steel and its union, United Steelworkers, in January 1994, citing an increase in imports market share from 15 percent in 1979 to 25 percent early in 1984 at a time of falling domestic sales and rising unemployment. In July 1984, by a three to two vote, the ITC determined that imports had been a substantial cause of serious injury in five of the nine major steel import categories. For relief it recommended a mixture of tariffs and quotas to be imposed for a five-year period. President Reagan had 60 days to implement, modify or reject the recommendation. It was election year.

On September 18 1994 USTR William Brock announced that the President was rejecting the ITC recommendation. However, the EC restrictions were to continue and the USTR might be authorized to negotiate restraint agreements with other countries. It was hoped that these actions would limit the level of steel imports to 18.5 percent of US steel consumption. Congress then legislated a target for fair import share: 17–20.2 percent of the US market. Agreements were then negotiated or reaffirmed with every major foreign seller, circumventing the fair-trade laws while imposing a national policy for the steel industry. So much for the free market rhetoric of the Reagan administration.

Table 10.3 chronicles the pattern of fair trade petitions through the course of the 1980s, showing sharply contrasting patterns. Countervailing duty cases rose in the first few years of the decade, peaked in 1982 and fell sharply after 1986. A large proportion of these petitions were steel cases targeted to force

*Table 10.3   Antidumping, countervailing-duty and section 201
investigations initiated, 1979–90*

Year	Antidumping cases	Countervailing-duty cases	Section 201 cases
1979	26	40	4
1980	21	14	2
1981	15	22	1
1982	65	140	3
1983	46	22	0
1984	74	51	7
1985	66	43	4
1986	71	27	1
1987	15	8	0
1988	42	11	1
1989	23	7	0
1990	43	7	1
Total	507	392	24

Source: Destler (1992: 166).

political solutions. Once that goal had been achieved, CVD petitions col-lapsed. By the end of the 1980s new CVD petitions were running at rates lower than those of the mid-1970s (Destler 1992: 166).

In contrast, antidumping petitions remained high, although they also peaked in the mid-1980s. There were more antidumping cases in 1988–90 than in 1980–2. Table 10.4 shows the post-1985 decline in the number of occasions where plaintiffs withdrew their petitions (to force political solutions). It also shows the rising success rates in winning relief under the antidumping statute itself. The ITA was finding dumping in the overwhelming majority of peti-tions submitted. The ITC was finding material injury in some 60 percent of all such petitions (Destler 1992: 167). In such circumstances, it is not sur-prising that escape clause cases had virtually disappeared by 1990, totally dominated by the less-burdensome and longer-lived antidumping relief mecha-nism.

10   Conclusions

In his book *Protectionism*, Jagdish Bhagwati (1988: 35) makes a case for 'the appropriate use of countervailing duties and antidumping actions to maintain, fair, competitive trade'. However, this is the ideal. Bhagwati goes on to

Table 10.4 Antidumping cases and results, 1980–89

Year	Total[a]	Cases withdrawn[b]	Cases completed[c]	Cases affirmed[d] No.[e]	Percent	Negative dumping[f] No.	Percent	No injury[g] No.	Percent
1980	21	9	12	3	25	1	8	8	67
1981	15	4	11	7	64	1	9	3	27
1982	65	24	41	14	34	3	7	24	59
1983	46	5	41	19	46	5	12	17	41
1984	74	42	32	12	38	5	16	15	47
1985	66	16	50	29	58	2	4	19	38
1986	71	7	64	44	69	3	5	17	27
1987	15	1	14	9	64	0	0	5	36
1988	42	0	42	22	52	3	7	17	40
1989	23	3	20	14	70	0	0	6	30
Total	438	111	327	173	53	23	7	131	40

Notes:
a Total number of petitions submitted
b Cases terminated by withdrawal of petition
c Cases followed through to an official finding
d Cases resulting in an antidumping action
e Number of cases completed
f Cases ending with finding of no dumping
g Cases resulting in finding of no injury to petitioners.

Source: Destler (1992: 168).

discuss the capture of the antidumping and countervailing-duty laws by the forces of protectionism during the 1970s and 1980s, especially in the United States. He views the capture of these laws as perhaps the most important development in trade policy in the past two decades. He attributes both the protectionist sentiment behind the capture of the trade laws and the search for *fairness* to the diminished giant syndrome of the United States as its economic dominance recedes relative to other nations. His book indeed exposes evil to sunlight. However, it does not go far enough.

We have endeavored to demonstrate in this chapter that there is no sound argument of a utilitarian nature to justify fair-trade laws either at the level of the nation state or in cosmopolitan terms. Therefore, even if the ITA and the ITC were to administer the US fair-trade laws in strict conformity with their legislative mandates, which demonstrably they have not done, they would wreak damage on the nation's wealth. We further suggest that their legislative mandate renders them predators on natural rights and enemies of individual liberty.

There is mounting evidence, however, that both the ITA and the ITC are influenced by congressional pressures into adopting a protectionist position well beyond the mandate of the fair trade laws, that they have become an illegal agent of trade protection malpractice. Such behavior is the predictable consequence of political market pressures and cannot be constrained by narrowing the legislative mandate. Only by eliminating the US fair trade laws in their entirety and by removing international trade from the reach of domestic politics can US consumers secure themselves from the harmful consequences of rent-seeking behavior on the part of special interests. Whether a sufficient vote majority of consumer interests has the will to cast down the fair trade laws that unequivocally oppress them is an as yet undetermined issue of late twentieth-century US politics.

References

Anderson, K.B. (1992) *Agency Discretion or Statutory Discretion: Decision Making at the U.S. International Trade Commission, Journal of Law Economic* 36(2): 915–36.

Baldwin, R.E. (1985) *The Political Economy of US Import Policy* (Cambridge, Mass.: MIT Press).

Bhagwati, J. (1988) *Protectionism* (Cambridge, Mass.: MIT Press).

Bovard, J. (1991) *The Fair Trade Fraud: How Congress Pillages the Consumer and Decimates American Competitiveness* (New York: St Martin's Press).

Coughlin, C.C. (1985) 'Domestic content legislation: House voting and the economic theory of regulation', *Economic Inquiry*, 23: 437–48.

Destler, I.M. (1986) *American Trade Politics: System Under Stress* (Washington, D.C.: Institute for International Economics).

Destler, I.M. (1992) *American Trade Politics*, Second Edition, (Washington, D.C.: Institute for International Economics.

Finger, J.M. (ed.) (1993) *Antidumping: How it Works and Who Gets Hurt* (Ann Arbor: University of Michigan Press).

Finger, J.M. and Murray T. (1993) 'Antidumping and countervailing duty enforcement in the

United States', in J.M. Finger (ed.) *Antidumping: How it Works and Who Gets Hurt* (Ann Arbor: University of Michigan Press), pp. 241–54.

Goldstein, J. (1986) 'The political economy of trade: institution of protection', *American Political Science Review*, 80: 161–84.

Hansen, W.L. (1990) 'The International Trade Commission and the politics of protectionism', *American Political Science Review*, 84: 21–43.

Horlick, G.N. (1993) 'The United States antidumping system', in J.H. Jackson and E.A. Vermulst (eds), *Antidumping: Law and Practice* (Ann Arbor: University of Michigan Press).

Horlick, G.N. and Oliver, G.D. (1989) 'Antidumping and countervailing duty law provisions of the Omnibus Trade and Competitiveness Act of 1988', *Journal of World Trade*, 23: 5–49.

Lenway, S.A. (1985) *The Politics of International Trade* (Marshfield: Pitman).

Moore, M.O. (1992) 'Rules or politics? An empirical analysis of ITC antidumping decisions', *Economic Inquiry*, 30: 449–66.

Nollen, S.D. and Iglarsh, H.J. (1990) 'Explanations of protectionism in international trade votes', *Public Choice*, 66: 137–53.

Rowley, C.K. and Thorbecke, W. (1995a) 'Congressional Influence over Decision Making at the ITC', in F. Schneider and J. Casas Pardo (eds), *Public Choice* (Dordrecht: Kluwer Academic Publishers).

Rowley, C.K., and Thorbecke, W. and Grote, K. (1995b) *The International Trade Commission and the Fair Trade Laws: A Public Choice Analysis* (Fairfax, Va.: Locke Institute).

Tullock, G. (1980) 'Efficient rent-seeking' in J.M. Buchanan, R.D. Tollison and G. Tullock (eds) *Toward a Theory of the Rent-Seeking Society* (College Station: Texas A&M University Press.

Weingast, B.R. and Moran, N.J. (1983) 'Bureaucratic discretion or congressional control?', *Journal of Political Economy*, 96: 132–63.

11   Regional trade politics

1   Introduction

Because it had been discriminated against throughout the 1918–39 interwar period, during which German and British bilateral systems dominated much of world trade, the United States government was firmly opposed to allowing discrimination in the GATT during the post-Second World War negotiations (Snape 1993: 7). The GATT compromised to the extent of agreeing to the continuation, but not the extension, of existing preferences and to preferential arrangements that involved essentially free trade among the participants: customs unions and free trade areas.

For essentially political reason the United States government supported the formation of the European Economic Community and the European Free Trade Association in the late 1950s. In the late 1960s, reluctantly, it agreed to the generalized system of preferences for developing countries, negotiated through the GATT. In general, however, it set itself resolutely against departures from the principle of non-discrimination as embedded in the most-favored-nation clause (MFN) of the GATT.

In contrast to this earlier position, since 1980 successive United States governments have been at the forefront in a new wave of preferential trading agreements that threaten seriously to distort the pattern of international trade and to undermine the multilateral trading order pursued by the GATT in eight successful rounds of negotiations. In 1983 the United States granted unilateral preferences to Caribbean countries. In 1985 it concluded a free trade agreement with Israel. In 1988 it concluded a free trade agreement with Canada. In 1993 it concluded the NAFTA agreement with Canada and Mexico. Both the Bush and the Clinton administrations have intimated that other Latin American countries may be candidates for similar agreements. Feelers have been extended in yet other directions (Snape 1993: 8).

Successive USTRs have explicitly stated throughout this latter period that bilateral and multilateral negotiations would proceed *pari passu*. They appear to believe that the two approaches are mutually reinforcing, that bilateral discriminatory trade agreements can be used as levers to force other nations into opening up their markets to US exports. In fact, the approach smacks of the crowbar mentality (Bhagwati 1991: 49) that now affects the US executive branch and that threatens seriously to undermine the multilateral trading system.

Preferences can be explicitly negative as well as positive. Sanctions imposed by the United States for political purposes against South Africa, Iran,

Iraq, and Haiti are examples of negative preferences. The Clinton administration flirted in 1994 with imposing similar sanctions against the People's Republic of China, but backed off because of domestic export pressures. Probably the most important explicitly negative preferences, however, are the section 301 and the now-expired Super 301 provisions of the 1988 Omnibus Trade and Competitiveness Act. Many of these provisions allow for GATT-illegal explicit discrimination against other countries in ways that are reminiscent of German and British policies during the 1930s.

In comparing non-discriminatory multilateral trade with trade discrimination, it is instructive to recall the role of the price system in a market economy (Snape 1993: 9). The market facilitates the depersonalization of trading. The foremost consequence of such depersonalization is a tendency towards economic efficiency. Non-market systems function through networks of obligations, responsibilities, love, hate, threats, war, queues, cooperation and favors. This is as true at the level of nations as it is at the individual level. Managed trade is political trade, extremely unlikely to be economically efficient, and not unlikely to end in open warfare between nation-states.

In this chapter, we review preferential trading agreements that manifest a regional form. Such preferential trading agreements are back in fashion. They constitute a continuing menace to the liberal trading order, especially now that the United States has thrown in the towel and joined the race to regional discrimination, through which outlet it can tout a corporatist industrial policy under the mask of managed trade.

2   The neoclassical theory of preferential reductions of trade barriers

Neoclassical theory does not come down unambiguously against preferential reductions of trade barriers by any group of countries, whether that preferential reduction is 100 percent (as required under Article XXIV of the GATT) or less. The uneasy case in favor of such preferential reductions rests on four related sets of analytical approaches (Bhagwati 1991: 59).

The first approach is due to Viner–Lipsey–Meade. In 1950, Jacob Viner distinguished between trade-creating and trade-diverting unions among subsets of countries that retained their respective external tariffs (or some average thereof). The trade-creating union would create trade among the member countries at the expense of inefficient industries in the member countries. The trade-diverting union would do so at the expense of more efficient industries in non-member countries.

Viner's contribution destroyed the 'fallacy that a preferential move toward freer trade was necessarily welfare-improving' (Bhagwati 1991: 59) (in the Paretian sense). It could also be interpreted, however, as showing that certain kinds of preferential moves might be welfare-improving. Two further points relevant to Article XXIV of the GATT have been drawn from Viner's insight

(Bhagwati 1991: 60). First, it is not necessary that preferential trade liberalization should be 100 percent for it to be welfare-improving. Second, as Meade (1955) demonstrated, as tariffs are progressively reduced within a customs union the incremental gain from trade creation falls while the probability of loss from trade diversion incrementally rises. Hence, Article xxiv, which insists on 100 percent trade liberalization as a preconditon for preferential groupings, arguably is inefficient.

The second approach, due to Murray Kemp and Henry Wan (1976), demonstrated that any group of countries could always form a customs union, with a common external tariff, that had two desired properties, namely (a) that non-members would have their welfare unchanged, and (b) that members would improve their own welfare. However, Kemp and Wan provided no guidance as to the necessary and sufficient conditions that such unions must satisfy. In the absence of such guidance, it is not possible to identify the specific real-world groupings that satisfy the Kemp–Wan conditions (Bhagwati 1991: 61).

The third approach, due to Cooper and Massell (1965, 1966) and Bhagwati (1968), reflected the concerns of small underdeveloped countries. They suggested that customs unions comprising such countries would foster import-competing industrialization while protecting members against the manufacturers of the developed countries. Specialization in manufactures within the union would be profitable even in the absence of scale economies. Following the logic of Kemp–Wan, such unions theoretically could be devised to satisfy the necessary and sufficient conditions for Pareto optimality (Bhagwati 1991: 61).

The fourth approach, due to Brecher and Bhagwati (1981), is more modest in scope, providing a mechanism to analyse the welfare effects of parametric and policy variations in customs unions with common external tariffs and with freedom of intra-union factor movements. As a customs union moves towards full integration, this analytical approach provides the requisite tools to calculate the costs and benefits of specific policy changes (Bhagwati 1991: 62).

Taken together, these four approaches offer something of an apology for customs unions and free trade areas, present a challenge to the multilateral free trade ideal espoused by the GATT, and rationalize the inclusion of Article xxiv of the GATT. Within the narrow, incrementalist logic of neo-classical economics, the case thus presented is superficially plausible. From the broader normative perspective of Virginia political economy, however, the case is less convincing, albeit somewhat predictable from the positive public-choice perspective.

3   The counter-argument for multilateralism

The Virginia arguments in favor of unilateral free trade for the United States (and indeed for any other nation) coupled with multilateralism in disbanding the network of regulations that currently strangles international trade have been outlined in detail in Chapters 1–3 of this book. Grounded as they are in a unique combination of methodological individualism, of the primacy of economic freedom over economic efficiency, of public choice and constitutional political economy, they stand apart from the principal preoccupation of neoclassical economics with social engineering in pursuit of utilitarian objectives. Suffice it to note that the Virginian case against trade protection holds equally at the level of the customs union and free trade area as at the level of the nation-state.

Even within the framework of neoclassical economics, however, a powerful counter-argument can be mounted against internationally negotiated discriminatory reductions of trade barriers and in favor of internationally negotiated non-discriminatory reductions as a second-best alternative to unilateral free trade policies. In essence, this counter-argument is based on global rather than incrementalist assessments of the gains and losses implicit in the two conflicting policies.

The principle reason for a nation state to undertake trade liberalization in the context of an international agreement – whether preferential or not – rather than to do so unilaterally is to obtain something in return from its trading partners (Snape 1993: 11). Such concessions provide a source of economic gain for the nation itself (to use a neoclassical concept). In addition, within the nation they provide a political counterbalance of obvious and concentrated gainers – exporters – against the obvious and concentrated losers – producers of import-competing industries in which there is trade-creation.

In addition to seeking concessions for its exports, a government may enter a negotiated international agreement in order to constrain its own policies. There are occasions when governments are able to execute policy relatively free from sectional pressures, most notably where external security considerations are paramount or in the immediate aftermath of electoral success. International commitments provide a bulwark against subsequent sectional pressures when the political market equilibrium shifts back to protectionism.

The case for non-discriminatory multilateralism, as compared with preferential schemes, is best advanced in fundamentalist terms (Snape 1993: 11). There are public-good aspects to compliance with a non-discriminatory world trading system. There is a constant threat that such a system will be eroded by free-riding. Any particular preferential trading agreement thus appears to be more attractive to the parties concerned, because they fail to recognize the harm to the wider trading system, than would be the case if they viewed preferential systems as a whole.

For any particular government choosing between discriminatory and non-discriminatory barrier reductions, the question is whether the extra *something in return* in a preferential agreement compensates for the trade diversion costs (Snape 1993: 12). Working on a broader canvas, however, governments can also consider the effect on the trading system as a whole of the development of preferential trading arrangements – the systemic affect – which can react on them adversely.

In particular, this should be a major concern for small countries. For, while small countries stand to gain from discrimination in their favor, they also stand to lose most from the collapse of a multilateral system. This is of particular importance when evaluating the development of a hub-and-spoke system of bilateral agreements centered on the United States.

While each of the partners with the United States in a hub-and-spoke system may benefit from its own bilateral relationship, an important question is what effect such a network will have on the multilateral trading system as a whole. In particular, will the United States inadvertently create a discriminatory, inefficient, hub-and-spoke trading structure that ultimately damages its partners and erodes prospects for future multilateral liberalization (Wonnacott 1990: 2)?

Each additional country embraced by a hub-and-spoke system reduces the gains for those already in it, with the exception of the hub country; for each new entrant reduces the advantages of the rim in trading with the hub, as bilateralism multiplies. Yet the more countries that are in the system, the greater the incentive for outsiders to join. If rim countries wish to develop a network of agreements among themselves to reduce the discrimination, the number of possible agreements increases rapidly as the number of rim countries grows.

Finally, the ability of the hub country's administration to focus on trade negotiations is limited, even in the case of the United States. Distraction of hub attention by hub-and-spoke dealings can stall, if not completely abort, important multilateral negotiations. This applies to a lesser extent to its potential partners, who may come to view a deal with the hub as an alternative to a multilateral agreement. This diversion effect was clearly evident in the 1990 stalling of the Uruguay Round when the United States became increasingly focused on the NAFTA negotiations. The entire GATT system was placed in jeopardy by the preoccupation of the United States government with a somewhat trivial hub-and-spoke negotiation.

The logic of collective action dictates that political markets will favor hub-and-spoke over multilateral negotiations, since the former provide concentrated benefits for the few and dispersed costs for the many, whereas the latter provide dispersed benefits to the many and often impose concentrated costs on the few. Only when the executive branch aggressively adheres to the bicycle theory of trade liberalization are multilateral negotiations likely to prevail over hub-and-spoke alternatives, given the institutional structure of the US Congress.

4   The GATT rules on preferential trading agreements

Article I of the GATT does not permit new preferential trading agreements between members of the GATT and any other country. It provides that any trade concession granted to any other country (not just any other contracting party) by a contracting party must be extended unconditionally to all other contributing parties. Note that the GATT itself extends MFN only to its members and hence falls short of worldwide multilateralism. However, the GATT membership is open to all countries that meet the criteria for admission and generally it has been inclusive rather than exclusive (Bhagwati 1991: 58), despite the invocation in the past of Article xxxv to deny the immediate benefits of membership to countries such as Japan.

Amendments to the GATT have qualified the MFN requirement by allowing preferences to be extended to developing countries without reciprocity. More important, however, from the viewpoint of regionalism is that Article xxiv qualifies Article I by permitting contracting parties to form preferential arrangements provided that:

1. they are in the form of customs unions (free trade internally and common barriers externally) or free trade areas (free trade internally and differential barriers externally) covering 'substantially all the trade in products' or are interim arrangements leading to these ends;
2. they do not result in raised barriers against non-participants (the 'general incidence' must not be raised in the case of customs unions); and
3. GATT is notified of the intention to form such arrangements.

Evidently, Article xxiv can be rationalized as reflecting a view that free trade areas and customs unions encompassing most trade among the member states will tend to be more trade-creating then trade-diverting, so that on balance they will be trade-liberalizing. Presumably, there is also an explicit judgement that the multilateralizm of the GATT as a whole will not be undermined by such arrangements. The fact that the exception is permitted only for the extremely difficult case, where all internal barriers to trade are eliminated, appears to preclude the possibility that the world might return to the bilateral discriminatory situation of the 1930s. The fact that the world's largest trading nation, the United States, was not viewed as a likely participant in Article xxiv negotiations further increased confidence in the multilateralism of the GATT rules.

The clear intent of those who drafted Article xxiv was to close all possible loopholes by which it could degenerate into a justification for preferential arrangements of less than 100 percent (Bhagwati 1991: 66). Paragraphs 4–10 of Article xxiv were written precisely for this purpose. In reality, however, the inherent ambiguity of these paragraphs, together with the political pressures for approval of substantial regional groupings of preferences of less than 100 percent have frustrated the original intent of the Article xxiv safeguards. Indeed, the leading expert on GATT law, John Jackson (1969), has observed that the accommodation of the European Economic Community's imperfect union, in disregard of the legal requirements of Article xxiv, was the beginning of the breakdown of the GATT's legal discipline.

Unfortunately, paragraph 8 of Article xxiv left sufficient scope for the original intent to be avoided by unscrupulous lawyers and government bureaucrats (Bhagwati 1991: 67). The first ambiguity lay in the directive that 'duties and other restrictive regulations of commerce' were to be 'eliminated with respect to *substantially all the trade* between the constituent territories'. The italicized phrase allowed a coach and horses to be driven through the intended safeguard. The second ambiguity concerned the time frame within which the 100 percent preferences were to be implemented. Paragraph 5 required 'a plan and schedule', and asked for the customs union or free trade area to be fully consummated 'within a reasonable length of time'. Once again, the laxity of definition offered a more than adequate opportunity for opportunism in the establishing of preferential trading agreements that should not have passed through the Article xxiv gateway (Bhagwati 1991: 68).

For the first 35 years of GATT's existence, the United States government resisted all temptations to resort to regionalism. In such circumstances, very few trade areas or customs unions were authorized by the contracting parties to the GATT. By late 1988, 69 preferential trading arrangements had been considered by the GATT under the provisions of Article xxiv. Of these, only four were deemed to be compatible with the Article. Yet, although the conditions have seldom been satisfied, no proposed agreement has been prohibited. For this reason, GATT surveillance must be viewed as lax; a weakness that has become serious since the early 1980s when the United States turned away from multilateralism in favor of hub-and-spoke regionalism.

5   The political and economic background: 1980–90

Although the performance of the international economy during the 1980s was positive – the value of trade grew by 50 percent as compared with a 30 percent growth in world gross product – it did not match the growth rates of the previous two decades. Unemployment became a much more serious problem rising from the 5–6 percent rates of the 1970s to 8 percent averages for OECD countries until the end of the 1980s, although the United States fared markedly better as a consequence of President Reagan's supply-side tax policies.

Despite its relatively robust economy, the United States underwent a series of economic shocks during the 1980s that stimulated protectionist pressures. Many large US banks experienced a deterioration in their financial position due to losses on loans to underdeveloped countries and to defaults in their domestic loan portfolios. Several bank failures occurred. The period of sustained high interest rates brought down a number of other financial institutions. Towards the end of the decade, the government's liability to recompense depositors in the failed institutions added tens of billions of dollars to an already out-of-control federal budget deficit (Hudec 1991: 104).

In the mid-1980s, the trading equilibrium of the United States was displaced by the emergence of a large trade deficit, with the US current account declining from a zero balance in 1982 to a $147 billion deficit by 1987. By the end of the decade, continuing trade deficits had moved the United States from a major creditor nation to the world's largest debtor nation.

The basic cause of the US trade deficit was not a loss of international competitiveness, but rather excessive domestic consumption fueled by a low savings rate and escalating federal budget deficits. The situation was worsened by a perverse movement in exchange rates, exacerbated by relatively high US rates of interest that were necessary to fund the budget deficits. By 1985, the US dollar had risen to 145 percent of its 1980 value, although it began to decline by end-1985 following the Plaza Agreement. The trade deficit continued at stubbornly high levels, despite the decline of the dollar, throughout the 1980s.

As a consequence of rising unemployment, increasing import penetration of domestic markets, the high value of the dollar, and the rising trade deficit, protectionist lobbying sharply increased in the United States at the end of the 1970s and continued throughout the 1980s. Such lobbying was markedly more effective with respect to Congress than to the executive branch. Congress became sharply more protectionist and demonstrated an increasing willingness to supply protectionist legislation. Yet in 1980, 1984, and 1988, the electorate favored Ronald Reagan (twice) and George Bush (once), both of whom campaigned on liberal trade platforms; and it decisively rejected Jimmy Carter, Walter Mondale, Richard Gephart, and Michael Dukakis, each of whom adopted protectionist-leaning positions.

Recognizing the policy divergence that was opening up between Congress and the executive branch, Congress began to involve itself much more actively in matters of trade policy. This transition began when Congress took control away from President Carter in designing the Trade Act of 1979 that implemented the Tokyo Round agreements. In 1984, Congress generated another protectionist trade act, overcoming stiff opposition from the executive branch. By the time of the Omnibus Trade and Competitiveness Act of 1988, which authorized US participation in the Uruguay Round, Congress had established a controlling position with respect to trade policy.

With control came a growing perception within Congress that the GATT had become ineffectual, and that the regional card should be played as a threat to those who would not move fast enough to change the GATT to suit America's desires and interests (Bhagwati 1991: 71). Since the process of change at the GATT was to prove always slower than Congress desired, the regional card would be played again and again, reinforcing a shift in US policy away from multilateralism.

6   The US regional card

In contrast to its earlier role as leader in developing a non-discriminatory trading system, the United States has been in the vanguard of a new wave of preferential trading agreements that threaten to destroy the multilateral liberal trading order cultivated by the GATT. The problem is no longer isolated in Congress but has permeated the executive branch, afflicting the USTR and the president as well as the congenitally protectionist departments of Commerce, Energy and the Environment.

Since 1984, successive USTRs have explicitly stated that bilateral and multilateral negotiations would proceed together. The position was clearly stated in the Reagan administration's statement on trade policy of September 22, 1985 (Snape 1993: 8):

> While our highest priority remains the improvement of the world trading system through a new round of multilateral trade negotiations, the United States is interested in the possibility of achieving further liberalization of trade and investment through the negotiation of bilateral free-trade arrangements such as the one recently concluded with Israel. We believe that, at times, such agreements could complement our multilateral efforts and facilitate a higher degree of liberalization, mutually beneficial to both parties, than would be possible within the multilateral context.

From the outset of Reagan's first term, the USTR, Ambassador Brock outlined the policy of strategic behavior that would be pursued by the US government throughout the 1980s and beyond:

> We will take into account the actions of other nations when they seek special privileges and special access to this market. I think that is something that needs to be understood and needs to be stated. I don't know how else to encourage other countries to participate as responsible members of the community. If people seek preferential access to our markets, then I think it is somewhat unbecoming of them to suggest that they should impose absolute and categorical barriers to the importation of our products. We will take those actions into account in our dealings with them (Destler 1992).

Perhaps the most explicit indication of the 'crowbar mentality' that has come to dominate US trade policy in the 1990s is to be found in the statement by Secretary of the Treasury, James Baker on June 22 1988 (Snape 1993: 8);

> [Our] approach is idealistic in aim, but realistic and often incremental in method. It seeks to move nations toward a more open trading system through a strategy of consistent, complementary, and reinforcing actions on various international fronts, bilateral and multilateral ... . [The trade agreement with Canada] is ... a lever to achieve more open trade. Other nations are forced to recognize that we will devise ways to expand trade – with or without them. If they choose not to open their markets, they will not reap the benefits.

In our view, regionalism and multilateralism are antithetical concepts and the recent outbreak of regionalism spearheaded by the United States constitutes a grave, unambiguous attack on the liberal trade order itself. Regionalism as practiced by the United States provides a mask behind which intervention-minded governments can develop highly protectionist industrial policies while explicitly subscribing to a false rhetoric of trade liberalization.

Early bilateral initiatives
Despite its general longer-range policy support for multilateralism and MFN, US policy-makers have been seriously tempted by bilateral approaches throughout the postwar period (Bhagwati 1991: 71).

One of the earliest such departures from MFN by the United States was its exclusion of communist countries from such treatment in 1951. This aberration could be excused as a weapon deployed in the Cold War. However, in the 1960s the United States initiated a bilateral move that related to its traditional GATT trading partners, developing and implementing in 1965 the US–Canada Automotive Products Agreements. The United States obtained a GATT waiver from its MFN obligations for this agreement.

In the Tokyo Round (1973–4), the United States government took steps that departed from unconditional MFN (Jackson 1989: 382). Congress mandated in the Trade Act of 1974 that the United States would withhold MFN treatment if countries failed to provide reciprocal advantages in a negotiated settlement. In addition, the United States refused to give unconditional MFN status to all GATT members in connection with the obligations of the countervailing duty code, the government procurement code and the standards code. In this respect, it came close to infringing GATT legality.

From the conclusion of the Tokyo Round, the United States has experienced an acrimonious relationship with Japan, aggressively pursued by the United States at a bilateral level. In 1979, the United States entered into bilateral negotiations with Japan for additional concessions under the Government Procurement Code for purchases by the Japanese telephone company,

NTT. Subsequently, bilateral meetings between the United States and Japan occurred frequently on a range of trade-related issues. For the most part, GATT has been completely sidestepped in these negotiations.

Even when the US was ostensibly implementing an MFN policy, a close examination sometimes exposes a strong bilateral effect. On the escape clause case on motorcycles (1983), for example, the quotas that were actually implemented primarily impacted on Japan. During the sequence of countervailing-duty cases on steel brought in 1982, the United States negotiated extensively with the European Community, bypassing the GATT in working out conflicts.

In 1983, through the Caribbean Basin Recovery Act, the United States implemented a bilateral trade relationship with the Caribbean basin. This was the first use of regional trade preferences under US trade law. The 1983 Act did not create a free trade area. However, it provided duty-free access to the US market for certain commodities not already covered by preferential treatment under the Generalized System of Preferences.

In 1985, the United States concluded with Israel its first free trade area agreement, signalling a policy shift towards regionalism which has now become a focal point of trade policy. Israel's trade with the United States is sufficiently small and sufficiently different from that of Latin American and East Asian countries as not to present significant trade-diversion risks. Its impact on most US industries has proved to be trivial, especially since many agricultural products are effectively excluded from the agreement. Undoubtedly, it constrains Israel's trade policy much more than it does that of the United States. Nevertheless, as the first spoke in the hub-and-spoke system it was a landmark event, although not remarked upon as such at the time that the legislation was passed.

The US–Canada Free Trade Agreement
The US–Canada free trade negotiations were initiated by Canada in 1984. Responding to this initiative, and using the bilateral fast-track authorization contained in the 1984 Act, President Reagan notified Congress in December 1985 of his intention to proceed. His initiative ran into serious opposition in a Senate Finance Committee that was frustrated by the administration's lack of responsiveness to its protectionist concerns (Destler 1992: 96).

Notwithstanding Republican control of that committee, Senate Finance took up a proposal to block fast-track treatment for the negotiations, rejecting that proposal in April 1986 only by a 10:10 tied vote, after assurances had been provided on softwood lumber and other issues. The Ways and Means Committee played an important facilitating role on behalf of the administration, offsetting opposition pressures on the House Floor.

The negotiations were rushed to completion by fall 1987, so that Congress could be pre-notified in early October as the law required, and so that the agreement could be signed on January 2 1988, the last day that the fast-track authority allowed. The administration once again upset Congress by defining major substantive provisions of the agreement in the period between the October notification and the January signing, despite the contrary intent of the fast-track legislation.

Thereafter, the implementing process was trouble-free. The administration promised not to submit legislation before June, provided that congressional leaders agreed to act between then and adjournment in October. 'Non-markups' were held in February through May, followed by a 'non-conference' to resolve differences between the House and Senate (Destler 1992: 97). Once agreement was reached, the legislation was formally introduced and approved, by 366 to 40 in the House and by 83 to 9 in the Senate. Ways and Means played a central role in tracking the details of the legislation. The Agreement was finally approved in September 1987, and came into force on January 2 1988. The Canadian government had to call an election over the agreement, which it won, but only by a plurality.

The US–Canadian Free Trade Agreement is one of the cleanest ever negotiated from a technical perspective of Article xxiv of the GATT. Even so, the Agreement provides a ten-year phase-in of liberalizing measures. Tariffs are expected to be eliminated by January 1998. However, a large number of non-tariff barriers are excluded from the trade-liberalization process. The Agreement is widely viewed as primarily trade-creating. The US gross national product is approximately four times the size of that of Canada. However, there is less of an imbalance in the value of trade between the two countries. Approximately 70 percent of Canada's total exports are destined for US markets, whereas only 21 percent of US exports are destined for Canadian markets. Overall, the United States is clearly the predominant trading partner, the hub nation with Canada on the rim.

Initially, Canada was much more protectionist, with an average tariff of 10.4 percent levied on US imports compared with an average US tariff on Canadian imports of only 3.3 percent. From the perspective of other countries concerned about the possible trade diversion with the US, the margin of preference for Canadian goods provided by the US ten years down the road must be viewed as relatively low, especially since the Uruguay Round has further reduced that preference. In isolation, therefore, the US–Canada Free Trade Agreement does not appear to constitute a major threat to the liberal trade order. Ominously, however, this Agreement is by no means the final play of the US regional card.

The North American Free Trade Agreement

In December 1990, the GATT Ministerial Conference in Brussels announced an impasse in the Uruguay Round negotiations, confirming that the US president could not expect to sign an agreement by June 1 1991 under the fast-track approval procedures provided by the 1988 Act. The Bush administration immediately turned its attention to the fallback provision of the 1988 Act, inserted with precisely this contingency in mind. Before March 1992, the president could seek a two-year extension of fast-track authority by declaring that progress had been made on the Uruguay Round and that additional time might allow the negotiations to succeed. As the law was written, he could gain the extension unless either house voted against it by June 1991. He would then have until June 1993 to sign a multilateral agreement.

There was one complicating factor (Destler 1992: 98). In the spring of 1990, Mexico's president, Carlos Salinas de Gortari, had broken with his country's protectionist, anti-US traditions by asking President Bush to negotiate a bilateral free trade agreement. President Bush had accepted this invitation, overruling trade advisers who preferred to await an accord in the Uruguay Round before entering into further hub-and-spoke trade negotiations. He had sent the required notification to Congress in September 1990. When the Canadian government expressed concern that a bilateral US–Mexico pact might undermine the US–Canada Free Trade Agreement, President Bush had agreed to include Canada in the projected negotiations, with the objective of creating a North American Free Trade Agreement (NAFTA). President Bush had notified Congress of this decision in February 1991.

A fast-track extension would apply to NAFTA as well as to the Uruguay Round since the fast-track procedures had been widened in 1984 to cover bilateral agreements, with similar consultation caveats and the same expiration date. The new timetable adopted in the 1988 Act also applied to both kinds of agreement. Therefore, any extension for the GATT talks must cover Mexico as well, even though no one had contemplated this possibility when the legislation was drafted. The prospect induced hostile lobbying from organized labor and from some environmental groups.

Organized labor portrayed itself as particularly threatened by open trade with a low-wage neighbor and claimed that US workers had already lost many low-skill, mass-production jobs to foreign competition. Its leaders were either unaware of the comparative-advantage theory of international trade or unwilling to defend the theory against strong populist pressures within the labor movement. Environmentalists contended that competition with Mexico would undermine US environmental regulations by providing a pollution haven for US firms located in Mexico, thus forcing a competitive relaxation of US antipollution laws. Both groups mobilized against fast-track extension, but failed to derail President Bush from formally requesting a general extension of the fast-track procedures.

Although the fast-track procedures had been law for over sixteen years, this was the first occasion that they would hold center stage on the House and

Senate floor (Destler 1992: 99). Previously, their details had been worked out in Finance and in Ways and Means, with Congress as a whole ratifying the results when it voted general trade legislation. This time also the issue could have been contained in committee; but not in the face of fierce and hostile lobbying. Both the committee and the chamber leaders determined that the issue must be voted up or down on the floors of Congress. To win an extension, President Bush, through USTR Carla Hills, would be obliged to bargain with Congress.

Because fast-track extension was subject to an extension disapproval resolution, there was no opportunity for statutory compromise. Lloyd Bentsen (Finance) and Dan Rostankowski (Ways and Means) therefore resorted to non-statutory bargaining, seeking assurances from President Bush on the overall economic impact of NAFTA, its effects on jobs and workers' rights, and its impact on the environment. They requested a reply by May 1 1991.

President Bush and USTR Carla Hills pressed business to be active, remobilized the old pro-trade coalition that had been demoralized by the Reagan trade deficit, and responded persuasively on May 1 to the questions posed, promising adjustment provisions to avert injurious effects, offering transition and safeguard mechanisms, and an adequately funded worker adjustment program. The statement also noted that the United States would ensure that its right to safeguard the environment was preserved in NAFTA.

The Bush statement shifted some environmental groups from opposition to support of NAFTA, using the negotiations as an opportunity to advance a pro-environment industrial policy. Labor remained in opposition but the AFL–CIO de-emphasized its lobbying. Ways and Means voted 27–9 against the disapproval resolution; Finance did likewise by 15–3. On May 23 1991, the House rejected the resolution 231–192. On May 24 1991, the Senate rejected the resolution 59–36. The northern Democrats for the most part were in favor. Representatives from California, Florida and Texas – states with large Hispanic populations – voted heavily against (Destler 1992: 102).

On December 17 1992, the United States, Canada and Mexico signed a historic trade accord. The North American Free Trade Agreement (NAFTA) is the most comprehensive free trade pact ever negotiated between regional trading partners. It is the first reciprocal free trade pact between an underdeveloped country and industrial countries. The last significant act of the Bush administration, the NAFTA was scheduled to enter into force on January 1 1994, following ratification by the three legislatures. Since the NAFTA is a trilateral agreement, it overcomes potential problems between the rim countries inherent in a strict hub-and-spoke system of preferential trade (Krueger 1993).

In essence, the NAFTA is an expanded version of the US–Canada Free Trade Agreement. In large part, the agreement involves commitments by

Mexico to implement the degree of trade and investment liberalization promised between its northern neighbors in 1988. However, the NAFTA goes further by addressing unfinished business from the 1988 Agreement, including protection of intellectual property rights, rules against distortions to investment (local-content and export-performance requirements), and coverage of transportation services.

The NAFTA provides for the phased elimination of tariff and most non-tariff barriers on regional trade within ten years, although a few import-sensitive products are allowed a fifteen-year transition period. US–Canada bilateral tariffs continue to be phased out according to the 1988 Agreement. The NAFTA establishes within fifteen years free trade in agricultural products between the United States and Mexico, immediately converting key US and Mexican agricultural restrictions into tariff-rate quotas, and sets a maximum fifteen-year period for the phase-out of the over-quota tariffs (Hufbauer and Schott 1993; Globerman and Walker 1992).

The investment obligations of the NAFTA accord national treatment to NAFTA investors, remove most performance requirements on investment in the region, and open up new investment opportunities in key Mexican sectors such as petrochemicals and financial services. Finally, the NAFTA offers less unambiguous liberalization in the case of textiles and apparel. On the one hand, it calls for the elimination of all tariffs and quotas on regional trade in textiles and apparel. However, the rules of origin established to qualify for duty-free treatment are highly restrictive and will be strongly trade-diverting.

Rules of origin have been aptly labelled *tools of discrimination* (Globerman and Walker 1992: 50). They penalize regional producers by forcing them to purchase from less-efficient suppliers located in the region, thereby undercutting the global competitiveness of the buying firms. This establishes a trade diversity precedent for other preferential trading pacts. For example, about 18 percent of US imports from Canada will not benefit from the Agreement as a consequence of tightly drawn rules of origin. The two sectors most seriously affected by this constraint are textiles and apparel, and automobiles; both have powerful protectionist lobbies in Washington.

Although less enthusiastic for NAFTA than President Bush, then-Governor Clinton endorsed the NAFTA in October 1992, rejecting any renegotiation of the text. However, he enumerated important qualifications which he pursued during the process of US ratification of the NAFTA following his election to the US presidency. He insisted on enacting five unilateral measures in the context of NAFTA implementing legislation:

1.   worker adjustment assistance;
2.   environmental funding;
3.   assistance to farmers;

4. providing US citizens with the right to challenge objectionable environmental practices;
5. an assurance that foreign workers would not be brought into the United States as strike-breakers.

In addition, he insisted on the creation of an Environmental Protection Commission with substantial powers and resources to protect the environment; the creation of a Labor Commission to protect worker standards and safety; and the establishment of a supplemental safeguards agreement to provide temporary protection against 'an unexpected and overwhelming surge' in imports from a partner country.

During the first half of 1993, President Clinton showed no interest in the NAFTA and lost control of the implementing agenda. By the time that he refocused attention on the issue, he faced major dissension among Democratic congressmen and was forced to rely on Republican support, especially in the House of Representatives, to win a very narrow majority for the Agreement. Recalcitrant Democrats extracted highly protectionist favors from the beleaguered president in return for their reluctant votes. A slew of organizations that normally advocate protectionism and regulation – especially the environmental lobbies – rushed to defend a bill whose principle thrust was recognized to be toward managed trade and investment and away from free trade. Passage of the NAFTA indeed was a black day for the multilateral trading order that previous United States governments had labored so mightily to achieve.

7 US regionalism in public-choice perspective

The public-choice model posits that legislators focus on issues of wealth distribution rather than economic efficiency when casting their votes on regional trade bills. In so doing, they reflect the interests of their respective electoral constituencies, ignoring or downplaying issues of broader public interest.

As Chapter 4 indicates, lobbying over trade bills may take the form of Ricardo–Viner (with import-competing industries lobbying against trade expansion, and export interests lobbying in favor) or of Stolper–Samuelson (with the abundant factor lobbying in favor of trade expansion and with the scarce factor lobbying against). Since regional hub-and-spoke legislation is likely to be long-lived, public choice suggests that Stolper–Samuelson is likely to be the more appropriate lens through which to view legislative trade politics (Thorbecke 1995).

An opportunity to test the Stolper–Samuelson model arises with respect to the vote in the US House of Representatives over NAFTA on November 17 1994. As Thorbecke (1995) notes, this vote produced strange political alliances. President Clinton, abandoned by the Democratic Party leadership, worked together with Republican Whip Newt Gingrich to secure passage. The Democratic Whip David Bonior worked to try to defeat the bill. In the final vote, 156 Democrats opposed the president's bill, while 132 Republicans supported it. Public choice explains this superficially puzzling pattern of coalitions.

Thorbecke (1995) modelled the redistributional impact of NAFTA using a three-factor Heckscher–Ohlin model in which capital and high-skilled labor (the abundant factors) are likely to gain from NAFTA, while low-skilled labor (the scarce factor) is likely to lose. He hypothesized that representatives whose constituents were primarily capital and high-skilled labor would tend to vote for NAFTA while those whose constituents were primarily low-skilled labor would not, irrespective of party affiliation.

His regression results were strongly supportive of Stolper–Samuelson. A representative whose district had a percentage of service workers one standard deviation above the mean was 8 percent less likely to vote for NAFTA; one whose district had a percentage of farmers one standard deviation above the mean was 10 percent more likely to vote for NAFTA; and one whose district had a percentage of college-educated constituents one standard deviation above the mean was 16 percent more likely to vote for NAFTA.

One whose district had an industry likely to gain from NAFTA was 22 percent more likely to vote for the bill; and one whose state adjoined Mexico (anti-immigration sentiment) was 21 percent more likely to favor it. Those whose League of Conservation Voters (LCV) ratings were one standard deviation above the mean were 10 percent more likely to vote for NAFTA; and those whose ADA ratings were one standard deviation above the mean were 29 percent more likely to oppose it.

The important implication of these votes is that the geographical and electoral constituencies exert an enormous impact on legislators' voting patterns. This explains the weak party allegiance demonstrated by House voting on the NAFTA bill, in a situation where the president was able to exert little influence over his own party. In such circumstances, the regional card will remain a growing factor in US trade politics irrespective of the general interest in multilateralism.

References

Bhagwati, J. (1968) 'Trade liberalization among LDCs, trade theory and GATT rules', in J. Wolfe (ed.), *Value, Capital and Growth: Papers in Honour of Sir John Hicks* (Edinburgh: University of Edinburgh Press).

Bhagwati, J. (1988) *Protectionism*, Cambridge: The MIT Press.

Bhagwati, J. (1991) *The World Trading System at Risk* (Princeton, N.J.: Princeton University Press).

Bhagwati, J. and Brecher, R. (1980) 'National welfare in an open economy in the presence of foreign-owned factors of production', *Journal of International Economics,* 10 (1): 103–17.

Brecher, R. and Bhagwati, J. (1981) 'Foreign ownership and the theory of trade and welfare', *Journal of Political Economy* 89 (3): 497–512.

Cooper, C.A. and Massell, B.F. (1965) 'A new look at customs union theory', *Economic Journal*, 75: 742–7.

Cooper, C.A. and Massell, B.F. (1965) 'Toward a general theory of customs unions for developing countries', *Journal of Political Economy*, 73 (5): 461–76.

Destler, I.M. (1992) *American Trade Politics* (New York: The Twentieth Century Fund).

Globerman, S. and Walker, M. (eds) (1992) *Assessing NAFTA: A Trinational Analysis* (Vancouver: Fraser Institute).

Hudec, R.E. (1991) *Enforcing International Trade Law: The Evolution of the Modern GATT Legal System* (Salem, N.H.: Butterworth Legal Publishers).

Hufbauer, G.C. and Schott, J.J. (1993) *North American Free Trade: Issues and Recommendations* (Washington, D.C.: Institute for International Economics).

Ito, T. and Krueger, A.O. (eds) (1993) *Trade and Protectionism* (Chicago: University of Chicago Press).

Jackson, J.H. (1969) *World Trade and the Law of GATT* (Indianapolis: Bobbs-Merrill).

Jackson, J.H. (1989) 'Multilateral and bilateral negotiating approaches for the conduct of US trade policies', in R.M. Stern (ed.), *U.S. Trade Policies in a Changing World Economy* (Cambridge, Mass.: MIT Press), pp. 377–401.

Kemp, M.C. and Wan, H. (1976) 'An elementary proposition concerning the foundation of customs unions', *Journal of International Economics*, 6: 95–8.

Krueger, A.O. (1993) 'American bilateral trading arrangements and East Asian interests', in T. Ito and A.O. Krueger (eds), *Trade and Protectionism* (Chicago: University of Chicago Press).

Meade, J. (1955) *The Theory of Customs Unions* (Amsterdam: North-Holland).

Snape, R.H. (1993) 'Discrimination, regionalism and GATT', in T. Ito and A.O. Krueger (eds), *Trade and Protectionism* (Chicago: University of Chicago Press).

Thorbecke, W. (1995) 'Explaining house voting on the North American Free Trade Agreement', *Public Choice* (forthcoming).

Viner, J. (1950) *The Customs Union Issue* (New York: Carnegie Endowment for International Peace).

Wonnacott, R.J. (1990) *U.S. Hub-and-Spoke Bilaterals and the Multilateral Trading System*, Commentary no. 23 (Ottawa: C.D. Howe Institute).

PART IV

FROM MANAGED
TO FREE TRADE

12 The political economy of the GATT

1 Introduction

The General Agreement on Tariffs and Trade (GATT) is the name of a trade agreement concluded in October 1947 between 23 governments. The signatories comprised thirteen leading Western developed countries (excluding Germany and Japan) and ten underdeveloped countries. The GATT agreement provided for a substantial reduction of tariffs among the signatories, together with a code of general rules limiting the right to use other trade restrictions. The United States and the United Kingdom were the driving forces behind the agreement. France also exercised considerable influence in its drafting.

To understand the GATT, it is important to remind ourselves of the general contours of the foreign trade policies that are followed by most market-economy governments. Typically, such governments impose a number of barriers to, and controls on, foreign trade transactions (Hudec 1991: 3). The most common barrier is a tariff, a tax levied on important goods at the time that they cross the border. Another common barrier is a quantitative restriction, or quota, which limits the quantity of specified goods allowed to cross the border during a given time period. Governments also exercise a range of other prohibitions and controls at the border for what they call public policy purposes – health, safety, morals, conservation, national security, and the like.

There is a further class of trade restrictions which governments impose on imported goods after they have crossed the border and entered domestic commerce. These internal restrictions take the form of internal taxes, such as a sales tax, or internal regulations, such as vehicle emission control, designed to impose a heavier burden on imported than on comparable domestic goods. Finally, governments apply two other types of trade policy measures to influence foreign transactions; namely, a subsidy to domestic products, and discrimination to provide competitive advantages to favored countries and/or competitive disadvantages to disfavored countries.

Following the Second World War, two major barriers stood in the way of restoring international trade to the levels that had prevailed prior to the disastrous Smoot–Hawley Tariff Act of 1930. The first obstacle was the high tariffs which had been imposed by many countries during the 1930s. In this respect, those of the United States were especially significant since they prevented foreign exporters earning much-desired US dollars for postwar reconstruction. The second obstacle was a tight network of quantitative restrictions erected by most governments during or immediately after the war to protect their foreign currency reserves from depletion through chronic trade imbalances.

The GATT was a multilateral trade agreement that provided for reductions in tariffs and for legal controls over a variety of non-tariff trade barriers including balance-of-payments restrictions. The most tangible accomplishment of this agreement was a substantial reduction in and a binding of tariff rates. The tariff reductions were negotiated through reciprocal bargaining, each government embodying its commitments in a Schedule of Concessions – a list of tariff rates, usually lower than its existing rates, that legally bound it not to exceed in the future.

The agreement also included a comprehensive code of rules limiting or prohibiting non-tariff measures, both border restrictions and internal restrictions. The signatories agreed to make the GATT's rules on non-tariff measures applicable to all products, whether or not a tariff concession had been granted on them. In this manner, the GATT code of rules became a general code of conduct applicable to all trade transactions.

The basic rules of the GATT code with regard to trade barriers can be summarized as follows (Hudec 1991: 5). First, with few exceptions, all internal restrictions are prohibited. Second, border measures are divided into two categories: non-tariff measures are generally prohibited, albeit subject to a range of exceptions; tariffs, on the other hand, are permitted and there is no formal limit to their level. The agreement provides a legal framework for negotiating reductions in tariff levels on a reciprocal basis. The underlying premise is that trade liberalization must be approached by a two-step process. First, governments should be required to collect all barriers to trade into one recognizable form – the tariff. Second, they should then be encouraged to reduce tariffs by means of voluntary negotiation.

The GATT allowed a number of important exceptions to its rules on trade barriers. With respect to its prohibition of internal restrictions, it allowed freedom to grant production subsidies to domestic producers; freedom to grant preferential treatment to domestic producers in government procurement; and freedom to impose internal quotas on the exhibition of foreign films. With respect to its prohibition of border quotas, it allowed freedom to use quantitative restrictions for balance-of-payments purposes; for economic development; for protection of agricultural price support programs; for protecting local industry from 'serious injury' due to increased import competition; and for public policy purposes such as health, safety, morals, and national security. These exceptions are sufficiently broad as to allow deviant governments to drive a coach and horses through the liberal trade constitution.

A basic principle of the GATT code of rules was the non-discrimination or most-favored-nation (MFN) principle. This principle required that every trade

advantage given to any country (GATT member or not) must be given immediately and unconditionally to every other GATT member. Once again, a
number of exceptions were allowed, the most important of which was freedom to form customs unions and free trade areas. Other exceptions included
freedom to retain existing colonial preferences; freedom to discriminate in
some balance-of-payments programs; freedom to discriminate in national
security matters; and freedom to discriminate against a number of essentially
'wrongful' actions such as dumping, subsidization and various other trade
practices considered to be harmful or noxious (Hudec 1991: 6). Once again,
these exceptions would allow deviant governments to discriminate among
foreign exporters without infringing the GATT rules.

In part because the GATT was perceived to be only a provisional arrangement between a small subset of the countries that would eventually participate in a Charter for an International Trade Organization (ITO), no formal
organizational structure was created. The signatory countries, known as the
contracting parties, gave themselves the power to make whatever decisions
were necessary to implement the agreement. Article XXIII provided that the
contracting parties could rule on claims of legal violation, could make recommendations for correction, and could authorize the aggrieved government
to withdraw concessions in response to unresolved violations. The rationale
of this legal design was reciprocity. It was essentially a diplomat's concept of
legal order (Hudec 1991: 7).

2   The flawed beginnings of the GATT

The major initiative culminating in the GATT was taken by the United States
government during the Second World War in cooperation with its allies,
particularly the United Kingdom. Two distinct strands of thought influenced
this initiative (Jackson 1969: 31). The first stemmed from the series of trade
agreements negotiated by the US under the auspices of the 1934 Reciprocal
Trade Agreements Act. Between 1934 and 1945, the US had entered into 32
bilateral trade agreements designed to liberalize international trade. The second stemmed from a recognition that protectionist economic policies during
the interwar period had contributed to the Great Depression and to the emergence of national socialism in Germany. Political leaders in the United States
and the United Kingdom determined to establish economic institutions that
would prevent a recurrence of such mistakes in the post-Second World War
era.

On this basis, the Bretton Woods conference was held in New Hampshire
during July 1–22 1944. The conference was devoted to monetary and bank-
ing issues and established the charters of the International Monetary Fund
(IMF) and the International Bank for Reconstruction and Development (World
Bank). It did not take up the issue of international trade, undoubtedly because

the conference was under the jurisdiction of the finance ministries and not the ministries responsible for trade policy. Nevertheless, the Bretton Woods conference recognized the need for a comparable institution for trade to complement the work of the IMF and the World Bank.

In 1945, the impetus to move on the trade front quickened. In the United States, Congress enacted a three-year renewal of the reciprocal trade agreements legislation. In December 1945, the US government invited a number of other countries to enter into negotiations to conclude a multilateral tariff-reduction agreement. In 1946, the United Nations adopted a resolution for a conference to draft a charter for an International Trade Organization. Simultaneously, the United States published a draft of a suggested ITO charter. A preparatory committee was formed which met in London in October 1946.

A total of four such preparatory meetings were held to complete a draft charter for an ITO. The principle meeting was held in Geneva from April to November 1947, and was followed by a meeting in Havana in 1948 to complete the ITO charter. Negotiations over the ITO and the GATT were completely intertwined at these meetings. As we have noted, the general clauses of the GATT imposed obligations on nations to refrain from a variety of trade-impeding measures.

However, the GATT was not intended to be an organization. Indeed, US negotiators were called to task by committees of Congress during 1947 for appearing to draft GATT clauses which implied the existence of an organization (Jackson 1969: 33). To obviate this criticism, the US negotiators redrafted the general GATT clauses, eliminating all references to an organization and substituting the term 'the contracting parties acting jointly'.

The negotiators at Geneva thus saw their task as to prepare a draft ITO charter to be completed in Havana in 1948, and to negotiate the GATT which was designed to operate under the ITO when the latter came into being. Indeed, the GATT contained a clause recognizing that, after the ITO charter was completed, parallel GATT clauses would be revised to bring them into conformity with those of the ITO charter.

Although delegates from 56 countries at the Havana Conference of 1948 completed the draft ITO charter, the organization never came into being and the charter was never ratified. The principal reason for this failure was the unwillingness of the US Congress to approve the charter. President Truman submitted it for congressional approval in April 1949. Congress was Republican-dominated, following the 1948 elections, and was controlled by special interests that were tilting back to normal peacetime protectionism. Wavering presidential leadership resulted in legislative stalemate. In April 1950, the House Committee on Foreign Affairs held hearings on President Truman's request for a joint resolution permitting US participation in the ITO. The committee never reported and the issue never reached the floor of the House. At the end of 1950, the State Department announced that the charter would not be resubmitted for congressional consideration. Like the League of Nations before it, the ITO had little chance of survival as an institution without the active participation of the United States (Low 1993: 41).

In addition to generalized protectionism within the United States, factors leading to the demise of the ITO initiative included the escape-clause mindedness of many underdeveloped countries, Commonwealth preferences, the creation of COMECON and of the OEEC. Any doubts about congressional attitudes toward the ITO were completely dispelled in 1956 when the Organization for Trade Cooperation was submitted for congressional consideration; it met with a fate similar to that of the ITO. The OTC had been drafted in the context of a GATT review session in 1955 which had been convened primarily to take stock of the trade situation in the light of the ITO's demise.

In consequence, although the GATT is popularly viewed as the most important treaty governing international trade relations, the GATT treaty as such has never come into force. Its authority technically lies in the Protocol of Provisional Application (PPA) through which the GATT is applied as a treaty obligation under international law. By this protocol, eight countries, including the United States, agreed to apply the GATT provisionally on and after January 1 1948, while the remainder of the 23 original GATT countries were to do so soon after.

The Protocol contained two important clauses that changed the impact of the GATT. First, the Protocol required only a 60-day notice period for withdrawal, compared to the six months required by the GATT agreement itself. In practice, this is unimportant since few countries have exercised the exit option, given the ease with which it is possible to break the rules. Much more important was the second clause implementation of the GATT.

Part I of the GATT, containing the MFN and the tariff concession obligations, and Part III, which was mainly procedural, were implemented fully without a PPA exception. However, the PPA called for implementation of Part II 'to the fullest extent not inconsistent with existing legislation'. Part II (Articles iii–xxiii) contained most of the principal substantive obligations, including those relating to customs procedures, quotas, subsidies, antidumping duties, and national treatment. Under the PPA, each GATT contracting party was entitled to 'grandfather rights' for any provision of its legislation in existence when it became a party and which was inconsistent with a GATT Part II obligation. Herein is the Achilles heel of the GATT.

The Part II exception solved for most countries the problem of executive authority to agree to the GATT without submitting the agreement for legislative approval. For, in most cases, the executives had authority to accept Articles i and ii of the GATT. The United States had such authority from its

1945 trade act extension. Whether the United States had authority fully to accept and implement the GATT on a definitive basis without submitting it to Congress is less clear-cut, although we shall argue with Jackson (1969) that such authority indeed existed.

3   US trade law and GATT law

A critical question concerning the GATT is whether these agreements have a direct application in the domestic law of signatory countries. The GATT language itself was certainly intended by negotiators to be precise enough for direct application by courts (Jackson 1969: 75). Its phraseology is such that US courts most probably would find the large majority of GATT clauses to be self-executing. However, the GATT as such is not in effect under international law. It is the Protocol of Provisional Application which brings the GATT into effect. This protocol contains language suggesting a requirement of an added governmental action to implement the GATT. Therefore, the language itself most probably would not be treated by a US court as self-executing.

The legal difference between a self-executing and a non-self-executing agreement is not simple. An international obligation is self-executing if it becomes directly applicable upon ratification. It is non-self-executing if it requires some additional act of domestic lawmaking to become applicable. Self-executing international agreements may take several forms. First, they may be treatises on which the Senate must give advise and consent, meaning approval by a two-thirds majority vote. Second, they may be Executive Agreements approved by both Houses of Congress. Third, they may be Executive Agreements entered into by the president pursuant to his constitutional powers to conduct foreign affairs.

According to Low (1993: 43), the first two agreements would have the equivalent legal force of all federal law, overriding all state law, past and future, and all past federal law. The authority of the third form of agreement has not yet been fully determined. Low argues that, while such agreements would be superior to all past and future state law, they would be inferior to all past and future federal law. The basic reasoning behind this argument is that it is difficult to imagine Congress allowing the president to change federal law on the basis of his own powers, without congressional participation in the decision.

Such reasoning is based upon confusion concerning the US Constitution. If the president acts within the limits of his constitutional authority, using his foreign policy powers, he surely could change federal law. The legislature is not superior to the executive branch but, rather, is separate but equal under the US Constitution, notwithstanding the judgment in *United States* v *Guy W. Capps Inc.* in 1953. If Congress wishes to override such an Executive Agreement it can do so by legislation that overrides any presidential veto.

The status of non-self-executing international agreements depends entirely upon the nature of the legal authority under which it is concluded. If it is implemented through a law of Congress, it will have the same force as federal law. If it results from executive action, such as a regulation, an Executive Order, or a Proclamation, legal status depends on the source of legislative authority behind the executive action. Even if the president does not have the authority to change federal law, Congress could grant him such authority.

The GATT itself would most probably be treated by US courts as not self-executing, given the wording of the PPA. However, the president negotiated the GATT under the authority of the Trade Agreements Act renewal of 1945, which contained the typical two-part authority: to accept an agreement and to proclaim it. In fact, the president has proclaimed all of the general language of the GATT except Part IV (added in the 1960s to address problems of underdeveloped countries).

Thus, the key parts of the GATT are all domestic US law because they have been proclaimed and not because they are self-executing. US courts, in deciding the issue of GATT direct applicability, have all held that the GATT is part of US domestic law. In so doing, they have failed to discuss the intermediate steps in the logic required for such a finding (Jackson 1989: 75).

From the Tokyo Round onwards, Congress and the executive anticipated questions concerning direct application and provided explicitly that the agreements approved would not be self-executing (Jackson 1993: 81). It is virtually certain that US courts will follow this intent. Thus the source of domestic US law in these cases is the implementing statute (for example, the Trade Agreement Act of 1979) and not the agreements themselves. However, the agreements are part of the legislative history of the statute. In addition, a well-accepted rule in US jurisprudence requires that courts should prefer the choice that is consistent with US international obligations when confronted with several possible choices for interpreting a statute.

Clarification is also necessary concerning the extent to which the executive branch is legally bound to abide by international agreements. Constitutionally, the president is required to implement US laws. Thus, if international obligations form part of these laws, the president must abide by them. Examples are self-executing Executive Agreements approved by Congress, and non-self-executing agreements whose execution depends on a law of Congress.

Suppose, however, that the implementing legislation simply empowers but does not oblige the president to act, a situation not uncommon with US trade legislation. In such circumstances, the president is free to decide whether or not to observe an international agreement. In addition, the president has powers permitting him to denounce certain kinds of self-executing international obligations, thereby nullifying their domestic legal effects (Low 1993: 45). Finally, the president has certain constitutional powers, whose limits are not clear, as commander-in-chief and head of state.

In summary, the GATT is a valid international agreement under US law. It is also part of US domestic law, as a non-self-executing executive agreement. The tariff commitments under the GATT entered US domestic law through presidential proclamation and, as such, may not be invulnerable to subsequent violation by a US president. The commercial policy provisions of the GATT also entered US domestic law through presidential proclamation. The Tokyo Round codes themselves are non-self-executing executive agreements.

4   The organization of the GATT

The original theory of the draftsmen of the GATT was that it was not to be an international organization. Indeed, this was the clear intent of the PPA that brought it into being. However, the failure to establish the ITO forced the GATT to assume a role for which it was not intended. In essence, that role became one of an organization for consultation, negotiation and application of rules regarding international trade (Jackson 1989: 45).

The 1947 agreement was concluded between 23 governments. The developed countries were Australia, Austria, Belgium, Canada, Czechoslovakia, France, Luxembourg, the Netherlands, New Zealand, Norway, Rhodesia, the United Kingdom and the United States. The underdeveloped countries were Brazil, Burma, Ceylon, Chile, China (the pre-1949 government), Cuba, India, Pakistan, Syria and Lebanon. Since the GATT was not an organization, these countries were contracting parties and not members, although we shall refer to them as members.

The accession of a new member country requires a two-thirds majority vote by the contracting parties (Article xxxIII). In a sense, Article xxxIII is inconsistent with the character of the agreement. Since trade benefits are granted to all members, it can be argued that a new member should only be accepted by unanimous vote (Meerhaeghe 1987: 104). However, a rule of unanimity might have resulted in members blocking membership applications from countries to which they exported comparatively little but which would compete against them for the markets of other members.

Members that do not assent to the accession of a given country are allowed to refrain from applying the provisions of the agreement if the two countries have not entered into tariff negotiations with each other. Therefore, membership does not necessarily imply a uniform tariff system across all participating countries. This opt-out provision (Article xxxv.1) was added on the initiative of India. It was exercised quite extensively against Japan and, by India, against South Africa.

Countries with a considerable production and export potential (such as Germany and Japan) have to make substantial concessions in exchange for membership. A majority of members will agree to its accession only if they are certain that increased exports to the new member will offset any fall in their exports to other GATT countries. This is known as 'negotiating the ticket of admission'.

A second path to membership also exists through Article XXVI (5c). This article provides that if a parent country has accepted the GATT in respect of a dependent customs territory (such as a colony), and if that customs territory later becomes independent, such territory can become a GATT contracting party merely through sponsorship by the parent country. Since the origin of the GATT, over 30 newly independent countries have entered GATT membership by this route, in some cases gaining access to GATT markets without having to make any tariff concessions .

As a result of decolonization, the number of member countries has greatly increased since 1947, rising from 37 in November 1957 to 91 in June 1986 and to 105 in July 1986. In April 1994 123 countries signed the Uruguay Round Agreement. Participation in the trade negotiation rounds is not confined to members of the GATT.

The GATT has a permanent headquarters building in Geneva. It has a small but highly regarded Secretariat of about 150 trade policy professionals and another 300 technical and service personnel. The majority of its members maintain permanent delegations to GATT who are resident in Geneva. The budget for the GATT in 1986 amounted to SwF60 million. The highest contribution was from the United States (15.5 percent), followed by Germany (10.1 percent), Japan (8.8 percent) and the United Kingdom (7.6 per cent). Despite major differences in budget contributions, each member has only one vote.

Acting jointly, the members would be governed by majority vote on many issues. However, in much of the business of the GATT there is a strong preference for consensus and some fear of using the formal vote mechanism, for the voting structure bears little resemblance to the underlying balance of economic power among the members. Therefore, the practice within the GATT is to avoid formal voting, although this practice is conditioned by the amending, membership and waiver language of the agreement which requires formal votes (or treaty acceptances).

Notwithstanding the desire for consensus, the legal structure of potential voting exercises a considerable influence. Negotiations over differences cannot be isolated from the participants' calculations of the likely outcome if the negotiations should fail. If the outcome were to be a vote, then the voting structure would influence any negotiated consensus; if not, the more powerful participants might simply bulldoze a consensus.

A consensus approach has other problems (Jackson 1989: 50). Strictly applied, it offers every country a veto power, thus lowering any feasible initiative to that of the lowest common denominator. If it is not strictly applied, there will be an inevitable deference to the underlying power structure. Such was the case, for example, during the Tokyo Round, when the actual negotiations often began with major decisions being made only by the United States, the European Community, and Japan. Other countries were excluded from real influence until the end of the drafting process, by which time it was difficult to make significant changes.

The voting–consensus issue has posed serious problems for the GATT dispute-settlement procedure. It has made it very difficult to obtain approval of a panel report in a dispute when a country dissatisfied with the outcome of such a report refuses to go along with a consensus for Council approval. A similar problem exists for many of the code agreements resulting from the Tokyo Round. Yet if simple majority voting were to be introduced along the lines foreshadowed for the World Trade Organization, the underdeveloped countries would comprise more than two-thirds of the GATT vote. It is extremely unlikely that the advanced countries would tolerate block voting by economically weak countries that was designed to redistribute wealth under the guise of trade initiatives.

In the light of the voting–consensus problem outlined above, the difficulty of amending the GATT is self-evident. Governed by Article xxx, amendments to Articles i, ii and xxix require unanimous acceptance. This has never occurred. Amending the remainder of the GATT requires two-thirds acceptance on the part of all contributing parties. However, such an amendment obligates only those members who accept it. In general, it has been considered impractical to attempt to amend the general clauses of the GATT. Thus, it was considered impossible, for example, to embody the non-tariff measure codes of the Tokyo Round into GATT amendments.

Yet, as Jackson (1989: 52) emphasizes, the development of 'side codes' or stand-alone ancillary treaties to enlarge and elaborate the GATT rules poses technical legal and administrative difficulties. Inevitably, complexities of interpretation will give rise to legal disputes among GATT members, and will be likely to hurt those members that cannot bring much expertise to problems of GATT representation. Whether the Uruguay Round agreements will help to resolve such problems remains to be seen.

If, formally and in a legal sense, the competence of the contracting parties remains unchanged, it has been modified in practice as a result of the development of the Council of Representatives, its committees, working parties and panels (Long 1987: 47).

The Council of Representatives

The Council was established by a decision of the members on June 4 1960. Legally, it is the intersessional body of the contracting parties. As such, it is authorized to take up all questions dealt with by members at their sessions, as well as any urgent matter. It is also authorized to establish subsidiary bodies and to determine their terms of reference. It oversees the work of the various committees, working parties and other subsidiary GATT bodies, examines their reports and makes appropriate recommendations to the members.

The Council consists of representatives of all members that request representation. Its chairman and other senior officials are elected by the members for one-year terms of office. Any decision of the Council can be appealed by a member and will be suspended until the appeal has been evaluated. In point of fact, this right of appeal has never been exercised. The Council, or its chairman, appoints panel members to settle GATT disputes. However, only when members adopt the annual report of the Council is a panel interpretation rendered legally authoritative.

Progressively the Council has become the central body directing the activities of the GATT, especially since November 1968, when the members called on it to make the maximum use of its powers to permit them to focus on major international trade issues. Since its establishment in 1960, the Council has never voted. It decides by consensus. It has 66 members, or some two-thirds of the contracting parties. It follows that a decision by the Council cannot easily be overturned. The Council meets on average nine times a year, much more frequently than the members, whose sessions have progressively shortened in duration.

Committees, working parties and panels

These subsidiary bodies are established by the members or by Council. Their membership is determined in the light of the particular circumstances and the nature of the task required.

Committees are established to examine important issues in depth, usually on a continuing basis. A number of such committees – for example, on balance of payments restrictions and on trade and development – are standing committees. The committees on trade negotiations are not permanent. They oversee the conduct of multilateral negotiations, and are chaired by the Director-General of the GATT.

Working parties are temporary bodies which deal with important issues as they arise. They draw their terms of reference from the Council, to which they submit reports and conclusions. Membership is open to all interested member countries. This implies that their conclusions reflect a high degree of consensus, making their adoption by Council highly predictable.

Panels of experts play an important role in the settlement of disputes between member governments. Members of panels act as independent experts and not as representatives of their government. Members do not always accept the judgements of the panels. Given the requirement of consensus in the GATT, recalcitrant members are thus able to defy panel judgements. This will change as the Uruguay Round agreement is ratified and as the proposed World Trade Organization replaces the GATT.

In July 1965, the GATT created the Group of Eighteen on a temporary basis. In 1979, this Group became a permanent feature of the GATT. The Group's membership is restricted to eighteen, including the United States, the European Community and Japan. Its composition is balanced so as to be representative of the GATT membership. The underdeveloped countries, with ten members, constitute a majority. It is a high-level Group, represented at its meetings by senior civil servants. It meets three or four times a year to examine the major issues of commercial policy.

The Group has neither power of decision nor executive power. It is a consultative body that operates by consensus. Nevertheless, legal rights and binding obligations can eventually result from positions taken in the Group.

5   The principles of the GATT system

The GATT is a multipurpose organization, aimed at promoting liberalization and guaranteeing stable conditions of market access through a set of rules and a dispute-settlement system (Low 1993: 148). The GATT does not claim to seek free trade. However, if trade policies move away from freer trade, as arguably is now the case, the GATT system would be failing in one of its basic objectives.

There are five primary mechanisms for promoting GATT objectives. These are: institutional arrangements to promote multilateral trade negotiations; binding attained levels of trade liberalization; guaranteeing non-discrimination; ensuring the rule that tariffs should be the only instrument of protection; and promoting accountability in multilateral trade policy. Through incremental trade liberalization, improvements in market access are achieved. Tariffs are then bound in schedules of concessions that form an integral part of the GATT. Such tariff binding can be renegotiated. However, any increase in a bound tariff must be compensated by a new or reduced tariff binding on some other product.

Tariff negotiations typically occur between countries with predominant supplying interests. They are then multilateralized on a non-discriminatory basis within the context of a negotiating round. More recently, a formula approach has been utilized, subjecting a range of tariffs to predetermined cuts by a number of countries. These tariff-cutting exercises have resulted in major tariff reductions since the GATT was first negotiated. Two rules dominate this GATT system of trade liberalization; namely, non-discrimination or the most-favored-nation principle, and the exclusivity of tariffs or taxes as the only permissible form of protection. Two other rules are also important; namely, the national treatment obligation, and the principle of reciprocity.

The most-favored-nation principle

Article I of the GATT prescribes most-favored-nation treatment in trade relations between the member countries: 'any advantage, favor, privilege or immunity granted by any contracting party to any product originating in or destined for any other country shall be accorded immediately and unconditionally to the like product originating in or destined for the territories of all other contracting parties'. This is the cornerstone of the GATT (Long 1987: 8).

The MFN obligation has a long history; indeed, it can be traced back to the twelfth century (Jackson 1989: 133). Growth of commerce during the fifteenth and sixteenth centuries generated MFN-type treaty clauses as European nations competed with each other to develop networks of trading relationships. The United States included an MFN clause in its first treaty, in 1778 with France. Because of this history, it has been debated whether there is any sort of MFN obligation, independent of a treaty clause, under customary international law. Most scholars now concur that such an obligation exists only when a treaty clause creates it. In the absence of such a treaty, countries have the sovereign right to discriminate against other countries as much as they desire.

A number of economic arguments have been advanced in favor of the MFN. First, non-discrimination minimizes distortions of the competitive market, thus enhancing the welfare economics case in favor of trade liberalization that was outlined in Chapter 1. Second, the MFN helps to generalize liberal trade policies by providing a multiplier effect on bilateral trade deals. Third, the MFN emphasizes general rules applicable to all participants, thus minimizing the cost of rule formation and avoiding prisoners' dilemma outcomes. Fourth, the MFN reduces border transaction costs since customs officials need not ascertain the origin of goods when assessing duties.

A political argument in favor of the MFN is that it inhibits (though, as Chapter 11 outlines, it does not prevent) the forming of discriminatory international groupings that tend to increase tensions between nations. The MFN also inhibits governments from pursuing short-term *ad hoc* trade policies that too often are tension-creating in a world already excessively exposed to such tensions (Jackson 1989: 135).

The MFN principle, notwithstanding these advantages, is not without its detractors. Underdeveloped countries not infrequently ask for trade preferences, either to compensate them for what they perceive to be an adverse bias in the system or, more honestly, as a request for charity. In reality, such preferences as are granted tend to be deployed to serve the short-sighted political objectives of the government and not the well-being of its subjects. Where the advanced nations accede to such deviations from MFN, they tend to deploy the preference system as part of their diplomatic bargaining.

More generally, there is an underlying problem with the unconditional MFN approach: hold-out nations can either prevent agreement or lower the agreement to some lowest common denominator. In such circumstances, if like-minded countries negotiate agreements, ignoring hold-outs while yet granting to them all the negotiated concessions, a serious free-rider incentive is created that may erode the MFN principle itself. These problems are not hypothetical. They continue to confront the GATT trade liberalization mission almost half a century after its inception, finding support in four broad categories of exception from the MFN rule, each of which erodes the authority of the GATT system.

GATT Article VI permits countries to apply antidumping or countervailing-duty measures if injurious dumping or subsidization occurs. The GATT rules seek to control the use of such measures, to ensure that unfair trade practices are proven, that antidumping or countervailing duties strictly respond to actual or threatened injury, and that there is clear causality between the injury and an unfair trade practice. However, as Chapter 10 demonstrates with respect to the United States, an unscrupulous government can manipulate Article VI to serve protectionist interests in a discriminatory, non-transparent manner.

GATT Articles XX and XXI offer further opportunities for GATT-legal discrimination. Article XX covers such matters as public health, safety, morals, the protection of patents, and the conservation of natural resources. Article XXI deals with national security consideration. Few disputes have arisen with respect to these exceptions, though clearly they are exploitable for protectionist purposes.

Preferential regional arrangements are yet another exception to the MFN, with Article XXIV of the GATT allowing the establishment of free trade areas and customs unions. The provisions are designed to ensure that any such arrangements stimulate the creation of new trading opportunities among the parties involved and do not divert trade away from third parties. However, Article XXIV is a serious defect of the GATT and has been exploited since the creation of the European Community in the late 1950s as a major discrimination opportunity. Chapter 11 outlines the major threat posed by this exception to multilateralism, especially since the United States has engaged actively in regional trade politics.

The fourth exception to the MFN principle concerns special arrangements for developing countries, acknowledging their particular financial, trade and development problems. Under the enabling clause, specific legal cover is provided for the Generalized System of Preferences (GSP), allowing for special and differential treatment under the Tokyo Round codes, for regional arrangements among underdeveloped countries, and for special treatment in favor of the most backward countries. The enabling clause has given rise to endless disputes within the GATT. One objective of the Uruguay Round agreement is to raise the level of obligations of the underdeveloped countries in the GATT.

The general elimination of quantitative restrictions

Article xi of the GATT prohibits the use of quantitative restrictions. At the time when it came into effect in 1948, such measures were in widespread use, effectively blocking the functioning of the market in international trade and acting as a major conduit for trade discrimination.

Most economists consider quantitative restrictions to be less desirable than tariffs as instruments of trade protection. First, quotas typically give rise to significantly greater losses than tariffs. Although it is possible in principle to create quotas that are equivalent to any specific tariff in efficiency terms, in practice it is extremely difficult to do so for information-cost reasons, even if a government was minded to do so.

Second, because quotas are less transparent than tariffs, and consumer resistance therefore is more muted, governments predictably will extend the protection margin beyond the tariff limit even in the absence of special interest lobbying.

Third, government procedures for administering quotas can be more easily abused by self-seeking customs officials, leading to widespread corruption, delays and other expenses in the processing of imports.

Fourth, because the rents created by quotas go directly to potential quota-holders, whereas the rents created by tariffs go first to the government, lobbying for quantitative restrictions will predictably exceed lobbying for an equivalent tariff. Public choice predicts for this reason alone that quota regimes will be more extensive and more protectionist than tariff regimes under otherwise identical conditions.

The experience of widespread quota use during the 1930s strongly influenced the draftsmen of the GATT to try to abolish this method of trade restraint. Yet the GATT's efforts to eliminate quantitative restrictions have been nowhere near as successful as its efforts to eliminate tariffs. One reason for this relative failure is the fact that the GATT prohibition of quantitative restrictions is riddled with exceptions, albeit exceptions that are supposed, by definition, to be of limited duration.

The first exception, under Article xi.2, is for agriculture and fisheries, and allows for the quantitative restrictions necessary for governments to stabilize national agricultural markets. This seed of agricultural protectionism was to propagate extensively in the years following the establishment of the GATT, buttressed as it was by the influential agricultural bloc vote in many Western democracies. This exception has aggravated a more general disregard for GATT discipline in the area of agricultural trade.

The second exception, under Articles xx and xxi, permits the use of quantitative restrictions for a variety of reasons, including health, public morals, conservation of exhaustible natural resources, participation in international commodity agreements, and national security. The third exception, under Article xii for industrial countries and under Article xviii:b for underdeveloped countries, permits the use of quantitative restrictions when foreign exchange is in short supply. In recent years, Article xii has not been used. However, underdeveloped countries continue to make extensive use of this exception. The Uruguay Round agreement should tighten discipline in this area.

The fourth exception, under Article xviii:c, permits underdeveloped countries to apply quantitative restrictions to foster the development of an industry: the GATT infant-industry provision. This exception has not been used extensively, primarily because the Article xviii:b balance of payments exception has proved easier and less costly to access. The fifth exception, under Article xix, permits quantitative restrictions to be deployed as safeguards when unexpectedly rapid import growth causes, or threatens to cause, serious injury to a domestic industry. This provision has fallen largely into disuse as countries increasingly resort to discriminatory measures of protection, often in the form of VERs, rather than submit to the discipline of Article xix.

The national treatment obligation

The national treatment obligation is expressed primarily in Article iii of the GATT, and requires the treatment of imported goods, once they have cleared customs and border procedures, to be no worse than that of domestically produced goods. This obligation applies to all products, not just to those that are tariff-bound. It is designed to prevent domestic taxes and regulations from being deployed as protectionist measures to defeat the intent of the MFN principle.

The national treatment rule is essential to the maintenance of definable market access commitments and transparency. Inevitably, it takes GATT commitments beyond national borders, impacting inevitably on governmental measures that are not designed primarily to restrain imports. Such a commitment is necessary, given the ingenuity with which national governments respond to the protectionist lobbying of domestic special interests. Under Article iii, it can be argued that even if a tax or regulation appears at face value to be non-discriminatory, if it has an effect of affording protection, and if this effect is not essential to the valid purpose, then such a tax or regulation is inconsistent with GATT regulations.

An important exception to the national treatment obligation is government procurement. The language of Article III generally exempts from national treatment obligations purchases by 'government agencies of products purchased for governmental purposes'. Apparently, government procurement was too close to sovereignty to permit regulation in 1947 (Jackson 1989: 199). This exception has become increasingly troublesome over time, not least because of the massive postwar expansion in government budgets and, in some countries, of the size of the non-market economy.

The problem was addressed in the Tokyo Round agreement in the form of a code of government procurement, designed to provide equal access to foreign supplies. However, the code only applies to the government entities appended by each signatory. Like the tariff binding schedule, the code is based on the principle of reciprocity. As such, it has achieved only limited success. In the United States, for example, there exists a multitude of 'Buy American' regulations both at the federal and at the state level. The United States is far from unique in deploying this instrument of discrimination.

Another important exception to the national treatment obligation relates to government subsidies, covered by Article XVI of the GATT as supplemented by the 1979 Tokyo Round code on subsidies and countervailing duties. The subsidy rules are intended to protect access commitments with respect to the domestic market. They are also intended to control intrusions into foreign markets via government assistance through subsidy payments.

The rules outlaw export subsidies on manufactured products. On primary products, they state only that they should be avoided. If subsidies are bestowed on primary products they should not result in a country acquiring more than a fair share of trade in the subsidized product. This rule has proved to be unenforceable. It is a major bone of contention with respect to agricultural trade. In general, GATT discipline has been weak with respect to trade-distorting subsidies.

The principle of reciprocity
Although reciprocity as a legal concept has not been defined by the contracting parties, it is a fundamental principle and occupies a central position in the GATT (Long 1987: 10). Its importance is clearly indicated in the Preamble. It is taken up again, under Article XXVIII, in the context of tariff negotiations directed on a reciprocal and mutually advantageous basis to the substantial reduction of the general level of tariffs.

Reciprocity is also referred to in connection with negotiations on the modification of tariff schedules (also under Article XXVIII. It is implicit in the provisions for accession of a new member country (Article XXXIII), which may accede 'on terms to be agreed between such government and the contracting parties.'

Reciprocity was viewed by the contracting parties as fundamental to achieving the liberal trading order that had been so badly eroded during the 1930s and that had been all but shut out during the Second World War. It has served the GATT well in lowering tariff schedules. Its spirit has been all but shattered by the United States-led shift towards aggressive unilateralism that commenced in earnest during the early 1980s and that now threatens to render the GATT's efforts at trade liberalization practically irrelevant.

6   The erosion of the GATT

Some 40 years after the world 'trade constitution' was launched as part of the post-Second World War Bretton Woods system, the central institution of that constitution, the GATT, is 'an organization which was not intended to be an organization, a treaty that is yet only "provisionally" in force, and an incredibly complex, tangled web of international agreements and provisions modifying, explaining or escaping those agreements' (Jackson 1989: 307).

That it works at all is really surprising. That its rules have been eroded or evaded to the point where its authority has all but disintegrated is highly predictable in a world where national governments have no built-in defenses against lobbying by special interest groups targeted on the liberal trade order (Moser 1990). The weakening of the GATT manifests itself in the increasing ineffectiveness of the MFN principle to the point where it has now been all but replaced by the national treatment obligation. This shift manifests itself in a marked increase in bilateralism and in the substitution of free trade by managed trade.

The demise of the most-favored-nation clause
The MFN principle is breaking down for two major reasons (Low 1993: 155). First, it is easier to organize a protectionist trade policy on a discriminatory basis, singling out specific countries for particular attention. Second, the MFN principle has become a victim of a weakening consensus concerning the appropriate nature of the rules of the game. Specifically, the United States and Western Europe have become overly critical of Japan's approach to trade policy, largely because the Japanese economy has outcompeted them in world markets. The discriminatory denial by these countries of MFN treatment to Japan constitutes a clear and present danger to the GATT system.

The demise of MFN is evident in four main areas: (a) first-order protectionism; (b) conditional MFN; (c) regionalism; and (d) special treatment for the underdeveloped countries (Low 1993: 155).

First-order protectionism If MFN can be safely ignored, protectionist policy is much easier to manage at a relatively low economic and political cost. From the late 1970s onwards, the United States government has led the retreat to first-order protectionism through the deployment of voluntary export restraints and similar export-restricting devices, through the misuse of the antidumping and countervailing-duty statutes, and through the strategy of aggressive unilateralism.

Part of the problem is the failure of the GATT system to provide countries with the necessary support to resist pressures for discriminatory trade restrictions. In the absence of any effective enforcement mechanism, the GATT must rely on consensus supported by moral persuasion to defer discrimination. This reliance has been subverted, notably by the United States government, through a cynical application of voluntary export restraints.

Protecting countries bribe the exporting countries with VER scarcity premia, when they could retain such premia for their own citizens by imposing import controls, as a means of silencing their victims and avoiding GATT litigation. In this sense, VERs are the highest expression of first-order discrimination promoted through discrimination (Low 1993: 157). VERs are clearly GATT-illegal; but they have never been challenged within the GATT, simply because there is no party with a clear interest in suing.

A variant on the VER is the voluntary import expansion arrangement (VIE). The VIE extends protection from the domestic market to favored imports. It is inherently discriminatory, welfare-reducing, and vulnerable to rent-seeking activities. The VIE must also be categorized as first-order protectionism. The United States government once again is active in this GATT-eroding exercise.

Absence of an effective enforcement mechanism has also enabled deviant governments to abuse the fair trade laws as a means of providing administered protection to failing domestic industries. When exporters challenge specific antidumping or countervailing-duty judgements as GATT-illegal, the dispute panels are often boycotted by the aberrant country. In such circumstances, the consensus requirement effectively prevents the GATT from rectifying even the most gross abuses of the fair trade laws.

Conditional MFN Conditional MFN arrangements are defined as the selective application of trade rules and disciplines. They do not include free trade areas and customs unions, which establish preferential market access on a geographical basis (Low 1993: 158).

Conditional MFN became a significant issue in the GATT during the Tokyo Round when it became increasingly evident that the side agreements (codes) would not be adhered to by the entire membership. Yet, for all the codes except that on government procurement, the presumption in GATT law was that even though not all members would subscribe, their benefits should be extended to all GATT members without discrimination.

In fact, the codes introduced into the trading system the potential for discrimination, a potential that has been exploited not least by the United States government. A good example is US policy toward the Subsidies Code. Prior to signature at the end of the Tokyo Round, the United States did not apply the injury test in countervailing-duty cases involving dutiable imports. In exchange for agreeing to bring its domestic policy into line with the GATT agreement, the United States insisted that it would grant the injury test only to countries that accepted a commitment to phase out export subsidies on manufactured goods. This policy was written into US law in the Trade Agreements Act of 1979. This legislation is a clear infringement of the MFN principle.

Conditional MFN policy first entered into US law in the Trade Act of 1974, which empowered the president to recommend the selective application of trade agreements where such applications were consistent with the terms of the agreement. In the Omnibus Trade and Competitiveness Act of 1988 this provision was tightened. The president now *must* recommend that trade agreements be applied on a conditional MFN basis. Conditional MFN is applied in relation both to the Code on Technical Barriers to Trade and to the Code on Government Procurement as well as to the Code on Subsidies.

The US government openly rationalizes conditional MFN as indispensable to the preservation of multilateralism and the liberal trading order. It castigates as free-riders and foot-draggers countries that threaten these ideals by refusing to play their part. Free-riders are the small (usually underdeveloped) countries that benefit from MFN without making any contribution to it. Foot-draggers are the large countries whose refusal to subscribe to an arrangement makes it inconceivable to extend an unconditional application of the benefits to all parties.

The error in this rationalization is the notion that a government deeply penetrated by special interest lobbying is in a position to deploy conditional MFN in a wealth-creating manner, even should the law of comparative advantage be deemed to be inapplicable. The Uruguay Round agreement, if ratified, may ameliorate the problem through the mechanism of the World Trade Organization. Much will depend on the ability of the WTO itself to withstand special interest rent-seeking. As a global bureaucracy, the prognosis cannot be optimistic.

Regionalism   The role played by preferential regional trading blocs in eroding the MFN principle of the GATT has been outlined and evaluated in Chapter 11. The particular role played in this exercise by the United States throughout the 1980s and early 1990s has also been reviewed. Suffice it to reiterate here that regional trade politics, whether in the form of customs unions or of free trade areas or of hub-and-spoke bilateralism, constitutes a grave menace to the liberal trading order. In particular, Article xxiv of the GATT has failed completely as a mechanism for protecting multilateralism from the worst abuses of regionalism.

In essence, the participants in regional trading blocs do not view their purpose as to open up trade opportunities to non-participants. Rather they energize themselves to close off opportunities to those outside the club. It is empirically clear that countries find it extremely difficult to focus simultaneously on regional agreements and on multilateralism. The European Community, for example, rarely or ever takes any initiative in the GATT to promote multilateralism. The United States almost sacrificed the Uruguay Round on the altar of the NAFTA. If Japan continues to be exposed to regional discrimination, it is predictable that its government also will eventually negotiate its way into a Pacific Rim trading bloc that surely would erode the credibility of the GATT.

Special treatment for underdeveloped countries   The nature of underdeveloped country participation has been a source of contention since the beginning of the GATT system. Initially, many underdeveloped countries were deterred from joining the GATT because of failure to ratify the charter of the International Trade Organization. They sought exceptions to GATT discipline and trade preferences, typically on infant-industry grounds.

However, it took ten years of lobbying before such preferences were recognized as a legitimate device, and some twenty years before full legal cover was granted to preferences in the framework of the Generalized System of Preferences. These preferences are extended unilaterally and selectively by the advanced nations. As such, they are harmful to the liberal trading order (Low 1993: 168).

To the extent that special treatment for developing countries has involved exceptions from rules, it has worked as a reverse conditional MFN, with conditionality being attached to the status of underdevelopment. For the most part, discrimination is intended to be temporary, or at least strictly circumstantial. However, its availability has diverted underdeveloped countries from participating fully in the GATT system.

From the mid-1980s onwards, many underdeveloped countries have adopted trade liberalization programs. As they have done so, they have become increasingly strident in protesting against the unwillingness of the advanced nations to honor their GATT commitments. The Uruguay Round negotiations addressed the issues posed by the perceived problems that have emerged between the advanced and the underdeveloped countries in GATT. Whether or not the agreement will lead to a greater emphasis on multilateralism is impossible to assess at this time.

The drive for national treatment   During the 1980s, a range of new issues attracted increasing attention among the major trading countries within the GATT. Such matters as trade in services, trade-related intellectual property rights, and trade-related investment measures simply were not accounted for by GATT rules. The United States, with its comparative advantage in many of these areas, led the initiative within the Uruguay Round to bring these matters within the domain of the GATT.

The pre-Uruguay Round GATT was concerned primarily with trade in goods. Services were relevant only where they were linked to goods. Rules concerning investment and cross-border flows of factors of production were all but non-existent. The challenge of the Uruguay Round was to develop rules that would discipline these new areas of concern at a time when the GATT system itself was subject to rule erosion. Central to the contradiction that threatened the viability of the GATT was the substitution of national treatment for MFN with respect to the new issues.

The new issues, by their nature, require negotiations about conditions encountered by producers rather than products (Low 1993: 171). As capital and labor cross frontiers, producers want to benefit from the same conditions on the other side of the frontier as do their domestic counterparts. This implies equal treatment with respect to domestic laws and regulations, once they cross the national border.

At first sight, the national treatment provision appears to play a supportive role to MFN and not to threaten its survival. But this is superficial. In practice, the emphasis on national treatment obligations blurs the distinction between non-discrimination among foreigners and non-discrimination between foreigners and domestic producers. In this sense, it weakens multilateralism and encourages bilateral negotiations, especially where the national treatment obligation is viewed as intruding on issues of national sovereignty.

Worse still, national treatment negotiated bilaterally introduces political pressures for industrial nations to demand standardization of domestic laws and regulations. The United States government, in particular, has taken advantage of such bargaining to demand of underdeveloped countries environmental regulations and wage policies that infringe their national sovereignty. To the extent that some countries reject coercive intervention, so the world trading system will fragment itself into regionalism and into hub-and-spoke systems of preferential trading. To the extent that such national treatment negotiations spill over into the broadening of domestic industrial policies across national borders, the market process increasingly will be dispensed with in favor of highly interventionist managed trade.

7 The achievements of the GATT Uruguay Round

The 1993 agreements negotiated in the Uruguay Round constitute the most comprehensive overhaul of the multilateral trading system since the GATT was initiated in 1948. They are intended to reinforce and extend multilateral rules for trade. However, they will not diminish the growing interest in regional arrangements nor do they confront the aggressive unilateralism pursued by the United States government since the mid-1980s.

The main impetus for the Uruguay Round stemmed from international concern about the growing interest of Congress in raising trade barriers to restrain imports, especially from Japan. The Reagan administration promoted a GATT round as a way of deflecting this pressure. At the same time, it encouraged anti-protectionist interest groups to support multilateral trade liberalization. Two such interests emerged: the US finance sector, which wanted multilateral rules to promote liberalization of global services markets; and the US pharmaceutical, information technology and recording industries, which wanted to graft rules into the GATT to promote protection of intellectual property. Many underdeveloped countries fiercely contested the inclusion of these items in the trade round (Oxley 1994: 47).

The Uruguay Round agreements will liberalize trade in the following ways:

1. by reducing tariffs globally by one-third over ten years;
2. by reducing protection in agriculture through: conversion of all trade barriers to tariffs; reduction over six years of budgets for agriculture by 36 percent; reduction of budgets for export subsidies by 36 percent; and reduction of produce exported by 21 percent;
3. by imposing new restrictions on subsidies, including the phase-down of directly trade-distorting subsidies;
4. by increasing the authority of the GATT dispute-settlement systems;
5. by authorizing the GATT Secretariat to review the trade policies of members;
6. by establishing new standards for intellectual property and providing for enforcement of those standards;
7. by establishing multilateral trade rules for the liberalization of trade in services;
8. by creating a World Trade Organization to administer the GATT and other trade agreements negotiated under GATT auspices (such as the agreements on services and intellectual property).

The tariff cuts will not mean much in the case of the industrialized countries (with the exception of Australia and New Zealand), since the average level of tariffs prior to the cuts is only 5 percent. However, they will have a marked effect in the case of the underdeveloped countries whose average tariff levels range from 20 to 50 percent. In general, the tariff cuts agreement continues the long-term trade-liberalizing contribution of the GATT.

Non-tariff barriers are scheduled to be phased out on agriculture and clothing and textiles, two areas where they are very high. In agriculture, all non-tariff barriers have to be converted immediately into tariffs. This will not reduce protection, since the US and the EC will replace their non-tariff barriers with tariffs set sufficiently high to maintain the effective level of protection, even after the general tariff cut takes place. In clothing and textiles, tariff quotas, which allow a specified quantity of a product to enter at a lower than normal tariff level, are to be deployed to effect the adjustment over a twelve-year period.

The agreements also affect other non-tariff barriers, such as voluntary restraint and orderly marketing arrangements, which the US and the EC have deployed notably in electronic consumer, automobile and steel markets. Both the US and the EC have agreed to phase out 'voluntary' arrangements to manage trade (although the EC has sought a specific exemption for its VRA on Japanese automobiles). However, this concession is offset by official assurances that the section 301 retaliations in the US Trade Act remain unaffected by Uruguay Round commitments.

The overall authority of the GATT (or its successor) should be enhanced as a consequence of the Uruguay Round agreement in the following significant ways. First, the means of regulating two major sectors of trade – agriculture and clothing and textiles – will be made to conform with GATT rules. Specifically, the US will surrender a formal authority that it secured in 1955 not to apply GATT rules to certain aspects of agricultural trade. The Multifiber Agreement, which provided GATT cover for the use of quotas on imports of clothing and textiles from developing countries, will also be formally abrogated.

Second, for the first time in GATT history, the underdeveloped countries have embraced GATT rules on tariffs. In addition, the right of these countries to impose trade barriers in order to protect their balance of payments has been significantly curtailed in a specific agreement on the terms of application of Article xviii of the GATT.

Third, the dispute-settlement authority of the GATT has been strengthened. Prior to the Uruguay Round, the system operated only if the parties to the dispute gave their consent. Virtually all small-country members of the GATT accepted the procedures. However, the US and the EC frequently did not. Post-Uruguay Round, all parties will be committed to respect the findings of the dispute panels.

Finally, the conversion of the GATT into the World Trade Organization is a significant constitutional change. It will bring under the umbrella of the one organization the operations of the two important new treaties, the General Agreement on Trade in Services and the Agreement on Trade-related Aspects of Intellectual Property. A common system of dispute settlement will be used to deal with disputes under these treaties.

Conclusions

The GATT has always been an instrument of managed rather than of free trade, as this chapter clearly demonstrates. On balance, its contributions have been strongly trade-liberalizing, although its agenda increasingly has been bypassed by new initiatives of a highly protectionist nature. When giant traders such as the United States and the European Community determine to play fast and loose with the GATT rules, there is a real danger that the entire GATT constitution will be destroyed. At the present time, the multilateral thrust of the GATT is gravely threatened by the misuse of non-tariff barriers, of the fair trade laws, and of regionalism not by the small but by the giant members of the GATT. Aggressive unilateralism is another potent weapon of protection that is being wielded without concern for the liberal trade order by a superpower that is reacting extremely badly to relative economic decline (Bhagwati 1988, 1989).

As yet, the World Trade Organization is little more than a twinkle in its GATT parent's eye. It brings questions as well as answers to the multilateral trading order. Will the one-nation-one-vote rule result in narrow majoritarian voting punctuated by periodic coercion from frustrated giant nations? Or will it give constitutional authority to the system of consensus on which the GATT system has relied? Will the new powers of the WTO include environmental safety and labor regulations that will extend the US regulatory industrial policies across national borders? Will such powers be used by the industrial nations to close off export opportunities for the underdeveloped countries?

These and other issues await resolution in the post-Uruguay Round environment. The way in which they are resolved will go far in determining whether a liberal trade order is feasible in the largely post-communist era (Tumlir 1985; Finger 1991).

References

Bhagwati, J.N. (1988) *Protectionism* (Cambridge, Mass.: MIT Press).

Bhagwati, J.N. (1989) 'US trade policy at the crossroads', *World Economy*, 12: 439–79.

Finger, J.M. (1991) 'The GATT as an international discipline over trade restrictions', in R. Vaubel and T. Willett (eds), *The Political Economy of International Organizations* (Boulder, Col.: Westview Press).

Hudec, R.E. (1991) *Enforcing International Trade Law: The Evolution of the GATT Legal System* (Salem, N.H.: Butterworth Legal Publishers).

Jackson, J. (1969) *World Trade and the Law of GATT* (Indianopolis: Bobbs-Merrill Company).

Jackson, J. (1989) *The World Trading System* (Cambridge: MIT Press).

Jackson, J. (1991) *The World Trading System: Law and Policy of International Relations* (Cambridge, Mass.: MIT Press).

Jackson, J. (1993) 'U.S. constitutional law principles and foreign trade law and policy', in M. Hilf and E.-U. Petersmann (eds), *National Constitutions and International Economic Law* (Deventer: Kluwer Law and Taxation Publishers).

Long, O. (1987) *Law and its Limitations in the GATT Multilateral Trade System* (Dordrecht: Martinus Nijhoff).

Low, P. (1993) *Trading Free: The GATT and US Trade Policy* (New York: Twentieth Century Fund).

Meerhaeghe, M.A.G. van (1987) *International Economic Institutions* (Dordrecht: Martinus Nijhoff).

Moser, P. (1990) *The Political Economy of the GATT* (St Gallan: Verlag Ruegger).

Oxley, A. (1994) 'The achievements of the GATT Uruguay Round', *Agenda*, 1(1): 45–54.

Tumlir, J. (1985) *Protectionism: Trade Policy in Democratic Societies* (Washington, D.C.: American Enterprise Institute).

13 The case for constitutional reform

1 Introduction

As Vincent Ostrom (1984) has explained, the use of governmental authority entails the use of an instrument of evil: power over other individuals, because of the good, peace and prosperity that can arise when that instrument is used properly. However, instruments of evil can also be used to promote evil; for example, when governmental authority is used not to prevent one person from violating someone else's rights, but to violate one individual's rights by conferring special favors on other individuals.

The use of state authority to provide a protective framework within which individuals can pursue their commercial activities is a time-honored legitimate function of government. The use of such state authority to protect individuals' ability to trade, however, can easily metamorphose into the strongly contrary use of state authority to protect some individuals from market competition by restricting the ability of other individuals to engage in commerce. In this respect, trade protection policies clash with policies designed to protect trade. This clash is a perfect illustration of the inescapably Faustian character of the use of governmental authority.

In Chapters 8–11 of this book, we have set out in considerable detail the evil aspect of this Faustian bargain as it has worked itself out with respect to US trade policies over the period 1930–94. We have demonstrated conclusively that a great deal of political activity regarding trade has been directed not at augmenting trade opportunities by securing property rights but at attenuating property rights in order to benefit rent-seeking interest groups by protecting them from free competition. We have outlined the precise terms on which the Faustian bargain has been played out and have demonstrated beyond any reasonable doubt that public choice and not public interest has been the primeval force in this sorry tale.

Those who have stayed through this chronicle no doubt are now disturbed by the manifest weakness and malfeasance that has been exposed. If the story is to end not in despair but in hope that there is a better way, that the Faustian bargain need not necessarily end in generalized dystopia, we must turn our attention from public choice, from 'politics as it is', to constitutional political economy: 'politics as it can and should be'.

2   What is at stake?

In order to make a case for constitutional reform, it is essential to chronicle the losses imposed on US citizens by the trade policies outlined in Chapters 8–11 of this book. Such losses may be categorized in terms both of wealth and of liberty. In this section, we shall attempt to define the magnitude of these losses, thus exposing the stakes that are on the table in the battle over US trade policy reform. Fortuitously, some of the domestic welfare (wealth) costs of US trade protection recently have been calculated in a path-breaking study by Hufbauer and Elliott (1994). We shall draw upon and augment this study to focus the case for constitutional reform.

Let us first briefly summarize the principal events that have given rise to the present US trade protection dilemma. In 1930, the US Congress passed the infamous Smoot–Hawley Tariff Act. By 1933, that legislation raised average US tariffs on dutiable imports to 59 percent, stimulating foreign retaliation and further contracting the demand for US goods thus intensifying the depth of the Great Depression.

In consequence, following the Second World War, the United States and its allies created the GATT as the foundation of a more enlightened international trade regime. As a result of multilateral negotiations, average US tariffs on dutiable imports declined from 20 percent in 1947 to 5 percent in 1992. Following the Uruguay Round agreement (1994) the average US tariff will decline further to 4 percent in 1995.

Despite this generally trade-liberalizing trend, a few favored interest groups – most noticeably agriculture, maritime services, and textiles and apparel – have managed to shield themselves against reductions through 50 years of multilateral negotiations. Meanwhile, pressures for increased protection on behalf of other import-competing industries have not disappeared, typically intensifying whenever the US economy slips into recession and whenever the US dollar appreciates against foreign currencies.

Such was the case during the early 1980s, with three years of negative or slow growth in US GNP accompanied by a 30 percent appreciation in the real, trade-weighted value of the dollar (Hufbauer and Elliott 1994: 1). Pressures for import relief intensified. The supply of protection took the form of voluntary export restraints on Japanese automobiles, and on steel imports from Japan, Europe and elsewhere. Import quotas were imposed on sugar, and the quantitative restrictions on textiles and apparel imports were tightened significantly. Voluntary export restraints were also negotiated with Japan and Taiwan to limit imports of machine tools into the United States.

Throughout the 1980s, the fair-trade laws were increasingly relied upon to protect US producers from foreign competition, with the antidumping and countervailing-duty statutes replacing the escape clause as the principal shield from market forces. Under pressure from such petitions, in 1985 the Japanese semiconductor producers raised prices and reduced exports. In 1986, Canada settled a countervailing-duty case brought by US industry by imposing a 15 percent export tax on shipments of softwood lumber to the United States.

In the early 1990s the US economy once again slipped into recession at a time when the Japanese yen depreciated against the dollar, stimulating record Japanese trade surpluses. Once again, pressures for protection intensified. Early in 1992, pressures from the US government forced Japan to lower the ceiling on its automobile VER from 2.3 million vehicles to 1.65 million vehicles per annum. In mid-1993, the ITC ruled that US steel producers had been injured by dumped and subsidized imports of cold-rolled, plate, and corrosion-resistant steel from a number of countries. Evidently, 1980s-style trade protection was to continue throughout the last decade of the twentieth century.

The economic costs

Hufbauer and Elliott (1994) estimated (for 1990) the potential consumer gains if the United States were to eliminate all tariffs and quantitative restrictions on imports. The study is grounded on a simple, computable partial equilibrium analysis with four key assumptions:

1.   the domestic good and the imported good are imperfect substitutes;
2.   the supply schedule for the imported good is perfectly elastic;
3.   the supply schedule for the domestic good is less than perfectly elastic (upwardly sloped);
4.   all markets are perfectly competitive.

The effects of removing a trade barrier are illustrated in Figures 13.1 and 13.2. For example, elimination of a tariff lowers the price of the import in the domestic market from Pm to Pm^1 in Figure 13.1. In Figure 13.2, the decrease in the price of the imported good causes an inward shift in the demand curve for the domestic commodity from Dd to Dd^1. This in turn leads to a decrease in the price of the domestic product from Pd to Pd^1. Returning to Figure 13.1, the decrease in the domestic price causes the demand schedule for the imported good to shift from Dm to Dm^1. In equilibrium, prices of both the imported good and the domestic good are lower, output of the domestic good is also lower (by $Qd - Qd^1$) and the quantity of imports is higher (by $Qm^1 - Qm$).

Hufbauer and Elliott (1994) used a methodology to quantify the welfare effects of trade liberalization based on work by Morkre and Tarr (1980). Because the imported and domestic goods are imperfect substitutes, the total gain to consumers must be calculated as the sum of the consumer surplus

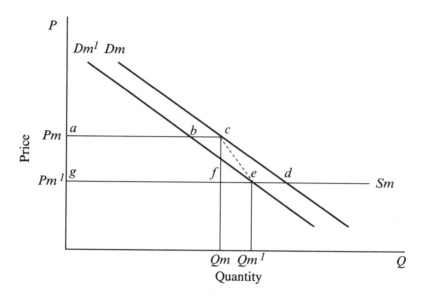

Figure 13.1   Effects in the import market of removing a trade barrier

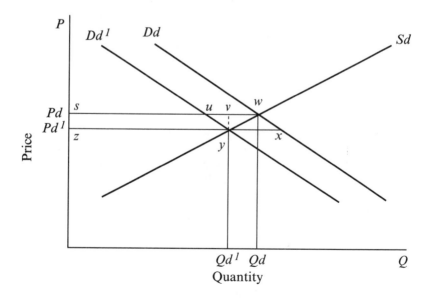

Figure 13.2   Effects in the domestic market of removing a trade barrier

gain in the two separate markets. In Figure 13.1, the consumer surplus gain from liberalization in the import market is approximated by the area *aceg*, which can be estimated by adding rectangle *acfg* to triangle *cef*.

If the form of protection is a tariff, the rectangular area *acfg*, according to Hufbauer and Elliott, represents a transfer from the government to consumers in the form of lost revenues, while the area of the triangle *cef* represents recovery of the deadweight efficiency loss. If quantitative restraints are used, and if all the quota rents previously were captured by foreign exporters, then area *acfg* is recovered from foreign interests. In that case, the consumer gain in the import market, measured by the area of the trapezoid *aceg*, is also equal to the net welfare gain.

Figure 13.2 identifies the domestic effects of trade liberalization. The consumer welfare gain from lower domestic prices is approximated by the area *swyz*. According to Hufbauer and Elliott, however, in the domestic market the consumer surplus gain is just offset by the producer surplus loss.

On this basis, Hufbauer and Elliott (1994) focused particular attention on the 21 US sectors protected by unusually high trade barriers (see Chapter 9 of this book), estimating demand and supply functions assumed to be linear in terms of their logarithms and incorporating terms of trade effects into their calculations. They estimated consumer surplus losses from trade barriers in these sectors to be in the neighborhood of $32 billion. To these losses they added an estimated $38 billion in consumer losses from the imposition of all other tariffs, which, in 1990, averaged 3.5 percent on other dutiable imports. Approximately one-third of US imports came in duty-free. *The potential consumer gains if the United States eliminated all tariffs and quantitative restrictions on imports, therefore, was in the neighborhood of $70 billion – about 1.3 percent of US GDP in 1990.*

In our view, this calculation, high though it may seem in absolute terms, seriously underestimates the true US economic gains from trade liberalization. It does so because certain perceived rents to US producers and to the US government derived from trade protection are tracked as simple transfers in calculating the net gain of free trade. Following Tullock (1980, 1993), this is an error. Let us suppose that the efficient rent-seeking model applies (see Chapter 4) and that resources are wasted in rent-seeking equal to the full total of domestic rents created by trade protection. In such circumstances, the *Tullock rectangles* must be added to the *Harberger triangles* to calculate the social cost of trade protection.

For the 21 most-protected sectors, Hufbauer and Elliott (1994: 28) calculated that the producers' surplus based on trade protection was $15.784 billion in 1990 and that tariff revenues were $5.861 billion. If so, then the rent-seeking waste in maintaining trade barriers in these sectors approximated $21.645 billion. If we approximate the rent-seeking waste from trade protection in the rest of the US economy in the ratio of consumer losses (38:32), this approximates to $25.640 billion.

By adding all rent-seeking waste to consumer surplus losses, we calculate that the welfare loss to trade protection in the United States in 1990 was in the neighborhood of $117 billion – about 2 percent of US GDP in 1990. This measure takes no account of any entrepreneurial or *x*-inefficiency welfare losses triggered by trade protection.

It is often argued that trade protection preserves jobs in the United States. If so, the cost to consumers of preserving such jobs is extremely high. In a quarter of the 21 sectors scrutinized by Hufbauer and Elliott (1994), the consumer cost per job saved was $500,000 or more. There was only one sector (costume jewelry) in which the estimated consumer cost of saving a job was less than $100,000. On average, the loss of consumer surplus per job saved was $170,000 per annum. In other words, consumers paid more than six times the average annual compensation of manufacturing workers to preserve jobs through import restraints. *Once rent-seeking costs are added on, the average social loss per job saved was approximately $287,000, or somewhat more than ten times the average annual compensation of manufacturing workers in the United States (in 1990).*

The loss of liberty
An often overlooked non-monetary cost of trade protection is the violation of economic freedom that occurs when governments intervene to reduce the range of contracts that consenting adults are able to enter into or to raise the cost of entering into such contracts (McGee 1993). Thus, a tariff that raises the price of a Japanese automobile by $2,000 on the US market forces consumers who choose to purchase that automobile to transfer $2,000 of their wealth to the government as a condition of entering into the contract. Such a transfer is a taking in all but name, although it is not treated as such by United States courts at the present time. If an import quota prevents certain consumers even from obtaining the automobile of their choice, a property right is violated, since property rights include the right to trade the fruits of one's labor. Once again, the United States courts are careless about such property rights at the present time.

While most economists view the free trade issue exclusively from a utilitarian perspective, the issue should also be viewed from a rights perspective. For those who endorse the Lockeian notion, written into the United States Constitution, that individuals possess inalienable rights to life, liberty and property, free trade follows as an inevitable implication, whether or not utility in some sense is or is not enhanced. Trade protection in any of its forms violates the right to property. In its quantitative forms, it violates the rule of law and opens up opportunities for bureaucrats to violate the liberty of individuals in pursuit of their own bureaucratic objectives. This view is in keeping with the classical liberal notion of government, which restricts government activity to the defense of life, liberty and property.

3   The constitutional political economy perspective

Constitutional political economy is a domain of inquiry and discourse among scientists who choose to perceive social interaction as a set of complex relationships, both actual and potential, among autonomous individuals, each of whom is capable of making rational choices (Buchanan 1990: 17). As such, the domain cannot be extended to include inquiry by scholars who choose to perceive social interaction differently, whether in purely conflictual or in purely idealistic visions. For these visions represent alternative windows on the world. We made it clear in Chapters 1 and 2 that the constitutional political economy perspective would be deployed in this book.

There is a categorical distinction to be made between constitutional political economy and non-constitutional political economy, a distinction that relates to the ultimate behavioral object of analytical attention. At one level, all political economy is concerned with choice and with the alternative institutional arrangements within which individuals make choices among alternatives. In non-constitutional political economy, analysis focuses on choices made *within* constraints that are exogenous to those individuals who are charged with making the choice. Such constraints may be imposed by nature, by history, by some sequence of past choices, by other individuals, by laws and institutional arrangements, by custom or by convention. Constitutional political economy instead directs attention to the *choice among constraints*, choices made by rational individuals that collectively bind them from undertaking certain avenues of decision-making in the post-constitutional environment.

At first sight, the notion that rational individuals may choose to constrain themselves and each other through a series of constitutional contracts that are difficult to disavow may seem to be counter-intuitive. Why would such individuals voluntarily constrain their future choice sets in the political market place? The answer lies in the potential for evil and social waste that is implicit in conflictual politics, the ever-present risk of the tyranny of the majority or even of the rent-seeking minority.

Individuals may be able to engage in far-sighted, wealth-enhancing contracts of a constitutional nature, even when they cannot do so in the day-to-day market place of politics, because the greater uncertainty associated with long-term contracts reduces the importance of particular circumstances that give rise to conflict in the immediate present. Such was the reasoning of Buchanan and Tullock in *The Calculus of Consent* (1962). Such is the perspective through which we advance the case for constitutional protection of unilateral free trade within the United States.

Central to the notion of constitutional political economy is the logic that free individuals will choose to restrict the domain and/or the range of democratically elected government, recognizing the potential for unconstrained democracies to usurp liberty and to destroy wealth in reaction to special interest pressures. Political philosophers indeed have anguished over this predilection for the minimal state to bloat itself into Leviathan since the early beginnings of modern democracy. Thus, an eighteenth-century Scottish historian, Alexander Tytler, was to conclude from his study of democracy in ancient Greece:

> A democracy cannot exist as a permanent form of government. It can only exist until a majority of voters discover that they can vote themselves largesse out of the public treasury. From that moment on, the majority always votes for the candidate who promises to them the most benefits from the public treasury, with the result that democracy always collapses over a loose fiscal policy. (Quoted in Niskanen 1978)

The United States Founding Fathers were well aware of this danger to liberty and wealth, and carefully prepared the ground for constitutional constraints that would ameliorate the adverse tendencies of special interest groups. In *The Federalist, no. 10*, James Madison described the *violence of faction*:

> By a faction I understand a number of citizens, whether amounting to a majority or minority of the whole, who are united and actuated by some common impulse of passion, or of interest, adverse to the rights of other citizens, or to the permanent and aggregate interests of the community.

Madison believed that the potential for such violence of faction could be averted by carefully devised constitutional rules. In *The Federalist, no. 51*, he succinctly defined the central problem of designing such a constitution and outlined an approach based on checks and balances that might serve to ameliorate it:

> Ambition must be made to counteract ambition. ... It may be a reflection on human nature that such devices should be necessary to control the abuses of government. But what is government itself but the greatest of all reflections on human nature? If men were angels, no government would be necessary. If angels were to govern men, neither external nor internal controls on government would be necessary. In framing a government which is to be administered by men over men, the great difficulty lies in this: you must first enable the government to control the governed; and in the next place oblige it to control itself. A dependence on the people is, no doubt, the primary control on the government; but experience has taught mankind the necessity of auxiliary precautions.

Madison correctly envisaged the supremacy of the legislature within a republican form of government and focused attention on the bicameral legislature as the basis for self-control. Thus, once again, in *The Federalist, no. 51*:

> In republican government, the legislative authority necessarily predominates. The remedy for this inconvenience is to divide the legislature into different branches; and to render them, by different modes of election and different principles of action, as little connected with each other as the nature of their common functions and their common dependence on the society will admit.

Madison also viewed the federal system of government as a means of reducing the violence of faction and advocated a constitution which would delegate different powers to the several states than would be delegated to the federal government. Thus in *The Federalist, no. 45*:

> The powers delegated by the proposed constitution to the federal government are few and defined. Those which are to remain in the State governments are numerous and indefinite ... The powers reserved to the several States will extend to all the objects which, in the ordinary course of affairs, concern the lives, liberties and properties of the people, and the internal order, improvements, and prosperity of the States.

The United States Constitution fully reflected Madison's genius and, for some 150 years, successfully inhibited the violence of faction. However, even by the mid-nineteenth century, Alexis de Tocqueville, in his great masterpiece, *Democracy in America* (1848), reflected a concern that the United States might not be able to avert what he called the 'tyranny of the majority'. Such a tyranny, according to Tocqueville, need not arise through the minority finding itself at the wrong end of rifles and bayonets. In his famous chapter, 'What Sort of Despotism Democratic Nations Have to Fear', Tocqueville described a form of democratic tyranny that:

> would be like the authority of a parent, if, like that authority, its object was to prepare men for manhood; but it seeks on the contrary to keep them in perpetual childhood; it ... provides for their security, foresees and supplies their necessities, facilitates their pleasures, manages their principle concerns, directs their industry, regulates the descent of property, and subdivides their inheritances ... The principal of equality has prepared men for these things; it has predisposed men to endure them, and often times to look on them as benefits.
>
> After having thus successively taken each member of the community in its powerful grasp, and fashioned them at will, the supreme power then extends its aim over the whole community. It covers the surface of society with a network of small complicated rules, minute and uniform, through which the most original minds and the most energetic characters cannot penetrate ... The will of man is not shattered, but softened, bent, and guided; men are seldom forced by it to act, but they are constantly restrained from acting; such a power does not destroy, but it compresses, enervates, extinguishes, and stupifies a people, 'til each nation is

reduced to be nothing better than a flock of timid and industrious animals, of which the government is the shepherd. (Tocqueville 1848)

4   The United States Constitution and economic rights

Thomas Hobbes, in his classic treatise *Leviathan* (1651), described the life of individuals in a society without laws and without government as 'solitary, poore, nasty, brutish and short'. Selfish and amoral individuals operating in such a state of nature, in his judgement, would endlessly predate upon each other's accumulation of property. Hobbes' justification of unlimited state powers to implement laws transforming the unconstrained individual pursuit of self-interest (the war of each against all) into a rule-ordered society was based on the assumption that the all-powerful governor (Leviathan) would respect his ultimate accountability to God and would act as a benevolent dictator.

Well before the War of Revolution, historical experience had forewarned the Founding Fathers that majoritarian democracies as much as absolute monarchs do not behave benevolently. Individuals may pursue their self-interests to the same extent and with greater impact in the public than in the private domain. Due to asymmetries in the organization and political representation of group interests, and the dependence of periodically elected governments on majority support, the narrow, short-term interests of members of such bodies may conflict with and overwhelm the long-term interests of the citizens at large (Petersmann 1993).

Constitutional law evolved in response to grievances and experiences of earlier times, with periodic restatements of the common-law tradition in England that was designed to protect the fundamental liberties of the individual during times of crisis. The Magna Carta of 1215, the Petition of Rights of 1628, the Habeas Corpus Act of 1679 and the Declaration of Rights of 1689 are the most important pre-revolutionary examples of such restatements.

The content of such deliberately incomplete written lists of individual rights was subject to change depending on the circumstances and the perceived nature of the constitutional challenge. An important implication of each such restatement was the notion that 'the state can acquire nothing by simple declaration of its will but must justify its claim in terms of the rights of the individuals whom it protects' (Epstein 1985: 12).

Hobbes attempted to justify absolutism, whether in the form of a monarch or of a Lord Protector (Hobbes always knew on which side his bread was buttered), as a reaction to the upheavals of the English civil war and to the perceived importance of a government monopoly of force to secure peace and order. These alien views were swiftly challenged by free-born Englishmen, notably by John Locke (1632–1704) in his recognition of inalienable human rights, and by Edmund Burke (1729–97) who challenged monarchical absolutism and established the case for parliamentary democracy.

The United States Founding Fathers had ready access to such received wisdom and were especially influenced by John Locke's view that the only role of government was to protect the inalienable rights of individuals to life, liberty and property. The Founders were rightly horrified, therefore, by the British Parliament's assertion, in 1766, of 'unlimited and unlimitable parliamentary sovereignty', which it justified on the ground that 'the nation did not need to be protected against its will' (Blackstone 1765). The Founders fell back on the wisdom of English common law and recognized that the fundamental rights of the people were prior to government. They clearly recognized that the individual would remain free only if the government and majoritarian politics were constitutionally restrained.

The Founding Fathers searched therefore for a constitutional solution focused on two central objectives; namely, to constitute government powers so as to protect individual rights, and to limit the exercise of all government powers by constitutional restraints. Unlike the English concept of parliamentary sovereignty, the US Constitution aimed at 'a government of laws, not of men' by subjecting all government powers to permanent constitutional rules with a higher legal ranking than ordinary legislation and government regulations.

Indeed, the most distinctive contribution of American constitutional law is its emphasis on the supremacy of individual rights over government powers. The fundamental rights of the people are recognized as being prior to government; they are not derived from government. In accordance with the constitutional principles of a limited government of enumerated powers and of protection of individual freedoms against government interference, the United States Constitution explicitly reserves certain powers to the states and to the people:

> The enumeration in the Constitution of certain rights shall not be construed to deny or disparage others retained by the people. (Ninth Amendment)

and

> The powers not delegated to the United States by the Constitution, nor prohibited by it to the States are reserved to the States respectively, or to the people. (Tenth Amendment)

The Ninth Amendment in particular recognizes the existence of legally enforceable rights not listed in the written Constitution but considered to be implicit in the concept of ordered liberty (Petersmann 1993: 12). In this sense, it reflects the notion that the common-law system supersedes the Constitution; that the Constitution itself is not the highest source of legal authority. The Amendment expresses the Lockeian idea that the citizens of a political society cede to government only limited, enumerated powers and retain their fundamental rights. The primary task of the judiciary is to protect the individual rights of the citizens and to make explicit the implied limitations on government powers.

More generally, the Bill of Rights amendments do not grant individuals any rights but, rather, protect their inalienable liberties, which are viewed as existing independently from and antedating the United States Constitution. Liberty of contract and the liberty to produce and distribute goods and services are both protected under the due-process clauses of the Fifth and Fourteenth Amendments, according to which no person shall be deprived of 'life, liberty and property without due process of law'. Until 1937, the US Supreme Court declared unconstitutional under these clauses many federal and state laws dealing with economic and social matters because they deprived a plaintiff of liberty or property without procedural or substantive due process of law.

The meaning of the unlisted natural rights ultimately will rest on judgments by the courts, hopefully irrespective of the behavior of Congress. Even though a major objective of the Constitution, as outlined in the Preamble, was 'to secure the blessings of liberty', the US Congress does not recognize an individual liberty to import and export, and has legislated in direct contravention of these liberties. Since 1937 (*West Coast Hotel Co.* v *Parrish*), the US courts have applied a judicial double standard which accords a higher level of scrutiny and of judicial protection to civil and political rights than to economic liberties.

Even before 1937, the US courts were reluctant to deprive Congress of a major source of taxation by denying it the authority to impose tariffs. Thus, in a 1904 decision (*Buttfield* v *Stranahan*), the US Supreme Court decided:

> that no one has a vested right to trade with foreign nations, which is so broad in character as to limit and restrict the power of Congress to determine what articles ... may be imported into this country and the terms upon which a right to import may be exercised.

As Petersmann (1993) has noted, this holding implies a *stare decisis* establishing the existence of 'a right to trade with foreign nations'. Subsequent court decisions, however, have quoted from the 1904 decision only that 'no one has a vested right to trade with foreign nations', thus denying a crucially important precedent in favor of individual liberty. In 1989 (*Arjay Associates Inc.* v *Bush*), the Court of Appeals for the Federal Circuit claimed that there had not been a single US Court decision over the preceding 200 years that had upheld a right of importers to overturn a congressional exclusion of any product from importation. The reason presented by the court for this absence of a right to trade was as follows:

When the people granted Congress the power '[t]o regulate Commerce with foreign Nations' they thereupon relinquished whatever right they, as individuals, may have had to insist upon the importation of any product.

This Hobbesian interpretation of the US Constitution is inconsistent with its Lockeian emphasis on inalienable rights. It is inconsistent with the concept of the Constitution as a protector of liberty even against legitimate authority, against the elected representatives of the people even when they act in good faith and in the public interest. Import restrictions which tax and restrict domestic consumers for the benefit of import-competing domestic producers surely fall within this protective shield provided by the Constitution.

The Founding Fathers explicitly limited the trade regulatory powers to constrain their potential abuse. Thus, the Constitution requires that 'all duties, imports and excises shall be uniform throughout the United States' (Article I), that 'no tax or duty shall be laid on articles exported from any State' (ibid.) and that 'no preferences shall be given by any regulation of commerce or revenue to the ports of one State over those of another' (ibid.).

Yet these protections evidently fell short, in the judgment of the courts, of a property right in the importation or exportation of goods and services sufficient to protect individuals against foreign trade restrictions. The commerce clause, which permits Congress to make laws 'to regulate commerce ... with foreign nations' has been construed as an unlimited plenary power enabling Congress to make whatever laws it chooses, including the power to prohibit imports and exports.

The US Supreme Court has declined to apply inter-state commerce precedents to the congressional foreign trade policy powers because such powers included 'the authority of Congress to absolutely prohibit foreign importations' (*Brolan* v *United States*). In the case of challenges to executive foreign trade restrictions, the courts will examine whether the executive action has exceeded the constitutional or statutory authority granted to the executive (for example, in *Youngstown Street & Tube* v *Sawyer*). However, if there is a legal basis for executive action, they will not review whether the foreign trade restrictions represents a disproportionate interference with an individual right to trade with foreign nations.

Some constitutional lawyers have argued from case law that nothing in the Constitution suggests that the rights of individuals with respect to foreign affairs differ from similar rights with respect to other exercises of governmental powers (Petersmann 1993: 17). Yet the United States government, the United States courts and prevailing constitutional doctrine view the individual freedom to import and export as a privilege and not as a right.

5   Parchment versus guns

In *The Federalist, no. 48*, James Madison, after describing how legislatures in Virginia and Pennsylvania had repeatedly violated their state constitution, concluded that 'a mere demarcation on parchment is not a sufficient guard against those encroachments which lead to a tyrannical concentration of all powers of government in the same hands'. Madison thus recognized clearly that merely to articulate constitutional principles, requirements and limitations will not ensure adherence to these principles. This recognition does not deny the value of the articulation of principles on parchment. Rather, it underlines the importance of placing the guns of individual and group self-interest so that they reinforce the parchment of the Constitution (Wagner 1993: vii).

The Founding Fathers attempted to reinforce the parchment of the United States Constitution by imposing a strict separation of powers as between the legislature, the judiciary, and the executive branches, by establishing a bi-cameral legislature and by creating a federal structure. Most important was their emphasis on a government of strictly enumerated powers, with all the other rights to be retained by the people. This experiment succeeded over a period of 150 years in protecting individual rights against encroachment by Leviathan. Since 1937, however, the balances have failed, with serious consequences for the erosion of individual liberties, as special interest groups have invaded parchment at some considerable cost to the general welfare.

The framers of the US Constitution intended to create a federal government of limited and enumerated powers with regard to foreign relations. Historically, the commerce clause (Article i) was intended to pre-empt state economic controls and to curb government regulations. Most certainly, it was not intended to confer large regulatory powers to the federal government (Petersmann 1993: 31). However, these good intentions have not survived the unlawful behavior of the United States judiciary.

With respect to foreign trade, the constitutional powers of Congress 'to regulate commerce with foreign nations', to levy 'taxes, duties, imposts and excises', and to enact legislation even in breach of international law are now construed by the courts to be so broad that no legislative foreign trade restriction has ever been declared void for lack of constitutional authority. The trade regulatory powers delegated by Congress to the president have also been allowed to provide for almost unfettered discretion. The executive has been allowed to impose non-transparent, discriminatory trade restrictions even when they seriously erode individual rights, and even when they promote foreign cartels. In such circumstances, the Constitution is failing to deliver on the promises of the Founding Fathers.

6 The cosmopolitan solution

In Chapter 2, we introduced the *cosmopolitan* version of the theory of free trade which requires free trade everywhere and does not endorse the unilateralist implications of the theory of comparative advantage. According to the cosmopolitan theory, any trade regime that is constructed must rule out artificial comparative advantage arising from outside interventions such as subsidies or protection. It must also rule out dumping as a technique employed to secure an otherwise untenable foothold in world markets. Jagdish Bhagwati (1989) presents an eloquent, if ultimately unconvincing, defense of the cosmopolitan approach, which he relates to the role played by the GATT in promoting multilateral trade liberalization through the principle of reciprocity.

For Bhagwati, the GATT represents a contractarian institution. Its underlying essence is a concept of symmetric rights and obligations for member states, rather than unilateralism in free trade. In this sense, the GATT also reflects, broadly, the notion of full reciprocity (i.e., a balance of market-access obligations by the contracting parties). However, the GATT also incorporates the notion of first-difference reciprocity (the level playing-field) as a matter of procedural practice. This tension between full and first-difference reciprocity has built into it the possibility of conflict should any major contracting party (Bhagwati clearly has the United States in mind) decide to reopen the question of balance in overall market access.

Bhagwati relies heavily upon the GATT as the engine of cosmopolitan multilateralism. Given its failure to contain protectionist forces, not least within the United States, there is little cause for optimism with respect to this reliance. The widespread abuse of the fair-trade laws, the emergence of aggressive unilateralism, the misuse of voluntary export agreements and the escalation of hub-and-spoke regionalism have all occurred during the GATT's watch, and have completely counteracted the impact of tariff reductions.

Bhagwati acknowledges the existence of a protectionist bias in the existing institutions of trade policy. He outlines a program of institutional reform designed to give more play to forces that favor freer trade. Unfortunately, his reform program reflects a welfare-state emphasis that is incompatible with the methodological individualism which directs our own thinking on the reform issue.

To minimize the capture of the fair-trade laws by protectionists, Bhagwati suggests a move toward more impartial institutions. Specifically, he calls for multilateral GATT panels to investigate relief; for the imposition of penalties on a petitioner whose complaints are viewed as frivolous; and for the settling of much higher threshholds before relief will be granted. To counteract the bias in safeguards actions, where relief tends to be granted without any accounting of its economic costs, Bhagwati advocates that the relevant institutions should be required to build in the costs of protection and, at some stage, to charge part of that cost to any industry that secures protection.

He urges the creation of institutional support mechanisms to ease the consequences of the decline and exit of firms in the emerging global economy. Although he acknowledges that adjustment assistance programs can be criticized as inefficient response mechanisms to economic change, nevertheless he considers such programs to be essential in a cosmopolitan world that differentiates between foreign and domestic communities. He suggests that governments should integrate the revenues that arise from the use of tariffs to provide adjustment assistance for those who suffer from foreign competition, albeit with a sunset provision. He claims that this solution is superior to the voluntary export restraints currently used to protect domestic industries. He suggests that such a provision should replace Article xix of the GATT, which has fallen into disuse.

Finally, Bhagwati urges a return to the multilateralism of the 1950s and away from the aggressive unilateralism of the 1980s, noting the importance of tolerating other countries' social objectives. He offers no specific mechanism to achieve this reform, relying instead on statesmanship and commitment to the goals of a liberal trading regime, presumably on the part of the United States. As this book has shown in some detail, it is unrealistic to rely on these qualities in the day-to-day process of United States politics.

The cosmopolitan approach, as outlined by Bhagwati (1989), seeks to have a nation convert the rest of the world to free trade before it practices free trade. The justification for this approach is that free trade everywhere is necessary to prevent trade based an artificial comparative advantage. In the absence of such a requirement, it is argued, a northern nation might encourage individuals to grow bananas in hothouses by subsidizing this activity, perhaps because energy and glass interest groups had lobbied for such an outcome. The nationalist approach, in Bhagwati's view, would have a southern nation accept the importation of such bananas to the extent that its residents chose to buy them.

There are a number of problems with Bhagwati's approach. First, we do not think that the distinction between nationalist and cosmopolitan perspectives provides a sufficiently rich vocabulary. Many economic nationalists are strongly opposed to free trade and in favor of managed trade, with trade barriers erected to support those interests and industries that the elite policy-makers deem to be deserving. In some cases, the objects of support may be culture-based, as in the French controversy over American cinema. In other cases, it may be historical, as in US concern to protect its rust-belt industries, such as steel production, from lower-cost competition.

Likewise, many cosmopolitans do not support free trade at all, but instead pursue global harmonization goals through some mechanism of international social democracy. Level playing-field arguments, in such circumstances, are rhetorical devices designed to curb the flight of individuals and of capital from less- to more-productive environments, from more- to less-oppressive regimes.

Second, it is by no means clear to us that the government of a trading nation can adopt simultaneously a classical liberal and a cosmopolitan outlook when it finds itself in a world engulfed in trade restrictions. In such circumstances, it is extremely difficult to adopt the *posture* of a pragmatic managed trader without becoming subverted to truly managed trade. The posture itself exposes the government to trade protectionist rent-seeking that must quickly induce trade protection well beyond what is justified by cosmopolitan considerations.

This danger becomes apparent once an examination is made of how claims for retaliation arise. Typically, retaliation claims arise because domestic producers, claiming injury, file complaints with the government. The foreign producer never announces that he is about to dump products on US markets. Rather, that producer simply exports products to the United States on terms agreed with US customers. The protectionist trigger, therefore, is at the fingertips of rent-seeking domestic interests, not those of the cosmopolitan government. Managed trade thus is driven by a process of private complaints, not by a process of governmental evaluation of whether the global playing-fields are level or tilted.

Third, we have major misgivings about Bhagwati's continuing faith in the GATT (even more so in its successor, the World Trade Organization) as a mechanism for promoting multilateral free trade. From the outset, the GATT was viewed as an organization to promote managed (if freer trade). It is not dedicated to the promotion of free trade. Admittedly, the norm of a market economy is embedded in the GATT rules' preference for tariffs over quotas, and the GATT's principled opposition to quotas is testimony to its commitment to the market economy. Yet the history of the GATT is that of failure to protect market economies from the tidal wave of quantitative restrictions that has followed swiftly upon the decline in tariff protection.

The GATT has been helpless to withstand such pressures because, for the most part, they have taken the form of victimless crimes, or rather of crimes that cannot be reported for fear of extra-legal revenge on the part of the bully nations. Furthermore, the GATT relies ultimately on financial appropriations from nations that themselves are in the vanguard in replacing free with managed commerce.

With its limited budget and lack of enforcement powers, the GATT has not been deemed worthy of capture by protectionist forces. All this will change, however, once the World Trade Organization is established. A well-heeled, powerful agency predictably will attract heavy rent-seeking on the part of protectionist interests. For, if trade can be restricted at the international level by a set of bureaucrats responding to budget maximizing goals (Niskanen 1994), the issue of freer trade can be removed from the domestic political market place.

7   The unilateral free trade solution

The United States was clearly founded on classical liberal principles, even if its post-1937 practice has often violated those principles. Recent practice notwithstanding, the rhetoric of policy is still largely classical liberal in orientation, at least to the extent that it does not expressly deny importance to economic rights. In a world where the international order is predominantly mercantilistic, with a good deal of state management of economic outcomes, what should be the posture of a major trading nation that seeks to affirm market processes over central direction while itself demonstrating vulnerability to social democratic pressure? Should it use its trading strength to nudge the international order in a classical liberal direction with the cudgel of reciprocity? Or should it lead by example and attempt unilaterally to do well for its citizens while doing good elsewhere?

In Bhagwati's (1989) formulation, the nationalistic approach to free trade would involve a major trading nation like the United States in pursuing a regime of open trade regardless of what nations were doing elsewhere. Regardless of whether other nations imposed quotas or subsidized exports, the unilateral free trader would continue to trade freely, taking the actions of other nations as an unalterable part of its environment. Such a nation would allow economic activities to be arranged in accordance with the common-law principles of property, contract and tort, regardless of the extent of mercantilist activities elsewhere.

In our judgement, unilateral free trade is the clearly preferred path once the problematical character of the Faustian bargain that government represents is properly appreciated. For it is a counsel of perfection, for which there are no listeners, to say that government should restrict trade only when appropriate. What government would ever claim to restrict trade when it should not do so? Governments always claim to use their power for good and never for bad. Yet the use of power for evil is inherent in the Faustian bargain itself.

The theory and evidence presented in this book clearly indicates that the United States government should be committed to unilateral free trade and that this should be a basic default setting of the constitutional order. Public choice informs us that unilateral free trade is an untenable political position in the present mercantilist environment in the absence of constitutional protection. For, unlike multilateralism, unilateralism cannot easily harness the export interests into some bicycle theory of trade liberalism. In the day-to-day political process, the generalized interests of consumers tend to be outflanked by the specific interests of the special interests. Therefore, even if some free-market US government were to *legislate* for unilateral free trade, that position assuredly would be eroded with the passage of rent-seeking time.

In order to provide significant constitutional protection against predictably unlawful behavior on the part of the judicial branch, it would be essential to make the necessary constitutional amendments as unambiguous as possible. We suggest that the following amendments to Article I, section 8 would suffice:

1. Delete the words 'with foreign nations' from the commerce clause.
2. Add the following clause: 'The Congress shall not lay any imposts or duties, nor shall it impose any quantitative restriction on imports or exports, except what may be absolutely necessary for executing its inspection laws or for protecting national security. Nor shall the Congress delegate any such authority to the president.'

Article v of the United States Constitution reads as follows:

> The Congress, whenever two-thirds of both Houses shall deem it necessary, shall propose Amendments to this Constitution, or, on the Application of the Legislatures of two-thirds of the several States, shall call a Convention for proposing Amendments, which in either case shall be valid to all Intents and Purposes, as Part of this Constitution, when ratified by the Legislatures of three-fourths of the several states, or by Conventions in three-fourths thereof, as the one or the other Mode of Ratification may be proposed by the Congress.

Article v thus provides two methods of amending the Constitution. Under the first method, the amendment is initiated by Congress. Under the second, the amendment is initiated by the States. In each method, the States must ratify the proposed amendment. The Constitution has been amended only 26 times since 1787; ten of those amendments concerned the Bill of Rights. In each case, the method employed was that of Congress initiative. Although several hundred resolutions have been submitted to Congress by the States requesting national constitutional conventions, none has proved successful. For this reason, the convention method has been called a 'constitutional curiosity' or 'one of the best-known "dead letter" clauses in the Federal Constitution' (Dirksen 1968).

It should not be supposed, however, that the convention clause is devoid of political influence. Upon occasion, Congress has initiated amendments in order to avoid the convention. For example, the Bill of Rights was proposed by Congress in 1789 in response to convention petitions by Virginia and New York. Similarly, the seventeenth amendment, which provided for the direct election of senators, was driven through a reluctant Senate by the presentation of a significant number of State petitions that threatened to activate the convention route.

Of course, neither route is ever easy; indeed, it is the essence of constitutionalism that it should not be so. It is especially difficult where economic interests are central and where rent-protection lobbying must be overcome by the general interest. In this respect, unilateral free trade roughly parallels the balanced-budget amendment (Rowley 1987: 391–406). This perceived difficulty has deterred leading scholars from pursuing much-needed constitutional reform. Most notably, Milton Friedman, who favored a 'Free Trade Amendment' to the US Constitution which would guarantee 'the right of the people to buy and sell legitimate goods and services at mutually acceptable terms' and which would limit the power of the US Congress to tax and restrict foreign trade, sheepishly concluded that it was 'visionary to suppose that such an amendment could be enacted now' (Friedman and Friedman 1979: 304).

Good scholars should never falter at the hurdle of political impossibility when their case is strong. If they do so, the case itself will fail, rightly, by default. The history of classical liberalism clearly demonstrates that there is no such thing as political impossibility. The theoretical, institutional and empirical case for unilateral free trade, as outlined in this book, is overwhelming. The American electorate, for the most part, is rational in its search for wealth and freedom. Let us carry our case to the electorate, in the hope and expectation that good ideas will drive out bad, that a broad interest will form behind the amendment proposal, and that the United States indeed will convert to free trade by the year 2000, just as Great Britain converted to free trade in 1846. If the United States electorate accepts this challenge to route the rentiers as we suggest, then we do not doubt that the twenty-first century will be acclaimed as the American Century, just as the nineteenth century rightly is enshrined as the British Century.

References

Arjay Associates Inc. v *Bush*, Court of Appeals for the Federal Circuit, 891 F.2d. 894, 1989.

Bhagwati, J. (1989) *Protectionism* (Cambridge, Mass.: MIT Press).

Blackstone, W. (1765) *Commentaries* 2 (original edition).

Brolan v *United States*, 236 U.S. 216, 22 (1915).

Buchanan, J.M (1990), 'The domain of constitutional economics', *Constitutional Political Economy*, I: 1–18.

Buchanan, J.M. and Tullock, G. (1962) *The Calculus of Consent* (Ann Arbor: University of Michigan Press).

Buttfield v *Stranahan*, 192 U.S. 470, 493 (1904).

Dirksen, E. (1968) 'The Supreme Court and the people', *Michigan Law Review*, 66.

Epstein, R.A. (1985) *Takings* (Cambridge: Harvard University Press).

Friedman, M. and Friedman, R. (1979) *Free to Choose: A Personal Statement* (New York: Harcourt Brace Jovanovich).

Hobbes, J. (1651) *Leviathan* (London: J.M. Dent).

Hufbauer, G.C. and Elliott, K.A. (1994) *Measuring the Costs of Protection in the United States* (Washington, D.C.: Institute for International Economics).

Locke J. (1690) *Two Treatises of Government* (New York: Cambridge University Press, 1991).

McGee, R.W (1993) 'An economic analysis of protectionism in the United States with implications for international trade in Europe', *George Washington Journal of International Law*, 26 (3): 539–73.

Morkre, M. and Tarr, D.G. (1980) *Effects of Restrictions on United States Imports: Five Case Studies and Theory* (Washington, D.C.: Federal Trade Commission).

Niskanen W.A. (1978) 'The prospect for liberal democracy', in J.M. Buchanan and R.E. Wagner (eds), *Fiscal Responsibility in Constitutional Democracy* (Leiden: Martinus Nijhoff), pp. 154–74.

Niskanen, W.A. (1994) *Bureaucracy and Public Economics* (Aldershot, Hants., and Brookfield, Vt.: Edward Elgar Publishing).

Ostrom, V. (1984) 'Why governments fail: an inquiry into the use of instruments of evil to do good', in J.M. Buchanan and R.D. Tollison (eds), *The Theory of Public Choice II* (Ann Arbor: University of Michigan Press).

Petersmann, E.-U. (1993) 'National constitutions and international economic law', in M. Hilf and E.-U. Petersmann (eds), *National Constitutions and International Economic Law* (Deventer: Kluwer Academic Publishers), pp. 3–52.

Rowley, C.K. (1987) 'The route to constitutional reform' in J.M. Buchanan, C.K. Rowley and R.D. Tollison (eds), *Deficits* (Oxford: Basil Blackwell), pp. 391–406.

Tocqueville, A. de (1848) *Democracy in America* (Oxford: Oxford University Press, 1965).

Tullock, G. (1980) 'Efficient rent-seeking' in J. Buchanan, R.D. Tollison and G. Tullock (eds), Towards a Theory of the Rent-seeking Society (College Station: Texas A & M University Press).

Tullock, G. (1993) *Rent Seeking*, Shaftesbury Paper 2 (Aldershot, Hants and Brookfield, Vt.: Edward Elgar Publishing).

Wagner, R.E (1993) *Parchment, Guns and Constitutional Order*, Shaftesbury Paper 3 (Aldershot, Hants., and Brookfield, Vt.: Edward Elgar Publishing).

West Coast Hotel Co. v *Parrish*, 300 U.S. 379 (1937).

Youngstown Sheet & Tube v *Sawyer*, 343 U.S. 579, (1952).

Index